OSCAR WILDE: THE CRITICAL HERITAGE

THE CRITICAL HERITAGE SERIES

GENERAL EDITOR: B. C. SOUTHAM, M.A., B.LITT. (OXON)
Formerly Department of English, Westfield College, University of London

---

Volumes in the series include

JANE AUSTEN	B. C. Southam
BROWNING	Boyd Litzinger and Donald Smalley
BYRON	Andrew Rutherford
COLERIDGE	J. R. de J. Jackson
DICKENS	Philip Collins
DRYDEN	James and Helen Kinsley
HENRY FIELDING	Ronald Paulson and Thomas Lockwood
THOMAS HARDY	R. G. Cox
HAWTHORNE	J. Donald Crowley
HENRY JAMES	Roger Gard
JAMES JOYCE (2 vols)	Robert H. Deming
KIPLING	Roger Lancelyn Green
D. H. LAWRENCE	R. P. Draper
MILTON	John T. Shawcross
SCOTT	John O. Hayden
SPENSER	R. N. Cummings
SWIFT	Kathleen Williams
SWINBURNE	Clyde K. Hyder
TENNYSON	J. D. Jump
THACKERAY	Geoffrey Tillotson and Donald Hawes
TROLLOPE	Donald Smalley
OSCAR WILDE	Karl Beckson

OSCAR WILDE

THE CRITICAL HERITAGE

Edited by
KARL BECKSON

Associate Professor of English
Brooklyn College
The City University of New York

NEW YORK
BARNES & NOBLE, INC.

First published in Great Britain 1970
Published in the United States of America 1970
by Barnes & Noble, Inc., New York, N.Y.
© *Karl Beckson 1970*
SBN 389 04059 2

Printed in Great Britain

General Editor's Preface

The reception given to a writer by his contemporaries and near-contemporaries is evidence of considerable value to the student of literature. On one side we learn a great deal about the state of criticism at large and in particular about the development of critical attitudes towards a single writer; at the same time, through private comments in letters, journals or marginalia, we gain an insight upon the tastes and literary thought of individual readers of the period. Evidence of this kind helps us to understand the writer's historical situation, the nature of his immediate reading-public, and his response to these pressures.

The separate volumes in the *Critical Heritage Series* present a record of this early criticism. Clearly for many of the highly productive and lengthily reviewed nineteenth- and twentieth-century writers there exists an enormous body of material; and in these cases the volume editors have made a selection of the most important views, significant for their intrinsic critical worth or for their representative quality—perhaps even registering incomprehension!

For earlier writers, notably pre-eighteenth century, the materials are much scarcer and the historical period has been extended, sometimes far beyond the writer's lifetime, in order to show the inception and growth of critical views which were initially slow to appear.

In each volume the documents are headed by an Introduction, discussing the material assembled and relating the early stages of the author's reception to what we have come to identify as the critical tradition. The volumes will make available much material which would otherwise be difficult of access and it is hoped that the modern reader will be thereby helped towards an informed understanding of the ways in which literature has been read and judged.

B.C.S.

Contents

Salomé (1893)

A Woman of No Importance (1893)

The Sphinx (1894)

An Ideal Husband (1895)

The Importance of Being Earnest (1895)

CONTENTS

Acknowledgments

I am indebted to the following for permission to reprint items included in this volume: The Society of Authors as literary representative of the Estate of Holbrook Jackson for No. 111, the Estate of Richard Le Gallienne for No. 31, and the Estate of Bernard Shaw for Nos 64 and 73; A. P. Watt & Son, Miss Anne Yeats, and Mr M. B. Yeats for Nos 35, 58, 123; A. P. Watt & Son and Miss Dorothy Collins for No. 105 (G. K. Chesterton); A. P. Watt & Son and the Owner of the Copyright for No. 127 (Arnold Bennett); *Times Literary Supplement* for Nos 92 and 103 (E. V. Lucas and Harold Child); Macmillan & Co. Ltd and Mrs Edward Shanks for No. 126; Granada Publishing Ltd and Harcourt, Brace and World for No. 15 and excerpts from *The Letters of Oscar Wilde*, ed. Rupert Hart-Davis (1962); William Heinemann Ltd and Mrs Eva Reichmann for Nos 86 and 93 (Max Beerbohm); John Johnson for No. 95 (R. B. Cunninghame Graham); Edward Colman for Nos 49 and 104 (Lord Alfred Douglas); Sidgwick & Jackson Ltd for No. 125 (John Drinkwater); Bertha Klausner International Literary Agency, Inc. for No. 121 (Upton Sinclair); Alfred Rice for No. 113 (James Gibbons Huneker); Mr J. C. Medley and Mr R. G. Medley for No. 119 (George Moore); The Bodley Head for No. 100 (R. A. Scott-James); Mrs Nona Hill for Nos 30, 80, and 102 (Arthur Symons); Laurence Pollinger Ltd for No. 115 (John Cowper Powys); Mrs Vera Newman for No. 77 (Ernest Newman).

In addition, I should like to express my gratitude to the following for their assistance in the making of this volume: Prof. Suheil Bushrui, Miss Margaret Campbell, Prof. Phyllis J. Fleming, Prof. Jules Gelernt, Prof. Helmut Gerber, Prof. Peter Irvine, Prof. Norman Kelvin, Dr Mary Lago, Mr George Lilley, Prof. James Mantinband, Prof. John M. Munro, Mr Walter W. Nelson, Prof. Alexander Preminger, Prof. Louis Salomon, and Prof. Arnold Schwab.

I am also grateful to the staffs of the New York Public Library and the Columbia University Library for providing me with photocopies of most of the items included in this volume.

Preface

Since the number of articles, reviews, and books on Wilde that have appeared since 1881 is overwhelming, this volume necessarily presents a representative selection of reviews, articles, excerpts from letters and memoirs which reveal the spectrum of reaction by Wilde's most critical readers. I have avoided quoting from books—either biographical or critical—entirely devoted to Wilde in the hope that such material is generally available to most readers.

Each selection is printed in its entirety whenever possible, except, of course, for reviews of Wilde's plays, which frequently give a summary of the plot and evaluate the acting. These parts of the reviews—not germane to our present purpose—I have omitted, as indicated by ellipses. In selecting items, I was guided by the dual standard of the intrinsic interest and representative importance of the critical statement concerned with Wilde's literary achievement rather than with his personality to provide, in the words of the General Editor of this series, 'an insight upon the tastes and literary thought of individual readers of the time'.

I have also chosen several reviews by such critics as William Archer, A. B. Walkley, and Shaw as well as reviews which appeared periodically in a single journal or paper in order to demonstrate how the critic or journal changed, or did not change, in its attitude toward Wilde. The Introduction to this volume, while drawing on the selections for a survey of the development of Wilde's reputation, also contains, as supplementary material, many additional excerpts from letters, memoirs, reviews, and articles (all documented) that are not in the body of this volume. Since Wilde's major works appeared within less than a decade and since his reputation underwent considerable change in the early twentieth century, I have included items dating as late as Arnold Bennett's review (No. 127) in 1927. In this way, the development of Wilde's reputation may be traced beyond the nadir that it reached in the years of his imprisonment and its sudden and dramatic regeneration in the years following his death.

For convenience, I have used the following abbreviations in the introduction and headnotes:

Letters	*The Letters of Oscar Wilde*, ed. Rupert Hart-Davis (1962)
Mason, *Bibliography*	Stuart Mason [Christopher Millard], *Bibliography of Oscar Wilde* (1914) (reprinted with the same pagination in 1967)
Mason, *Art and Morality*	Stuart Mason, *Art and Morality* (1912)

Finally, selections from journals, newspapers and books, unless otherwise indicated, were originally published in London.

Introduction

Despite the fact that Oscar Wilde has probably been written about more than most nineteenth-century writers, his place and reputation continue to be uncertain. Wilde's extraordinary personality and wit have so dominated the imaginations of most biographers and critics that their estimates of his work have too often consisted of sympathetic tributes to (or attacks on) a writer whose literary production was little more than a faint reflection of his brilliant talk or the manifestation of what a reviewer for the *Times Literary Supplement* (No. 92) called his 'lawlessness'. Characteristic is Richard Le Gallienne's opening remark in his introduction to *The Works of Oscar Wilde* (New York, 1909): 'The writings of Oscar Wilde, brilliant and even beautiful as they are, are but the marginalia, so to say, of a striking fantastic personality.' Indeed, Wilde's remark—as reported by André Gide—that he had put his genius into his life and only his talent into his art has provided support to those who regard his life as the primary object of interest.

In addition, late nineteenth-century critics habitually judged Wilde's work by a standard now held in disrepute—namely, its 'sincerity', which, for the Victorians, implied moral earnestness and fidelity to 'inner' feeling. Aware that sincerity, as a standard of value, was irrelevant to the aesthetic experience, Wilde wrote in 'The Critic as Artist': 'A little sincerity is a dangerous thing. All bad poetry springs from genuine feeling.' For Wilde, style, not sincerity, was essential to the experience of art; 'insincerity', as he said in *The Picture of Dorian Gray*, was 'merely a method by which we multiply our personalities'— the idea of the mask, which Yeats later developed as a major aspect of his metaphysical vision. The poet, Francis Thompson, in a letter to a friend in August 1890, reveals the critical bias of the Victorians in his judgment of Wilde: 'A witty, paradoxical writer, who, nevertheless, *meo judicio*, will do nothing permanent because he is in earnest about nothing' (*The Letters of Francis Thompson*, ed. John Evangelist Walsh, New York, 1969, p. 44). One wonders, in view of such an objection, voiced frequently by his critics, whether Wilde deliberately entitled his play *The Importance of Being Earnest*—his most 'insincere' and artificial play—to compound the critics' distress over his lack of earnestness.

I

Another critical objection centred on his 'imitation' of other authors; indeed, on occasion he was accused of plagiarism—a more strongly pejorative term for 'imitation'—most notably by Whistler (No. 14). The whole question of borrowed images and ideas haunted Wilde who, on more than one occasion publicly defended himself (see No. 15). Privately, he once said facetiously to Max Beerbohm: 'Of course I plagiarize. It is the privilege of the appreciative man' (*Max Beerbohm's Letters to Reggie Turner*, ed. Rupert Hart-Davis, London, 1964, p. 36). However, the alchemy involved in the creative process was suggested by Arthur Symons, who, with irony and insight, wrote in a review of Wilde's *Intentions* (No. 30):

At his best, to our thinking, when he is most himself—an artist in epigram—he can be admirable even when his eloquence reminds us of the eloquent writing of others. He is conscious of the charm of graceful echoes, and is always original in his quotations.

If the alchemy did not always succeed, it was not the fault of the borrowing but of the alchemist, for as T. S. Eliot (who also had to defend himself against similar charges) wrote in *The Sacred Wood* (1920):

One of the surest of tests is the way in which a poet borrows. Immature poets imitate; mature poets steal; bad poets deface what they take, and good poets make it into something better or at least something different.

By this standard, Wilde was perhaps less than a mature poet, but a good critic, and a splendid playwright.

Many late nineteenth- and early twentieth-century reviewers and critics of Wilde's work, unprepared to grasp his unique gifts, thus judged his achievement within a critical frame of reference dominated by considerations of literature as a form of moral enlightenment in which sincerity was essential. In the theatre, however, Wilde's reputation rose as the result of such influential and enlightened critics as William Archer, A. B. Walkley, and, of course, Shaw. With the publication of *The Ballad of Reading Gaol* and *De Profundis*, his reputation continued to rise, particularly on the Continent; *Salomé* and *De Profundis* were, in fact, hailed as masterpieces in Germany and France.

But since the early part of this century Wilde's reputation as a poet (aside, perhaps, from *The Ballad of Reading Gaol*) has steadily declined—though it was never very high—and W. H. Auden's recent anthology, *19th-century British Minor Poets* (New York, 1966), does not include any of Wilde's poems, suggesting, apparently, that Wilde was unworthy of even being regarded as minor. But overriding most disputes about Wilde's literary achievement is the general consensus concerning *The Importance of Being Earnest*, which has a firm place among the great comedies in English drama.

Wilde's position as a critic has had a less certain history. In recent years his importance as a spokesman for artistic autonomy has risen considerably. The cultural historian Jacques Barzun, in a preface to a new edition of *De Profundis* (New York, 1964) has stated that Wilde was 'first and foremost a critic—one of *the* critics thanks to whose exertions Western art is unique in being an object not only of enjoyment but also of self-aware contemplation . . . an interpreter of life and art who made clear and unforgettable most of the moral and artistic assumptions on which we still live' (pp. xv, vi). Yet other critics, stressing Wilde's lack of originality, have called him merely a witty synthesizer of other men's ideas.

For the literary historian, then, Wilde is a writer whose reputation eludes fixity and demands fresh evaluation.

I

1881–8: POEMS, VERA; OR THE NIHILISTS, and THE HAPPY PRINCE AND OTHER TALES

Wilde's first volume of verse, *Poems* (1881), was eagerly awaited by those who had followed his career of self-advertisement from Oxford to the pages of *Punch*, which had made his poses the object of national hilarity. On 25 June 1881, two days after the appearance of *Poems*, *Punch* published an illustration depicting Wilde's head at the centre of a sunflower under which appeared a quotation of supposed literary judgment:

> Aesthete of Aesthetes!
> What's in a name?
> The poet is Wilde,
> But his poetry's tame.

Further comment on Wilde's verse followed on 23 July 1881, when *Punch*, noting the imitations of various authors in *Poems*, concluded—a brief review titled 'Swinburne and Water', with: 'There is a certain amount of originality about the binding, but that is more than can be said for the inside of the volume' (p. 26)—an observation echoed by a number of other reviews.

The *Athenaeum* (No. 1), which saw imitation everywhere in the volume, could detect no 'distinct message' from the 'apostle of the new worship' of Beauty. The worst faults, the review noted, were 'artificiality and insincerity'—the very characteristics that Wilde would later hold to be the central virtues of his art. The *Saturday Review* (No. 2), though admitting 'cleverness and astonishing fluency' in the young poet, likewise noted the imitated mannerisms of greater poets, adding the now familiar comment: 'The great fault of all such writing as this is the want of literary sincerity . . .'

But if the volume did not fare well among some of the reviewers, the Cambridge don, Oscar Browning, whom Wilde had asked to review the book, lent the weight of his name in the prestigious literary journal the *Academy*. His sympathetic review (No. 3), clearly designed to correct the judgments of previous reviews, was not, however, simply an elaborate puff, for while Browning found in the poems a 'fresh, vigorous mind' and announced that 'England is enriched with a new poet', he also noted the volume's 'extravagance and imitation'. Attacks on the volume, however, continued. The *Spectator*'s review (No. 5) declared that Wilde should never have conceived the poems or had them published, for they were 'trash'.

But the greatest praise for the volume occurred in the pages of some American newspapers and journals. In Chicago, the *Dial* (No. 4), which, to be sure, noted the affectation and lack of 'exaltation that can come alone from a high and sincere poetic purpose', declared the poems 'remarkable . . . striking in form and treatment'; in New York, the *Century* said of one of the poems, 'Ave Imperatrix': 'How an Englishman can read it without a glow of pride and sigh of sorrow is beyond comprehension. Mr. Wilde can comfort himself. "Ave Imperatrix" outweighs a hundred cartoons of *Punch*' (November 1881, xxiii, p. 153). The *New York Times*, also greatly impressed by 'Ave Imperatrix', but spelling Wilde's name 'Wylde' throughout the review, offered the following judgment:

He has written an ode on England such as Tennyson has not and cannot. . . .
In Wylde England has a new poet, who, if not of the first order of power, is so true a poet underneath whatever eccentricity of conduct or cant of school that his further persecution in the press must be held contemptible (14 August 1881, p. 10).

Despite the generally unfavourable or mixed reviews in England, the book went through five editions (totalling 1250 copies), which, if not overwhelming, was an impressive beginning for a new poet at a time when a first volume of poems was expected to sell between 300 and 500 copies, though, no doubt, some of the public interest had as much to do with Wilde's personality as with his poetic accomplishment.

Wilde's notoriety as personality and poet in 1882 may be gauged not only by the coverage in the popular press of his lecture tour in the United States and Canada but also by the inclusion of a lengthy chapter on Wilde in Walter Hamilton's *The Aesthetic Movement in England* (No. 6), which itself went through several editions. Wilde, who was only twenty-eight at the time, was thus ranked—if only in notoriety—with such figures as Rossetti, Ruskin, and Morris. Wilde was no doubt delighted by such recognition, but in Boston the *Woman's Journal* published a signed front-page attack by the reformer T. W. Higginson (No. 7), who called Wilde's verse not only 'very mediocre' but also indecent. The attack was serious, for Higginson was too greatly renowned a figure to ignore. Furious, Wilde, in a letter to Joaquin Miller, alludes to Higginson's urging that he be ostracized: 'This apostle of inhospitality, who delights to defile, to desecrate, and to defame the gracious courtesies he is unworthy to enjoy' (*Letters*, p. 98). But Wilde had his defenders against such attacks: in addition to Miller, Julia Ward Howe, author of *The Battle Hymn of the Republic*, who had entertained him at her home in Boston, published a signed defence in the *Boston Daily Globe* on 15 February 1882.

When Wilde returned to the United States in August 1883, to witness the production of *Vera; or the Nihilists*, he had high hopes of scoring a success in the theatre. The reviews, however, were crushing. The *New York Times*, noting that his 'labor [was] altogether out of proportion to his reputation', found the play 'unreal, longwinded, and wearisome' (No. 9); the *New York Daily Tribune* (No. 10) substantially agreed, and the *New York Herald*, echoing the other two prominent newspapers, concluded: 'It is long-drawn, dramatic rot, a series of disconnected essays and sickening rant, with a coarse and common kind of cleverness' (21 August 1883, p. 10).

The lone voice to oppose the prevailing opinion of the play came from the *New York Mirror*, but the extraordinarily high praise and the irrelevant allusions to the abuse and contempt suffered by Wilde on his lecture tour in the previous year suggest that the reviewer seems less interested in accurately judging the value of the play than in purging the collective guilt of the American people:

There was a great surprise in store for the people who gathered at the Union Square Theatre on Monday night. They had come to laugh. They remained to applaud. If Oscar Wilde desired any vindication for the abuse, ridicule, and contempt with which he was met on his first visit to this country, it was handsomely secured to him by the triumph of his play. . . . It has been the pleasure of the newspapers and that portion of the public which revels in its ignorance and flaunts its vulgarity to assail Mr. Wilde with every manner of coarse, cheap and indecent indignity. . . . It is not the first instance in history of the crucifixion of a good man on the cross of popular prejudice and disbelief. . . . From a literary, as well as a dramatic point of view, *Vera* is a work that takes rank among the highest order of plays. (25 August 1883, p. 7.)

The review and a letter of protest to the *New York Times* by Marie Prescott (see No. 9), who had performed the role of Vera, could not save the play, for it closed within the week. *Punch*, noting the disaster, quipped that from all accounts the play was 'Vera Bad' and suggested that Oscar become a drama critic (1 September 1883, p. 99).

In 1888, Wilde published *The Happy Prince and Other Tales*, the critical reaction to which no doubt did much to heal the wounds suffered over the failure of *Vera*. A letter from Walter Pater (No. 11), filled with high praise for the stories, likewise filled Wilde with high spirits. (One wonders whether Pater would have offered such praise had he committed himself to print.) The reviews (see Nos. 12 and 13) were generally quite favourable, the *Universal Review*, for example, stating that the volume 'shows Mr. Oscar Wilde's genius at its best' (June 1888, ii, 305). Not only did Wilde's volume provoke favourable prose but also laudatory verse. In 1889, Thomas Hutchinson's *Jolts and Jingles: A Book of Poems for Young People* contained the following dedication:

> TO OSCAR WILDE
> To you who wrote THE HAPPY PRINCE,
> The sweetest tale of modern tales,
> In individual gratitude
> For hours of tearful happiness
> I dedicate these Children's Rhymes.

And in 1890, Justin Huntly McCarthy, who was not always an admirer of Wilde's later works, included a poem titled 'The Happy Prince', dedicated to Wilde, in his *Harlequinade: A Book of Verses*, which contains the lines:

Long have I lingered an enchanted guest
In the green garden of your fairy tales . . .

Wilde's volume sold well, for after the first edition, published by
David Nutt, had exhausted its initial printing of 1000 copies, the second
edition appeared in January 1889. Following Wilde's death, five
editions were issued by Nutt between 1902 and 1910, an indication of
renewed interest in Wilde's work. In the United States, Roberts
Brothers of Boston, who had published *Poems*, issued three impressions
between 1888 and 1894.

II

1890–1: THE PICTURE OF DORIAN GRAY, THE DUCHESS OF PADUA, INTENTIONS, LORD ARTHUR SAVILE'S CRIME AND OTHER STORIES, and A HOUSE OF POMEGRANATES

In the first year of Wilde's final decade, when Decadence in literature
was bruited about in *avant-garde* circles, *The Picture of Dorian Gray*
appeared, complete, in the July issue of *Lippincott's Monthly Magazine*.
Its appearance created the first of several literary sensations in the 1890s.
The popular Press, outraged by the novel's suggestion of perverse
sexuality, attacked it as decadent and immoral. The first of these
attacks occurred in the *St. James's Gazette* on 24 June within four days of
Dorian Gray's appearance (No. 17). The anonymous reviewer, Samuel
Jeyes, referring to the novel's 'esoteric prurience', made the famous
comment which has conferred on Jeyes a renown otherwise impossible,
'The writer airs his cheap research among the garbage of the French
Décadents like any drivelling pedant', ironically expressing the hope
that the Vigilance Society would not prosecute the book. In a letter to
the paper, Wilde argued, with extraordinary restraint, that the reviewer
had not grasped the nature or intent of the novel; indeed, said Wilde,
the public, on hearing that it was a wicked book, would rush to read it:
'But, alas! they will find that it is a story with a moral . . . a terrible
moral . . . which the prurient will not be able to find in it, but which
will be revealed to all whose minds are healthy', concluding, ironically,
that the moral was the only artistic error in the book (*Letters*, p. 259).
  Wilde's letter resulted in further remarks by Jeyes and, in turn, three
further letters from Wilde—the former continuing his abuse, the latter

maintaining his restraint (see No. 17). But as Wilde had suggested in his first response, such an attack would no doubt result in increased sales of the magazine. Robert Ross, writing to Wilde, reported that eighty copies of *Lippincott's* were sold in one day by a bookseller in the Strand, where usually three copies were sold in a week (*Robert Ross: Friend of Friends*, ed. Margery Ross, 1952, pp. 20–21).

On 30 June, the *Daily Chronicle* published a review (No. 18) which in vitriol equalled that of the *St. James's Gazette*. Pointing to the novel's 'effeminate frivolity, its studied insincerity, its theatrical cynicism, its tawdry . . . and garish vulgarity', the reviewer denied what Wilde had insisted on—its 'moral'. In response, Wilde wrote to the editor:

> . . . so far from wishing to emphasize any moral in my story, the real trouble I experienced in writing the story was that of keeping the extremely obvious moral subordinate to the artistic and dramatic effect. . . . I think the moral too apparent. When the book is published in a volume I hope to correct this defect. (*Letters*, p. 263.)

When the novel appeared in book form in the following year, with six additional chapters which did little to minimize the too obvious moral, Wilde added the famous 'Preface', designed, as he wrote in a letter to J. S. Little, 'to teach [those 'wretched journalists' who had 'so ignorantly and pruriently' assailed the novel] to mend their wicked ways' (*Letters*, p. 290).

The briefest notice of the novel, but one which launched a debate involving not only Wilde but the reviewer and several readers and which filled the correspondence columns from July through September, appeared in W. E. Henley's *Scots Observer* (later the *National Observer*). Calling the novel 'ingenious, interesting, full of cleverness, and plainly the work of a man of letters', the reviewer (No. 19) nevertheless called it an offence to 'public morals'. Again, Wilde took to his pen in the continuing debate over the relationship between morality and art; Henley did not enter the flow of letters, though one of his staff, Charles Whibley, did, as well as the reviewer, who debated with Wilde under the pseudonym of 'Thersites' (see No. 19, headnote).

The *Speaker* convinced that the 'conception' of the story was 'exceedingly strong', took exception to the moral objections and innuendoes of those reviewers who were obsessed by Wilde's depiction of Dorian:

> It has been insinuated that this story should be suppressed in the interest of morality. Mr. Wilde has answered that art and ethics have nothing to do with

each other. His boldness in resting his defence on the general proposition is the more exemplary, as he might fairly have insisted on the particular proposition—that the teaching of his book is conspicuously right in morality. If we have correctly interpreted the book's motive—and we are at a loss to conceive what other can be devised—this position is unassailable. (5 July 1890, ii, 25.)

Though occasionally laboured in some descriptive passages, the novel, the review concludes, is a 'work of serious art, strong and fascinating, in spite of its blemishes' (*Ibid.*, p. 26).

In the *Christian Leader* of 3 July, the reviewer, convinced that Wilde's motive in writing the novel was laudable, states that in portraying 'the gilded paganism which has been staining these latter years of the Victorian epoch with horrors that carry us back to the worst incidents in the history of ancient Rome', Wilde has 'performed a service to his age'. And the reviewer sees the salutary effect of the novel in no uncertain terms:

We can only hope that it will be read and pondered by those classes of British society whose corruption it delineates with such thrilling power, and that it may be the means of preserving many young lives from the temptations by which they are surrounded. (Quoted in Mason, *Art and Morality*, pp. 137–138.)

Thus, Wilde, who later insisted in his added 'Preface' that 'All art is useless', was praised as a hoped-for deterrent to evil.

Wilde's novel was not widely reviewed in the United States, but praise came from the pages of *Lippincott's* itself in a review by Julian Hawthorne (No. 22), son of the novelist, who called *Dorian Gray* 'a remarkable book . . . which everybody will want to read'. But the influential *Chicago Tribune* offered a dissenting opinion, not because of the absence of a moral but because of its tone:

The moral of Mr. Wilde's book is meant to be good; at least he deals out to sin its proverbial wages. But the tone is pernicious, and the punishment of the author should be severe. He should be subjected at once to a curtain lecture from his wife. (6 July 1890, p. 26.)

The extraordinary attention to a novel that had appeared in a monthly magazine and not yet in book form (Wilde boasted that he had received 216 reviews and notices) was, to some extent, the result of a carefully cultivated notoriety. But once the object of attack, he responded with commendable restraint and wit. He also revealed good business sense, for when Ward, Lock and Company, the London publisher of *Lippincott's*, decided to publish the novel in book form,

Wilde suggested that additional chapters be added to improve its sale. Having followed the controversy in the Press between Wilde and the outraged reviewers the publisher George Lock suggested in a letter to Wilde on 7 July 1890:

> Could you not make Dorian live longer with the face of the picture transferred to himself and depict the misery in which he ends his days by suicide or repents and becomes a better character. Lord Henry too goes off the scene very quickly. Could not he also have a little longer and you could make an excellent contrast between the deaths of the two men. (Mason, *Bibliography*, p. 105.)

Wilde rightly rejected both of these suggestions, added six additional chapters (without substantially affecting the nature of the novel), and a preface, which epigrammatically stated his ideas on art.

When *Dorian Gray* appeared in book form in April 1891, it was not as widely reviewed as the first version had been. The *Theatre* contained a notice (No. 23) which described the novel as 'undeniably clever and even brilliant' but with an 'almost utter lack of true humanity'; still, it was 'wonderfully ingenious and even fascinating'. The *Athenaeum*, however, agreeing with those reviews which had attacked the first version of the novel, used the now-familiar adjectives in its very brief notice: 'unmanly, sickening, vicious, and tedious' (No. 24). But coming late in 1891, the lengthy review by Pater (No. 25) contained the most perceptive insights into the nature of Wilde's novel. Praising the artistry as 'first-rate', Pater finds Dorian 'a beautiful creation' with a 'very plain moral pushed home'. In its skill, 'the real subtlety of art', the novel, Pater concludes, may be favourably compared to the work of Poe, Mallarmé, whom Wilde regarded as being one of France's great writers and to whom Wilde had sent an inscribed copy of his novel, responded in a letter to Wilde with an appreciation of the novel's rare refinement of intellect and 'perverse atmosphere of beauty' which was a 'miracle that you have accomplished by employing all the arts of the writer!' (Quoted in *Letters*, p. 298.) We have no recorded reaction by Wilde to these critical judgments by Pater and Mallarmé, but we may surmise that he regarded them as the ultimate accolades.

Despite the publicity given to Wilde's novel, it took (according to Stuart Mason) five years to sell the 1000 copies published in 1891, the result, perhaps, of the wide sale of the first version in *Lippincott's* in the previous year. Yet the publishing history of *Dorian Gray* is extraordinary by any standards. Mason had in his private collection 142 different editions of the novel, many in foreign languages. Between

1895, when it appeared in French, and 1911, it had already been translated into thirteen foreign languages, including Yiddish (published in London) and Russian. It has become a favourite of limited edition clubs, a recent edition (New York, 1957), is sumptuously printed and boxed, with an introduction by André Maurois, who writes: 'the transmutation into beauty of a diffuse and disquieting sensuality partly explains the lasting nature of its hold on us'.

Early in 1891, Wilde's second play, *The Duchess of Padua* (which had been privately printed in 1883), was produced in New York under the title *Guido Ferranti*. Wilde's name was withheld from the playbills and programmes, but the author of the play was widely known. The reviews were respectful but not generally enthusiastic. The *New York Times* (No. 26) noted the lack of inspiration but commended some passages as 'full of the fire of eloquence'. The review in the *New York Daily Tribune* (No. 27) reported that the verse was melodious, 'often eloquent', but it was critical of the melodrama in the play, concluding that the defect of the work was 'insincerity . . . no one in it is natural' —a comment that, for Wilde, would be praise of the highest order for his later dramatic efforts.

The play ran for twenty-one performances, a veritable triumph after the dismal failure of Wilde's first play in 1882. Revivals of the play have been rare. Performances were given in Germany, where Wilde's reputation was second only to Shakespeare, in 1904 and 1906; the first English publication of the play was by Methuen in Wilde's collected works (1908).

In May 1891, less than a month after book publication of *Dorian Gray*, *Intentions* appeared. Thus, having produced a volume of lyric poetry, a volume of fairy tales, two plays, and a novel, Wilde now decided to collect his previously published essays (the first as early as 1885) to make his mark as a literary theorist. No genre was to be left untouched by his genius. He had decided to become a 'man of letters', having devoted a good many years to book reviewing for the *Pall Mall Gazette*. But Wilde could not escape his self-imposed image as poseur. Meredith, in a letter to a friend, wrote on 25 February 1889: 'It is a curious comment on our system of reviewing that the *Pall Mall* critic should be Oscar Wilde' (*Letters of George Meredith*, edited by his son, vol. ii, New York, 1912, p. 422). But Shaw could penetrate the pose and note the achievement of Wilde's reviews. In a letter to the journalist David O'Donoghue on 9 May 1889, he wrote: '. . . all the long reviews of distinctly Irish quality during the 1885-8 period may, I think, be set down either to me or to Oscar Wilde, whose reviews were sometimes credited to me. His work was exceptionally finished in style and very amusing' (*Collected Letters: 1874–1897*, ed. Dan Laurence, New York, 1965, p. 210).

In its review of *Intentions,* the *Pall Mall Gazette* (No. 28) took Wilde to task for his facile method of constructing paradoxes—a criticism that was repeated endlessly when his social comedies began to appear—but praised *Intentions* as a 'fascinating, stimulating book, with more common sense in it than he would perhaps care to be accused of'. The *Athenaeum* (No. 29), which in three weeks would condemn *Dorian Gray* as 'vicious', agreed with the *Pall Mall Gazette* that Wilde had emerged as an important critic; indeed, after Vernon Lee, the reviewer contended: 'hardly any one has a better claim than Mr. Wilde to be named as a contributor of something fresh, something original and stimulating, amongst the matter about art that has been written during the last twenty years'. In the *Speaker,* Arthur Symon's unsigned review (No. 30) states that Wilde 'has gained a reputation for frivolity which does injustice to a writer who has at least always been serious in the reality of his devotion to art'—a comment about Wilde rarely seen in the literary reviews. Once believing that Wilde was little more than 'a flighty-brained poseur' (letter to Churchill Osborne, 4 October 1887, Princeton University Library), Symons concludes his review: '. . . after achieving a reputation by doing nothing', Wilde 'is in a fair way to beat his own record by real achievements'. In the *Academy* (No. 31), Richard Le Gallienne, admirer and disciple of Wilde, finds *Intentions* 'delightful reading' in a review which contains obvious but graceful puffery. William Butler Yeats, not noted as one easily given to facile judgments, said of *Intentions* in a later review of Wilde's *Lord Arthur Savile's Crime and Other Stories* (No. 35) that 'it hides within its immense paradox some of the most subtle literary criticism we are likely to see for many a long day'.

The praise that greeted *Intentions* in England was also heard in the United States. In reviewing the American edition, the *Photographic American Review* for July 1891 said of Wilde:

He is one of the cleverest men who ever touched our shores, and his words have had an influence which has been felt . . . in the artistic life given to almost every trade and manufacture upon which his new presentation of artistic creed could touch. We have not, as a nation, come to the recognition of the value of this man to us. . . . And now, after poems and novels, he again, in clever satire, in the reversal of ideas, in the charm of literary style which is fascinating to the cultured, presents new thoughts in new ways in the volume just issued. (Quoted in Mason, *Bibliography*, p. 359.)

An even more extraordinary tribute to *Intentions* appeared in the *North American Review*, written by the well-known essayist, Agnes Repplier, who had been invited to nominate the best book of 1891 (No. 32). Finding two of the four essays to have 'real and permanent value', she declares that the volume contains 'that finer criticism which is one with art and beauty'.

The first edition of *Intentions*, published by Osgood, McIlvaine & Co., consisted of 1500 copies, of which 600 were issued in New York by Dodd, Mead & Co.; the sale was sufficiently brisk and continuing interest in Wilde sufficiently strong to warrant another printing in 1894, consisting of 1000 copies, of which 500 were again issued by the same American publisher.

With two major books published in 1891, Wilde saw two more through the press, books which demonstrated his versatility in widely divergent genres. The first of these, *Lord Arthur Savile's Crime and Other Stories*, which appeared in July, was received, however, with some disappointment. William Sharp, in a signed review in the *Academy* (No. 34), observed that the stories 'will not add to their author's reputation'. Except for 'The Model Millionaire', the stories, Sharp noted, lacked 'cleverness'. Yeats, in *United Ireland* (No. 35), also confessed his disappointment with the volume; though the title story was 'amusing enough', Yeats thought that the others were 'quite unworthy of more than a passing interest'. The *Graphic* (No. 33) found the volume 'excellent', but reserved its highest praise for the title story, which was 'worth all Mr. Wilde's serious work put together'.

Osgood, McIlvaine & Co. published 2000 copies, of which 500 were issued in America by Dodd, Mead & Co.; of the sale of this volume, no information is available.

When *A House of Pomegranates* appeared in November 1891, it was greeted by the *Pall Mall Gazette* (No. 36) with small praise, the reviewer questioning whether the volume, with its highly coloured style—'something between a "Swinburnian ecstasy" and the catalogue of a high art furniture dealer'—was intended for children. Again Wilde, unable to remain indifferent to the taunts of reviewers, wrote to the paper: 'Now in building this *House of Pomegranates*, I had about as much intention of pleasing the British child as I had of pleasing the British public' (*Letters*, p. 302). But such remarks had the effect of amusing some and alienating others, particularly those who took Wilde's wit as a form of masked aggression. The unfortunate result was that Wilde's reputation as a writer continued to suffer because of his penchant for entertaining the public at the expense of the reviewers.

Other mixed reactions—in the *Saturday Review* (No. 37) and the *Athenaeum* (No. 38)—commented on the excessive artifice of style and the pleasing inventiveness of the plots. Frequently cited for its interest was 'The Fisherman and his Soul', which George Saintsbury, in a brief signed notice in the *New Review*, called 'the best thing Mr. Wilde has yet done' (January 1892, vi, 121).

The volume, of which 1000 copies were issued by Osgood, McIlvaine & Co. (and by Dodd, Mead & Co. in New York), sold poorly. Around 1904, the remaining stock of copies was sold as 'remainders' for disposal by booksellers.

III

1892–3: LADY WINDERMERE'S FAN, SALOMÉ, A WOMAN OF NO IMPORTANCE

If, in Wilde's literary career, notable achievement had not yet overtaken notoriety, Wilde was soon to find a suitable means of expressing his genius and silencing those who had attacked his 'sickly aestheticism'. In the theatre, the writing of society comedies, within the framework of the well-made play, was to provide him with his most stunning successes. The first of these, *Lady Windermere's Fan*, opened on 20 February 1892, to generally enthusiastic reviews, though to some critics Wilde's paradoxical wit seemed a facile, easily constructed device. The poet, William Watson, in an attempt to demonstrate how Wildean wit could be easily imitated, wrote a letter to the *Spectator*, which printed it under the title 'Wilde and Whirling Words' on 26 March 1892, p. 429, listing seventeen epigrams he had composed in half an hour—all of them rather lame, conclusively demonstrating that true wit was not a matter of simply inverting commonplaces.

Henry James, who attended the opening performance, wrote to a friend:

. . . there was so much drollery—that is 'cheeky' paradoxical wit of dialogue, and the pit and gallery are so pleased at finding themselves clever enough to 'catch on' to four or five of the ingenious—too ingenious *mots* in the dozen, that it makes them feel quite '*décadent*' . . .

Though Wilde did not always succeed at epigram, 'those that hit', wrote James, 'are very good indeed. This will make, I think, a success—possibly a really long run' (quoted in Leon Edel's *Henry James: The Treacherous Years*, 1895–1904, Philadelphia and New York, 1969, p. 44).

Of the critical reviews, the most enthusiastic was by A. B. Walkley (No. 39), one of the most respected and influential drama critics of his day, who found the play and its 'brilliant talk' entirely successful. *Black and White* (No. 41) thought that the play, despite the obvious formula of the well-made play, was 'very amusing', and the *Westminster Review* (No. 43) opened its review with the observation that 'Mr. Oscar Wilde is nothing unless brilliant and witty.' Like *Black and White*, the *Westminster Review* questioned whether *Lady Windermere's Fan* was a play or a series of brilliant paradoxes, but concluded: 'To any one interested in plays we certainly say, if you have not yet been to see it, go at once.'

However, some reviewers were less impressed. The sullen Clement Scott (whom Shaw caricatured in his play *The Philanderer*, 1893) devoted much of his review (No. 40) in the *Illustrated London News* to chastizing Wilde for bad manners in appearing before the curtain, after the play had concluded, with a cigarette in his hand and for the 'cynicism' which he detected in the play. 'Meanwhile', he concludes, 'society at large will rush to see his play'—an accuracy of judgment rare for Scott. Justin McCarthy's signed notice (No. 44) in *Gentleman's Magazine* was also concerned more with Wilde than with the play—an indication that, to these critics, Wilde, not the play, was the thing.

Lady Windermere's Fan ran for five months before it was taken on tour of the provinces. Since renown invites burlesque Wilde's play was no exception: Charles Brookfield, the actor who, it is believed, later gathered evidence against Wilde in the case involving the Marquess of Queensberry, wrote, in collaboration with J. M. Glover, *The Poet and the Puppets: A Travesty*, suggested by *Lady Windermere's Fan*, produced in May 1892. An early indication that Wilde's fame as a dramatist was known on the Continent occurs in a letter, dated 5 September 1892, to Wilde from J. T. Grein, founder of the Independent Theatre, who drew up, on Wilde's behalf, a contract with a Dr O. Blumenthal for the sole right of production of *Lady Windermere's Fan* in Austria and Germany, half of all fees and other royalties to go to Wilde (Item 122 in Dulau & Co.'s Catalogue No. 161: *A Collection of Original Manuscripts, Letters, and Books of Oscar Wilde* [1928]).

Publication of the play occurred in November 1892, by the Bodley

Head, and in 1900 an acting edition was published by Samuel French, reissued twice in 1905; in New York there were issues in 1907 and 1910. The play was first translated into French in 1913.

When the New York production of the play opened on 6 February 1893, the drama critics of the leading dailies were generally restrained in their judgments, some, such as the critic on the *New York Daily Tribune* (7 February), judging Wilde rather than the play:

The achievement was personal. It probably pleased the writer. It is of no consequence to anybody else. It imparts the idea of a clever, satirical man who has not yet got over his youth, and who wants to make a sensation.

Despite the lack of critical enthusiasm, the play had a highly successful run of several months.

Following Wilde's death, revivals of the play at the St James's Theatre, were given in 1902, 1904, and 1911. In the latter year, Vanderheyden Fyles, tracing its stage history in an article titled 'The Course of a Modern Classic', called the play 'a masterpiece of comedy . . . as truly an epoch-making play as *The Second Mrs. Tanqueray*' (*Green Book Album* [Chicago], December 1911, vi, 1240).

Clearly, *Lady Windermere's Fan* was a stunning recovery from Wilde's two previous theatrical failures, and since this was his first play produced in England, the triumph was of singularly greater significance. His next venture, *Salomé*, rehearsals for which were proceeding in June with Sarah Bernhardt in the leading role, encountered the displeasure of the Examiner of Plays for the Lord Chamberlain, who refused to license it since it contained biblical characters. The result was another *cause célèbre*. This time, however, Wilde, who was perhaps the most talked-about writer in England, though not the most widely read, expressed his anger with less than his usual restraint, no longer concerned with merely humouring his detractors with witticisms.

Of the few to protest publicly against the ban was William Archer, among the foremost drama critics of his day, who published a letter in the *Pall Mall Gazette* on 1 July 1892, deploring the power of the censor, whom he called the 'Great Irresponsible', in suppressing 'a serious work of art'. Urging Wilde not to flee England for France (which Wilde had, in a lapse of composure, threatened to do) where he would be only one among a number of talents, Archer wrote: 'Here, on the other hand, Mr. Wilde's talent is unique. We require it and we appreciate it—those of us, at any rate, who are capable of any sort of artistic appreciation.'

Writing to Archer, Wilde thanked him for his letter, 'not merely for its very courteous and generous recognition of my work, but for its strong protest against the contemptible official tyranny that exists in England in reference to the drama' (*Letters*, p. 319). And in a letter to his publisher, John Lane, Wilde complained bitterly that the ordinary English newspapers—the *St. James's Gazette* was the 'most scurrilous'— were 'trying in every way to harm *Salomé*, though they have not read it' (*ibid.*).

When the play was published in French in February 1893, Wilde, staying at Babbacombe Cliff, wrote to the actor Oswald Yorke, 'I hear London is like some grey monster raging over the publication of *Salomé*, but I am at peace for the moment' (*Letters*, p. 335). The Times (No. 46), on the day following publication of *Salomé*, called it 'morbid, bizarre, repulsive', though admitting that it was 'vigorously written in some parts'. Wilde's letter to *The Times*, designed to correct an apparent error in the notice—that the play was written expressly for Sarah Bernhardt—contained the rather extraordinary statement: 'The opinions of English critics on a French work of mine have, of course, little, if any, interest for me' (*Letters*, p. 336).

In its review of the play, the *Pall Mall Gazette* (No. 48), pointing to Wilde's indebtedness to Flaubert, among other 'masters', concludes that *Salomé* lacks 'freshness' in both idea and presentation, conceding, however, that it does have 'cleverness'—that fatal word which reviewers relied upon in discussing Wilde's works. But it is the daily Press itself, the 'mouthpiece of Philistinism', that Lord Alfred Douglas accuses of 'pompous absurdities' in its condemnation of *Salomé* (No. 49). Clearly a puff for Wilde, the review declares the play a 'perfect work of art, a joy for ever'. A more thoughtful review appeared in *Black and White* by William Archer (No. 50), who, in defending Wilde's possible borrowing of technique from Maeterlinck, sees *Salomé* as superior to anything by the Belgian poet. When, however, the English translation of *Salomé* appeared in 1894, the influential conservative American journal the *Critic* published a brief notice (No. 51), calling Wilde a 'humbug', his play merely 'stupid and vulgar', but admitting that Wilde did have 'cleverness'.

Salomé was first given in Paris in 1896. According to Henry-D. Davray (see No. 88) it was a poor production but received respectful notices. The play was not produced in England, however, until 1905, when Max Beerbohm, reviewing it for the *Saturday Review*, found the staging faulty; indeed, he was convinced that the play read better than it acted, for the 'tragic thrill' of the action had to be imaginatively experienced (13 May 1905, xcix, 623). On the Continent, *Salomé* was performed in most of the major cities between 1902 and 1912, where it was widely regarded as Wilde's masterpiece, but in America, its first production in 1905, by an *avant-garde* group, was poorly received.

A Woman of No Importance, Wilde's second play produced in London (19 April 1893), attracted a glittering first-night audience, though, as Beerbohm's description in a letter to his friend, Reggie Turner, indicates, it did not wholly approve of the play (or perhaps of Wilde):

The first night was very brilliant in its audience. . . . Balfour and Chamberlain and all the politicians were there. When little Oscar came on to make his bow there was a slight mingling of hoots and hisses. . . . The notices are better than I had expected: the piece is sure of a long, of a very long run, despite all that the critics may say in its favour. (*Max Beerbohm's Letters to Reggie Turner*, ed. Rupert Hart-Davis, London, 1964; letter dated 21 April 1893).

Despite Max's enthusiasm, the play ran until only 16 August, a month less than that enjoyed by *Lady Windermere's Fan*. The reviews, as Max ironically indicates, were surprisingly good, considering the fact that the play was weaker than *Lady Windermere's Fan*.

William Archer (No. 52), contending that Wilde's dramatic work 'stands alone . . . on the very highest plane of modern English drama', praised the play but lamented that Wilde's 'pyrotechnic wit' was 'one of the defects of his qualities', adding that he looked forward to the day when Wilde would 'take himself seriously as a dramatic artist'—which, for Archer, would presumably mean that Wilde should become a disciple of Ibsen. Archer's praise of Wilde, however, brought such adverse criticism from various quarters that he felt compelled to defend himself in a review of Pinero's *The Second Mrs. Tanqueray* (No. 53), in which he reaffirmed his contention that Wilde was a writer 'of the first rank'.

Walkley's review (No. 54), much like Archer's, praises Wilde's 'true dramatic instinct', but he confesses that the witty paradoxes began to tire him by their sheer number. The *Saturday Review* (No. 55), typical of the more thoughtful reviews, declared that Wilde 'has more or less fairly earned his right to be taken seriously as a dramatist'. A similar reaction to the play occurs in an open letter in the *Theatre* (No. 56), which, convinced that Wilde had the capacity to do 'great work', urges him to take his art seriously—a familiar comment at the time among those critics who could not believe that Wilde was serious about anything except notoriety. Other reviews, such as that in the *Westminster Review* (No. 57) and Yeats's review of the published version (No. 58) are noteworthy: the latter praises Wilde's excellent talk but deplores his reliance on worn-out theatrical conventions while the former is critical of the characters, who are unnatural poseurs without the 'spontaneity of natural motives'. Wilde's wit, concludes the *Westminster Review*, is amusing for a while, but the playwright has 'blighted some of our great expectations'.

Despite the minority opinion, the play was widely regarded as a success. Sir William Rothenstein, in *Men and Memories: 1872–1900* (1931), recalls seeing the play, 'which had taken the town by storm':

> Oscar was delighted, as he had been on the success of his first play, *Lady Windermere's Fan*. At last he had achieved a popular success. In addition, he was making a great deal of money. In Paris he had been rather apologetic about his first play; as though to write a comedy were rather beneath a poet. When I saw it I thought, on the contrary, here is the genuine Wilde, making legitimate use of the artifice which was, in fact, natural to him; like his wit, indeed, in which his true genius lay. (pp. 132–3.)

This was precisely what many early critics could not (or would not) comprehend—the naturalness of Wilde's artifice—or, to put it another way, the truth of masks.

The American production of *A Woman of No Importance* opened in New York on 11 December 1893 to audiences that appeared to be amused but to drama critics who seemed even more grudging in their reactions than before in their response to *Lady Windermere's Fan*. The play's audacity—particularly its sympathy for the unmarried mother—seemed particularly repugnant to some. The *New York Times*, for example, referred to Wilde as one 'whose mind seems to be as impure as the River Thames by London Bridge' (12 December 1893, p. 5).

IV

1894–5: THE SPHINX, AN IDEAL HUSBAND, and THE IMPORTANCE OF BEING EARNEST

In June 1894, Wilde published his lengthy poem, *The Sphinx*, portions of which he had written as early as 1874, while a student at Oxford. Despite Wilde's reputation as a dramatist, it was not widely reviewed.

The reviews included in this volume are characteristic of the lack of enthusiasm for the poem. Henley's review (No. 60) is clearly an attempt to discredit Wilde rather than to evaluate the poem honestly; the *Athenaeum* (No. 61), while not impressed, does admit that the poem has some skill and ingenuity; and the *Pall Mall Budget* (No. 59) comes closest to praise in its description of the poem's 'beautiful words strangely shaped and coloured'.

The Sphinx did little to advance Wilde's reputation; coming after the success of *A Woman of No Importance*, it was perhaps an error of judgment on Wilde's part to commit to print, at a high point in his career as a playwright, a poem conceived and partly written in his youth. Critics such as Reginald Golding Bright were prepared to condemn such a work designed to attract attention by its strangeness. In a letter to Bright on 19 November 1894, Shaw defended Wilde— more for his plays, one suspects, than for *The Sphinx*:

You must give up detesting everything pertaining to Oscar Wilde or to anyone else. The critic's first duty is to admit, with absolute respect, the right of every man to his own style. Wilde's wit and his fine literary workmanship are points of great value. (*Collected Letters: 1874–1897*, ed. Dan H. Laurence, New York, 1965, pp. 460–1.)

In the year of his trial and imprisonment, Wilde saw his last two plays produced on the London stage. *An Ideal Husband*, which opened on 3 January 1895 at the Theatre Royal, did not draw praise from H. G. Wells (No. 62), who had begun reviewing plays for the *Pall Mall Gazette*. Declaring it 'very poor', Wells was in agreement with Clement Scott (No. 65), who was never able to see much value in Wilde as a playwright. But Archer, Shaw, Walkley, and William Dean Howells (Nos. 63, 64, 66, 68) all agreed that it was work of a high order, despite some obvious weaknesses in its characterization or in the lessened output of Wilde's 'epigram-factory', as Archer called it. Even *Punch*, in a review free of the usual facetiousness (indeed, *Punch* grew more respectful as Wilde's career developed), declared that the play, 'though in sharp dialogue not up to Mr. Wilde's high spirits-and-water mark, is an unmistakable success' (2 February 1895, cviii, 54).

An Ideal Husband had a run of 111 performances, closing on 6 April (the day following Wilde's arrest, though announcements had been made beforehand that the play would soon close to permit production of another play); it reopened at the Criterion Theatre on 13 April and was withdrawn on 27 April.

In New York, *An Ideal Husband*, which opened at the Lyceum Theatre on 12 March 1895, was judged by most of the critics as Wilde's best play to date. A notable feature of the reviews is that they contain fewer personal attacks than in the past. Characteristic is the review in the *Sun*, which stated: 'The actors rendered the evening pleasurable with Mr. Wilde's pedantic, assuming, and sometimes irritating composition, so it will not do to say that he has no cleverness as a playwright' (13 March 1895, p. 7). What particularly irritated the critics, however, was that the audiences seemed to enjoy the play.

With the production on 14 February 1895 of *The Importance of Being Earnest*, Wilde achieved his greatest theatrical triumph. The audience at the St James's Theatre on opening night was reduced to spasms of laughter. Years later, the actor Allan Aynesworth, who had played the role of Algernon Moncrieff, told Hesketh Pearson: 'In my fifty-three years of acting, I never remember a greater triumph than the first night of *The Importance of Being Earnest*. The audience rose in their seats and cheered and cheered again' (*The Life of Oscar Wilde*, 1946, p. 257).

Most critics were equally impressed. Wells (No. 69), who had been disappointed with *An Ideal Husband*, found Wilde's new play thoroughly delightful; Archer (No. 71), intrigued by its curiously elusive wit, declared the play as 'an absolutely wilful expression of an irrepressibly witty personality'; the reviewer for *Truth* (No. 72), observing that Wilde dominates the play, saw it as highly amusing precisely because he does. Indeed, in perceiving that Wilde makes no attempt at individual characterization, the reviewer seems to grasp the nature of Wilde's dandiacal world. Walkley (No. 74), one of Wilde's staunchest defenders, begins his review for the *Speaker* by announcing that Wilde has at last 'found himself . . . as an artist in sheer nonsense . . . and better nonsense, I think, our stage has not seen'.

But some critics dissented from this widespread praise. Shaw (No. 73), who had delighted in *An Ideal Husband*, found *The Importance* amusing but insisted that 'the general effect is that of a farcical comedy dating from the seventies'. Moreover, added Shaw, the play lacked 'humanity'—a quality, presumably, which Shaw would associate with his own drama of social and political reform. But, curiously, Shaw seems to have overlooked the obvious and significant point that Wilde, like Shaw himself, had taken conventional dramatic form and infused it with a new vitality. *Punch* printed a fictitious interview with Wilde to suggest its attitude towards his new play and a common attitude towards his wit:

Q. Why give a play such a title?
A. Why not?
Q. Does the trivial comedy require a plot?
A. Nothing to speak of.
Q. Or characterization?
A. No, for the same kind of dialogue will do for all the company—for London ladies, country girls, justices of the peace, doctors of divinity, maid-servants, and confidential butlers.
Q. What sort of dialogue?
A. Inverted proverbs and renovated paradoxes.

(23 February 1895, p. 260.)

But, clearly, 'inverted proverbs and renovated paradoxes' do not regularly result in comic masterpieces, yet the belief that this was Wilde's literary trick—a simple device used with a minimum of facility—persisted through the 1890s. The most damning review is to be found in the pages of the *Theatre* (No. 75), which judged the play to be poor, designed, as were Wilde's other plays, for the 'less intelligent section of the public,' an extraordinary reaction to a work now generally regarded as one of the wittiest in the language. But such minority opinions obviously were being disregarded by playgoers, for the drama critic of *The Times*, Hamilton Fyfe, reported to the *New York Times* (No. 70) that the 'universal assumption is that it will remain on the boards here for an indefinitely extended period'.

Despite Wilde's arrest on 5 April, the play ran until 8 May for a total of eighty-six performances, Wilde's name having been removed from the playbills and programmes—against which the playwright Sydney Grundy protested in a letter to the *Daily Telegraph* on 8 April 1895. George Alexander, the actor and manager who played the role of Worthing, attributed the loss of almost £300 on this production to the scandal of Wilde's arrest. In 1902, he revived the play (having bought the copyright before Wilde died) at the St James's Theatre, but this production was not too successful financially although it had been critically well received. Beerbohm, reviewing it for the *Saturday Review*, describes the play as

fresh and exquisite as ever, and over the whole house almost every line was sending ripples of laughter—cumulative ripples that became waves, and receded only for fear of drowning the next line. In kind the play always was unlike any other, and in its kind it still seems perfect. I do not wonder that now the critics boldly call it a classic, and predict immortality. And (timorous though I am apt to be in prophecy) I join gladly in their chorus. (18 January 1902, xciii, 75.)

In 1909, the second revival staged by Alexander, acting the role of Jack again, and Allan Aynesworth as Algernon, ran for eleven months and made a profit of over £21,000. Writing to Robert Ross, Alexander delightedly reported: 'You will be glad to hear that dear E has really caught on: we had splendid houses yesterday, and turned money away from the "pit and gallery"—how this would have pleased him [Wilde]!' (*Robert Ross: Friend of Friends*, p. 173.) Further revivals were presented by Alexander at the St James's Theatre in 1911 and 1913.

Unlike the London production, the New York production, which opened on 22 April 1895, two days before Wilde's trial, at the Empire Theatre was not well received by the critics. William Winter, the well-known critic for the *New York Daily Tribune* who usually disapproved of Wilde's work, did not even review the play. *The Sun* was the only daily to write favourably of the production:

The audience did not give the smallest indication that it knew or cared anything about the playwright, further than to appreciate the fact that he had written an exceedingly clever piece. (23 April 1895, p. 7.)

Despite the generally unfavourable reception from most of the critics, the play ran for a few weeks, but its closing marked the beginning of a period of oblivion for Wilde in America that would last for ten years.

V

1895–8: The Silent Years and THE BALLAD OF READING GAOL

From the time of Wilde's conviction in late May 1895, until his death, his name was little mentioned in English literary journals or in the popular Press, even with the publication of *The Ballad of Reading Gaol* in 1898. This was, as Holbrook Jackson has described it, 'the great silence' (No. 110). There were, however, notable instances which shattered it. Within a week of Wilde's conviction, the *Free Review* published a lengthy article on Wilde as a genius in paradox by Ernest Newman (No. 77), with its daring attack on the 'stupid' and 'prejudiced' British public:

If the public howls a man down or grins him down, he is certain to be possessed of genius. . . . it is very hard to say anything original about genius, and still harder to say anything original about the British public.

Shaw also invoked Wilde's name in several theatre reviews written during Wilde's imprisonment. In October 1895, for example, in a review of Jerome K. Jerome's *The Rise of Dick Halward*, Shaw points to a 'remarkable scene' in *An Ideal Husband* to illustrate a point; and in October 1897, in reviewing Charles Hawtrey's *Mr. Martin*, Shaw wrote: 'It cannot be compared to the comedies of Mr. Oscar Wilde, because Mr. Wilde has creative imagination, philosophic humour, and original wit, besides being a master of language . . .' (*Our Theatres in the Nineties*, ii, 1932, 217).

When, on 6 November 1897, the *Academy* proposed the founding of an Academy of Letters and published a list of proposed nominees, omitting Wilde, Shaw wrote two letters to the journal, one of which (published 13 November, p. 402) comments: 'The only dramatist, besides Mr. Henry James, whose nomination could be justified is Mr. Oscar Wilde.' H. G. Wells, calling the *Academy*'s list a 'parlour game', also wrote to the editor inquiring why Wilde's name had been omitted (*ibid.*).

In France, where Wilde's career had been followed more closely than in most other European countries, such journals as *La Revue Blanche*, *La Plume*, and *Le Mercure de France* published articles in defence of Wilde—as martyred artist—(see, for example, Hugues Rebell's 'Défense d'Oscar Wilde', *Mercure de France*, August 1895, xv, 182–90), but the popular Press, as Léon Lemonnier has pointed out, was sharply divided over Wilde (see 'La Condamnation d'Oscar Wilde et l'opinion française', *La Revue mondiale*, 15 January 1931, ccii, 139–51). Lemonnier concludes that if the arrest of Wilde and the revelation of his vice alienated him from many Frenchmen, the excessive punishment brought a sympathetic response, such as Jean de Tinan's in a review of the first production of *Salomé* in 1896 at the Théâtre de l'Œuvre, which concludes: '. . . not to have been there, not to have seen his *Salomé*, more beautiful and more terrible than he had dreamed, was for Oscar Wilde the cruellest misfortune which for an artist must be inconsolable' (*Mercure de France*, March 1896, xvii, 417).

In October 1897, when Wilde completed *The Ballad of Reading Gaol* —his 'great poem', as he called it in a letter to Reginald Turner (*Letters*, p. 556)—he attempted to place it with an American newspaper, having already accepted Leonard Smithers's offer to publish it in England. In August 1897, Robert Sherard, the journalist and later Wilde's first biographer, had apparently suggested that he could arrange to have the poem published in the *New York World* for a considerable sum (*Letters*,

p. 632). But in November, Wilde was telling Robert Ross of his 'unsaleable poem': 'I had no idea that there were such barriers between me and publication in America' (*Letters*, p. 673); and to Ada Leverson: 'I find that I cannot get my poem . . . accepted even by the most revolting New York paper' (*Letters*, p. 674). By late November, he wrote to More Adey: 'Of course I am depressed by the difficulty of reaching an audience; the adventures of my American poem have been a terrible blow to my ambition, my vanity, and my hopes' (*Letters*, p. 687).

In January 1898, Smithers asked Elizabeth Marbury, the agent who had handled all of Wilde's theatrical productions in New York, to secure serialization of *The Ballad* with or without Wilde's name. She replied on 25 January: 'Nobody here seems to feel any interest in the poem, and this morning I received from the *Journal* their final offer, which, alas, is only $100. The *World* refused to give us anything and no syndicate will handle it' (Mason, *Bibliography*, p. 416). But the offer from the *Journal* did not, finally, result in publication. Wilde's name, as Wilde himself wrote to Smithers, had terrified the American newspapers (*Letters*, p. 698).

When *The Ballad* appeared in February 1898, its author given as 'C.3.3' (Wilde's cell-block number), Wilde was convinced that the Press would ignore it, but to his surprise and delight, there were a number of favourable reviews. Some of them, however, as in the case of the *Daily Chronicle* and the *Echo*, regarded the poem, in Wilde's distressed words, as 'a pamphlet on prison-reform' (*Letters*, p. 704). Reviews in the *Academy*, the *Pall Mall Gazette*, and the American journal the *Critic* (Nos. 78, 81, 82)—the latter being the only publication to give Wilde's name as author—are generally favourable, but the uncertainty of response is particularly notable. The greatest praise came from Arthur Symons (No. 80), who concluded that the poem was a 'very powerful piece of writing', indicative of an 'extraordinary talent'. Wilde, who was enormously pleased, wrote to Frank Harris, editor of the *Saturday Review*, that he was 'greatly touched' by the review (*Letters*, p. 716). In France, Henry-D. Davray, an admirer who reviewed English books for the *Mercure de France* and who later wrote a book on Wilde, suitably puffed the poem in the April issue, and in *La Revue Blanche*, Laurence Jerrold (an Englishman who was Paris correspondent for the *Daily Telegraph*) wrote that *The Ballad* was 'splendid', discussing the background of the poem and identifying Wilde as its author (15 April 1898, xv, 635-6).

Once fearful that the Press would ignore the poem, Wilde wrote to Ross: '. . . really the Press has behaved very well' (*Letters*, p. 720), but he was furious with Henley for his attack (No. 79). He was convinced, however, that Henley's review was having an opposite effect (*Letters*, p. 720). The critical reaction caused Frank Harris, in his biography of Wilde, to exclaim, somewhat inaccurately: 'The enthusiasm with which *The Ballad* was accepted in England was astounding. . . . No word of criticism was heard: the most cautious called it a "simple poignant ballad . . . one of the greatest in the English language". This praise is assuredly not too generous' (*Oscar Wilde: His Life and Confessions*, New York, 1918, p. 388).

Despite Wilde's facetious remark to Smithers that 'the popularity of the poem will be largely increased by the author's painful death by starvation' since the public 'love poets to die in that way' (*Letters*, p. 687), *The Ballad* sold out the first edition's 800 copies within a few days. (When Smithers had planned on only 400 copies for the first edition, Wilde wrote to Ross that his publisher was 'so fond of "suppressed" books that he suppresses his own'—*Letters*, p. 705.) A second edition of 1000 copies appeared within the same month, and in March a special third edition of ninety-nine copies appeared (priced at 8s. more a copy), each signed by Wilde. Also in March, the fourth, fifth, and in May the sixth editions (each 1000 copies) were issued by Smithers—a notable demand by the public. In March 1899, Smithers wrote to Wilde that he was planning to print more copies of the poem in case he ran short; he also asked Wilde whether he had any objection to the author's name appearing on the title page. Wrote Smithers: 'I think the time has now come when you should own the "Ballad"' (Mason, *Bibliography*, p. 422). In June, the seventh edition of 2000 copies consequently appeared with Wilde's name in square brackets; in this edition, also, the printer identified himself for the first time. Thus, wide public acceptance had broken the taboo—if only momentarily—of Wilde's name. This was the last 'authorized' edition, for after Wilde's death, Smithers, in financial distress, issued several unauthorized editions until his own death in 1907. Other editions continued to appear (chiefly through Methuen) until 1910.

In his exhaustive study of the publishing history of *The Ballad*, Abraham Horodisch has discussed its phenomenal reception on the Continent and in the United States, where there were nineteen reprints of the poem. Translations of *The Ballad* have been rendered in virtually every European language and several non-European, including Hebrew,

Japanese, and Arabic. None of Wilde's other works, except, perhaps, *The Picture of Dorian Gray*, has had a similar publishing history. But aside from its importance to Wilde as a means of restoring his creative impulse, *The Ballad* provided the means of reminding the literary world and the general public that he still existed and that he was capable of creative work.

VI

Wilde's Posthumous Reputation

With Wilde's sudden death on 30 November 1900, journalists and critics were presumably released from the stigma of Wilde's name. But in a number of estimates of his work both in England and America, doubt over the quality of his achievement persists and the lingering disgrace clings to his name. *The Times*, characterizing Wilde as 'the once brilliant man of letters', briefly summarized his career in its obituary column under the death notice of a German army officer (No. 84). The *Pall Mall Gazette* (No. 85) described Wilde's plays 'as full of bright moments but devoid of consideration as drama'. Indeed, the notice concludes: 'nothing that he ever wrote had strength to endure.' On a back page under the heading 'Dramatic Gossip', the *Athenaeum* offers eleven lines on Wilde's passing, noting that his plays are 'still remembered', and, ignoring his Irish origins, concludes: 'His death further reduces the small number of Englishmen capable of writing comedy' (8 December 1900, p. 768). A sympathetic notice appeared in the *Literary World*:

Mr. Oscar Wilde, a once famous novelist, poet, and playwright, has survived by five years the blow which justice dealt in May, 1895, to his career. . . . The names of Mr. Wilde's works were at one time almost household words in literary circles, but they have fallen into obscurity since his disappearance from society. Few sadder histories have been than his . . . (7 December 1900, lxii n.s., 468.)

In Dublin, the leading literary journal, *Irish Monthly*, devoted no space to Wilde's death.

Notable literary estimates of Wilde's achievement came from Max Beerbohm (No. 86) and J. T. Grein (No. 87). Beerbohm had to ask permission of Herbert Hodge, editor of the *Saturday Review*, to include a tribute to Wilde in his regular review of London openings, a tribute which concludes that Wilde's downfall was 'a lamentable loss to dramatic literature'. In France, Davray, in the *Mercure de France* (No. 88), called Wilde 'a pure artist and a great writer'. Stuart Merrill, the American poet and critic who lived most of his life in France, wrote in *La Plume* that Wilde 'died a victim of the moralists', concluding:

In the presence of the death of the most unfortunate man of our times, I cry out for compassion and invoke oblivion. He who was the prisoner C.3.3 is never prisoner of the great Jailer. Let the work of Oscar Wilde appear to us henceforth in the serene beauty of anonymity. Let us be at least as pitiable as the grave! (15 December 1900, p. 739.)

Despite the passionate rhetoric of such a request, Merrill's wish was only partly fulfilled, for while in the ensuing years critics began to examine the work rather than the man, others, such as Lord Alfred Douglas, would not let Wilde rest in peace. In 1904, there was still discomfort associated with Wilde's memory, for when Althea Gyles, the artist who had designed covers for several of Yeats's books, wished to publish a volume of her own verse with the dedication 'to the beautiful memory of Oscar Wilde', the publisher, refusing to proceed, asked her to remove 'beautiful'. When she refused, the manuscript was returned. Indeed, as late as 1938, E. M. Forster, in a review of Frank Harris's life of Wilde, which finally appeared in England sixteen years after its publication in the United States, pleaded: '. . . it is time Wilde took his place in English literature and English social history, apart from either scandal or *réclame* . . .' ('The Feast of Tongues', *The Spectator*, 29 July 1938, clxi, 194).

The appearance in 1905 of *De Profundis*, extensively cut by Robert Ross, mistakenly convinced many that Wilde had turned repentant sinner. The book was widely reviewed with sympathy under such titles as 'A Soul's Awakening' (J. Tyssul Davis, in the *Inquirer*, 12 August) and 'A Book of Penitence' (by Rev. William Barry in the *Bookman*, April). Wilde's friends (No. 91) also responded with expected sympathy, but Shaw's letter to Robert Ross is particularly interesting in calling *De Profundis* 'all comedy'. Shaw was the only writer at the time to see that Wilde's prison letter—even in its cut version—did not reveal any fundamental change in Wilde at all but was an expression of an artistic temperament. In the United States, the *Critic* stated that *De Profundis* 'has done a good deal to reinstate Wilde in public opinion, not as a man, perhaps, but as a writer' (November 1905, xlvii, 405).

And in France, André Gide wrote that he could not read the work without tears ('Le *De Profundis* d'Oscar Wilde', *L'Ermitage*, 15 August 1905, ii, 65).

The sale of the volume was phenomenal. Between 1905 and 1913, Methuen published twenty-eight editions, the first edition alone consisting of 10,000 copies. In America, Putnam reprinted the work sixteen times between 1905 and 1914. *De Profundis* was quickly translated on the Continent, where Wilde's literary reputation soared.

In *Home Life in Germany* (New York, 1908), Mrs Alfred Sidgwick wrote that Ruskin and Wilde were the 'two popular modern authors' in Germany. And Sir Herbert Beerbohm Tree, the actor and manager, on his return from a tour of Germany, stated that there the three great dramatists in English were Shakespeare, Shaw, and Wilde (Mason, *Art and Morality*, p. 24). Wilde's fame was further enhanced in Germany by Richard Strauss's musical setting of *Salomé* in 1905, when it created a sensation in Dresden. (The American critic James Huneker, writing to a friend, complained: 'It's the music that speaks, not that wretched mediocrity Wilde'—*Letters of James Gibbons Huneker*, ed. Josephine Huneker, New York, 1922, p. 56. For Huneker's general deprecation of Wilde, see No. 113.) The extraordinary popularity of Wilde in Germany is also described by Percival Pollard, who noted, in his introduction to *In Memoriam: Oscar Wilde* (Greenwich, Conn., 1905):

When you went beyond the theatre, eyeing the windows of the booksellers, you saw Wilde's name everywhere,—his *De Profundis* was the most famous book of the season in Berlin, as in France and England; or at any rate, the booksellers seemed to intimate that; they positively plastered their showcases and windows with Wilde literature. (pp. 10–11.)

Carl Dietz, in a lengthy article in the *Preussische Jahrbücher*, states that at the time of Wilde's trial in 1895, little was known of him in Germany, and little mention of his death was made in the German Press, but by 1905, hardly a week passed when a German newspaper did not mention his name (April 1906, cxxiv, 1–41). In Trieste, Joyce, capitalizing on the widespread interest in Wilde on the Continent and on the occasion of the performance of Strauss's opera in that city, published an article in *Il Piccolo della Sera* (24 March 1909), largely a biographical account but with the judgment that Wilde's comedies were 'brilliant' (*The Critical Writings of James Joyce*, ed. Ellsworth Mason and Richard Ellmann, New York, 1964, pp. 201–5). The special correspondent for the *Boston Evening Transcript*, attempting to account for Wilde's extraordinary popularity on the Continent among the Germans, French, and Italians, suggested that good translations were partly responsible but also that Wilde's sophisticated wit and intelligence combined with the tragic legend of his life associated him with Poe and Byron, who had long fascinated Continental readers ('Oscar Wilde Redivivus', 28 August 1907, p. 15). (For a further discussion of Wilde's reputation on the Continent, see Archibald Henderson, No. 98.)

In other European countries interest in Wilde was less extensive but none the less present. In Sweden, for example, Wilde was little known before the early 1890s. *Intentions*, the first of Wilde's works to be translated, appeared in 1893. The critic Ekvard Alkman translated *Salomé* in the same year but had considerable difficulty in finding a publisher. By the late nineties, however, some Swedish critics were comparing *Lady Windermere's Fan* and *The Importance of Being Earnest* to the works of Congreve and Sheridan. But when a translation of *The Picture of Dorian Gray* appeared in 1905, only three major newspapers out of fifteen reviewed it. In Denmark, *Dorian Gray*, appearing in the same year, received some praise, but the Danes appear to have been little interested in Wilde, only *Salomé* having been previously translated. (See Walter Nelson, *Oscar Wilde in Sweden and Other Essays*, Dublin, 1965.) The critical activity of the Swedish critic Ernst Bendz, who wrote in three languages and published widely in Europe, was later responsible for a renewed interest in Wilde. A representative continental scholar-critic, he regarded Wilde as a major writer (see Nos. 112, 116).

Wilde's fame, however, has not been confined to Europe, as Japanese and Hebrew translations have testified. (Yeats once reported that he had heard that Wilde's 'Soul of Man Under Socialism' was much read in China. See No. 123.) In the Middle East, Wilde is one of the most frequently translated authors, *Dorian Gray*, *The Happy Prince*, and *An Ideal Husband* having been translated into Arabic several times; and *Lady Windermere's Fan*, *Lord Arthur Savile's Crime*, and *Salomé* having been translated at least once. (Professor Suheil Bushrui, of the American University of Beirut, recalls a comment made to him by Mrs Yeats that when *The Happy Prince and Other Tales* was translated and widely read in Arabia, Yeats considered that the climax of Wilde's success.)

In America, little attention was paid to Wilde between 1895 and 1905, but in that year the publication of *De Profundis* stimulated renewed interest in his works. As a result of the great success of *De Profundis*, New York booksellers were calling him 'the greatest Irishman of letters since Swift'. Many critics, however, were reluctant to revise their estimates of his achievement. When the Progressive Stage Society, an *avant-garde* group of volunteer actors, staged *Salomé*, William Winter, who had refused to review *The Importance of Being Earnest*, wrote in the *New York Daily Tribune*:

> Oscar Wilde was a person of slender talent and of no lasting importance, and, considering the baleful associations that hang about his name, it would be 'progressing' in the right direction to allow his works and all memory of him to pass at once into the oblivion that surely awaits them. (14 November 1905, p. 7.)

When *Salomé* was given a professional production in 1906 at the Astor Theatre, it was again condemned, *The Sun* calling it 'bloodily degenerate' (6 November 1906), and Winter again denouncing it as a 'repulsive composition . . . decadent stuff, and unworthy of notice' (*Tribune*, 16 November 1906).

But the attraction (and repulsion) of *Salomé* persisted. Strauss's opera, given at the Metropolitan Opera House in January 1907, created a sensation (indeed, twenty-seven years were to pass before another production of *Salomé* was seen there). And in 1909, another production of Wilde's play was seen in New York. By 1910, Wilde's fame was widespread: between that year and 1918, all of the major plays were successfully revived on the New York stage and elsewhere in the United States. Wilde's reputation as a playwright had reached its zenith. In the 1920s, however, it declined as native American drama developed.

In the years following Wilde's death a growing number of notable critics—as the present volume indicates—were attracted to the complexities of Wilde's art. The seriousness of Wilde's devotion to a life of art and the art of life had been perceived by some in the 1890s, but in the years before the First World War the critical response moved in a direction that would have surprised many earlier critics. Archibald Henderson (No. 99), for example, treated Wilde's plays seriously as important documents in the history of the drama, and Alice Wood (No. 114) discussed Wilde as a significant critic, writing that 'even a *flâneur*, one who trifled with and abused life, is worthy of study by those who would observe the modern spirit in its growth'.

But a number of Wilde's fellow writers saw little of value in his work. Edmund Gosse (No. 107) regarded Wilde as a 'mediocre figure'. After having read Gide's study of Wilde in 1910, John Galsworthy confided his visceral reaction to his diary on 4 May that he could 'never stomach Wilde's personality nor his writings' (H. V. Marrot, *The Life and Letters of John Galsworthy*, 1935, p. 281). The distinguished American critic James Huneker (No. 113) could only lament in 1914 that since Wilde's death 'the number of volumes dealing with his glittering personality, quite negligible verse and more or less insincere prose, have been steadily accumulating; why, I'm at a loss to understand'. A. E. Housman, in a letter dated 21 June 1928, expressed the idea—indicative, clearly, of his general estimate of Wilde—that 'parts of *The Ballad of Reading Gaol* are above Wilde's average, but I suspect they were written by Lord Alfred Douglas . . .' (quoted in Laurence Housman, *A.E.H.: Some Poems, Some Letters, and a Personal Memoir*, 1937, p. 200). And Arnold Bennett, like most of the writers here quoted, regarded Wilde as merely a successful mediocrity (No. 127).

Yet Wilde has survived, and since the Second World War, the man and his work have attracted such major critics as W. H. Auden, Edmund Wilson, Eric Bentley, Louis Kronenberger, Richard Ellmann, James Agate, René Wellek, and the novelist Kingsley Amis, who wrote in 1956 that Wilde's 'stock probably stands as high today as any time since the earlier 1890s' ('Introduction' to *Oscar Wilde: Poems and Essays*, p. 15). James Laver, in a British Council monograph (1954), has written, however, that though Wilde has a 'permanent niche' in literary history, his reputation remains uncertain:

Oscar Wilde is still a controversial figure. On the continent of Europe his reputation stands as high as ever it did, and his name is probably, after Shakespeare's, the best known in English letters. Englishmen are inclined to think this estimate exaggerated . . . (p. 7.)

The most recent evaluations of Wilde's work contain a new appreciation and understanding of his ironic methods, his use of masks, and the psychology and strategy of the artist—which many Victorians either completely misunderstood or barely grasped. Wilde's reputation, therefore, continues to undergo revision, as the tensions of the Victorian age become clearer to us and as we clarify our understanding of Wilde's symbolic relation to that age and to our own.

POEMS

June 1881

1. Unsigned review, *Athenaeum*

23 July 1881, pp. 103–4

Mr. Wilde's volume of poems may be regarded as the evangel of a new creed. From other gospels it differs in coming after, instead of before, the cult it seeks to establish. It has thus the advantage of answering objection as well as propounding dogma, and its rebuke of irreverence, instead of being vague and discursive, is exact and to the point. One drawback from these advantages is that what should be promulgation of truth takes occasionally a form that might be mistaken for apology, and that querulous protest disappoints at times those who anticipate a clarion note of defiance. That the mind of the poet has been vexed, and the soul of the teacher troubled by 'shallow wit' is obvious. In one of those poems of fourteen lines which find occasional acceptance as sonnets Mr. Wilde declares:—

[quotes 'Theoretikos']

The kind of neutrality indicated in the last line of this poem corresponds with and recalls that invoked by the hero of a Western adventure with a 'grizzly,' who, without asking for any direct aid from the superior powers, urged them at least not to 'side with the b'ar.'

In the 'Garden of Eros' the doctrine of the new worship is promulgated intelligibly, if not very musically:—

[quotes from 'Spirit of Beauty! tarry still a-while' to 'Its new-found creeds so sceptical and so dogmatical'.]

This at least is challenge. It is a little difficult to know what the 'slain of Waterloo' have to do in the matter, or why their phantoms should rise in wrath to combat with the ancient votaries of the Spirit of Beauty who

are not yet dead. Since the days of Macbeth a state of affairs which the
thane understood to have existed before his time, that

When the brains were out the man would die,

has returned, and the slain of Waterloo, or those of them buried in
England, will scarcely hear the 'pother o'er their heads' created by
modern aestheticism. 'Victories' is a singularly bad rhyme to 'votaries,'
and the last line of the quotation affords a notable instance of bathos.
Still, if the verses have not much poetry they at least show courage. In a
sonnet entitled 'Taedium Vitae' the protest seems most directly
personal:—

[quotes sonnet]

Worship of beauty, whatever shape it may take, is not likely to be a
thing of which to be ashamed, and those by whom it is derided may
well be chargeable with offences far more mischievous than a little
false aestheticism. We fail to see, however, that the apostle of the new
worship has any distinct message. With Wordsworth and with some
other men Mr. Wilde holds we should be the better for the return of
Milton. With the Laureate as with Wordsworth he disapproves strongly
of the commercial tendencies of the age. With others besides poets he
does not quite know what to make of modern demagogism, with some
aspects of which he sympathizes, while others are wholly repellent to
him; and he is greatly exercised by the position of the Pope at Rome.

It is doubtful, however, how far familiarity with the nudities of
passion will go towards setting the world straight. A study so clever as
Manon Lescaut has not done much to check the movement towards
feminine suffrage. We doubt, then, whether any number of rhapsodies
like 'Charmides' will serve a purpose such as Mr. Wilde seems to desire
when he sighs for a return of Milton.

Turning to the execution of the poems, there is something to admire.
Mr. Wilde has a keen perception of certain aspects of natural beauty.
Single lines might be extracted which convey striking and accurate
pictures. The worst faults are artificiality and insincerity, and an
extravagant accentuation of whatever in modern verse most closely
approaches the *estilo culto* of the sixteenth century. Imitation of previous
writers goes far enough seriously to damage the claim to originality,
and the workmanship is slovenly in the sense that those half rhymes
which in pre-Tennysonian days were tolerated in the writings of the
best poets are employed with a freedom that deprives the task of writing

verse of the greater portion of its difficulty. A single page affords
instances not only of such rhymes as 'Thessaly' and 'virginity' and
'armoury' and 'poesy,' but of such altogether unpardonable attempts to
force a rhyme as 'worshipper' and 'conqueror.' 'Sicily' and 'uncon-
sciously,' and 'sovereignty' and 'eternity,' are weak and unsatisfactory.
in fact rhymes of this description abound. In dealing, meanwhile, with
imitation we pass over the use, in two consecutive lines, of such epithets
directly taken from Milton as 'swinked' shephered and 'wattled'
sheep- 'cotes.' Does Mr. Wilde suppose he could ever have written the
verses in 'Ave Imperatrix' commencing,—

> But the sad dove, that sits alone
> In England—she hath no delight.

> In vain the laughing girl will lean
> To greet her love with love-lit eyes:
> Down in some treacherous black ravine,
> Clutching his flag, the dead boy lies,—

if the Laureate [Tennyson] had not given us the noble picture in 'In
Memoriam,'

> Oh somewhere, meek, unconscious dove, &c.?

The sonnet on the 'Massacre of the Christians in Bulgaria' reflects
Milton's sonnet on the 'Massacres in Piedmont.' The 'Garden of Eros'
recalls at times Mr. Swinburne—at times Alexander Smith. In the
descriptions of flowers which occur in the poem last named there is
direct and reiterated imitation of Shakspeare.

> Some violets lie
> That will not look the gold sun in the face
> For fear of too much splendour

reminds one of the

> Pale primroses
> That die unmarried, ere they can behold
> Bright Phœbus in his strength.

Mr. Wilde's

> Budding marjoram which but to kiss
> Would sweeten Cytheræa's lips,

and his

> Meadow-sweet
> Whiter than Juno's throat,

35

bring back the

> Violets, dim,
> But sweeter than the lids of Juno's eyes
> Or Cytherea's breath;

and the 'rustling bluebells'—'rustling bluebells' 'is a vile phrase'—that come

> Almost before the blackbird finds a mate
> And overstay the swallow,

are but the daffodils

> That come before the swallow dares.

Traces of this kind of imitation abound, and there is scarcely a poet of high mark in the present century whose influence is not perceptible.

What, however, impresses most unfavourably the reader is the over-indulgence in metaphor, in affected neologisms, and in conceits behind which sense and reason are obscured. Gradually during recent years this style has grown upon us, until the poetic literature of the latter half of the nineteenth century seems likely to be classed with that produced by Lyly and the Euphuists. Of whatever is most vicious in a style which grows out of a misunderstanding worship of Keats, Mr. Wilde supplies abundant illustrations, and the whole is as inflated and insincere as it can well be. Work of this nature has no element of endurance, and Mr. Wilde's poems, in spite of some grace and beauty, as we have said, will, when their temporary notoriety is exhausted, find a place on the shelves of those only who hunt after the curious in literature. They may perhaps serve as an illustration in some chapter on the revival in the nineteenth century of the Gongorism of the sixteenth.

2. Unsigned notice, *Saturday Review*

23 July 1881, lii, 118

Mr. Wilde's verses belong to a class which is the special terror of reviewers, the poetry which is neither good nor bad, which calls for neither praise nor ridicule, and in which we search in vain for any personal touch of thought or music. The author possesses cleverness, astonishing fluency, a rich and full vocabulary, and nothing to say. Mr. Wilde has read Messrs. Tennyson, Swinburne, Arnold, and Rossetti with great pleasure, and he has paid them the compliment of copying their mannerisms very naïvely; indeed, it might be fairly said that his book is little more than a cento of reminiscences from these poets. The great fault of all such writing as this is the want of literary sincerity that it displays. For instance, Mr. Wilde, brings in to his verse the names of innumerable birds and flowers, because he likes the sound of their names, not because he has made any observation of their habits. He thinks that the meadow-sweet and the wood-anemone bloom at the same time, that that shy and isolated flower the harebell 'breaks across the woodland' in masses 'like a sudden flush of sea,' and that owls are commonly met with in mid-ocean. But worse than this profuse and careless imagery is the sensual and ignoble tone which deforms a large proportion of the poems, and for which the plea of youth is scarcely sufficient excuse. So much talk about 'grand cool flanks' and 'crescent thighs' is decidedly offensive, and we have no wish to know that the writer ever 'paddled with the polished throat' of his lady-love. The book is not without traces of cleverness, but is marred everywhere by imitation, insincerity, and bad taste.

3. Oscar Browning on *Poems*

1881

Signed review in the *Academy* 30 July 1881, xx, 85.
Oscar Browning (1837–1923), Cambridge don from 1876 to 1909, published studies on such figures as Dante, Napoleon, Goethe, and George Eliot. Wilde, who had known Browning since 1879, asked him, in a letter probably written in June 1881, to review his forthcoming volume of poems, adding: 'Books so often fall into stupid and illiterate hands that I am anxious to be really criticised: ignorant praise or ignorant blame is so insulting.' (*Letters*, p. 77.)

This volume has for many reasons been looked for with interest. Mr. Wilde has rightly or wrongly been marked out as representing the newest development of academic aestheticism. He has had to undergo the irrational abuse and ridicule, and the still more irrational flattery, earned by principles and tendencies with many of which he can have but little sympathy. His poems will therefore be read with the twofold purpose of discovering what these new teachers have to say, and what claim Mr. Wilde has to be heard by the public whom he addresses. That the latter claim will be conceded no one who has read these poems can doubt. They are the product of a fresh, vigorous mind, dowered with a quick perception of the beauties of nature, with a command of varied and musical language, with a sympathetic sensuousness which would gain rather than lose by the vesture of a thicker veil. Critics may blame or praise; they cannot speak of Mr. Wilde's work with contempt. But the message of the new gospel is not delivered with so clear a note. We are bewildered by the irregular pulsations of a sympathy which never wearies. Roman Catholic ritual, stern Puritanism, parched Greek islands, cool English lanes and streams, Paganism and Christianity, despotism and Republicanism, Wordsworth, Milton, and Mr. Swinburne, receive in turn the same passionate devotion. Perhaps this inconsistency is more attributable to the author than to the school. Keats has told us that the imagination of a boy is healthy, and the mature imagination of a man is healthy, but there is a space of life between in which the soul is in a ferment, the character undecided, the way of life uncertain, the ambition thick sighted.

Let us remember this, and be charitable and patient.

The book is artistically arranged, as might be expected from its brilliant binding and its luxury of type and paper. As at a cunning concert, songs and ballads alternate with longer flights of melody. 'Eleutheria,' a collection of small poems, mainly sonnets, more or less concerned with freedom, is followed by the 'Garden of Eros,' a graceful tribute to Swinburne, Morris, and Rossetti. Up to this point we are checked by many faults, both of extravagance and imitation. Then follows a spell of songs under the name of 'Rosa mystica,' a flower of Italian travel, which shows, if nothing else, the poet's love for Italy, and his command of the 'large utterance' which befits her praise. Then succeeds an exquisite poem, 'The Burden of Itys,' a dissolving view of Greece, Italy, and England fused into one by the song of the nightingale common to all. Here, however, the discord which shrieks so untuneably in 'Charmides' is first heard. Mr. Wilde's audacious sensuousness should have felt that 'the Venus of the little Melian farm' and the *Dawn* of Michaelangelo were too sacred to be profaned by passion.

A batch of smaller poems, including a sweetly musical tribute to the poet's college, Magdalen, and some stanzas for music, of which we are glad not to have the setting, is followed by 'Charmides,' the longest poem in the volume. It is full of music, beauty, imagination, and power; but the story, as far as there is one, is most repulsive. Mr. Wilde has no magic to veil the hideousness of a sensuality which feeds on statues and dead bodies. Let him learn a lesson from the *Vénus d'Ille* of Mérimée, where the ground-thought is a *bourdon*[1] of horror through the whole of the dreadful story. Then come more songs, tributes to Keats and Shelley, to Florence and Greece, very musical and passionate, and some mediaeval ballads which would be more effective if Mr. Calverley had never taught us the burden of 'butter and eggs and a pound of cheese.'

We must hurry on to the last long poem, 'Humanitad' (why not Humanidad?), a praise of those who have fallen martyrs to the enthusiasm of humanity, and of that enthusiasm itself as the conqueror and expeller of baser passions. We think that as Mr. Wilde's work progresses this poem will be found to mark a transition to a deeper and fuller tone than he has yet had strength to strike.

[1] Ground-note.

The volume ends with a lament on the bitter-sweet of love, written in a lingering metre, a trochaic Alexandrian, full of melody and pathos.

> Ah! what else had I to do but love you: God's
> own mother was less dear to me,
> And less dear the Cytherean rising like an argent
> lily from the sea.
> I have made my choice and lived my poems, and
> though youth is gone in wasted days,
> I have found the lover's crown of myrtle better
> than the poet's crown of bays.

We have no space to justify our opinion by quotations, but we lay down this book in the conviction that England is enriched with a new poet. If Mr. Wilde, keeping his passion, his sense of beauty, his gifts of language and metre, will apply to himself the stern self-discipline through which alone those whom he admires have obtained the excellence which is theirs, there is no boyish dream of fame or ambition which he may not at some time satisfy. But if he continues to prefer the meed of the lover to that of the poet, emotion to reason, extravagance to chastity of taste, he will find that the Byronic despair which lends grace to the work of five-and-twenty turns to a most unpoetical reality in maturer years.

4. Unsigned review, *Dial*

1881

Unsigned review, titled 'The Poetry of an Aesthete', in the *Dial* [Chicago], August 1881, ii, 82–5. The following extracts are taken from a rather extensive review, most of which consists of long illustrative passages from *Poems*.

. . . That a man could go about the streets wearing long hair and unheard-of garments and bearing lilies in his hands, and give afternoon tea-parties and astonish his guests with the fantastic novelty of his apartments and the ethereal nonsense of his conversation, all as a carefully-studied preliminary to the publication of a volume of poems, would seem at first thought surprising. But the surprise lessens when we recall the early history of Bulwer and Disraeli and other literary dandies and eccentricities, and the possibility that this young man from Dublin —whose mother is Lady Wilde, an Irish poetess, and whose father was a physician, knighted for distinguished services—may have chosen to attempt his march to fame by the Disraelian route.

This might not be the theory most worthy of acceptance were the poems themselves less worthy of consideration. Affected and strained though they often are, and lacking the exaltation that can come alone from a high and sincere poetic purpose, they are scarcely what one would expect from a hare-brain or a guy. Coming from a new and unknown writer, they are certainly remarkable. Striking in form and treatment, and polished in workmanship, while they fail to move those deeper human chords inaccessible to their studied artificiality, they often surprise us with their virility and freedom, and are never, except in disconnected passages, ridiculous. There are some intense lines which are dangerously near the breakers, but these are usually rescued before their sense is wrecked. Most tastes will reject such phrases as 'unvintageable sea' and 'paddled with the polished throat,' though the latter finds its justification, and doubtless found its suggestion, in Shakespere's 'paddling in your neck,' etc. That the poems are often overweighted

41

and turgid in their straining for effect is no more than could be expected of so affected a person. And that they are altogether, lacking in humor is still more needless to state, since it is precisely the lack of this quality in an Æsthete that can alone prevent him from perceiving his own ridiculousness.

The poems are sixty in number, ranging from sonnets—of which there is a considerable number—to 'Charmides,' comprising forty pages, the longest piece in the collection. This poem especially illustrates the author's fondness for Greek themes and treatment—a fondness which is the dominant spirit of the book, and in which he almost surpasses Swinburne. Suggestive, too, of Swinburne, and of a gross 'fleshly' rather than æsthetic school, are many of the stanzas; others are very beautiful, and most are full of power. . . .

We think that after these extracts most readers of poetic taste will agree that there is something in this young man from Dublin not dis-covered by the caricaturist of *Punch*; and that if we are to have more of this Æsthete's philosophy it is desirable by all means to have it in the form of his poetry.

5. Unsigned review, *Spectator*

13 August 1881, liv, 1048–50

The reading of this book fills us with alarm. It is evidently the work of a clever man, as well as of an educated man, but it is not only a book containing poems which ought never to have been conceived, still less published, but it is almost wholly without thoughts worthy of the name, entirely devoid of true passion, with very few vestiges even of genuine emotion, and constituted entirely out of sensuous images and pictures strung together often with so little true art that they remind one more of a number of totally different species of blossoms accumu-lated on the same stem, than of any cluster of natural flowers. It is quite a shock to find that so much talent as is needed to produce such a book as this, is not also enough to prevent a book on the whole so worthless, from being written.

Mr. Wilde's usual mood is one of lackadaisical despair that he does not live in Greece, and see the images with which Greek poetry has filled his mind. He shakes off the dust of this modern world from his feet, in the following very superior sonnet:—

[quotes 'Theoretikos']

But even in this reprobation of our modern world, Mr. Wilde is not clear. We hardly know what he means by 'wisdom and reverence' being 'sold at mart,'—not, we suppose, that they are eagerly demanded and bought in the market-place, because with that he would hardly find fault, but probably that the people of this country are willing to strip themselves of their own wisdom and reverence for the sake of getting other people's money, for he adds that the 'rude people rage with ignorant cries against an heritage of centuries.' But as he does not give us the slightest hint as to the particular forms of wisdom and reverence of which we are stripping ourselves for gain, we do not believe that he has given us the true reason why he thus abjures the world he is so dissatisfied with, and devotes himself to what he calls the world of Art, really, in his case, a world of fragments of coloured glass, hardly even arranged, as the child's kaleidoscope arranges them, into something like harmonious form. Mr. Wilde begins his life 'apart' by a poem called 'The Garden of Eros,' in which there is a very curious medley of inconsistent flowers with capricious 'dreams of Art.' It is the heart of June, he says, though a daffodil and some violets have outstayed the spring; the harebells are out, and the columbines and the red holly-hock; it is a place Persephone ought to tread, when she is wearied of 'the flowerless fields of Dis;' but soon it appears that anemones, and convolvulus, and hyacinths, and purple clematis, and foxgloves, and oxlips, and irises, and 'the snowy primrose of the night,' which is, we suppose, a white evening primrose, are all out together; and finally, to our great astonishment, we are told that 'the almond-blossoms gleam' 'against the pallid shield of the wan sky,'—almond-blossoms which, so far as we know, are never seen later than March or the very earliest days of April. However, this world of inconsistent flowers is made the scene of various pictures in which we may perhaps detect why Mr. Oscar Wilde is ill-pleased with the world as it is. The spirit of beauty is entreated to tarry, in spite of the deficiency of Greek foliage and Greek trees, on our 'bleak hills:'—

[quotes from 'The Garden of Eros', stanzas 21–4: 'Yet tarry! for the boy who loved thee best' to 'And the new Sign grows grey . . .']

Thus the spirit of poetry is conjured to tarry, because Keats is dead, and only Mr. Swinburne,—with whom Mr. Wilde afterwards associates the names of Mr. Morris and Mr. Rossetti—is left to us; and it appears that the great claim of Mr. Swinburne on our gratitude is that he had discrowned Christ, and restored the worship of the Greek divinities. Would not that achievement be tolerably fitly described as one of those feats of the 'vile traffic-house,' in renouncing 'wisdom and reverence' and the 'heritage of centuries,' which Mr. Wilde had previously assigned as his reason for turning away from the modern world altogether? Yet it is represented as constituting the greatest possible claim upon the gratitude of the artist, instead of as the deed of a barbarian. After this tribute to Mr. Swinburne, Mr. Morris, and Mr. Rossetti, Mr. Wilde returns to his desolate mood, and begins to complain of science:—

[quotes stanzas 36–7: 'But they are few . . .' to 'Because rude eyes peer at my mistress through a telescope!']

We cannot imagine any one offering a sillier suggestion, than that Mr. Wilde should lose all hope because there are lunar astronomers who examine the moon through a telescope, nor do we suppose that Mr. Wilde himself would ever have made it, if it had not occurred to him as a novel sort of sneer against men of science. But whom should we accuse of wasting the heritage of centuries, if not the man who first praises Mr. Swinburne for having discrowned the Galilean, and then attacks science for dispelling,—what needed no dispelling,—the illusions of Greek fable? If it is true that Christianity is false, and that science is deadly, what heritage of wisdom and reverence have the centuries left us worth preserving? The truth is that all Mr. Wilde cares about is to have some sort of excuse for a lackadaisical melancholy, without substance and without character. He complains of the age for ignoring the past, without feeling what he writes; and then he praises the most destructive writers of the age precisely for ignoring the riches we have inherited from the past, again, as we believe, without feeling in the least what he expresses. There is, indeed, no trace of genuine emotion in any one of these poems.

In one poem Mr. Wilde breathes out execrations against Italy for the irreverence done to the Pope, and in another panegyrises Mazzini for driving the Pope out of Rome:—

[quotes 'Italia']

Now read this:—

[quotes from 'Humanitad', stanzas 39–42: 'One such indeed I saw, but, Ichabod!' to 'Breathe through my melancholy pipe thy sweetest threnody!']

If Mr. Wilde has changed his mind, why did he perpetuate in the same volume two states of opinion so violently opposed? Probably he has not changed his mind, but only his mood, and thinks one mood as good as the other. So far as we can understand him by the aid of this volume, that is likely enough to be his real condition of thought, and it is somewhere about the truth, neither mood being of the slightest weight or worth, and one just as good as the other. But what in the world does he mean, —probably he has no meaning,—in saying that Mazzini,—for, of course, all this refers to Mazzini,—'being man, died for the sake of God?' He died at the age of sixty-three in Pisa, and, so far as we know, as other men of sixty-three die. Mr. Wilde does not care too much whether he has a meaning or not in what he writes.

A clever man, with a host of sensuous pictures in his mind, some-times passing into pure sensuality,—that is what this volume displays. To our mind, there is no poetry in it, and no genuine lyrical feeling, from one end to the other. If Mr. Wilde were a less clever man, we should think less badly of his book. But as it is, it is clear he must and does know how artificial and pumped-up it is, and he publishes it, nevertheless, without scruple, as likely to pass current with the world. For a fresh instance, take the continuation of the passage we have just quoted about Mazzini:—

> Breathe through the tragic stops such melodies
>   That Joy's self may grow jealous, and the Nine
> Forget awhile their discreet emperies,
>   Mourning for him who on Rome's lordliest shrine
> Lit for men's lives the light of Marathon,
> And bare to sun-forgotten fields the fire of the sun!
>
> O guard him, guard him well, my Giotto's tower,
>   Let some young Florentine each eventide
> Bring coronals of that enchanted flower
>   Which the dim woods of Vallombrosa hide,
> And deck the marble tomb wherein he lies
> Whose soul is as some mighty orb unseen of mortal eyes.

Some mighty orb whose cycled wanderings,
   Being tempest-driven to the farthest rim
Where Chaos meets Creation and the wings
   Of the eternal chanting Cherubim
Are pavilioned on Nothing, passed away
Into a moonless void,—and yet, though he is dust and clay,

He is not dead, the immemorial Fates
   Forbid it, and the closing shears refrain,
Lift up your heads, ye everlasting gates!
   Ye argent clarions sound a loftier strain!
For the vile thing he hated lurks within
Its sombre house, alone with God and memories of sin.

Is it possible for a clever man to write worse stuff than that? No doubt, 'discreet emperies' is a noble phrase, and will impress the vulgar. But will even the vulgar be impressed by the stellar metaphor? Mazzini's soul is as some mighty orb, tempest-driven to the border-land between chaos and creation, where the cherubim are pavilioned upon nothing; and he passed away into a 'moonless void,'—as if the void beyond the borders of 'creation' were at all likely to be moonlit,—and 'yet' he is not dead,—the 'yet' implying, we suppose, that, as a rule, mighty orbs which are tempest-driven 'to the furthest rim where chaos meets creation,' *are* dead when they go out into the 'moonless' void beyond. In Mazzini's case, the 'immemorial fates' forbid the possibility of Death. We should have attached somewhat more meaning to the sentence, if it had been said that it was the memorial fates which forbade it. 'Immemorial' means, we suppose, 'beyond the reach of memory;'—at least 'time immemorial' certainly means time reaching back beyond what human memory can record. But why should Fates which reach beyond the limits of memory have anything special to say to Mazzini's death or immortality? If the veto on his death were not founded on the gloriousness of his achievements, it was not a tribute to his greatness. And if it were, then it was not the immemorial character of the Fates on which their decree was founded. And what is the significance to be attached to the words, 'the closing shears refrain?' We had always thought that the shears of Atropos only determined the length of the life on earth, but had nothing to say to immortality. Then, again, is there any drift, unless it be a species of blasphemy, to be attached to the last four lines? The 'argent clarions' are, we suppose, to sound for the entrance of Mazzini into some dwelling-place of immortal fame; but if so, what is the meaning of the reason given for the lifting up of the gates and the sounding of the 'argent clarions?'

> For the vile thing he hated lurks within
> Its sombre house, alone with God and memories of sin.

The vile thing Mazzini hated was, we suppose, tyranny of some kind; Mr. Wilde surely does not mean that Mazzini was going to enter into the dwelling of tyranny; and if not, then 'the sombre house' where tyranny lurked 'alone with God and memories of sin' must be, we suppose, a totally different place from that whose gates are to be lifted up for Mazzini to enter; and what connection the one dwelling has with the other, or the gates of that other, we have not the remotest idea.

Mr. Oscar Wilde is no poet, but a cleverish man who has an infinite contempt for his readers, and thinks he can take them in with a little mouthing verse. Perhaps he is right for the moment; but this we can say with some confidence, that the book is the trash of a man of a certain amount of mimetic ability, and trash the trashiness of which the author is much too cultivated not to recognise quite clearly.

6. Walter Hamilton on *Poems* as 'aesthetic poetry'

1882

Extracts from a chapter on Wilde in *The Aesthetic Movement in England* (1882), pp. 85–110, which consists of an account of Wilde's life, his significance in the Aesthetic Movement, and lengthy illustrations from *Poems*.

Walter Hamilton (1844–99), critic and bibliophile, published a study of Poe, a treatise on book-plates, and a history of English drama. The fact that Hamilton devoted a lengthy chapter to Wilde (other chapters are on such figures as William Morris and Rossetti) after one volume of verse amply testifies to his notoriety at this time.

. . . Now I have no intention of comparing Mr. Wilde with any of our greater poets, but I do wish to call attention to the fact that he is still a very young man; the early works of Shelley, Keats, Byron and Tennyson, were pronounced by the critics, also, to be 'poor and pretentious stuff,' so Mr. Wilde need not be greatly disturbed by these spiteful criticisms, especially as his poems have already run through four editions. . . .

The longest poem in the volume tells how Charmides obtained access into the sacred secret temple of Minerva, and the terrible vengeance the haughty virgin goddess took upon him, and the maid who loved him. This poem abounds with both the merits and the faults of Mr. Oscar Wilde's style—it is classical, sad, voluptuous, and full of passages of the most exquisitely musical word painting; but it is cloying from its very sweetness—the elaboration of its details makes it over luscious. It is no mere trick to be able to write thus; it betrays a luxuriant fancy and a great command of language; youth is apt to be exuberant, age will mellow down his muse, and then Mr. Wilde's undoubted genius will produce something finer even than Charmides.

Poets do not at all times express their own individual opinions in their works, nor is it advisable they should; theirs it is to portray many minds, and many moods of many men; yet, without doubt, the ideas expressed in '*Ave Imperatrix*' are those of Mr. Wilde, and they show him to be a Republican, not of the noisy and blatant, but of the quiet and patient kind, content to wait till the general spread of democracy, and the absorption of governing power by the people, shall peacefully bring about the changes they desire, and remove the abuses of our present *régime*. . . .

But those who would find the true ring of *Æsthetic* poetry, must indeed go to the book itself; even a Philistine may find delight in its perusal, if *he will*; or if he prefer to scoff and jibe so let it be. For such a one nothing but pity should be felt—for truly the gift of appreciating the beautiful in nature, or in art, is not given to every man, and he who has it not is as one who is colour-blind; he is sense-blind, or sound-blind, and deserves commiseration.

7. T. W. Higginson on Wilde's 'unmanly' poetry

1882

Signed article by Thomas Wentworth Higginson, 'Unmanly Manhood', the *Woman's Journal* [Boston], (4 February 1882), xiii, 33.

Higginson (1823–1911), a prolific author, an ardent social reformer and champion of woman's suffrage, here attacks Wilde's *Poems* as offensive to decency and morality. Wilde, who was in America on his celebrated lecture tour, alluded to Higginson (in a letter to Joaquin Miller, dated 28 February 1882) as 'this scribbling anonymuncule in grand old Massachusetts who scrawls and screams so glibly about what he cannot understand.' (*Letters*, p. 98.)

We say that the clergy are the appointed guardians of the public morals. Yet what clergyman in preaching a funeral discourse over an eminent or opulent parishioner, ever admits that he had a vice? Almost every Doctor of Divinity who now speaks publicly of Daniel Webster bows down before 'the especial greatness of his moral nature,' and utterly ignores or denies the questionable personal habits which were a matter of common notoriety, thirty years ago. It is needless to particularize about these habits; they were almost as notorious, though probably not so great, as those of Aaron Burr; and are, like his, now incapable of direct proof, since at a man's hundredth birthday it is hard to produce personal evidence of misdeeds. Yet I have not seen a reference to these things among those clergymen who now celebrate his towering moral nature: and it is left for a layman, a literary man, a man of the world, like Henry Cabot Lodge, manfully to recognize and deplore these drawbacks to which the others have shut their eyes. This is surely no guardianship of the public morals. 'One is almost led to ask,' said a business man to me, the other day, 'whether the clergy have really the same moral standard with other men?'

But the moral of all this goes farther. Women are as distinctively recognized as the guardians of the public purity as are the clergy of the public morals. Yet when a young man comes among us whose only distinction is that he has written a thin volume of very mediocre verse, and that he makes himself something very like a buffoon for notoriety and money, women of high social position receive him at their houses and invite guests to meet him; in spite of the fact that if they were to read aloud to the company his poem of 'Charmides,' not a woman would remain in the room until the end. In the vicious period of the English Georges, Byron was banished from society, Moore was obliged to purify his poems, for less offences against common decency than have been committed by Oscar Wilde. There are pages in his poems which, as a witty critic says, 'carry nudity to a point where it ceases to be a virtue.' In all else Mr. Wilde imitates Keats, but in Keats there is nothing in the least like these passages; they can indeed be paralleled in Whitman, but Whitman's offences rest on a somewhat different ground and need not here be considered. Mr. Wilde may talk of Greece; but there is nothing Greek about his poems; his nudities do not suggest the sacred whiteness of an antique statue, but rather the forcible unveiling of some insulted innocence. We have perhaps rashly claimed that the influence of women has purified English literature. When the poems of Wilde and Whitman lie in ladies' boudoirs, I see no evidence of the improvement.

And their poetry is called 'manly' poetry! Is it manly to fling before the eyes of women page upon page which no man would read aloud in presence of women? But there is another test of manhood: it lies in action. 'It makes a great difference to a sentence,' said the clear-sighted Emerson,' 'whether there be a man behind it or no.' Each of these so-called 'manly' poets has had his opportunity of action and waived it. I am one of many to whom Whitman's 'Drum-Taps' have always sounded as hollow as the instrument they counterfeit, simply because their author, with all his fine physique and his freedom from home-ties, never personally followed the drum, but only heard it from the comparatively remote distance of the hospital. There was a time when the recruiting-officers wanted men; their test was final, or at least so far final that he who did not meet it, no matter for what good reasons, had best cease boasting about his eminent manhood. So of this young Irish poet, who speaks, I observe, of 'us Englishmen.' His mother, Lady Wilde, has written poems upon the wrongs of Ireland that are strong and fervid enough, one would say, to enlist an army; especially her poem on the Irish exodus, 'A million a decade.' There is now Ireland on the verge of civil war; her councils divided, her self-styled leaders in jail; she needs every wise head and brave heart she has ever produced, to contribute, according to their best light, to some solution of her hard problem. Is it manhood for her gifted sons to stay at home and help work out the problem; or to cross the Atlantic and pose in ladies' boudoirs or write prurient poems which their hostesses must discreetly ignore? What would Sir Philip Sidney have thought of these new definitions of manhood; he of whom it was written, 'This bright and accomplished cavalier might, if he please, in his day, have set the fashion of a shoe-tie, or have altered the fashion of any man's peruque in the country; but he thought it more becoming his manhood and his greatness of soul, to hold out a brave example of virtue and religion?' For one, I should like to hear, if the so-called 'English Renaissance' is good for anything, more of the gospel of Sir Philip Sidney and less of the gospel according to Oscar Wilde.

8. Ambrose Bierce on Wilde as 'sovereign of insufferables'

1882

Unsigned comment from a column titled 'Prattle' in the *Wasp* [San Francisco], 31 March 1882; reprinted in *The Ambrose Bierce Satanic Reader*, edited by Ernest Jerome Hopkins (New York, 1968), pp. 5–6.

Bierce (1842–1914?), American journalist and author, best known for *The Devil's Dictionary* (1911), was chief editor of the *Wasp* at the time of Wilde's appearance in San Francisco to lecture on the Aesthetic Movement. Bierce's attitude toward Wilde was widely shared at the time, but the expression of that attitude was unparalleled as an example of creative vituperation.

That sovereign of insufferables, Oscar Wilde, has ensued with his opulence of twaddle and his penury of sense. He has mounted his hind legs and blown crass vapidities through the bowel of his neck, to the capital edification of circumjacent fools and foolesses, fooling with their foolers. He has tossed off the top of his head and uttered himself in copious overflows of ghastly bosh. The ineffable dunce has nothing to say and says it—says it with a liberal embellishment of bad delivery, embroidering it with reasonless vulgarities of attitude, gesture and attire. There was never an impostor so hateful, a blockhead so stupid, a crank so variously and offensively daft. Therefore is the she fool enamored of the feel of his tongue in her ear to tickle her understanding.

The limpid and spiritless vacuity of this intellectual jellyfish is in ludicrous contrast with the rude but robust mental activities that he came to quicken and inspire. Not only has he no thoughts, but no thinker. His lecture is mere verbal ditch-water—meaningless, trite and without coherence. It lacks even the nastiness that exalts and refines his verse. Moreover, it is obviously his own; he had not even the energy and independence to steal it. And so, with a knowledge that would equip an idiot to dispute with a cast-iron dog, an eloquence to qualify

53

him for the duties of caller on a hog-ranch and an imagination adequate to the conception of a tom-cat, when fired by contemplation of a fiddle-string, this consummate and star-like youth, missing everywhere his heaven-appointed functions and offices, wanders about, posing as a statue of himself, and, like the sun-smitten image of Memnon, emitting meaningless murmurs in the blaze of women's eyes. He makes me tired.

And this gawky gowk has the divine effrontery to link his name with those of Swinburne, Rossetti and Morris—this dunghill he-hen would fly with eagles. He dares to set his tongue to the honored name of Keats. He is the leader, quoth'a, of a *renaissance* in art, this man who cannot draw—of a revival in letters, this man who cannot write! This littlest and looniest of a brotherhood of simpletons, whom the wicked wits of London, haling him dazed from his obscurity, have crowned and crucified as King of the Cranks, has accepted the distinction in stupid good faith and our foolish people take him at his word. Mr. Wilde is pinnacled upon a dazzling eminence but the earth still trembles to the dull thunder of the kicks that set him up.

VERA; OR THE NIHILISTS

First produced: 20 August 1883

---

9. Unsigned review, *New York Times*

21 August 1883, pp. 4–5

Extracts from 'Mr. Oscar Wilde's Play', a lengthy review, half of which consists of an editorial on the blessings of freedom in the United States and the terrors of Nihilism.

In a letter to the *New York Times* (24 August 1883, p. 3), Marie Prescott, the actress who performed the role of Vera, reported the 'indignation' on the part of 'prominent citizens' over the treatment of Wilde's play by the New York critics. Despite such indignation, the play closed in a week.

. . . We do not doubt the sincerity of Mr. Oscar Wilde, who, nevertheless, has given us cogent reason to doubt his sincerity. He is a very clever young man, whose labor is altogether out of proportion to his reputation. He is, undoubtedly, alert enough to understand this. Fortunately, his chicanery has not quite destroyed our faith in him. In the midst of his foolish, green-sick business as a *poseur*, versifier, and apostle—he is certainly an apostle of things which others have made evident to us—he has shown a suggestive talent which no one cares to underrate. He has accomplished as little as possible, but we have been willing to believe that he could accomplish more. His one fine and truehearted poem, 'Ave Imperatrix', is worth all the lectures and instructions that he has imposed upon us. In popular aesthetics, moreover, he has done much that is right to acknowledge. But he has, probably, made his most serious effort in the play which was acted at the Union-Square Theatre last night. . . .

. . . Mr. Wilde believes, apparently, that Nihilism is an imposing force of the age. At any rate, he does not see the ludicrous side of it. He accepts it all solemnly enough. His play is meant to be impressive; meant to prove that liberty is a glorious thing when it is preached and spouted from the stage. . . . The fine poetic charm and the strength of the final situation redeem, one is almost willing to say, the other four acts of *Vera*. Yet this would be saying too much. The Nihilism which is presented in *Vera* is a stupid and tiresome element of the work. These rapid fellows who talk like lunatics, swear the most preposterous oaths, and act like children give no dramatic force to the play. It should be observed clearly that they do not act—they talk. They yell their theories of liberty. They argue and quarrel. What one asserts another is bound to repeat. The monotony of the second and fourth acts of *Vera* is simply depressing. The everlasting garrulity of these Nihilists, one is forced to believe, is like the constant babble of the brook—only less musical. In the third act the Czar and his son have a vivacious dispute, which carries on the peculiar argumentative purpose of the play. Fortunately, the Czar is disposed of before his loquacity ends. Mr. Wilde's play is, in fact, an energetic tirade against tyrants and despots; it is full of long speeches in which the glory of liberty is eloquently described; each of the characters has his 'preaching' to do, and each does it with extraordinary vigor; the play is, we may suggest, a kind of pulpit from which Mr. Wilde utters his declamatory dictum upon freedom and the rights of man. But all this does not make a dramatic play, and *Vera* is not dramatic. Yet there is constantly suggested in it a dramatic motive which is not shown concretely. The first act or prologue, for example, opens well as an exposition. It is then felt that the drama lies between Vera and Alexis, in their love and tragic passions. But the body of the play does not exhibit this drama, which appears only in the last act. This fact, and the fact that the Nihilists are dull haranguers, kill the interest of the play, which seems hollow and unsatisfactory. Yet there is a great deal of good writing in *Vera*, and Mr. Wilde exhibits cleverness and wit in a character like Prince Paul—which is considerably sharper than M. de Talde in *The Danicheffs*. But this cleverness stops short of dramatic art. His play is unreal, longwinded, and wearisome. It comes as near failure as an ingenious and able writer can bring it. We do not think that such a play can be popular. . . .

10. Unsigned review, *New York Daily Tribune*

21 August 1883, p. 5

The reviewer's comment on Wilde's play being 'untimely launched' refers to a lengthy description, in the previous paragraph, of the unbearable heat in the theatre.

A new play, entitled *Vera*, written by Mr. Oscar Wilde, was presented last night at the Union Square Theatre . . . and was seen by an audience that completely filled the house, notwithstanding a sudden accession of midsummer heat had made life almost intolerable and rendered a crowded place repugnant even to contemplate. The piece poorly rewarded the public curiosity, however, by a display of several queer scenes, picturesque at points, but mostly ugly, and by the exposition of a fanciful, foolish, highly peppered story of love, intrigue and politics, invested with the Russian accessories of fur and dark-lanterns, and overlaid with bantam gabble about freedom and the people. . . .

Mr. Wilde's play of *Vera*, thus untimely launched, is clumsily constructed according to the accepted principles of modern melodrama. That is to say, its author has aimed to compose it of strong incidents, surprises and theatrical situations. Such a piece, if acted a hundred years ago, or less, would have been interspersed with songs and illustrated or emphasized with frequent outbursts of instrumental music. To-day the melodious accompaniment is virtually discarded, but the same old literary fashion remains. The writer of melodrama is not constrained to square his ideas with probability, or to maintain a nice and exact observance of nature in his portraiture of the development and display of character under the stress of emotions and the pressure of circumstances. Without venturing into the realm of the ideal, he nevertheless steers as widely as he likes away from the realm of the actual.

He generally assumes, indeed, to deal with the facts of some specific phase of social life, but he does not scruple to wrest those facts to the theatrical purposes of his melodrama—making the conduct of individuals and the occurrence of events to take any course that may happen to be preferred by his fancy or enjoined by the necessities of the play. Hence it is that if we were to take our knowledge of countries and peoples and distant aspects of civilization from contemporary melodrama, we should depart away from the theatre with extraordinary ideas. But, indeed, the melodrama does not aim to teach. Its object is to surprise, dazzle, and excite. It begins and ends in sensation, and if this be attained it does not trouble itself about the means that were used to effect this result.

Mr. Wilde, as true as he can be to the traditions of the craft, which he seems carefully to have observed without having as yet conquered, has built up his play upon a central idea which is incredible and preposterous, but which, nevertheless, is useful as the motive or spring of climacteric situations; and these situations he has devised freely and with occasional slight felicity. *Vera* is high-stepping, wordy, and long-winded; but it is, in substance, and after much condensation shall have formed it, a practical piece of a common-place order. . . .

THE HAPPY PRINCE AND
OTHER TALES

May 1888

---

11. Walter Pater on *The Happy Prince*

1888

Letter to Wilde, dated 12 June 1888 from Brasenose College, Oxford, quoted in Stuart Mason's *Bibliography of Oscar Wilde* (1914), p. 334.

Walter Horatio Pater (1839–94), Fellow and Tutor of Brasenose College and critic, published the widely heralded *Studies in the History of the Renaissance* in 1873. The famous 'Conclusion' urging its readers 'to be forever curiously testing new opinions and courting new impressions', to 'burn always with this hard, gemlike flame', and to cultivate a love of 'art for art's sake', was omitted by Pater in the second edition 'as I conceived it might possibly mislead some of those young men into whose hands it might fall'. Wilde, who had studied with Pater at Oxford, called *The Renaissance* (as it was subsequently called) his 'golden book'. When Pater wrote to praise *The Happy Prince*, Wilde, overjoyed, told Alfred Nutt, the publisher, 'Mr. Pater has written me a wonderful letter about my prose, so I am in high spirits.' (*Letters*, p. 219.)

My dear Wilde,

I am confined to my room with gout, but have been consoling myself with *The Happy Prince*, and feel it would be ungrateful not to send a line to tell you how delightful I have found him and his companions. I hardly know whether to admire more the wise wit of 'The Wonderful

[Remarkable] Rocket,' or the beauty and tenderness of 'The Selfish Giant': the latter certainly is perfect in its kind. Your genuine 'little poems in prose,' those at the top of pages 10 and 14, for instance, are gems, and the whole, too brief, book abounds with delicate touches and pure English.

I hope to get away in a day or two, and meantime am a debtor in the matter of letters.

Ever

Very sincerely yours

WALTER PATER

12. Unsigned notice, *Athenaeum*

1 September 1888, p. 286

The gift of writing fairy tales is rare, and Mr. Oscar Wilde shows that he possesses it in a rare degree. *The Happy Prince, and other Stories*, are full of charming fancies and quaint humour. Though with a distinct character of their own, they are not unworthy to compare with Hans Andersen, and it is not easy to give higher praise than this. There is a piquant touch of contemporary satire which differentiates Mr. Wilde from the teller of pure fairy tales; but it is so delicately introduced that the illusion is not destroyed and a child would delight in the tales without being worried or troubled by their application, while children of larger growth will enjoy them and profit by them. The illustrations are charming.

13. Alexander Galt Ross, review, *Saturday Review*

20 October 1888, lxvi, 472

Ross (1860–1927), elder brother of Robert Ross (1869–1918), later Wilde's literary executor, was, like his brother, born in Canada and educated in England. The elder Ross, a frequent contributor to the *Saturday Review*, moved in the literary circles of the Savile Club and became a founder in the Society of Authors, serving as honorary secretary in its early years until he left to enter business. At the time of this review, which was unsigned, both Rosses were friends of Wilde.

One of the chief functions of the true fairy story is to excite sympathy. Whether they are princes, peasants, or inanimate objects (Was the immortal tin soldier an inanimate object?), the joys and sorrows of the heroes and heroines of fairyland will always be real to those persons, whatever their age may be, who love the fairy story, and regard it as the most delightful form of romance. Mr. Oscar Wilde, no doubt for excellent reasons, has chosen to present his fables in the form of fairy tales to a public which, though it should count among its numbers most persons who can appreciate delicate humour and an artistic literary manner, will assuredly not be composed of children. No child will sympathize at all with Mr. Wilde's *Happy Prince* when he is melted down by order of the Mayor and Corporation in obedience to the dictum of the art professor at the University that, since 'he is no longer beautiful, he is no longer useful.' Children do not care for satire, and the dominant spirit of these stories is satire—a bitter satire differing widely from that of Hans Andersen, whom Mr. Wilde's literary manner so constantly recalls to us. This quality of bitterness, however, does not repel the reader (except in the story of the 'Devoted Friend,' which is at once the cleverest and least agreeable in the volume), inasmuch as Mr. Wilde always contrives to leave us at the end of every tale with a very pleasant sensation of the humorous. Perhaps the best example of Mr.

Wilde's method is to be found in 'The Nightingale and the Rose.' Here the nightingale has sacrificed its life in order to obtain a red rose for the student. The student repairs with the nightingale's gift to the daughter of the Professor, in order to present the rose to her:—

> But the girl frowned.
> 'I am afraid it will not go with my dress,' she answered; 'and besides, the Chamberlain's nephew has sent me some real jewels, and everybody knows that jewels cost far more than flowers.'

Then the student, having thrown away the rose, returns to a great dusty book, reflecting:—

> 'What a silly thing Love is. It is not half as useful as Logic, for it does not prove anything, and it is always telling one of things that are not going to happen . . . In fact, it is quite unpractical, and, as in this age to be practical is everything, I shall go back to Philosophy and study Metaphysics.

It may be remarked in connexion with this story that, in order to get the desired effect at the conclusion, Mr. Wilde has gone dangerously near the region of sham sentiment. It is the only place in the book where his artistic sense has stumbled a little along with his natural history.

14. James Abbott McNeill Whistler on Wilde as a plagiarist

1890

Signed letter to *Truth*, 2 January 1890, xxvii, 4–5.
Whistler (1834–1903), American painter, etcher, and author, had delivered his famous 'Ten O'Clock' lecture (at the unusual hour of 10 p.m.) in 1885, in which he urged a break with the prevailing tradition in art of the imitation of nature—an idea that Wilde was to exploit in his essay 'The Decay of Lying' (1889). See Nos 15 and 16 for Wilde's response and Whistler's reply. These three letters were reprinted by Whistler in his *The Gentle Art of Making Enemies* (1890). (Henry Romeike, mentioned in Whistler's letter, founded a press cutting agency in 1881.)

Most Valiant *Truth*—Among your ruthless exposures of the shams of to-day, nothing, I confess, have I enjoyed with keener relish than your late tilt at that arch-imposter and pest of the period—the all-pervading plagiarist!

I learn, by the way, that in America he may, under the 'Law of '84,' as it is called, be criminally prosecuted, incarcerated, and made to pick oakum, as he has hitherto picked brains—and pockets!

How was it that, in your list of culprits, you omitted that fattest of offenders—our own Oscar?

His methods are brought again freshly to my mind, by the indefatigable and tardy Romeike, who sends me newspaper cuttings of Mr. Herbert Vivian's *Reminiscences*, in which, among other entertaining anecdotes, is told at length, the story of Oscar simulating the becoming pride of author, upon a certain evening, in the club of the Academy students, and arrogating to himself the responsibility of the lecture, with which, at his earnest prayer, I had, in good fellowship, crammed him, that he might not add deplorable failure to foolish appearance, in his anomalous position, as art expounder, before his clear-headed audience.

He went forth, on that occasion, as my St. John—but, forgetting that humility should be his chief characteristic, and unable to withstand the unaccustomed respect with which his utterances were received, he not only trifled with my shoe, but bolted with the latchet!

Mr. Vivian, in his book, tells us, further on, that lately, in an article in the *Nineteenth Century* on the 'Decay of Lying,' Mr. Wilde has deliberately and incautiously incorporated, 'without a word of comment,' a portion of the well-remembered letter in which, after admitting his rare appreciation and amazing memory, I acknowledge that 'Oscar has the courage of the opinions . . . . of others!'

My recognition of this, his latest proof of open admiration, I send him in the following little note, which I fancy you may think *à propos* to publish, as an example to your readers, in similar circumstances, of noble generosity in sweet reproof, tempered, as it should be, to the lamb in his condition:—

Oscar, you have been down the area again, I see!

I had forgotten you, and so allowed your hair to grow over the sore place. And now, while I looked the other way, you have stolen *your own scalp!* and potted it in more of your pudding.

Labby has pointed out that, for the detected plagiarist, there is still one way to self-respect (besides hanging himself, of course), and that is for him boldly to declare, '*Je prends mon bien là où je le trouve.*'[1]

You, Oscar, can go further, and with fresh effrontery, that will bring you the envy of all criminal *confrères*, unblushingly boast, '*Moi, je prends son bien là où je le trouve!*'[2]

---

[1] 'I take what I need where I find it', a variant of a remark attributed to Molière in Jean Léonor Le Gallois de Grimarest's *La Vie de Molière* (1704).
[2] 'I take *his* where I find it!'

15. Wilde's response to Whistler's charge of plagiarism

1890

Signed letter to *Truth*, 9 January 1890, xxvii, 51; reprinted in Rupert Hart-Davis's edition of Wilde's letters.

SIR—I can hardly imagine that the public are in the very smallest degree interested in the shrill shrieks of 'Plagiarism' that proceed from time to time out of the lips of silly vanity or incompetent mediocrity.

However, as Mr. James Whistler has had the impertinence to attack me with both venom and vulgarity in your columns, I hope you will allow me to state that the assertions contained in his letters are as deliberately untrue as they are deliberately offensive.

The definition of a disciple as one who has the courage of the opinions of his master is really too old even for Mr. Whistler to be allowed to claim it, and as for borrowing Mr. Whistler's ideas about art, the only thoroughly original ideas I have ever heard him express have had reference to his own superiority as a painter over painters greater than himself.

It is a trouble for any gentleman to have to notice the lucubrations of so ill-bred and ignorant a person as Mr. Whistler, but your publication of his insolent letter left me no option in the matter.—I remain, Sir, faithfully yours,

OSCAR WILDE

16. Whistler's final word on the question of Wilde's plagiarism

1890

Signed letter to *Truth*, 16 January 1890, xxvii, 97.

O TRUTH!—Cowed and humiliated, I acknowledge that our Oscar is at last original. At bay, and sublime in his agony, he certainly has, for once, borrowed from no living author, and comes out in his own true colours—as his own 'gentleman.'

How shall I stand against his just anger, and his damning allegations! for it must be clear to your readers, that, beside his clean polish, as prettily set forth in his epistle, I, alas! am but the 'ill-bred and ignorant person,' whose 'lucubrations' 'it is a trouble' for him 'to notice.'

Still will I, desperate as is my condition, point out that though 'impertinent,' 'venomous,' and 'vulgar,' he claims me as his 'master'—and, in the dock, bases his innocence upon such relation between us.

In all humility, therefore, I admit that the outcome of my 'silly vanity and incompetent mediocrity,' must be the incarnation: 'Oscar Wilde.' *Mea culpa!* the Gods may perhaps forgive and forget.

To you, *Truth*—champion of the truth—I leave the brave task of proclaiming again that the story of the lecture to the students of the Royal Academy was, as I told it to you, no fiction.

In the presence of Mr. Waldo Story did Oscar make his prayer for preparation; and at his table was he entrusted with the materials for his crime.

You also shall again unearth, in the *Nineteenth Century Review* of Jan. 1889, page 37, the other appropriated property, slily stowed away, in an article on 'The Decay of Lying'—though why Decay!

To shirk this matter thus is craven, doubtless; but I am awe-stricken and tremble, for truly, 'the rage of the sheep is terrible!'

THE PICTURE OF DORIAN GRAY

First published version: 20 June 1890

17. Unsigned review, *St. James's Gazette*

1890

The first published version of Wilde's novel, which contained thirteen chapters, appeared in *Lippincott's Monthly Magazine* [Philadelphia and London] (July 1890), xlvi, 3–100; when published as a separate volume in 1891, the novel contained six new chapters and many revisions.

The review, written by Samuel Henry Jeyes (1857–1911), journalist and biographer, and titled 'A Study in Puppydom', appeared on 24 June 1890, xx, 3–4; reprinted in Mason, *Art and Morality*. According to Sidney Low (1857–1932), editor of the *St. James's Gazette*, who wrote a prefatory memoir to a volume of Jeyes' writings titled *Samuel Henry Jeyes*, ed. W. P. Ker (1915), Jeyes

waged strenuous warfare against the fads and freaks which were shooting through the intellectual and artistic atmosphere in the last decade of the nineteenth century. For Yellow-Bookism, Water-Paterism, aestheticism, and all other 'isms' and cults sprouting so bounteously from the soil at that period, he had no indulgence. (p. 32.)

Wilde responded to Jeyes' attack (which Low calls 'a brilliant piece of slashing criticism') with a letter to the editor which provoked a series of responses and replies. In his first letter (dated 25 June; appeared 26 June), Wilde objected to the reviewer's moralistic criticism of the novel, stating what he was to repeat, in various ways, in succeeding letters: 'The sphere of art and the sphere of ethics are absolutely distinct and separate.' In his memoir, Low states that he asked Jeyes to comment on Wilde's response. Accordingly, Jeyes appended a note to the published letter, stating, in part: 'We are quite aware that ethics and aesthetics are different matters, and that is why the greater part of our criticism was devoted not so much to the nastiness of *The Picture of Dorian Gray*, but to its dulness and stupidity.' Incensed, Wilde wrote a second letter on 26 June (which was published on 27 June) charging that the review contained 'the most unjustifiable attack that has been made upon any man of letters for many years', and elaborately defended his novel. Jeyes, appending a comment to this letter, in turn defended the right of critical judgment:

We simply say that every critic has the right to point out that a work of art or literature is dull and incompetent in its treatment—as *The Picture of Dorian Gray* is; and that its dulness and incompetence are not redeemed because it constantly hints, not obscurely, at disgusting sins and abominable crimes—as *The Picture of Dorian Gray* does.

Again, Wilde responded in a long letter (dated 27 June; appeared 28 June), discussing censorship, the malice of the reviewer, and the difference between art and life–to which Jeyes again added a comment insisting that prosecution should not be taken 'against a book which we believed to be rendered innocuous by the tedious and stupid qualities which the critic discovered and explained.' Wilde concluded his fourth letter (dated 28 June; appeared 30 June):

. . . let me ask you not to force on me this continued correspondence, by daily attacks. It is a trouble and a nuisance. As you assailed me first, I have the right to the last word. Let that last word be the present letter, and leave my book, I beg you, to the immortality that it deserves. (*Letters*, pp. 252–262, *passim*.)

Time was (it was in the '70's) when we talked about Mr. Oscar Wilde; time came (it came in the '80's) when he tried to write poetry and, more adventurous, we tried to read it; time is when we had forgotten him, or only remember him as the late editor of *The Woman's World*— a part for which he was singularly unfitted, if we are to judge him by the work which he has been allowed to publish in *Lippincott's Magazine* and which Messrs. Ward, Lock & Co. have not been ashamed to circulate in Great Britain. Not being curious in ordure, and not wishing to offend the nostrils of decent persons, we do not propose to analyse *The Picture of Dorian Gray*: that would be to advertise the developments of an esoteric prurience. Whether the Treasury or the Vigilance

Society will think it worth while to prosecute Mr. Oscar Wilde or
Messrs. Ward, Lock & Co., we do not know; but on the whole we
hope they will not.

The puzzle is that a young man of decent parts, who enjoyed (when
he was at Oxford) the opportunity of associating with gentlemen,
should put his name (such as it is) to so stupid and vulgar a piece of
work. Let nobody read it in the hope of finding witty paradox or racy
wickedness. The writer airs his cheap research among the garbage of
the French *Décadents* like any drivelling pedant, and he bores you un-
mercifully with his prosy rigmaroles about the beauty of the Body
and the corruption of the Soul. The grammar is better than Ouïda's;
the erudition equal; but in every other respect we prefer the talented lady
who broke off with 'pious aposiopesis' when she touched upon 'the
horrors which are described in the pages of Suetonius and Livy'—not
to mention the yet worse infamies believed by many scholars to be
accurately portrayed in the lost works of Plutarch, Venus, and Nicodemus, especially Nicodemus.

Let us take one peep at the young men in Mr. Oscar Wilde's story.
Puppy No. 1 is the painter of the picture of Dorian Gray; Puppy No. 2
is the critic (a courtesy lord, skilled in all the knowledge of the Egyp-
tians and aweary of all the sins and pleasures of London); Puppy No. 3
is the original, cultivated by Puppy No. 1 with a 'romantic friendship.'
The Puppies fall a-talking: Puppy No. 1 about his Art, Puppy No. 2
about his sins and pleasures and the pleasures of sin, and Puppy No. 3
about himself—always about himself, and generally about his face,
which is 'brainless and beautiful.' The Puppies appear to fill up the
intervals of talk by plucking daisies and playing with them, and sometimes drinking 'something with strawberry in it.' The youngest
Puppy is told that he is charming; but he mustn't sit in the sun for fear
of spoiling his complexion. When he is rebuked for being a naughty,
wilful boy, he makes a pretty *moue*[1]—this man of twenty! This is how
he is addressed by the Blasé Puppy at their first meeting:

'Yes, Mr. Gray, the gods have been good to you. But what the gods
give they quickly take away. . . . When your youth goes, your beauty
will go with it, and then you will suddenly discover that there are no
triumphs left for you. . . . Time is jealous of you, and wars against
your lilies and roses. You will become sallow, and hollow-cheeked,
and dull-eyed. You will suffer horribly.'

[1] Pout.

Why, bless our souls! haven't we read something of this kind somewhere in the classics? Yes, of course we have? But in what recondite
author? Ah—yes—no—yes, it *was* in Horace! What an advantage it is
to have received a classical education! And how it will astonish the
Yankees! But we must not forget our Puppies, who have probably
occupied their time in lapping 'something with strawberry in it.'
Puppy No. 1 (the Art Puppy) has been telling Puppy No. 3 (the Doll
Puppy) how much he admires him. What is the answer? 'I am less to
you than your ivory Hermes or your silver Faun. You will like them
always. How long will you like me? Till I have my first wrinkle, I
suppose. I know now that when one loses one's good looks, whatever
they may be, one loses everything. . . . I am jealous of the portrait
you have painted of me. Why should it keep what I must lose? . . . .
Oh, if it was only the other way! If the picture could only change,
and I could be always what I am now!'

No sooner said than done! The picture *does* change: the original
doesn't. Here's a situation for you! Théophile Gautier could have made
it romantic, entrancing, beautiful. Mr. Stevenson could have made
it convincing, humorous, pathetic. Mr. Anstey could have made it
screamingly funny. It has been reserved for Mr. Oscar Wilde to make it
dull and nasty. The promising youth plunges into every kind of mean
depravity, and ends in being 'cut' by fast women and vicious men. He
finishes with murder: the New Voluptuousness always leads up to
blood-shedding—that is part of the cant. The gore and gashes wherein
Mr. Rider Haggard takes a chaste delight are the natural diet for a
cultivated palate which is tired of mere licentiousness. And every
wickedness or filthiness committed by Dorian Gray is faithfully
registered upon his face in the picture; but his living features are un-
disturbed and unmarred by his inward vileness. This is the story which
Mr. Oscar Wilde has tried to tell; a very lame story it is, and very
lamely it is told.

Why has he told it? There are two explanations; and, so far as we
can see, not more than two. Not to give pleasure to his readers: the
thing is too clumsy, too tedious, and—alas! that we should say it—too
stupid. Perhaps it was to shock his readers, in order that they might cry
Fie! upon him and talk about him, much as Mr. Grant Allen recently
tried in *The Universal Review* to arouse, by a licentious theory of the
sexual relations, an attention which is refused to his popular chatter
about other men's science. Are we then to suppose that Mr. Oscar
Wilde has yielded to the craving for a notoriety which he once earned

by talking fiddle-faddle about other men's art, and sees his only chance of recalling it by making himself obvious at the cost of being obnoxious, and by attracting the notice which the olfactory sense cannot refuse to the presence of certain self-asserting organisms? That is an uncharitable hypothesis, and we would gladly abandon it. It may be suggested (but is it more charitable?) that he derives pleasure from treating a subject merely because it is disgusting. The phenomenon is not unknown in recent literature; and it takes two forms, in appearance widely separate —in fact, two branches from the same root, a root which draws its life from malodorous putrefaction. One development is found in the Puritan prurience which produced Tolstoy's *Kreutzer Sonata* and Mr. Stead's famous outbursts. That is odious enough and mischievous enough, and it is rightly execrated, because it is tainted with an hypocrisy not the less culpable because charitable persons may believe it to be unconscious. But is it more odious or more mischievous than the 'frank Paganism' (that is the word, is it not?) which delights in dirtiness and confesses its delight? Still they are both chips from the same block—*The Maiden Tribute of Modern Babylon* and *The Picture of Dorian Gray*—and both of them ought to be chucked into the fire. Not so much because they are dangerous and corrupt (they are corrupt but not dangerous) as because they are incurably silly, written by simpleton *poseurs* (whether they call themselves Puritan or Pagan) who know nothing about the life which they affect to have explored, and because they are mere catchpenny revelations of the non-existent, which, if they reveal anything at all, are revelations only of the singularly unpleasant minds from which they emerge.

18. Unsigned review, *Daily Chronicle*

30 June 1890, p. 7

The review (which appeared in a column titled 'Magazines' and was reprinted in *Art and Morality*, ed. Stuart Mason) provoked a response from Wilde in a lengthy letter dated 30 June (published in the *Daily Chronicle* on 2 July). Taking up the reviewer's interpretation of the 'moral' of the novel, Wilde stated: 'The real moral of the story is that all excess, as well as renunciation, brings its punishment', adding that the moral 'realises itself purely in the lives of individuals and so becomes simply a dramatic element in a work of art, and not the object of the work of art itself'. (*Letters*, pp. 263–9.) Unlike the *St. James's Gazette*, the *Daily Chronicle* declined to pursue the question.

Dulness and dirt are the chief features of *Lippincott's* this month. The element in it that is unclean, though undeniably amusing, is furnished by Mr Oscar Wilde's story of *The Picture of Dorian Gray*. It is a tale spawned from the leprous literature of the French *Décadents*—a poisonous book, the atmosphere of which is heavy with the mephitic odours of moral and spiritual putrefaction—a gloating study of the mental and physical corruption of a fresh, fair and golden youth, which might be horrible and fascinating but for its effeminate frivolity, its studied insincerity, its theatrical cynicism, its tawdry mysticism, its flippant philosophisings, and the contaminating trail of garish vulgarity which is over all Mr Wilde's elaborate Wardour Street æstheticism and obtrusively cheap scholarship.

Mr Wilde says his book has 'a moral.' The 'moral,' so far as we can collect it, is that man's chief end is to develop his nature to the fullest by 'always searching for new sensations,' that when the soul gets sick the way to cure it is to deny the senses nothing, for 'nothing,' says one of Mr Wilde's characters, Lord Henry Wotton, 'can cure the soul but the senses, just as nothing can cure the senses but the soul.' Man is half angel and half ape, and Mr Wilde's book has no real use if it be not to inculcate the 'moral' that when you feel yourself becoming too angelic you cannot do better than rush out and make a beast of yourself. There is not a single good and holy impulse of human nature, scarcely a fine feeling

72

or instinct that civilisation, art, and religion have developed throughout the ages as part of the barriers between Humanity and Animalism
that is not held up to ridicule and contempt in *Dorian Gray*, if, indeed,
such strong words can be fitly applied to the actual effect of Mr
Wilde's airy levity and fluent impudence. His desperate effort to vamp
up a 'moral' for the book at the end is, artistically speaking, coarse and
crude, because the whole incident of Dorian Gray's death is, as they say
on the stage, 'out of the picture.' Dorian's only regret is that unbridled
indulgence in every form of secret and unspeakable vice, every resource
of luxury and art, and sometimes still more piquant to the jaded young
man of fashion, whose lives 'Dorian Gray' pretends to sketch, by every
abomination of vulgarity and squalor is—what? Why, that it will leave
traces of premature age and loathsome sensualness on his pretty face,
rosy with the loveliness that endeared youth of his odious type to the
paralytic patricians of the Lower Empire.

Dorian Gray prays that a portrait of himself which an artist, who
raves about him as young men do about the women they love not wisely
but too well, has painted may grow old instead of the original. This is
what happens by some supernatural agency, the introduction of which
seems purely farcical, so that Dorian goes on enjoying unfading youth
year after year, and might go on for ever using his senses with impunity
'to cure his soul,' defiling English society with the moral pestilence
which is incarnate in him, but for one thing. That is his sudden impulse
not merely to murder the painter—which might be artistically defended
on the plea that it is only a fresh development of his scheme for realising
every phase of life-experience—but to rip up the canvas in a rage, merely
because, though he had permitted himself to do one good action, it had
not made his portrait less hideous. But all this is inconsistent with
Dorian Gray's cool, calculating, conscienceless character, evolved
logically enough by Mr Wilde's 'New Hedonism.'

Then Mr Wilde finishes his story by saying that on hearing a heavy
fall Dorian Gray's servants rushed in, found the portrait on the wall as
youthful looking as ever, its senile ugliness being transferred to the foul
profligate himself, who is lying on the floor stabbed to the heart. This is
a sham moral, as indeed everything in the book is a sham, except the
one element in the book which will taint every young mind that comes
in contact with it. That element is shockingly real, and it is the plausibly
insinuated defence of the creed that appeals to the senses 'to cure the
soul' whenever the spiritual nature of man suffers from too much purity
and self-denial.

19. Unsigned notice, *Scots Observer*

5 July 1890, iv, 181

Wilde responded to this brief notice, which appeared in a column titled 'Reviews and Magazines', with a letter to the *Scots Observer* (12 July issue) in which he expounded on his often repeated distinction between art and morality: 'An artist, sir, has no ethical sympathies at all. Virtue and wickedness are to him simply what the colours on his palette are to the painter.' In closing, Wilde remarked acidly:

That the editor of the *St. James's Gazette* should have employed Caliban as his art-critic was possibly natural. The editor of the *Scots Observer* [W. E. Henley] should not have allowed Thersites to make mows in his review. It is unworthy of so distinguished a man of letters.' (*Letters*, pp. 266–67).

Rupert Hart-Davis identifies 'Thersites' as Charles Whibley (1860–1930), journalist and biographer on the staff of the *Scots Observer*, but this seems unlikely, for Whibley himself published a letter in the journal (19 July 1890) commenting on the unsigned notice: 'Your criticism of *Dorian Gray* seems to me more than fair. . . . You find in it art and no morals; I detect in its pages lots of morality and no art.' In the 26 July number, the writer of the notice, now identifying himself as 'Thersites', wrote to the editor of the *Scots Observer* commenting on Whibley's letter. Wilde re-entered the debate after Whibley published another letter; the correspondence continued to fill columns of the journal through the beginning of September with further letters from Whibley and Wilde (see *Letters*, pp. 268–72), one from William Archer, and several from less-known letter writers. Wearied by the discussion, Wilde wrote to Arthur Conan Doyle in the spring of 1891:

The newspapers seem to me to be written by the prurient for the Philistine. I cannot understand how they can treat *Dorian Gray* as immoral. My difficulty was to keep the inherent moral subordinate to the artistic and dramatic effect, and it still seems to me that the moral is too obvious. (*Letters*, p. 292.)

Why go grubbing in muck-heaps? The world is fair, and the proportion of healthy-minded men and honest women to those that are foul, fallen, or unnatural is great. Mr. Oscar Wilde has again been writing stuff that were better unwritten; and while *The Picture of Dorian Gray*, which he contributes to *Lippincott*, is ingenious, interesting, full of cleverness, and plainly the work of a man of letters, it is false art—for its interest is medico-legal; it is false to human nature—for its hero is a devil; it is false to morality—for it is not made sufficiently clear that the writer does not prefer a course of unnatural iniquity to a life of cleanliness, health, and sanity. The story—which deals with matters only fitted for the Criminal Investigation Department or a hearing *in camera*[1] is discreditable alike to author and editor. Mr. Wilde has brains, and art, and style; but if he can write for none but outlawed noblemen and perverted telegraph boys, the sooner he takes to tailoring (or some other decent trade) the better for his own reputation and the public morals.

[1] In secret.

20. Unsigned review, *Punch*

19 July 1890, xcix, 25

The review, written by 'The Baron de Book-Worms' under the title 'Our Booking-Office', was believed by Wilde to have been authored by Francis Cowley Burnand (1836–1917), editor of *Punch* (1862–1906) and playwright. However, in a letter to Henry Lucy (1845–1924), a writer on the staff of *Punch* who signed his articles as 'Toby M.P.', Wilde revealed that he had discovered the author of the review, which greatly annoyed him by 'its offensive tone and horridness'. (*Letters*, p. 267.) However, Lucy deleted the name Wilde gave in the letter.

The Baron has read Oscar Wilde's Wildest and Oscarest work, called *Dorian Gray*, a weird sensational romance, complete in one number of *Lippincott's Magazine*. The Baron recommends anybody who revels in *diablerie*, to begin it about half-past ten, and to finish it at one sitting up; but those who do not so revel he advises either not to read it at all, or to choose the daytime, and take it in homœopathic doses.

The portrait represents the soul of the beautiful Ganymede-like Dorian Gray, whose youth and beauty last to the end, while his soul, like John Brown's, 'goes marching on' into the Wilderness of Sin. It becomes at last a devilled soul. And then Dorian sticks a knife into it, as any ordinary mortal might do, and a fork also, and next morning

Lifeless but 'hideous' he lay,

while the portrait has recovered the perfect beauty which it possessed when it first left the artist's easel.

If Oscar intended an allegory, the finish is dreadfully wrong. Does he mean that, by sacrificing his earthly life, Dorian Gray atones for his infernal sins, and so purifies his soul by suicide? 'Heavens! I am no preacher,' says the Baron, 'and perhaps Oscar didn't mean anything at all, except to give us a sensation, to show how like Bulwer Lytton's old-world style he could make his descriptions and his dialogue, and what an easy thing it if to frighten the respectable Mrs Grundy with a Bogie.' The style is decidedly Lyttonerary. His aphorisms are Wilde, yet forced. Mr Oscar Wilde says of his story, 'it is poisonous if you like, but you cannot deny that it is also perfect, and perfection is what we artists aim at.'[1] Perhaps; but 'we artists' do not always hit what we aim at, and despite his confident claim to unerring artistic marksmanship, one must hazard the opinion, that in this case Mr Wilde has 'shot wide.' There is indeed more of 'poison' than of 'perfection' in *Dorian Gray*.

The central idea is an excellent, if not exactly novel, one; and a finer art, say that of Nathaniel Hawthorne, would have made a striking and satisfying story of it. *Dorian Gray* is striking enough, in a sense, but it is not 'satisfying' artistically, any more than it is so ethically. Mr Wilde has preferred the sensuous and hyperdecorative manner of 'Mademoiselle de Maupin,' and without Gautier's power has spoilt a promising conception by clumsy, unideal treatment.

His 'decoration' (upon which he plumes himself) is indeed 'laid on with a trowel.' The luxuriously elaborate details of his 'artistic hedonism' are too suggestive of South Kensington Museum and æsthetic Encyclopædias. A truer art would have avoided both the glittering conceits, which bedeck the body of the story, and the unsavoury suggestiveness which lurks in its spirit.

Poisonous! Yes. But the loathly 'leperous distilment' taints and spoils, without in any way subserving 'perfection,' artistic or otherwise. If Mrs Grundy doesn't read it, the younger Grundies do; that is, the Grundies who belong to Clubs, and who care to shine in certain sets wherein this story will be much discussed. 'I have read it, and, except for the ingenious idea, I wish to forget it,' says the Baron.

[1] Quoted from Wilde's letter to the *Daily Chronicle* in protest over their unfavourable review of *The Picture of Dorian Gray*. (See *Letters*, pp. 263–4.)

21. John Addington Symonds, letter to Horatio Brown

1890

Letter dated 22 July 1890, from Davos, Switzerland, in *Letters and Papers of John Addington Symonds,* ed. Horatio Brown (New York, 1923), p. 240.

Symonds (1840–93), biographer, poet, and historian, whose *The Renaissance in Italy* (7 vols, 1875–86) is his best-known work, received a copy of *Lippincott's Monthly Magazine,* which contained Wilde's novel, from its author. On 22 July, the same day that he wrote a letter to Brown, Symonds wrote to Edmund Gosse to voice his displeasure at 'the morbid and perfumed manner of treating such psychological subjects' as Wilde had dramatized in his novel (Phyllis Grosskurth, *The Woeful Victorian: A Biography of John Addington Symonds,* New York, 1964, p. 267).

Oscar Wilde has sent me his novelette, *The Picture of Dorian Gray.* It is an odd and very audacious production, unwholesome in tone, but artistically and psychologically interesting. If the British public will stand this, they can stand anything. However, I resent the unhealthy, scented, mystic, congested touch which a man of this sort has on moral problems.

22. Julian Hawthorne, review, *Lippincott's*

1890

Signed review, titled 'The Romance of the Impossible', *Lippin-cott's Monthly Magazine* [Philadelphia and London], September, 1890, xlvi, 412–15.
Hawthorne (1846–1934), American man of letters and biographer of his father, Nathaniel, has an appreciation of the originality of *Dorian Gray* rather than its reliance on French and English sources. (Omitted at the end of this selection is Hawthorne's summary of the plot.)

Mr Oscar Wilde, the apostle of beauty, has in the July number of *Lippincott's Magazine* a novel or romance (it partakes of the qualities of both), which everybody will want to read. It is a story strange in con-ception, strong in interest, and fitted with a tragic and ghastly climax. Like many stories of its class, it is open to more than one interpretation; and there are, doubtless, critics who will deny that it has any meaning at all. It is, at all events, a salutary departure from the ordinary English novel, with the hero and heroine of different social stations, the preda-tory black sheep, the curate, the settlements, and Society. Mr Wilde, as we all know, is a gentleman of an original and audacious turn of mind, and the commonplace is scarcely possible to him. Besides, his advocacy of novel ideas in life, art, dress, and demeanour had led us to expect surprising things from him; and in this literary age it is agreed that a man may best show the best there is in him by writing a book. Those who read Mr Wilde's story in the hope of finding in it some compact and final statement of his theories of life and manners will be satisfied in some respects, and dissatisfied in others; but not many will deny that the book is a remarkable one, and would attract attention even had it appeared without the author's name on the title page.

The Picture of Dorian Gray begins to show its quality in the opening pages. Mr Wilde's writing has what is called 'colour,'—the quality that forms the mainstay of many of Ouïda's works,—and it appears in the sensuous descriptions of nature and of the decorations and environments of the artistic life. The general aspect of the characters and the tenor of their conversation remind one a little of *Vivian Gray* [*sic*] and a little of *Pelham*, but the resemblance does not go far: Mr Wilde's objects and philosophy are different from those of either Disraeli or Bulwer. Meanwhile his talent for aphorisms and epigrams may fairly be compared with theirs: some of his clever sayings are more than clever, —they show real insight and a comprehensive grasp. Their wit is generally cynical; but they are put into the mouth of one of the characters, Lord Harry, and Mr Wilde himself refrains from definitely committing himself to them; though one cannot help suspecting that Mr Wilde regards Lord Harry as being an uncommonly able fellow. Be that as it may, Lord Harry plays the part of Old Harry in the story, and lives to witness the destruction of every other person in it. He may be taken as an imaginative type of all that is most evil and most refined in modern civilisation,—a charming, gentle, witty, euphemistic Mephistopheles, who deprecates the vulgarity of goodness, and muses aloud about 'those renunciations that men have unwisely called virtue, and those natural rebellions that wise men still call sin.' Upon the whole, Lord Harry is the most ably portrayed character in the book, though not the most original in conception. Dorian Gray himself is as nearly a new idea in fiction as one has nowadays a right to expect. If he had been adequately realised and worked out, Mr Wilde's first novel would have been remembered after more meritorious ones were forgotten. But, even as 'nemo repente fuit turpissimus,'[1] so no one, or hardly any one, creates a thoroughly original figure at a first essay. Dorian never quite solidifies. In fact, his portrait is rather the more real thing of the two. . . .

[1] 'No one ever became evil overnight.' (Juvenal, *Satire II*, line 63.)

THE PICTURE OF DORIAN GRAY

Second published version: April 1891

---

23. Unsigned review, *Theatre*

1 June 1891, xvii, 295

Dorian Gray, as the finished work of a literary exquisite, must command a certain attention. It is the very genius of affectation crystalised in a syrup of words. Reading it, we move in a heavy atmosphere of warm incense and slumbering artificial light. We thread our way through a mob of courtier epigrams, all bowing, all murmuring to the white lily of beauty, all forced to premature growth in the hothouse of a somewhat sickly fancy. We long to push on to the light, and the blowing wind, and the clean air of honest commonplace that Mr. Wilde's cultured puppets cry faugh! to. The author and his following have nothing in common with the lilac and violet they belaud. Their most fragrant speech stirs no one of the breezy plumes: nor is the spirit of the dank ghostly wood an open secret to them. Not for them is 'A green thought in a green shade,' but rather that comfortable mystic pessimism, which 'the bliss of being sad made melancholy.' Power is here, but rather the inventive power of the engineer than the creative force of the artist. Still, to say that only an age that had produced the wild study of Dr. Jekyl's dual personality could give birth to a *Dorian Gray* is not necessarily to disparage the latter. That shrewd knowledge of the weight and value of words that Mr. Stevenson has taught us, has pierced the cuticle of many a man of letters who would be loth to acknowledge his teacher. But that disciples may outdo their masters is an obvious truism, and *Dorian Gray* may remain a psychical curiosity when Dr. Jekyl is forgotten. It is at least undeniably clever, and even brilliant—as a sick man's eye. Looking at it from the point of view of dramatic possibilities, we are bound to recognise in it great attractions, saving, alone, in its almost utter lack of true humanity. As a book, it is from cover to finish, an elaborate work of art, extremely clever, wonderfully ingenious, and even fascinating; but not convincing, from that same absence of human interest.

24. Unsigned notice, *Athenaeum*

27 June 1891, p. 824

Mr. Oscar Wilde's paradoxes are less wearisome when introduced into the chatter of society than when he rolls them off in the course of his narrative. Some of the conversation in his novel is very smart, and while reading it one has the pleasant feeling, not often to be enjoyed in the company of modern novelists, of being entertained by a person of decided ability. The idea of the book may have been suggested by Balzac's *Peau de Chagrin*, and it is none the worse for that. So much may be said for *The Picture of Dorian Gray*, but no more, except, perhaps, that the author does not appear to be in earnest. For the rest, the book is unmanly, sickening, vicious (though not exactly what is called 'improper'), and tedious.

25. Walter Pater on *Dorian Gray*

1891

Signed review, titled 'A Novel by Mr. Oscar Wilde', in the *Book-man* (November 1891), i, 59–60; reprinted in Pater's *Sketches and Reviews* (1919).
Pater's review is the most perceptive of the early reviews of *The Picture of Dorian Gray* in its grasp of Wilde's intentions. The occasion permitted Pater to demonstrate his moral concerns in literature in addition to aesthetic considerations—a fact which many contemporary critics of Pater had misunderstood.

There is always something of an excellent talker about the writing of Mr. Oscar Wilde; and in his hands, as happens so rarely with those who practise it, the form of dialogue is justified by its being really alive. His genial, laughter-loving sense of life and its enjoyable intercourse, goes far to obviate any crudity there may be in the paradox, with which, as with the bright and shining truth which often underlies it, Mr. Wilde, startling his 'countrymen,' carries on, more perhaps than any other writer, the brilliant critical work of Matthew Arnold. *The Decay of Lying*, for instance, is all but unique in its half-humorous, yet wholly convinced, presentment of certain valuable truths of criticism. Conversational ease, the fluidity of life, felicitous expression, are qualities which have a natural alliance to the successful writing of fiction; and side by side with Mr. Wilde's *Intentions* (so he entitles his critical efforts) comes a novel, certainly original, and affording the reader a fair opportunity of comparing his practise as a creative artist with many a precept he has enounced as critic concerning it.

A wholesome dislike of the common-place, rightly or wrongly identified by him with the *bourgeois,* with our middle-class—its habits and tastes—leads him to protest emphatically against so-called 'realism' in art; life, as he argues, with much plausibility, as a matter of fact, when it is really awake, following art—the fashion an effective artist sets; while art, on the other hand, influential and effective art, has never

83

taken its cue from actual life. In *Dorian Gray* he is true certainly, on the whole, to the æsthetic philosophy of his *Intentions*; yet not infallibly, even on this point: there is a certain amount of the intrusion of real life and its sordid aspects—the low theatre, the pleasures and griefs, the faces of some very unrefined people, managed, of course, cleverly enough. The interlude of Jim Vane, his half-sullen but wholly faithful care for his sister's honour, is as good as perhaps anything of the kind, marked by a homely but real pathos, sufficiently proving a versatility in the writer's talent, which should make his books popular. Clever always, this book, however, seems to set forth anything but a homely philosophy of life for the middle-class—a kind of dainty Epicurean theory rather—yet fails, to some degree, in this; and one can see why. A true Epicureanism aims at a complete though harmonious development of man's entire organism. To lose the moral sense therefore, for instance, the sense of sin and righteousness, as Mr. Wilde's heroes are bent on doing so speedily, as completely as they can, is to lose, or lower, organisation, to become less complex, to pass from a higher to a lower degree of development. As a story, however, a partly supernatural story, it is first-rate in artistic management; those Epicurean niceties only adding to the decorative colour of its central figure, like so many exotic flowers, like the charming scenery and the perpetual, epigrammatic, surprising, yet so natural, conversations, like an atmosphere all about it. All that pleasant accessory detail, taken straight from culture, the intellectual and social interests, the conventionalities, of the moment, have, in fact, after all, the effect of the better sort of realism, throwing into relief the adroitly-devised supernatural element after the manner of Poe, but with a grace he never reached, which supersedes that earlier didactic purpose, and makes the quite sufficing interest of an excellent story.

We like the hero, and in spite of his somewhat unsociable devotion to his art, Hallward, better than Lord Henry Wotton. He has too much of a not very really refined world in and about him, and his somewhat cynical opinions, which seem sometimes to be those of the writer, who may, however, have intended Lord Henry as a satiric sketch. Mr. Wilde can hardly have intended him, with his cynic amity of mind and temper, any more than the miserable end of Dorian himself, to figure the motive and tendency of a true Cyrenaic or Epicurean doctrine of life. In contrast with Hallward, the artist, whose sensibilities idealise the world around him, the personality of Dorian Gray, above all, into something magnificent and strange, we might say that Lord Henry, and even more the, from the first, suicidal hero, loses too much in life to be a true

Epicurean—loses so much in the way of impressions, of pleasant memories, and subsequent hopes, which Hallward, by a really Epicurean
economy, manages to secure. It should be said, however, in fairness,
that the writer is impersonal: seems not to have identified himself
entirely with any one of his characters: and Wotton's cynicism, or
whatever it may be, at least makes a very clever story possible. He becomes the spoiler of the fair young man, whose bodily form remains
un-aged; while his picture, the *chef d' œuvre*[1] of the artist Hallward,
changes miraculously with the gradual corruption of his soul. How
true, what a light on the artistic nature, is the following on actual personalities and their revealing influence in art. We quote it as an example
of Mr. Wilde's more serious style.

I sometimes think that there are only two eras of any importance in the world's
history. The first is the appearance of a new medium for art, and the second is the
appearance of new personality for art also. What the invention of oil-painting
was to the Venetians, the face of Antinous was to late Greek sculpture, and the
face of Dorian Gray will some day be to me. It is not merely that I paint from
him, draw from him, sketch from him. Of course I have done all that. But he is
much more to me than a model or a sitter. I won't tell you that I am dissatisfied
with what I have done of him, or that his beauty is such that art cannot express
it. There is nothing that art cannot express, and I know that the work I have
done, since I met Dorian Gray, is good work, is the best work of my life. But
in some curious way his personality has suggested to me an entirely new manner
in art, an entirely new mode of style. I see things differently, I think of them
differently. I can now recreate life in a way that was hidden from me before.

Dorian himself, though certainly a quite unsuccessful experiment in
Epicureanism, in life as a fine art, is (till his inward spoiling takes visible
effect suddenly, and in a moment, at the end of his story) a beautiful
creation. But his story is also a vivid, though carefully considered, exposure of the corruption of a soul, with a very plain moral, pushed
home, to the effect that vice and crime make people coarse and ugly.
General readers, nevertheless, will probably care less for this moral, less
for the fine, varied, largely appreciative culture of the writer, in evidence from page to page, than for the story itself, with its adroitly
managed supernatural incidents, its almost equally wonderful applica-
tions of natural science; impossible, surely, in fact, but plausible enough
in fiction. Its interest turns on that very old theme, old because based on
some inherent experience or fancy of the human brain, of a double life:
of Döppelgänger—not of two *persons,* in this case, but of the man and

[1] Masterpiece.

his portrait; the latter of which, as we hinted above, changes, decays, is spoiled, while the former, through a long course of corruption, remains, to the outward eye, unchanged, still in all the beauty of a seemingly immaculate youth—'the devil's bargain.' But it would be a pity to spoil the reader's enjoyment by further detail. We need only emphasise, once more, the skill, the real subtlety of art, the ease and fluidity withal of one telling a story by word of mouth, with which the consciousness of the supernatural is introduced into, and maintained amid, the elaborately conventional, sophisticated, disabused world Mr. Wilde depicts so cleverly, so mercilessly. The special fascination of the piece is, of course, just there—at that point of contrast. Mr. Wilde's work may fairly claim to go with that of Edgar Poe, and with some good French work of the same kind, done, probably, in more or less conscious imitation of it.

THE DUCHESS OF PADUA

First produced: 26 January 1891

26. Unsigned review, *New York Times*

27 January 1891, p. 4

In 1882, Wilde had been commissioned by the American actress Mary Anderson to write a five-act tragedy. The play, *The Duchess of Padua*, completed in March 1883, was subsequently refused. In that year, Wilde published the play privately at his own expense. When the distinguished American actor-manager Lawrence Barrett (1859–91), who had been interested in Wilde's play since 1882, produced it on 26 January 1891 in New York, he changed the title to *Guido Ferranti*, probably to give greater significance to his own role. Because Wilde was 'anxious to have the play judged entirely on its own merits' (*Letters*, p.283), its authorship was not revealed, though judging from the reviews, it was a well-known secret.

The author of *Guido Ferranti*, the sombre romantic play produced at the Broadway Theatre last night by Mr. Lawrence Barrett, has a gift that the author of *Ganelon* seems to lack, namely, the gift of melody. If he is, indeed, a poet, he is probably at his best in writing lyrics. His five-act play is not altogether poetical. A dramatic poet who is equal to his task is not compelled to seek in the graveyard of dead forms of speech for phrases and metaphors. There are lots of reminiscent lines in *Guido Ferranti*. They actually speak in it of a 'foul, unnatural murder';[1] there is an oath of vengeance that is a reminder of a dozen almost forgotten tragedies, but there are some passages full of the fire of eloquence. The

---

[1] From *Hamlet*, Act I, scene 5, line 25, in which the Ghost commands Hamlet: 'Revenge his foul and most unnatural murder.'

rhythm is there, if there is not much in the matter. One of the speeches of Beatrice, Duchess of Padua, is something like this:

> I care not if you either stay or go,
> For, if you stay, you steal my love from me,
> And, if you go, you take my love away!
> Guido, if all the morning stars could sing at once
> They could not tell the measure of my love!

This may not be real poetry, but it is much more like poetry than the machine-made iambics of *Ganelon*. . . . The authorship of *Guido Ferranti* has been attributed by a competent authority to Oscar Wilde. It is said that Mr. Wilde wrote the play ten years ago or more, and that it was then called *The Duchess of Padua*. . . .

The plots of most tragedies are not of much account. It is always the manner rather than the matter that counts. The manner of this work is, as we have said, better than the ordinary. If we are sometimes reminded of Sheridan Knowles, we are, nevertheless, more frequently reminded of Browning. The author, whoever he is, does not live wholly in the past. There are a number of well-imagined and skilfully wrought scenes in his play, and many passages that must have been written in a glow of excitement. If this poet was not inspired, he at least tried very hard to be, and certainly thought he was.

It is not likely that *Guido Ferranti* will be a popular play 'on the road'. You will notice that many of the reviewers will condemn it as being highly improbable. Probability and improbability in art, like realism and idealism, are largely matters of personal illusion. It all depends on the point of view. Tragedy does not aim to picture manners, but to depict the battle of the human soul with relentless fate. *Guido Ferranti* has a hard time with Fate, and Fate, as usual, is the only real conqueror in the catastrophe. . . .

27. Unsigned review, *New York Daily Tribune*

27 January 1891, p. 6

In the Broadway Theatre last night, in presence of a numerous, eagerly attentive, and often kindly responsive audience, Lawrence Barrett . . . produced another new piece, under the name of *Guido Ferranti*. The performance was followed with deep interest and at certain telling points was rewarded with earnest applause. . . . The new play is deftly constructed in five short acts, and is written in a strain of blank verse that is always melodious, often eloquent, and sometimes freighted with fanciful figures of rare beauty. It is less a tragedy, however, than a melodrama—by which is meant a drama of situation. To this ingredient everything is moulded and sacrificed. The inevitable consequence ensues. The radical defect of the work is insincerity. No one in it is natural. . . .

The authorship of *Guido Ferranti* has not been disclosed. There need not have been any hesitation about it—for he is a practised writer and a good one. We recognize in this work a play that we had the pleasure of reading several years ago in manuscript. It was then called *The Duchess of Padua*. The author of it is Oscar Wilde.

INTENTIONS

2 May 1891

---

28. Unsigned review, *Pall Mall Gazette*

12 May 1891, p. 3

In his dialogue on 'The Critic as Artist', Mr. Oscar Wilde relates what he calls the legend of the Remorseful Academician—an expression which curiously illustrates his bent towards paradox, since the natural epithet for an Academician is clearly not 'remorseful' but 'impenitent'. 'It seems that a lady once gravely asked the remorseful Academician if his celebrated picture of "A Spring Day at Whiteley's", or "Waiting for the Last Omnibus", or some subject of that kind, was all painted by hand.' 'And was it?' interjects the second speaker. A similar question forces itself to out lips as we wander through Mr. Wilde's Paradise of Dainty Paradoxes. Are they all hand-made, these quaint perversions of the obvious? Are they not turned out by machinery at so much the gross? May we not suspect them to be the result of a facile formula, a process of word-shuffling, rather than of genuine insight into the facts of art and life? M. Jules Lemaître has given an ingenious recipe—'Every Man his own Larochefoucauld' he might have called it—by which the veriest dullard can concoct epigrammatic maxims in any quantity. In the same way, it should not be difficult to lay down a set of rules—under the rubric 'Every 'Arry his own Oscar'—by means of which the merest penny-a-liner should be able to *épater le bourgeois*[1] with all the sweet unreasonableness of our latter-day Sage of Chelsea. For instance you take two interlocutors, Tweedledum and Tweedledee, you make one of them enunciate a truism, such as 'Fine words butter no parsnips,' and then you set the other to prove in fifteen florid pages that fine words are the only possible butter for the parsnips of life, nay that parsnips have no right to exist save as an occasion and excuse for fine words, and that, in

[1] Startle the middle-class man.

sum, the Artist regards the whole Universe as his Parsnip, created by the something not ourselves that makes for Art, to the single end that that Art should butter it. Of course this does not exhaust Mr. Wilde's method. He has many other devices for the production of paradox, some of them even simpler. Indeed it is in the simplicity of his technique that his art is truly great. He has long ago recognized that, to the class of readers among whom his intellectual lot is cast, paradox is the subtlest form of flattery. Any fool can talk plain sense and understand it, but it needs a quite superior order of intelligence to disguise sense as nonsense and to see through the disguise. Take, for example, the assertion that Nature imitates Art, and that this is 'the one thing that keeps her in touch with civilized man'—an amplification, by the way, of Mr. Whistler's reluctant admission that 'Nature's creeping up'. The writer who addresses us in such terms pays us the compliment of assuming our familiarity with a coterie-speech—not to say a jargon—current only on the highest heights of culture. If we read with comprehension, we feel ourselves of the initiated; and even if our comprehension be none of the clearest, the occasional detonation of an epigrammatic paradox serves, like a fog-signal, to keep us awake and attent. But in truth Mr. Wilde's perversities are none of them very baffling. He writes so well, that from page to page he may be called lucid, even if his carelessness of consistency prove somewhat bewildering in the long run. Whatever else it may be, his book is entertaining. He has every qualification for becoming a popular Pater. Indeed, if he would condescend to suppress some over-complacent allusions to the artistic value of 'sin'—a favourite word of his—he might fairly be described as a Pater-familias.

Mannerism apart, there is much excellent matter in Mr. Wilde's dialogues and essays. His criticisms are often just and sometimes luminous; his wit, except where we smell the formula, is very pretty indeed. For example: 'I took the Baroness Bernstein down to dinner last night, and, though absolutely charming in every other respect, she insisted on discussing music as if it were actually written in the German language.' And again: 'Every great man nowadays has his disciples, and it is always Judas who writes the biography.' In point of style Mr. Wilde is very unequal. He can write (and generally does) with silken delicacy, but is apt now and then to strive eagerly after a plushy lusciousness, deep-piled with epithets. For instance: 'We come across some noble grief that we think will lend the purple dignity of tragedy to our days, but it passes away from us and things less noble take its place, and on some grey windy dawn, or odorous eve of silver and of silence, we find ourselves looking with callous wonder, or dull heart of stone, at the tress of gold-flecked hair that we had once so wildly worshipped and so madly kissed.' He is not—who is?—entirely irreproachable on the score of mixed metaphor, but he seldom sins so flagrantly as in the following case:—'When, at the Renaissance, Greek literature dawned upon Europe, the soil was in some measure prepared for it.' It is strange to find this sworn foe to the obvious indulging, not very infrequently, in such cheap epithets as this: 'The tradesman's creed did not prevent France and Germany from clashing together in *blood-stained* battle'— but consistency is the last virtue to which Mr. Wilde would dream of laying claim. He has written a fascinating, stimulating book, with more common sense in it than he would perhaps care to be accused of.

29. Unsigned review, *Athenaeum*

6 June 1891, p. 731

In spite of his showy paradoxes, Mr. Oscar Wilde, in his volume of essays called *Intentions* (Osgood, McIlvaine & Co.), succeeds in proving that he has something to say, and it is a pity that he should think, or find, it necessary to resort to the tricks of the smart advertiser in order to attract attention to his wares. He runs the risk of making his readers throw down his book in disgust, and he spoils his style by making it mechanical. To call Mr. Wilde's favourite rhetorical figure by the name of paradox is really too complimentary; he carries his joke too far, and makes paradox ridiculous. The form of language in which he chooses to conceal his thoughts is easily described. His method is this: he takes some well-established truth, something in which the wisdom of centuries and the wit of the greatest men have concurred, and asserts the contrary; then he whittles his assertion down, and when at his best arrives at the point which might have been reached by starting at the other end. Piquant at first, but soon wearisome, his method does sometimes succeed in that illumination of the commonplace which constitutes originality. The first essay, called 'The Decay of Lying' (which means the growth of realism), is by far the cleverest. Here Mr. Wilde, in the intervals of his labour over paradoxes and self-contradictions, has spared time to think for himself. In speaking of writers about art Mr. Ruskin must, of course, be left in the place which he incontestably occupies by himself. But speaking of lesser people, after 'Vernon Lee' hardly any one has a better claim than Mr. Wilde to be named as a contributor of something fresh, something original and stimulating, amongst the mass of matter about art that has been written during the last twenty years. Next to 'The Decay of Lying' comes a paper on Wainewright the poisoner, which is not much above the ordinary level of magazine padding, and then Mr. Wilde returns to art matters. In two essays on 'The Critic as Artist' his besetting habit holds the mastery over him, and the reader becomes heartily weary of it. Making every allowance for Mr. Wilde's tiresome way of expressing himself, one cannot extract anything of much value from these two papers. In the 118 pages which they occupy Mr. Wilde has attempted to make sense of a number of propositions such as these:—that it is more difficult to talk about a thing than to do it, and that to do nothing at all is the most difficult thing in the world; that all art is immoral, and all thought dangerous; that criticism is more creative than creation, and so on. He is at times naturally driven to desperate assertions. He says that ordinary people have a glib, ignorant way of saying, 'Why should we read what is written about Shakespeare and Milton? We can read the plays and the poems. That is enough.' The obvious truth is, of course, that ordinary people say and do just the reverse. And ordinary people, too, who write spend their labour in writing about literature instead of labouring to write literature. Again, what can Mr. Wilde have been thinking of, except effect, when he said that bad artists always admire each other's work, as a summary of his theory that good ones do otherwise? Had he forgotten his Vasari and the evidence of the golden age of the great Italian artists? His statement that 'to the æsthetic temperament the vague is always repellent' is almost as reckless. When he speaks of Matthew Arnold's definition of 'literature' as a criticism of life he is worse than reckless. When he speaks of the Caffè Florian at Venice as 'Florio's', of the author of the 'Ode to Evening' as Collin, and of Wainewright's being in 'gaol,' he shows, perhaps, that strict accuracy is beneath him. But these are trifles. No one can read Mr. Wilde's book without being convinced of the strong ability which he does so much to hide, and without hoping that he has now sufficiently sown his literary wild oats and will some day devote himself to writing something more solid and reasonable and not less brilliant than *Intentions*.

30. Arthur Symons on *Intentions*

1891

Unsigned review in the *Speaker* (4 July 1891), iv, 27; reprinted, in revised form, in Symons's *A Study of Oscar Wilde* (1930).

Arthur Symons (1865–1945), poet, critic, playwright, and translator, became, in the 1890s, a spokesman for the Decadent Movement and the foremost interpreter of the French Symbolists. Indeed, his first article on a French Symbolist poet—Villiers de l'Isle Adam—was published in *Woman's World* in 1889, then recently edited by Wilde, who had invited Symons to contribute after having read his article on Pater in 1887. Symons, however, thought of Wilde as 'a flighty-brained enthusiast and *poseur*' (letter to C. Churchill Osborne, 4 October 1887), but clearly, as this review indicates, he had revised his estimate of Wilde after reading *Intentions*.

'I cannot but be conscious,' says Mr. Wilde in one of his essays, 'that we are born in an age when only the dull are treated seriously, and I live in terror of not being misunderstood.' To be precisely accurate, it is one of the characters in a dialogue who makes this remark. It is no doubt meant to have a personal application—it certainly has. Mr. Wilde is much too brilliant to be ever believed; he is much too witty to be ever taken seriously. A passion for caprice, a whimsical Irish temperament, a love of art for art's sake—it is in qualities such as these that we find the origin of the beautiful farce of æstheticism, the exquisite echoes of the *Poems*, the subtle decadence of *Dorian Gray*, and the paradoxical truths, the perverted common sense, of the *Intentions*. Mr. Wilde, with a most reasonable hatred of the *bourgeois* seriousness of dull people, has always taken refuge from the commonplace in irony. Intentionally or not—scarcely without intention—he has gained a reputation for frivolity which does injustice to a writer who has at least always been serious in the reality of his devotion to art. The better part of his new book is simply a plea for the dignity, an argument for the supremacy, of imaginative art.

The first essay, 'The Decay of Lying', is a protest against realism—
'against the monstrous worship of facts.' It presents certain æsthetic
doctrines, which Mr. Wilde probably partly believes. We are told, for
example, that

Art never expresses anything but itself. It has an independent life, just as Thought
has, and develops purely on its own lines. . . . All bad art comes from returning
to Life and Nature, and elevating them into ideals. Life and Nature may sometimes be used as part of art's rough material, but before they are of any real
service to art, they must be translated into artistic conventions. . . . Life imitates
Art far more than Art imitates Life. . . . It follows, as a corollary from this, that
external Nature also imitates Art. The only effects that she can show us are effects
that we have already seen through poetry, or in paintings. . . . The final revelation is that Lying, the telling of beautiful untrue things, is the proper aim of Art.

All this, startling as it sounds, needs only to be properly apprehended, to
be properly analysed, and we get an old doctrine, indeed, but a doctrine
in which there is a great deal of sanity and a perfectly reasonable view of
things. The two long dialogues called 'The Critic as Artist' present a
theory of criticism which might certainly be justified by the practice of
some of the most perfect among critical writers.

'To the critic,' we are told, 'the work of art is simply a suggestion for a new
work of his own, that need not necessarily bear any obvious resemblance to the
thing it criticises. The one characteristic of a beautiful form is that one can put
into it whatever one wishes, and see in it whatever one chooses to see; and the
beauty, that gives to creation its universal and aesthetic element, makes the critic
a creator in his turn, and whispers of a thousand different things which were not
present in the mind of him who carved the statue or painted the panel or graved
the gem.'

The essay on 'The Truth of Masks' is a learned argument from Shakespeare in favour of the beautiful and appropriate use of archæology in
the mounting of the Shakespearian drama—an argument which seems
to us obviously just, in spite of the warning with which it concludes:
'Not that I agree with everything that I have said in this essay. There is
much with which I entirely disagree. The essay simply represents an
artistic standpoint, and in æsthetic criticism attitude is everything.'
Then, finally, there is a paper on Wainewright, the artist in 'Pen, Pencil,
and Poison', a paper which suffers from the lack of intrinsic interest in
its subject. A pretentious, affected writer does not become interesting
merely because he commits a murder.

A book like this, with its curious convolutions of sentiment, its in-
tricacies of mood and manner, its masquerade of disguises, cannot

OSCAR WILDE

possibly receive adequate notice in the space of a brief review. Mr.
Wilde is always suggestive; he is interesting even when he is provoking.
At his best, to our thinking, when he is most himself—an artist in
epigram—he can be admirable even when his eloquence reminds us of
the eloquent writing of others. He is conscious of the charm of graceful
echoes, and is always original in his quotations. His criticism is often
just as well as amusing: over and over again he proves to us the truth of
masks. By constantly saying the opposite of sensible opinions he proves
to us that opposites can often be equally true. While he insists on producing his paradox, sometimes for no other reason than that it is a
paradox, and would rather say something that is clever than something
that is merely true, it is surprising how often he contrives to illustrate a
mathematical figure by an intellectual somersault, and how often he
succeeds in combining truth and cleverness. After achieving a reputation by doing nothing, he is in a fair way to beat his own record by real
achievements. He is a typical figure, alike in the art of life and the art of
literature, and, if he might be supposed for a moment to represent anything but himself, he would be the perfect representative of all that is
meant by the modern use of the word Decadence.

31. Richard Le Gallienne on *Intentions*

1891

Signed review in the *Academy* (4 July 1891), xl, 7–9.
Le Gallienne (1866–1947), poet and critic, was an admirer, like Wilde, of Walter Pater and moved, like Wilde, in the literary circles of the Aesthetes and Decadents of the 1890s. Le Gallienne first met Wilde in 1887 and sent him a copy of his first volume of poems, *My Ladies' Sonnets and 'Vain and Amatorious' Verses*, published that year.

Mr. Wilde, in speaking of the methods open to the critic, well says that Mr. Pater's narrative is, of course, only criticism in disguise: his figures are but personifications of certain moods of mind, in which he is for the time interested, and which he desires to express. Now I have been wondering whether one should not, similarly, regard Mr. Wilde essentially as a humorist who has taken art-criticism for his medium, just as Carlyle was a humorist in the odd disguise of a prophet. Certainly, I am inclined to think that much of his intricate tracery of thought and elaborate jewel-work of expression is simply built up to make a casket for one or two clever homeless paradoxes. 'The fact of a man being a poisoner is nothing against his prose.' Mr. Wilde somehow struck that out, and saw that it was deserving of a better fate than to remain a waif of traditionary epigram; so he went to work on Lamb's strange friend, Thomas Griffiths Wainewright, one of the subtlest art-critics and poisoners of his time, unearthed his curious history, made selections from his criticism, and then set his own epigram, diamond-wise, in the midst of a biographical essay. Various readers solemnly add to their historical knowledge, discuss the strange character of the man, study his criticism; but Mr. Wilde sits and watches his epigram sparkling far within. About Wainewright he cares far less than the reader, about his own epigram—far more.

Of course this is not the whole truth about these *Intentions*; the whole truth is a many-coloured thing about a personality so complex as

97

that of the author of *Dorian Gray*. Had Ernest read Mr. Pater, to whom Mr. Wilde makes the continual affectionate reference of a disciple, or had he 'with a little rod'[1] touched what the Laureate calls the 'honey-poison' of France—chanced, for instance, on a passage in which M. Anatole France says that

la critique est, comme la philosophie et l'histoire, une espèce de roman à l'usage des esprits avisés et curieux, et tout roman, à le bien prendre, est une auto-biographie; (and continues) Le bon critique est celui qui raconte les aventures de son âme au milieu des chefs-d'œuvre—[2]

had Ernest been twenty-five instead of presumably nineteen, or had he even at that age possessed a larger measure of the artistic temperament, that night in the Piccadilly library would have lost none of its charm, but it would hardly have been so spiritually dislocating for the poor boy. For the 'autobiographical' theory of criticism is no more the secret of M. Anatole France or Mr. Pater than of Mr. Wilde: it belongs to every subtly developed temperament, and has unfortunately been practised in England all too much by men who are anything but subtle. Every small author is eager to give us 'les aventures de son âme au milieu des chefs-d'oeuvre'; but exquisite things happen on that quest to few—to Mr. Pater, to Mr. Henry James, occasionally to Mr. Henley, and certainly to Mr. Wilde. He himself does not take Ernest seriously. It is part of the fun of dialogue as a form for criticism, he says, that the critic 'can invent an imaginary antagonist and convert him when he chooses by some absurdly sophistical argument'.

One must not forget that the form is dialogue, and therefore dramatic. Otherwise, we may be inclined to resent some of Gilbert's information, besides missing the subtle pleasure of watching a young innocent soul undergoing initiation. It was for that—among other things—that Mr. Wilde wrote these two 'colloquies', as they used to be called, on 'The Critic as Artist'; it was not to tell us that creation is as essential a part of criticism as criticism is of creation. All the same, we are glad of the definition of criticism as 'a creation within a creation', and of this clear-sighted illustration of its operation.

But it is the dominant tendency among many others hardly less powerful. Mr. Wilde's worship of beauty is proverbial, it has made a

[1] From Wilde's poem 'Hélas!'

[2] 'Criticism is, like philosophy and history, a kind of romance designed for those who have sagacious and curious minds, and every romance rightly taken, is an autobiography. The good critic is he who relates the adventures of his soul among masterpieces.' (From 'M. Jules Le Maître', *La Vie littéraire*, II, 1890.)

latter-day myth of him before his time; and yet, at least in these essays, his gift of comic perception is above it, and, rightly viewed, all his 'flute-toned' periods are written in the service of the comic muse. Where he is not of malice aforethought humorous, where he seems to be arguing with serious face enough, is it not simply that he may smile behind his mask at the astonishment, not to say terror, of a public he has from the first so delighted in shocking? He loves to hear it call him 'dangerous' as some men delight to be called 'roué'.

There will be many who will, as the phrase is, take him seriously; but let me assure them that Mr. Wilde is not of the number. It all depends what one means by the phrase; for I, for one, take Mr. Wilde very seriously as a creator of work which gives me much and various new pleasure: he is so absolutely alive at every point, so intensely practical— if people could only see it—and therefore so refreshingly unsentimental; he is wittier than is quite fair in a man of his nationality, and he often writes prose that one loves to say over for mere pleasure of ear—his own literary touchstone. The artistic temperament should delight in him, for the serious in the pursuit of literary pleasure he is as serious as every new joy must be; it is only in the domain of thought where it is rather funny to see him taken with such open mouth. Not that Mr. Wilde is not a thinker, and a very subtle one too; but it is rather, so to say, as a dama-scener of thought, than a forger of it, that he is to be regarded. Of course all things are relative; and to the unsophisticated Ernest of Mr. Wilde's dialogue on 'The Critic as Artist' it is certain that the brilliant half-truths with which the sadder and wiser Gilbert lit up their all-night colloquy, as with weird fireworks, were 'strange things' and dangerous to the younger man.

You have told me many strange things tonight, Gilbert. You have told me that it is more difficult to talk about a thing than to do it, and that to do nothing at all is the most difficult thing in the world; you have told me that all art is immoral, and all thought dangerous; that criticism is more creative than crea-tion, and that the highest criticism is that which reveals in the work of art what the artist had not put there; that it is exactly because a man cannot do a thing that he is the proper judge of it; and that the true critic is unfair, insincere, and not rational. My friend, you are a dreamer.

The critic occupies the same relation to the work of art that he criticises as the artist does to the visible world of form and colour, or the unseen world of passion and of thought. He does not even require for the perfection of his art the finest materials. Anything will serve his purpose. And just as out of the sordid and sentimental amours of the silly wife of a small country doctor in the squalid village of Souville l'Abbaye, near Rouen, Gustave Flaubert was able to create a classic, and make a masterpiece of style, so, from subjects of little or no importance . . . the true critic can, if it be his pleasure so to direct or waste his faculty of contemplation, produce work that will be flawless in beauty and instinct with intellectual subtlety.

Mr. Wilde is speaking of criticism in its highest form, in the same sense as Matthew Arnold spoke of poetry as 'a criticism of life'. Of the humbler form of it known as reviewing, he makes one or two common-sense remarks—

'As a rule,' he says, 'the critics . . . are far more cultured than the people whose work they are called upon to review. This is, indeed, only what one would expect, for criticism demands infinitely more cultivation than creation does. . . . The poor reviewers are apparently reduced to be the reporters of the police courts of literature, the chroniclers of the doings of the habitual criminals of art. It is sometimes said of them that they do not read all through the works they are called upon to criticise. They do not; or at least, they should not. . . . Nor is it necessary. To know the vintage and quality of a wine one need not drink the whole cask.'

It belongs to Mr. Wilde's paradoxical method that he should continually play on the convertibility of terms. Thus, the whole contention of his essays on criticism is that criticism and creation are essentially one and the same, or, at least, that they necessarily dovetail one into the other; and yet towards the end of this essay we find Gilbert saying 'it is certain that the subject-matter at the disposal of creation is always diminishing, while the subject-matter of criticism increases daily.' Here we have the two terms crystallized once more to their hard and fast everyday meaning, while all through they have been used as convertible. This is apt to bewilder. As a rule, however, Mr. Wilde gains his effects by adhering to the concrete signification of words. This reduces some of his contentions to a mere question of terms. One often feels: Now, if that word were but changed for another, for which it really stands, there would be nothing further to say. But that, of course, would not do for Mr. Wilde, nor, indeed, for us, to whom, presumably, subject is nought and treatment is all. Occasionally, by this means, it follows that Mr. Wilde seems to beg the question; as, for instance, in his remarks on morality in art. When he says, 'All art is immoral', he is using the word in its narrow relative sense; he does not mean by it the same as those who use it seriously against certain schools and forms of art: though they say 'immoral' they mean 'unspiritual', and that is the meaning many people will attach to the word in Mr. Wilde's phrase.

They will thus be quite unnecessarily shocked by a mere quibble of words, and their real position is left unassailed; the real question at issue being whether or not there is certain art which is dangerous to the spirit, of which one should feel as Mr. Pater says in *Marius*: 'This is what I may not look at.' If life be really a struggle between higher and lower, if art is anything more than a form of sensuous indulgence, this is a question to be answered. Mr. Wilde does not leave us quite clear as to his side in the matter, though he seems to lay over-much stress on the sensuous side of art, a side which is, after all, external and impossible without an informing, formative soul. He echoes, too, Gautier's tirades against 'virtue', and Mr. Swinburne's

> What ailed us, oh gods, to desert you
> For the creeds that refuse and restrain?

and says hard things of chastity and self-sacrifice—really a very 'young' and quite illogical position in an age which has accepted evolution. He quotes M. Renan to the effect that 'Nature cares little about chastity'; but does that prove anything save that Nature is always behind the age, as Mr. Wilde tells us in another place? Surely it is by such ideals, of which, once seen, the beauty haunts him through all his sinnings, that man evolves at all, striving and failing and striving, till slowly what was once the ideal becomes the instinct.

But I am not recking my own rede, and am in danger of growing quite 'heated', as they say of politicians, while Mr. Wilde is doubtless smiling in his sleeve.

Let us leave contention and enjoy. I have referred to two or three of the interesting qualities in these papers. They are so absolutely alive. Every sentence is full of brain. There is no padding, no vagueness, all is 'thought out', as the painters say. One has that safe, untroubled feeling in reading that Matthew Arnold's calm dissecting method gives us—though, needless to say, the austerity of the *Essays in Criticism* is a very different thing from this luxuriously coloured prose: however difficult the thesis, we leave it to the writer with perfect confidence that he will speedily make all clear. Mr. Wilde has, indeed, a rare power of keeping his eye steadily 'on the object'. It is doubtless, too, a part of his perversity that while, as we have seen, he will, when it suits him, adhere rigidly to the fixed signification of words, he can at other times exercise a quite remarkable power of reducing them to their elements, of remorselessly forcing them to say what they really mean. 'You must not be frightened by words,' said Gilbert to his young neophyte; and certainly, if you set such words as 'unpractical', 'dangerous', or 'dreamer' on to Mr. Wilde they will come in for the same summary dissection that befel the lion which attacked the strong man in Holy Writ.

Mr. Wilde's delight in words for their own sake is quite Rabelaisian. He loves so to spread them in heaps, like a child bathing its hands in rich, many-coloured beads, that sometimes he is in danger of a lack of proportion, and catalogues that remind us of the Whitmanese. But some of his tapestries in which, in a brief pageant, he shows us again the Trojan war, or Dante threading the circles of his great dream, are beautiful: and in passages such as the following his technical knowledge of artistic methods, especially handicraft, give us a sense of sure-footedness, a pre-Raphaelite distinction of impression very quickening to the imagination:

The sculptor hewed from the marble block the great white-limbed Hermes that slept within it. The waxers and gilders of images gave tone and texture to the statue, and the world, when it saw it, worshipped and was dumb. He poured the glowing bronze into the mould of sand, and the river of red metal cooled into noble curves, and took the impress of the body of a god. With enamel or polished jewels he gave sight to the sightless eyes. The hyacinth-like curls grew crisp beneath his graver. . . . All subtle arts belonged to him also. He held the gem against the revolving disk, and the amethyst became the purple couch for Adonis, and across the veined sardonyx sped Artemis with her hounds. . . . The potter sat in his shed, and, flower-like from the silent wheel, the vase rose up beneath his hands.

This comes of an almost Renaissance gift of curiosity and a power of various appreciation, which is one of Mr. Wilde's surprises, as it is one of the most robust signs about his work. His reverence for Milton means much. In fact, since 'The Decay of Lying', which is here reprinted, Mr. Wilde has become quite newly significant. One hardly knows yet what to expect of him, but we may be quite sure that these essays and *Dorian Gray* are but preludes. At present a delicate literary affectation, which is probably irritating to most, but rather a charm to those who know what it means, a suggestion of insincerity, a refusal to commit himself, to be 'the slave of his own opinions', makes him somewhat of a riddle. Will it seem too serious to remind Mr. Wilde of one of his earliest sonnets—'Is that Time Dead?' I think not.

Meanwhile, these *Intentions* are delightful reading, especially, as was said at the beginning, for their humour; and if I have failed to do them justice, it is but a proof of Mr. Wilde's paradox that it is impossible to do justice to anything we care about.

32. Agnes Repplier on *Intentions*

1892

Signed article in the *North American Review* [New York] (January 1892), cliv, 97–100: reprinted in her *Essays in Miniature* (New York, 1893).
Agnes Repplier (1855–1950), American essayist and biographer, had been invited to submit an article to a symposium on 'The Best Book of the Year'.

Ever since the first printers with misguided zeal dipped an innocent world in ink, those books have been truly popular which reflected faithfully and enthusiastically the foibles and delusions of the hour. This is what is called 'keeping abreast with the spirit of the times', and we have only to look around us at present to see the principle at work. With an arid and dreary realism chilling us to the heart, and sad-voiced novelists entreating us at every turn to try to cultivate religious doubts, fiction has ceased to be a medium of delight. Even nihilism, which is the only form of relief that true earnestness permits, is capable of being overstrained, and some narrowly conservative people are beginning to ask themselves already whether this new development of 'murder as a fine art' has not been sufficiently encouraged. Out of the midst of the gloom, out of the confusion and depression of conflicting forms of seriousness, rises from London a voice, clear, languid, musical, shaken with laughter, and speaking in strange sweet tones of art and beauty, and of that finer criticism which is one with art and beauty, and claims them forever as its own. The voice comes from Mr. Oscar Wilde, and few there are who listen to him, partly because his philosophy is alien to our prevalent modes of thought, and partly because of the perverse and paradoxical fashion in which he delights to give it utterance. People are more impressed by the way a thing is said than by the thing itself. A grave arrogance of demeanor, a solemn and self-assertive method of reiterating an opinion until it grows weighty with words, are weapons more convincing than any subtlety of argument. 'As I have before expressed to the still reverberating discontent of two continents,' this is the mode in which the public loves to have a statement offered to its ears, that it may gape, and wonder, and acquiesce.

Now, nothing can be further from such admirable solidity than Mr. Wilde's flashing sword-play, than the glee with which he makes out a case against himself, and then proceeds valiantly into battle. There are but four essays in his recent volume, rather vaguely called *Intentions*, and of these four only two have real and permanent value. 'The Truth of Masks' is a somewhat trivial paper, inserted apparently to help fill up the book, and 'Pen, Pencil, and Poison' is visibly lacking in sincerity. The author plays with his subject very much as his subject, 'kind, light-hearted Wainewright,' played with crime, and in both cases there is a subtle and discordant element of vulgarity. It is not given to our eminently respectable age to reproduce that sumptuous and horror-laden atmosphere which lends an artistic glamour to the poisonous court of the Medicis. This 'study in green' contains, however, some brilliant passages, and at least one sentence—'The domestic virtues are not the true basis of art, though they may serve as an excellent advertisement for second-rate artists'—that must make Mr. George Moore pale with envy when he reflects that he missed saying it, where it belongs, in his clever, truthful, ill-natured paper on 'Mummer-Worship'.

The significance and the charm of Mr. Wilde's book are centred in its opening chapter, 'The Decay of Lying', reprinted from the *Nineteenth Century*, and in the long two-part essay entitled 'The Critic as Artist', which embodies some of his most thoughtful, serious, and scholarly work. My own ineffable content rests with 'The Decay of Lying', because under its transparent mask of cynicism, its wit, its satire, its languid mocking humor, lies clearly outlined a great truth that is slipping fast away from us—the absolute independence of art—art nourished by imagination and revealing beauty. This is the hand that gilds the grayness of the world; this is the voice that sings in flute tones through the silence of the ages. To degrade this shining vision into a handmaid of nature, to maintain that she should give us photographic pictures of an unlovely life, is a heresy that arouses in Mr. Wilde an amused scorn which takes the place of anger. 'Art' (he says) 'never expresses anything but itself. It has an independent life, just as Thought has, and develops purely on its own lines. It is not necessarily realistic in an age of realism, nor spiritual in an age of faith. So far from being the creation of its time, it is usually in direct opposition to it, and the only history that it preserves for us is the history of its own progress.'

That we should understand this, it is necessary to understand also the 'beautiful untrue things' which exist only in the world of fancy; the things that are lies, and yet that help us to endure the truth. Mr. Wilde repudiates distinctly and almost energetically all lying with an object, all sordid trifling with a graceful gift. The lies of newspapers yield him no pleasure; the lies of politicians are ostentatiously unconvincing; the lies of lawyers are 'briefed by the prosaic.' He reviews the world of fiction with a swift and caustic touch; he lingers among the poets; he muses rapturously over those choice historic masterpieces, from Herodotus to Carlyle, where 'facts are either kept in their proper subordinate position, or else entirely excluded on the general ground of dulness.' He laments with charming frankness the serious virtues of his age. 'Many a young man,' he says, 'starts in life with a natural gift for exaggeration which, if nurtured in congenial and sympathetic surroundings, or by the imitation of the best models, might grow into something really great and wonderful. But, as a rule, he comes to nothing. He either falls into careless habits of accuracy, or takes to frequenting the society of the aged and the well-informed. Both things are equally fatal to his imagination, and in a short time he develops a morbid and unhealthy faculty of truth-telling, begins to verify all statements made in his presence, has no hesitation in contradicting people who are much younger than himself, and often ends by writing novels that are so like life that no one can possibly believe in their probability.' Surely this paragraph has but one peer in the world of letters, and that is the immortal sentence wherein De Quincey traces the murderer's gradual downfall to incivility and procrastination.

'The Critic as Artist' affords Mr. Wilde less scope for his humour and more for his erudition, which, perhaps, is somewhat lavishly displayed. Here he pleads for the creative powers of criticism, for its fine restraints, its imposed self-culture, and he couches his plea in words as rich as music. Now and then, it is true, he seems driven by the whips of our modern Furies to the verge of things which are not his to handle—problems, social and spiritual, to which he holds no key. When this occurs, we can only wait with drooping heads and what patience we can muster until he is pleased to return to his theme; or until he remembers, laughing, how fatal is the habit of imparting opinions, and what a terrible ordeal it is to sit at table with the man who has spent his life in educating others rather than himself. 'For the development of the race depends on the development of the individual, and where self-culture has ceased to be the ideal, the intellectual standard is instantly lowered, and often ultimately lost.' I like to fancy the ghost of the late rector of Lincoln, of him who said that an appreciation of Milton was the reward of consummate scholarship, listening in the Elysian Fields, and nodding his assent to this much-neglected view of a much-disputed question. Everybody is now so busy teaching that nobody has any time to learn. We are growing rich in lectures, but poor in scholars, and the triumph of mediocrity is at hand. Mr. Wilde can hardly hope to become popular by proposing real study to people burning to impart their ignorance; but the criticism that develops in the mind a more subtle quality of apprehension and discernment is the criticism that creates the intellectual atmosphere of the age.

LORD ARTHUR SAVILE'S CRIME AND OTHER STORIES

July 1891

33. Unsigned notice, *Graphic*

22 August 1891, xciv, 221

The humour of Oscar Wilde's *jeu d'esprit* thus entitled is of a very different order. As pure farce—and what can be better than farce at its best?—it deserves to live; for it is independent of passing circumstances, and is written with all the grave, simple, matter of fact seriousness which is more essential to farce than to tragedy. Nobody with the slightest sense of humour, or, for that matter, nobody with the strongest, can fail to enjoy the story of a man to whom murder presented itself in the light of a simple duty. It is worth all Mr. Wilde's serious work put together. The stories which follow are also excellent, and their author is to be congratulated on having introduced an entirely new and original ghost to the world—no slight feat in these days. But for its degeneration into sentiment, the story in which it appears would be almost as good in its way as that of 'Lord Arthur's Crime'.

34. William Sharp on *Lord Arthur Savile's Crime*

1891

Signed review, *Academy* (5 September 1891), xl, 194.

William Sharp (1856–1905), Scottish journalist, biographer, and poet, who, inspired by the Celtic revival in the 1890s, wrote stories and plays under the pseudonym of 'Fiona Macleod', the identity of whom was disclosed after Sharp's death. In his edition of *Sonnets of this Century* (1886), Sharp included two poems by Wilde.

Lord Arthur Savile's Crime, and its three companion stories, will not add to their author's reputation. Mr. Oscar Wilde's previous book, though in style florid to excess, and in sentiment shallow, had at least a certain cleverness; this quality, however, is singularly absent in at least the first three of these tales. Much the best of the series is the fourth, the short sketch entitled 'A Model Millionaire', though even this brief tale is spoilt by such commonplace would-be witticisms as 'the poor should be practical and prosaic', 'it is better to have a permanent income than to be fascinating.' There is much more of this commonplace padding in the story that gives its name to the book, *e.g.* 'actors can choose whether they will appear in tragedy or comedy,' &c., 'but in real life it is different. Most men and women are forced to perform parts for which they have no qualifications,' and so on, and so on, even to the painfully hackneyed 'the world is a stage, but the play is badly cast.' This story is an attempt to follow in the footsteps of the author of *New Arabian Nights*. Unfortunately for Mr. Wilde's ambition, Mr. Stevenson is a literary artist of rare originality. Such a story as this is nothing if not wrought with scrupulous delicacy of touch. It is, unfortunately, dull as well as derivative. 'The Sphinx without a Secret' is better. 'The Canterville Ghost' is, as a story, better still, though much the same kind of thing has already been far better done by Mr. Andrew Lang; but it is disfigured by some stupid vulgarisms. 'We have really everything in common with America nowadays, except, of course, language.' 'And manners,' an American may be prompted to add. A single example may suffice:

The subjects discussed were merely such as form the ordinary conversation of cultured Americans of the better class, such as the immense superiority of Miss Fanny Davenport over Sara Bernhardt as an actress; the difficulty of obtaining green corn, buckwheat cakes, and hominy, even in the best English houses . . . and the sweetness of the New York accent as compared to the London drawl.

It is the perpetration of banalities of this kind which disgusts Englishmen as well as 'cultured Americans'. One should not judge the society of a nation by that of a parish; the company of the elect by the sinners of one's own acquaintance. Mr. Wilde's verbal missiles will serve merely to assure those whom he ridicules that another not very redoubtable warrior has bestirred himself in the camps of Philistia.

35. W. B. Yeats on *Lord Arthur Savile's Crime*

1891

Signed review, titled 'Oscar Wilde's Last Book', *United Ireland*, 26 September 1891, p. 5.

William Butler Yeats (1865–1939), who first met Wilde around 1887, wrote of that first encounter: 'My first meeting with Wilde was an astonishment. I never before heard a man talking with perfect sentences, as if he had written them all overnight with labour and yet all spontaneous.' (*Autobiography*, 'Four Years: 1887–1891', part eight.) As Yeats became increasingly involved in the Irish literary revival in the 1890s, he saw less of Wilde. (The allusion to the 'coldblooded Socialist' in the second paragraph is, of course, to Shaw.)

We have the irresponsible Irishman in life, and would gladly get rid of him. We have him now in literature and in the things of the mind, and are compelled perforce to see that there is a good deal to be said for him. The men I described to you the other day under the heading, 'A Reckless Century', thought they might drink, dice, and shoot each other to their hearts' content, if they did but do it gaily and gallantly, and here now is Mr. Oscar Wilde, who does not care what strange opinions he defends or what time-honoured virtue he makes laughter of, provided he does it cleverly. Many were injured by the escapades of the rakes and duellists, but no man is likely to be the worse for Mr. Wilde's shower of paradox. We are not likely to poison any one because he writes with appreciation of Wainewright—art critic and poisoner—nor have I heard that there has been any increased mortality among deans because the good young hero of his last book tries to blow up one with an infernal machine; but upon the other hand we are likely enough to gain something of brightness and refinement from the deft and witty pages in which he sets forth these matters.

'Beer, bible, and the seven deadly virtues have made England what she is,' wrote Mr. Wilde once; and a part of the Nemesis that has fallen upon her is a complete inability to understand anything he says. We should not find him so unintelligible—for much about him is Irish of the Irish. I see in his life and works an extravagant Celtic crusade against Anglo-Saxon stupidity. 'I labour under a perpetual fear of not being misunderstood,' he wrote, a short time since, and from behind this barrier of misunderstanding he peppers John Bull with his peashooter of wit, content to know there are some few who laugh with him. There is scarcely an eminent man in London who has not one of those little peas sticking somewhere about him. 'Providence and Mr. Walter Besant have exhausted the obvious,' he wrote once, to the deep indignation of Mr. Walter Besant; and of a certain notorious and clever, but coldblooded Socialist, he said, 'he has no enemies, but is intensely disliked by all his friends.' Gradually people have begun to notice what a very great number of those little peas are lying about, and from this reckoning has sprung up a great respect for so deft a shooter, for John Bull, though he does not understand wit, respects everything that he can count up and number and prove to have bulk. He now sees beyond question that the witty sayings of this man whom he has so long despised are as plenty as the wood blocks in the pavement of Cheapside. As a last resource he has raised the cry that his tormentor is most insincere, and Mr. Wilde replies in various ways that it is quite an error to suppose that a thing is true because John Bull sincerely believes it. Upon the other hand, if he did not believe it, it might have some chance of being true. This controversy is carried on upon the part of John by the newspapers; therefore, those who only read them have as low an opinion of Mr. Wilde as those who read books have a high one. *Dorian Gray* with all its faults of method, is a wonderful book. *The Happy Prince* is a volume of as pretty fairy tales as our generation has seen; and *Intentions* hides within its immense paradox some of the most subtle literary criticism we are likely to see for many a long day. To this list has now been added *Lord Arthur Savile's Crime and other Stories* (James R. Osgood, M'Ilvaine, and Co.). It disappoints me a little, I must confess. The story it takes its name from is amusing enough in all conscience. 'The Sphinx without a Secret' has a quaint if rather meagre charm; but 'The Canterville Ghost' with its supernatural horse-play, and 'The Model Millionaire', with its conventional motive, are quite unworthy of more than a passing interest. . . .

Surely we have in this story something of the same spirit that filled Ireland once with gallant, irresponsible ill-doing, but now it is in its right place making merry among the things of the mind, and laughing gaily at our most firm fixed convictions. In one other Londoner, the socialist, Mr. Bernard Shaw, I recognize the same spirit. His account of how the old Adam gradually changed into the great political economist Adam Smith is like Oscar Wilde in every way. These two men, together with Mr. Whistler, the painter—half an Irishman also, I believe—keep literary London continually agog to know what they will say next.

paper, they put on about as much invisibility as is possible to things visible, and as they are arranged, neither facing letterpress nor with the usual tissue guard, but with a blank sheet of paper of the same tint and substance opposite them, a hasty person might really open the leaves and wonder which side the illustration was. Nevertheless, we rather like them, for when you can see them, they are by no means uncomely, and they suit their text—a compliment which we are frequently unable to pay to much more commonplace instances of the art of book illustration.

In the case of the text, also, hasty judgment is likely to be unduly harsh judgment. The pomegranates that compose the house—the grains that make up the pomegranate would have been a better metaphor—are four in number, and are all tales of the *Märchen* order,[1] though one is something even more of a *fabliau*[2] than of a *Märchen*. This is called 'The Birthday of the Infanta', and tells, to put it very shortly, how a certain little Spanish princess had an ugly dwarf who loved her, and died of a broken heart when he found out, not only how ugly he himself was, but how his beloved mistress thought of him as nothing but a fantastic toy. 'Tis an ower true tale. But we are not sure that Mr. Wilde's manner of telling it is quite the right one. The first and the last of the four, 'The Young King', and 'The Star Child', are pretty enough moralities; the first of half-mediaeval, half-modern Socialist strain. The other tells how a child was cured of cruelty, partly by some metaphysical aid, partly (we do not know whether Mr. Wilde intended to draw this part of the moral, but he has) by sound beatings and a not excessive allowance of bread and water.

But the third piece, 'The Fisherman and his Soul', is much longer, as long, indeed, as any two of them, and to our fancy a good deal better. It tells how a fisherman fell in love with a mermaid, and, to gain her, consented to part with, but not in the ordinary fashion to sell, his soul; how after a time he grew weary of his happiness, went to look after his soul, and found her, divorced as she was from his or any heart, a rather unpleasant, not to say immoral, companion; how he in vain endeavoured to return once more to his mermaid and only found her dead, when he and she and the soul were reunited once for all; and how, when the dead bodies of the pair were found and buried in unhallowed ground, there came a miracle converting to charity the

---

[1] That is, in the manner of German fairy tales.

[2] A medieval French verse tale, often comic, sometimes ribald. Its English counterpart may be seen in Chaucer's 'Miller's Tale'.

heart of the parish priest who had cast them out. The separate ingredients of the piece are, of course, not very novel; but, to tell the truth, the separate ingredients of a story of this kind hardly can be, and Mr. Wilde has put them together with considerable skill, and communicated to the whole an agreeable character. The little mermaid is very nice, both when she is caught literally napping, and when she sings, and when she explains the necessity of her lover parting with his soul if he will have her. Also the young witch (to whom, when the parish priest has, not unnaturally, declined to unsoul him, the fisherman goes) is pleasing. She had red hair, and in gold tissue embroidered with peacock's eyes and a little green velvet cap she must have looked very well. The Sabbath, too, is good (there are too few Sabbaths in English), though the gentlemanly Satan is not new. Good, too, is the business-like manner in which the fisherman separates his soul from him by a device not impossibly suggested by one Adelbert von Chamisso, a person of ability. The adventures of the discarded and heartless soul are of merit, and it is a very good touch to make the fisherman's final, and hardly conscious, desertion of his mermaid-love turn on nothing more than a sudden fancy to dance, and the remembrance that she had no feet and could not dance with him. It is particularly satisfactory to learn that the mermaid's tail was of pearl-and-silver. There has been an impression in many circles that mermaids' tails are green, and we have always thought that it would be unpleasant to embrace a person with a green tail. But pearl-and-silver is *quite* different.

38. Unsigned notice, *Athenaeum*

6 February 1892, p. 177

In connection with the reviewer's opening remark, see No. 36.

Mr. Oscar Wilde has been good enough to explain, since the publication of his book that it was intended neither for the 'British Child' nor for the 'British Public', but for the cultured few who can appreciate its subtle charms. The same exiguous but admiring band will doubtless comprehend why a volume of allegories should be described as *A House of Pomegranates*, which we must confess is not apparent to our perverse and blunted intellect. It consists of four storeys (we mean stories), 'The Young King', 'The Birthday of the Infanta', 'The Fisherman and his Soul', and 'The Star-Child', each dedicated to a lady of Mr. Wilde's acquaintance, and all characterized by the peculiar faults and virtues of his highly artificial style. The allegory, as we have had occasion to remark on former occasions, when discussing the work of Lady Dilke and Miss Olive Schreiner in this particular field, is one of the most difficult of literary forms. In Mr. Wilde's *House of Pomegranates* there is too much straining after effect and too many wordy descriptions; but at the same time there is a good deal of forcible and poetic writing scattered through its pages, and its scenes have more colour and consistence than those which we criticized in 'Dreams' and 'The Shrine of Love'. Mr. Wilde resembles the modern manager who crowds his stage with aesthetic upholstery and *bric-à-brac* until the characters have scarcely room to walk about. Take this inventory of the contents of a chamber in the young king's palace, which reads for all the world like an extract from a catalogue at Christie's:—

After some time he rose from his seat, and leaning against the carved penthouse of the chimney looked round at the dimly-lit room. The walls were hung with rich tapestries representing the Triumph of Beauty. A large press, inlaid with agate and lapis-lazuli, filled one corner, and facing the window stood a curiously wrought cabinet with lacquer panels of powdered and mosaiced gold, on which were placed some delicate goblets of Venetian glass and a cup of dark-veined onyx. Pale poppies were broidered on the silk coverlet of the bed, as though they had fallen from the tired hands of Sleep, and tall reeds of fluted ivory bare up the velvet canopy, from which great tufts of ostrich plumes sprang, like white foam, to the pallid silver of the fretted ceiling. A laughing Narcissus in green bronze held a polished mirror above its head. On the table stood a flat bowl of amethyst.

The adornment of these 'beautiful tales,' as Mr. Wilde modestly calls them, has been entrusted to Messrs. C. Ricketts and C. H. Shannon, and for combined ugliness and obscurity it would be hard, we imagine, to beat them. The full-page illustrations are so indistinctly printed that whatever excellence they may possess is lost to view, while the grotesque black-and-white woodcuts are hideous to behold. It is, perhaps, as well that the book is not meant for the 'British Child'; for it would certainly make him scream, according to his disposition, with terror or amusement.

LADY WINDERMERE'S FAN

First produced: 20 February 1892

---

39. A. B. Walkley on *Lady Windermere's Fan*

1892

Review signed 'A. B. W.', the *Speaker* (27 February 1892), v, 257–8.
Arthur Bingham Walkley (1855–1926) was a drama critic on such publications as the *Star* (1888–1900), reviewing under the pseudonym of 'Spectator', and *The Times* (1900–26) as well as the *Speaker*. One of the most influential drama critics of his day, Walkley was a long and continuing admirer of Wilde's plays.

'It is well that a change should from time to time be made in old customs,' said M. Renan the other day, 'as life would otherwise be too monotonous.' This profound truth explains some things, and excuses others. It explains M. Renan. It excuses Mr. Oscar Wilde. Here is a gentleman who devotes brilliant talents, a splendid audacity, an agreeable charlatanry and a hundred-Barnum-power of advertisement, to making a change in old customs and preventing life from being monotonous. He does this in innumerable ways—by his writings, his talk, his person, his clothes, and everything that is his. He has aimed at doing it in his play, *Lady Windermere's Fan*, and has been, to my mind, entirely successful. It is by no means a good play: its plot is always thin, often stale; indeed, it is full of faults—oh! dear, yes! glaring faults—faults that would leap to the eyes of the man in the street or of the old applewoman round the corner. Yet, again, it *is* a good play, for it carries you along from start to finish without boring you for a single moment. While it is a-playing, it convinces you, in spite of yourself, that life is not monotonous. If we have had more sparkling dialogue on the stage in the present generation, I have not heard it. It presents at least one fresh and piquant study of character. And it breaks long-established laws of the theatre—makes, as M. Renan would say, a change in old customs, with light-hearted indifference. If these qualities do not constitute a good play, they constitute a very diverting one. The man or woman who does not chuckle with delight at the good things which abound in *Lady Windermere's Fan* should consult a physician at once: delay would be dangerous.

For the staleness of the incidents one has only to refer to half a dozen familiar French plays. As to the stage laws which are broken, they are two: one invented by Sarcey, the other by Diderot and promulgated by Lessing, while—but perhaps it will be better to tell the story and make my comments as I go along. Lady Windermere is a guileless young bride who, like M. Dumas' Françillon, believes in an equal law of fidelity for both husband and wife. She has perfect confidence in her husband, but if ever that confidence is betrayed it is pretty clear that she will act on Françillon's principle of reprisals—an eye for an eye, a tooth for a tooth. The time comes when she has reason to suspect that her confidence is betrayed. An unprincipled man of the world—unprincipled, for he divides mankind not into the good and the bad, but 'the charming and the tedious,' and 'can resist everything, except temtation'—with designs of his own upon Lady Windermere, hints to her —only hints, for he holds that 'to be intelligible is to be found out'—that her husband is too intimate with a certain Mrs. Erlynne. Who is Mrs. Erlynne? She is a *demi-mondaine* in the original Dumasian sense of that much-abused term:[1] or, as a certain gossiping Duchess puts it, one of those people 'who form the basis of other people's marriages.' The suspicions thus aroused are confirmed when the wife tears open her husband's bankbook: the creature is in his pay! More than that, he insists upon her being admitted as a guest to one of his wife's receptions. 'If she comes, I will strike her in the face with my fan,' says the indignant wife. 'How hard you good women are!' 'How weak you wicked men are!' 'If she only knew!' sighs Lord Windermere.

She does not know; if she did, there would be no piece. But are we, we spectators, not to know? Orthodox theatrical practice says, yes; Mr. Wilde, ever bent on 'making a change in old customs,' says, no. Diderot, to be sure (the curious will find the passage in the preface to his

---

[1] The term 'demi-monde' was coined by Alexandre Dumas *fils* for the title of his play *Le Demi-Monde* (1855), which the French Academy defined as 'the society of women with slight morals'.

Père de Famille), warned the dramatist against 'surprises,' and his warning has since been petrified into a hard-and-fast law. But this, really, is
to misunderstand Diderot himself, who, in the very same passage, goes
on to say:—

O faiseurs de règles générales, que vous ne connaissez guère l'art, et que vous
avez peu de ce génie qui a produit les modèles sur lesquels vous avez établi ces
règles, qu'il est le maître d'enfreindre quand il lui plaît![1]

Does Mr. Oscar Wilde prove himself such a *maître* in this play? I
think he does. It is all a question of pleasure, of interest. If he gives us
more pleasure by teasing our curiosity about Mrs. Erlynne than by
satisfying it, then is he entirely justified. We do not know who Mrs.
Erlynne is until the very end of the play. If we were told at the outset, I,
for one, should not view her conduct and Lord Windermere's in forcing her upon his wife with half the interest which these things afford
me while still in the dark. (I put this as a personal view, because the
general opinion is very possibly against me. So at least Mr. Wilde
would seem to think, for it appears that, since the first night, the story
has been so modified that the audience are no longer kept in the dark.
But, of course, I shall continue to discuss the only version of the play
which I have seen.)

Well, then, Mrs. Erlynne is duly ushered into Lady Windermere's
drawing-room, and we have the spectacle of an adventuress bearing
herself bravely, captivating all the men, and outshining all the women,
in the presence of a hostile hostess. This, of course, is Act I. of Dumas'
L'Etrangère over again: Mrs. Erlynne is Mrs. Clarkson, and Lady
Windermere is the Duchesse de Septmonts. But yet there is a difference—a difference which again shows Mr. Wilde 'making a change in
old customs.' Dumas introduces this incident for the sake of a *scène-à-
faire*,[2] beloved of Sarcey. For a corresponding *scène-à-faire* in Mr.
Wilde's play, we should have to see the hostess keeping her word about
the fan, and administering a slap in the face to her guest. We have no
such scene. Instead of imitating the Duchesse de Septmonts, when she
breaks the cup out of which Mrs. Clarkson has drunk, Lady Windermere elects again to imitate Françillon: she will leave her husband's
roof—naturally for that of Lord Darlington.

[1] 'O makers of general rules, how little you know of art and how little of that genius
you have which has produced the models on which you have established these rules, rules
which the genius of a master is free to break when it suits him!'
[2] The 'obligatory scene', which the dramatist must present to his audience in order to
resolve the conflicts of the play satisfactorily.

Thither she is followed by Mrs. Erlynne, who alone knows of her flight, and is determined to save her. Why? Because she feels that the very same tragedy which once happened to herself is now in danger of happening to this other woman—see (and the resemblance will seem more complete to you when you know all Mrs. Erlynne's secret) M. Jules Lemaître's *Révoltée*. She appeals, first to the young wife—in vain; then to the young mother—and prevails. But it is too late. The women have only just time to hide before Lord Darlington, Lord Windermere, and a party of men enter the room. Here, once more, Mr. Wilde poses as the law-breaker. He calmly suspends his action, while the men sit down to a long talk. But you do not notice its length, for it is a perpetual coruscation of epigrams. All the men talk like Mr. Oscar Wilde. Everything is discussed paradoxically, from the connection between London fogs and seriousness—'whether London fogs produce the serious people or serious people the London fogs'—to the connection between feminine frivolity and feminine charms—'nothing is so unbecoming to a woman as a Nonconformist conscience'; from cynicism —'the cynic is the man who knows the price of everything and the value of nothing'—to married womanhood—'nothing is so glorious in life as the devotion of a married woman; it is a subject about which no married man knows anything.' Then, just before we are in danger of getting a little tired of epigrams, just *before*—for did I not say that Mr. Wilde never lets you be bored?—it is discovered that a lady is in hiding. Here is her fan—'my wife's!' says Lord Windermere, much as the Prince de Bouillon recognises his wife's bracelet in *Adrienne Lecouvreur*. But we have had a much more recent parallel than that in Mr. Haddon Chambers's *Idler*, produced at this very theatre. In fact, henceforward, if any stage-heroine carries a fan, I shall know at once what the plot is going to be. But the fan does not betray Lady Windermere, for it is Mrs. Erlynne who comes forward to claim it, while the wife glides away, unperceived.

Now you are nearing the end of the play, you are to be told Mrs. Erlynne's secret, and I will hark back, if you please, to my mention of M. Lemaître's *Révoltée*. In that play a divorced woman, believed by her daughter to be dead, intervenes to save the girl from the very fate which she herself suffered. That is the case here: Mrs. Erlynne is Lady Windermere's mother. But M. Lemaître gets a *scène-à-faire* out of this: the mother reveals herself to her daughter. That is not Mr. Wilde's way. He lets the truth about Mrs. Erlynne slip out, quite casually, in a conversation between the lady and Lord Windermere, and so we now know how it is she has been able to blackmail him; but she never tells her child. She has had enough of virtuous self-sacrifice and of playing at motherhood. 'How could I pass for a woman of twenty-nine or thirty—twenty-nine when there are pink shades, thirty when there are not—with a grown up daughter?' And, thank goodness, she doesn't repent—stage repentances are so tedious! No, she retires laughing from the scene, a true *demi-mondaine* to the last; and with the reconciliation of husband and wife the play ends.

As I began by saying, the faults of this piece are glaring enough. Mrs. Erlynne has really no better reason for forcing her way into her daughter's drawing-room than Mr. Wilde's recollection of that scene in *L'Etrangère*. Lord Windermere is an impossibly foolish person for risking his whole domestic happiness rather than let his wife know her mother was a divorced woman. But then, if Mrs. Erlynne did not force her way in, if Lord Windermere were not an impossibly foolish person, there would be no play, and Mr. Oscar Wilde would not have broken the monotony of life so gallantly as he has. It is no use telling me of the constructive faults, the flimsy plot, the unreasonable conduct of the characters. My answer is, 'I know all that; but the great thing is, that the play never bores me; and when a dramatist gives me such a perpetual flow of brilliant talk as Mr. Wilde gives, I am willing to forgive him all the sins in the dramatic Decalogue, and the rest.' Someone this week has compared the talk with Sheridan's; but that is, perhaps, a little 'too steep.' The style of the play suggests to me rather the Lyttonian, the Disraelian, the style of the Age of the Dandies. And a very delightful style, too! Meretricious, you say? Oh, yes! undeniably meretricious. But meretricious wit is better than the usual jog-trot, philistine stupidity of the stage. Anything for a change. . . .

40. Clement Scott on
Lady Windermere's Fan

1892

Signed review, *Illustrated London News* (27 February 1892), c, 278.
Clement Scott (1841–1904), was a drama critic on the *Daily Telegraph* as well as the *Illustrated London News*, an adapter of French plays, and a vigorous opponent of Ibsen. In a letter dated 27 February 1895 to Richard Mansfield (1854–1907), the actor-manager, George Bernard Shaw revealed that one of the characters in *The Philanderer* was modelled on Scott: 'Cuthbertson is a caricature of Clement Scott, whose double you must have somewhere on the New York press.' (*Collected Letters: 1874–97*, ed. Dan Laurence, p. 488.) In his review, Scott devotes a lengthy opening paragraph to an expression of indignation over Wilde's conduct at the opening night of *Lady Windermere's Fan* (he had appeared on stage following the final curtain with cigarette in hand to congratulate the audience on its good sense in liking his play) and similar 'condescension' on the part of other playwrights.

. . . But supposing, after all, Mr. Oscar Wilde is a cynic of deeper significance than we take him to be. Supposing he intends to reform and revolutionise society at large by sublime self-sacrifice. There are two sides to every question, and Mr. Oscar Wilde's piety in social reform has not as yet been urged by anybody. His attitude has been so extraordinary that I am inclined to give him the benefit of the doubt. It is possible that he may have said to himself, 'I will show you and prove to you to what an extent bad manners are not only recognised but endorsed in this wholly free and unrestrained age. I will do on the stage of a public theatre what I should not dare do at a mass meeting in the Park. I will uncover my head in the presence of refined women, but I refuse to put down my cigarette. The working-man may put out his pipe when he spouts, but my cigarette is too "precious" for destruction. I will show no humility, and I will stand unrebuked. I will take greater liberties with the public than any author who has ever preceded me in history. And I will retire scatheless. The society that allows boys to puff cigarette-smoke into the faces of ladies in the theatre-corridors will condone the originality of a smoking author on the stage.' This may be the form of Mr. Oscar Wilde's curious cynicism. He may say, 'I will test this question of manners and show that they are not nowadays recognised.'

Having proved by a test so strong as this the indifference of society to what used to be called good manners and good breeding, Mr. Oscar Wilde may say, 'I will show you also how unsentimental is the age in which we live. I cannot help it. I am not responsible for it, but there it is. I can only write for people as they are, not for people as they ought to be. I will prove to you by my play that the very instinct of maternity—that holiest and purest instinct with women—is deadened in the breasts of our English mothers. I will paint for you a young English mother who adores her husband, who has a firstborn child scarcely yet weaned from the breast, who has been brought up in a strictly decorous society, who has high views on religion and honour, and I will show how, without seeking reflection at her child's bedside, she will leave her husband, her home, her firstborn, her character, her reputation—and for what? For the arms of a man she does not profess to love. And for what reason? Because she has learned from the tittle-tattle of her friends that her husband has been false to her! This shall be accepted as the Gospel truth. I tell you that the mothers in society will not consider that I have outraged their sex or expressed anything but the truth. But this is not the only type of mother I will paint for you. You have seen how the good mother can desert her new-born infant without a pang. You shall see how the worldly mother shall, having recognised her lost child, part from her as she parts from the atelier of a Bond Street milliner. I will show you a mother who leaves her daughter for ever, unkissed, and goes downstairs to accept the hand of a roué admirer on her deserted daughter's doorstep. I tell you that society will not say one word except that it is all very amusing. Amusing they will consider it, but un-natural—never. It is society that is at fault, not I. I paint what I see; I am not a sentimentalist, but a cynic. The best test of the justice of my picture is found in the fact that society does not reprimand it.' And then Mr. Oscar Wilde, pursuing this train of thought, may go on to say, 'And I will prove to you also how inartistic are these people for whom I write. They have no nice sense of proportion. They don't understand balance of effect or light and shade. They are quick, and they will laugh at what is clever. They love "smart people" and "smart things". They have canonised the word "smart." They don't care one brass farthing if the elderly man talks like the callow boy or the innocent girl like the blasée woman. They must all be up to date and smart. "To be intelligible is to be found out." I have never since I left Oxford and won the Newdigate with my poem on "Ravenna" been wholly intelligible. And I have never been found out.' Thus might argue Mr. Oscar Wilde in his own defence. Meanwhile, society at large will rush to see his play.

41. Unsigned review, *Black and White*

27 February 1892, iii, 264

The Red Lamp, which the reviewer compares with Wilde's play, was by W. Outram Tristram and in it the actor-manager H. Beerbohm Tree scored a notable success.

Mr. Oscar Wilde's play belongs to the school of which *The Red Lamp* is a conspicuous example. It is, like *The Red Lamp*, a play which owes its title and its theme to a piece of domestic furniture. In the one piece the fortunes of a Russian Princess depended upon the position of a lamp as scarlet as the cry of Montanaro's passionate parrot. In the other piece the fortunes of an Englishwoman depend upon the proprietorship of a fan as white as Lady Windermere's fortuitous innocence. As a rule plays built up round some inanimate object are rather boring; but that could not be said of *The Red Lamp* or of *Lady Windermere's Fan*. On the contrary both are very amusing plays. Mr. Wilde's pictures of exalted London life are as faithful as Mr. Tristram's studies of St. Petersburg society; if Mr. Tristram was more adventurous, Mr. Wilde is more epigrammatic. Indeed, it is obvious that Mr. Wilde regards a play as a vehicle merely for the expression of epigram and the promulgation of paradox. *Lady Windermere's Fan* is not really a play; it is a pepper-box of paradoxes. The piece is improbable without being interesting. It is a not too ingenious blend of the *Eden* of Mr. Edgar Saltus, with *The Idler* of Mr. Haddon Chambers, and the *Francillion* of Alexander Dumas the Younger. Its people act in an unnatural manner without arousing sympathy or hostility by their actions. The situations are weatherworn. But the paradox is the thing, not the play. The Great God Paradox has his impassioned prophet in Mr. Wilde and all Mr. Wilde's puppets chant his litany. It has a quaint effect to find, in this Cloud-Cuckoo-Town of Mr. Wilde's, all its inhabitants equally cynical, equally paradoxical, equally epigrammatic. Were the trick to become too stale it might prove tiresome, for it is, after all, but a question of inverted vocabulary. Mr. Wilde's figures talk a Back Slang of their own; once accept the conditions of the game, and the fantastic becomes the familiar. Black is white, day is night; well and good, by all means. But what next? While it is fresh, however, this kind of fantasy is exceedingly diverting. . . .

42. Frederick Wedmore on *Lady Windermere's Fan*

1892

Signed review in his column, 'The Stage', *Academy* (5 March 1892), xli, 236–7.
Wedmore (1844–1921), author and critic, published a life of Balzac, several books on art, and many short stories. For thirty years, he was art critic on the *Standard*; in 1912, he was knighted.

Lady Windermere's Fan—which, as I was unable to be present on the first night, it was impossible to notice last week, while it was absolutely a novelty—shall receive to-day a brief, though by no means an unfavourable comment. In it Mr. Oscar Wilde—whose unconventionalities (of speech and cigarette, for instance) lie, after all, very much upon the surface—has managed to write a play by no means so extra-ordinarily unlike other people's as he might enjoy to believe, and as certain of the critics, on whom the speech and the cigarette appear to have made a great impression, have good-naturedly and gently as-sumed. The construction, the story, even the very moral of the story—unassisted even by speech and cigarette—these things could have been much as they are. Many a dramatist would have been capable of them. The 'incident of the fan' has recalled to everybody quite a recent work of Mr. Haddon Chambers's; but it has hardly, I suppose, occurred to the least intelligent to suggest plagiarism. There is here doubtless a mere coincidence, and it is only worth mentioning because it is an instance of the extent to which Mr. Wilde and the dramatist who is confessedly accepted and 'popular' have travelled the same road. *Nuances* of treat-ment there are certainly—apart altogether from his unrelaxed smartness of dialogue—yes, yes, let me say, also, certain boldnesses of conception, which separate Mr. Wilde, in this the most serious of his efforts, from even the clever playwright who is bent upon conciliating the sym-pathies of the upper boxes, and who has it upon his mind to square the conduct and final disposition of his characters with the views of life which may obtain among the readers of Mr. William Black and Dr. George Macdonald. There is the character of Mrs. Erlynne, for example: a woman not without good points, though with infinite faults and a past that she knows has been disgraceful. The dramatist bent upon conciliation would have made her repentant; Mr. Wilde does nothing of the kind. He recognises the nature of the woman, and is faithful to the formula that the leopard does not change her spots. Much more than Bohemian—for Bohemia has room for unselfishness, and exacts, as the very condition of its citizenship, a capacity for impulsive affection—more, much more than Bohemian, *demimondaine* in the true sense—the sense of Dumas *fils*[1] what would Mrs. Erlynne do among the proprie-ties and domesticities? Did she repent at the end, her's could be only such a taming and a penitence as that of the down-trodden Jew in 'Holy Cross Day,' whose penances and humiliations had no meaning and no heart in them, but were devised simply that they might

> Usher in worthily Christian Lent.

Others of the characters, however, are conceived in more ordinary fashion and, though they express themselves with a brightness that is, alas, not customary, the spirit of their dialogue is that of the habitual

[1] See No. 39, note 1.

society satire. The Duchess of Berwick, for instance—and here the comedy becomes a little farcical—believes in nothing but a good marriage. That is well. But her idea of a good marriage—a good marriage for her daughter—is a marriage with a millionaire from Australia. And the daughter—however much of a *débutante* she may be—can you conceive her in the colours of a French *ingénue*, with her eternal 'Yes, mamma'? And the Duchess's brother. Natural enough, I have no doubt —natural, but ordinary. And so on, with the rest.

But why carp, when on the whole there is so much to enjoy! The play, if not a revelation, is a pleasure. . . .

43. Unsigned review, *Westminster Review*

April 1892, cxxxvii, 478–80.

George Alexander (1858–1918), actor and theatre manager, acted in several of Wilde's plays. He was knighted in 1911. As the review indicates, he was known for his grave style.

Mr. Oscar Wilde is nothing unless brilliant and witty. He has written in a light satirical vein, cultured and refined, and in good taste. There is no particular point about his characters, but they serve as mouths to enunciate the author's exquisitely funny remarks on society; and this is all that was expected of them. The St. James's Theatre is, to Mr. Wilde, what the charitable institution is to the amateur dramatic company, a means to an end. Though the remarks of the cynical young men about town, and the garrulous duchess of Berwick, may show a keen appreciation of the vices of society, we are inclined to think that a drama conceived on the lines of *Lady Windermere's Fan*, though successful for once, should not be attempted too often, for really, clever and entertaining as it undoubtedly is, it is scarcely a play at all! Mr. Alexander was much perplexed, and did not come up to our expectations in consequence. He was condemned to be good, which was very hard considering the shallow, insincere, cynical throng in which he was mixed up. He is made to do various very silly things in the interests of justice, and evinces throughout the play the knowledge of the world of the average country curate. This is, of course, the author's fault, not his; but why need Mr. Alexander make the simile more striking by adopting a slightly pulpit style of oratory in all the earnest passages? Here is a question to which there seems no reply. Indeed, we should not have been much surprised had he, on more than one occasion, finished his speech with the ominous words, 'and here endeth the first lesson.' That is only one aspect of the question; there are others by which *Lady Windermere's Fan* may be condemned. It is very improbable—impossible, one might almost add. Surely a good moral woman, such as Lady Windermere is made out to be, would not desert her husband because of the mere gossip of a scandalmongering old lady. Lord Windermere also would never have allowed matters to come to a crisis without taking his wife into confidence, and explaining to her a little sooner, her relationship with Mrs. Erlynne. But this is not Mr. Wilde's idea. He is anxious to express to the world his reflections on things in general, to lash the petty vices of people of fashion, and does not, in the least, wish to tell a good story. So the plot does not matter, as the whole interest lies in the conversation, which is as if many Wildes, male and female, were talking together. So far, then, the author is successful. The dialogue is exquisitely funny, is satirical without being aggravating to the audience. It is biting, and at the same time genial and good-humoured. . . .

We give this brief outline of the plot in order to elucidate our previous criticisms, for such of our readers as have not yet been to see *Lady Windermere's Fan* at the St. James's. To any one interested in plays we certainly say, if you have not yet been to see it, go at once. You will be well entertained by an original, clever, and ridiculous piece portraying London society as seen through the spectacles of Mr. Oscar Wilde.

44. Justin Huntly McCarthy on
Lady Windermere's Fan

1892

Signed notice in *Gentleman's Magazine* (April 1892), cclxxii, 476.
Justin Huntly McCarthy (1860–1936), historian, novelist, and
Member of Parliament (1884–92), whose best-known work, *If I
Were King* (1901), became the basis for the operetta *The Vagabond
King*.

Mr. Oscar Wilde is inclined to be peevish with his critics. Yet his critics
were very patient with him. He wrote what he called a play, and he
peppered it with not unamiable paradox, and diverted a considerable
number of persons. But it takes more than this to convert an adventurous Bœotian into the ideal blend of, let us say, Goethe, Shakespeare, and
Baffo, which appears to be Mr. Wilde's own image of himself. Mr.
Wilde has in his time aroused the gaiety of English-speaking countries.
It delights him—as the performance delights the spectators—to masque
as an Athenian. But he is no Athenian. George Meredith brands one of
his creations as 'An Epicurean whom Epicurus would have scourged out
of his Garden.' The Athenians would not have been tolerant of this
sham Athenian. Mr. Wilde seems most to resemble the man in Charles
de Bernard's ablest novel, who always has Art upon his lips because he
had so little in his soul. Mr. Wilde has called his play a work of art. That
of course it is not, could not be. Mr. Wilde is many things needless to
enumerate, but he is not an artist. His utterances upon art must be regarded with a delicate disdain.

SALOMÉ

22 February 1893

---

45. Edgar Saltus on Wilde's reading of *Salomé* in manuscript

1917

From Edgar Saltus's *Oscar Wilde: An Idler's Impression* (Chicago, 1917), p. 20.

Saltus (1855–1921), American author and aesthete, first met Wilde in 1882 when the latter was on his lecture tour of America.

In his hand was a manuscript, and we were supping on 'Salomé.'

As the banquet proceeded, I experienced that sense of sacred terror which his friends, the Greeks, knew so well. For this thing could have been conceived only by genius wedded to insanity and, at the end, when the tetrarch, rising and bundling his robes about him, cries: 'Kill that woman!' the mysterious divinity whom the poet may have evoked, deigned perhaps to visit me. For, as I applauded, I shuddered, and told him that I had.

Indifferently he nodded and, assimilating Hugo with superb unconcern, threw out: 'It is only the shudder that counts.'

46. Unsigned notice, *The Times*

23 February 1893, p. 8

The reviewer, in his column 'Books of the Week', preceded his notice of *Salomé* with one of Ibsen's *The Master Builder*, which he characterized as 'intolerably dull as a drama and repulsively morbid as a picture of human nature'. (Ollendorff's exercises were a popular method of language instruction stressing repetitive patterns.)

Of Mr. Oscar Wilde's *Salomé: Drame en un Acte* (Elkin Mathews and John Lane), we are constrained to express an equally unfavourable opinion. This is the play, written for Mme. Sarah Bernhardt, for performance in this country. It is an arrangement in blood and ferocity, morbid, *bizarre*, repulsive, and very offensive in its adaptation of scriptural phraseology to situations the reverse of sacred. It is not ill-suited to some of the less attractive phases of Mme. Bernhardt's dramatic genius, as it is vigorously written in some parts. As a whole, it does credit to Mr. Wilde's command of the French language, but we must say that the opening scene reads to us very like a page from one of Ollendorff's exercises.

47. Max Beerbohm, letter to Reginald Turner

1893

Extract from letter written on 25 February 1893, to Reginald Turner, published in *Max Beerbohm's Letters to Reggie Turner*, ed. Rupert Hart-Davis (London, 1964), p. 32.

Beerbohm (1872–1956) had met Wilde in 1889, but not until 1893 did he come to know him well. Turner (1869–1938), also an admirer of Wilde, had left Merton College, Oxford, in 1892 and was reading for the Bar. One of Wilde's intimate circle, he was present when Wilde died in Paris. Turner later published twelve unsuccessful novels and, like Beerbohm, lived for many years in Italy.

The book that they have bound in Parma violets and across whose page is the silver voice of the Master made visible—how could it not be lovely? I am enamoured of it. It has charmed my eyes from their sockets and through the voids has sent incense to my brain: my tongue is loosed in its praise. Have you read it? In construction it is very like a Greek play, I think: yet in conception so modern that its publication in any century would seem premature. It is a marvellous play. If Oscar would re-write *all* the Bible, there would be no sceptics. I say it is a marvellous play. It is a lovely present.

But oh did you see (perhaps inspired?) a paragraph in the *Daily Telegraph*, saying that Mr Wilde had distorted the facts of one of the most straightforward of Biblical tales and that his version of it left an unpleasant taste in the mouth? This criticism appeared this morning. What will be done to the writer? Dismissal would be too good for him. . . .

48. Unsigned review, *Pall Mall Gazette*

27 February 1893, p. 3.

Rehearsals for the production of *Salomé* had been in progress (with Sarah Bernhardt in the leading role) in 1892 when, in June, the Examiner of Plays for the Lord Chamberlain refused to license the play because it contained biblical characters. Outraged, Wilde, who in a letter to William Rothenstein characterized the Examiner, Edward F. Smyth Piggott, as one 'who panders to the vulgarity and hypocrisy of the English people, by licensing every low farce and vulgar melodrama' (*Letters*, p. 316), announced his intention to renounce his British citizenship and depart for France, where his play could be produced.

The suppression, prohibition, excommunication of any work of art or of anything professing to be a work of art always lends to the thing suppressed a kind of reputation. The Examiner of Plays saw fit, in the exercise of his discretion, to forbid the production of *Salomé* on the stage of a London theatre, and his action made *Salomé* a matter of talk. So long as the State maintains such an officer, it would be hard to see how the Examiner of Plays could have acted otherwise. He would have acted equally in obedience to the duties of his office in preventing the presentation of any piece upon the stage which could give offence to the followers of Mahommed, for the British Empire is a Mussulman Empire as well as a Christian Empire, and the creeds of an Empire are not toys to be trifled with by any seeker after notoriety. But the soreness which Mr. Wilde felt at the action of the Examiner of Plays—a soreness which at one time tempted him to change his nationality—is soothed by the publicity of print, and neither the creed of Christendom nor the decorum of the commonweal will reel under the shock.

Salomé is a mosaic. Mr. Wilde has many masters, and the influence of each master asserts itself in his pages as stripes of different colours assert themselves in stuffs from the East. The reader of *Salomé* seems to stand in the Island of Voices and to hear around him and about the utterances of friends, the whisperings of demigods. Now it is the voice of Gautier, painting pictures in words of princesses and jewels and flowers and unguents. Anon it is Maeterlinck who speaks—Maeterlinck the Lord of the Low Countries—with his iterations and reiterations, his questions and conundrums, that make so many of his pages—and so many of Mr. Wilde's pages—recall the Book of Riddles that Master Slender sighed for. The chorus seems to be swelled by the speech like silver of Anatole France, perchance by the speech like gold of Marcel Schwob. But the voices that breathe the breath of life into *Salomé* are dominated by one voice, the voice of Flaubert. If Flaubert had not written *Salammbô*, if Flaubert had not written *La Tentation de Saint Antoine*—above all, if Flaubert had not written *Hérodias*, *Salomé* might boast an originality to which she cannot now lay claim. She is the daughter of too many fathers. She is a victim of heredity. Her bones want strength, her flesh wants vitality, her blood is polluted. There is no pulse of passion in her.

There is no freshness in Mr. Wilde's ideas; there is no freshness in his method of presenting those ideas. Flaubert long ago exhausted all that was to be got out of making John the Baptist the hero of a story of sensualism. When the adaptors of Flaubert put his story upon the stage they well-nigh exhausted the possibilities of shocking any shockable Christian by the device of skirting blasphemy. But the imitation which dominates the play follows it into particulars. The appearance of Salomé before the soldiers seems but a reminiscence of the appearance of Salammbô before the mercenaries, chilled in the process of reproduction. Herodias has her hair powdered with blue, another effect from Flaubert. Was not Salammbô's hair powdered with a violet dust when she first appeared before the eyes of Matho; was not the hair of the Queen of Sheba powdered with blue when she appeared, a phantasm, before the eyes of Anthony in the desert? The squabbles of the Jews among themselves do but parody the squabbles of the Christians in the *Tentation*. The passion of the young Syrian for Salomé is a recollection of Gautier in the mood of *Une Nuit de Cléopâtre*. As for the portions that belong to Maeterlinck—the jugglery with the moon's resemblances, the short, repeated sentences in the phrase-book manner—they, in the words of Celia, are laid on with a trowel.

All this would be of no moment if Mr. Wilde's work wore no sign of grace, were quite without ability. But there is a cleverness in the way in which the thing is done that must make the reader wish it had been done otherwise. The talent that has been employed in the preparation of a pastiche might in all probability have created something belonging to

Mr. Wilde himself, not to Maeterlinck and Gautier, to France and to Flaubert. As it is, Mr. Wilde resembles some traveller who contents himself with making a dissected map at home when he might be exploring the Land East of the Sun, West of the Moon, or sailing to the Islands of Felicity. For it can be in no sense admitted as a proof of Mr. Wilde's originality that he has written his *Salomé* in French. That may be a success in linguistics, that may be a proof of elegance and taste, but it does not add one jot either to the merits or to the defects of *Salomé*. It has no more to do with any possible value that the piece may have as a work of art than would the fact that Mr. Wilde had written *Salomé* while standing on one leg, after the example of a predecessor of old time. A work that professes to be a work of art must win or lose by its art, not by its author's skill in tongues.

But, because of its faults, *Salomé* is a play that will appeal to the Philistine, especially to the Philistine who shams an acquaintance with the literature of the France of to-day. It might flutter the dovecots of the suburbs; it might trouble readers, whose simplicity surpassed their intelligence, with a sense of boldness; it might tickle their untempered palates with suggestions of voluptuousness; it might please their sluggishness with its catalogues of objects of price, with its largesse of adjectives, with its tricks of colour and odour and simile. Indeed, to the Philistine of the Philistines, he who longs to wear the lion's skin, who seeks to be what he calls 'in the movement,' *Salomé* will be a treasure beyond estimation. For in it Mr. Wilde has given, as it were, the quintessence of a school of writing. In this regard it is a library in itself, or perhaps it would be better to say a handbook to a library, a Primer, as it were, wherefrom the Philistine 'at which we dedicate him particularly' may suck out no small advantage. It will equip him for his part of lion, and he need not be at the pains of reading a great number of other authors. But the wise will only regret that Mr. Wilde has wasted his wit. He has shown, not for the first time, that he can mimic, where he might have shown—for the first time—that he could create.

49. Lord Alfred Douglas on *Salomé*

1893

Extracts from a signed review in *Spirit Lamp* [Oxford] (May 1893), iv, 21–7.

Douglas (1870–1945), the son of the Marquess of Queensberry, was editor, while at Oxford, of *The Spirit Lamp* ('An Aesthetic, Literary and Critical Magazine'), to which Wilde occasionally contributed. (Douglas had first met Wilde in 1891.) In addition to some volumes of verse, Douglas later published several books on his liaison with Wilde. Douglas also translated *Salomé* into English for publication in 1894. In the review that follows, a lengthy section, consisting of a summary of the plot, has been omitted.

That mouthpiece of Philistinism, the daily press, surpassed itself in the stern and indignant condemnation of the book which it had not read and the play which it had not seen; never before it declared had such an outrage on decency and good taste been committed, never had a more infamous plot against morality and the Bible been nipped in the bud. For it *was* nipped in the bud, the censor had refused to license its production, England was saved from lasting disgrace. The daily press positively swelled with pride, it metaphorically slapped its chest and thanked God it was an Englishman. It is hard to understand the attitude taken up by the anonymous scribblers who propounded these pompous absurdities. Why it should be taken for granted that because a writer takes his subject from a sublime and splendid literature, he should necessarily treat it in a contemptible manner, is a mystery it is hard to solve. Apparently it never occurred to these enlightened beings that the very sublimity and grandeur of such a subject would be a sufficient guarantee that the artist had put his very best work into it, and had done his utmost to exalt his treatment to the high level his subject demanded. To a man who takes for the scene of a vulgar farce, the back drawing-room of a house in Bloomsbury, and who brings on to the stage a swindling

138

stockbroker or a rag-and-bone merchant, they are ready to listen with delighted attention, to laugh at his coarse jokes and revel in his cockney dialogue; good healthy English fun they call it. But a man who actually takes for the scene of a tragedy the gorgeous background of a Roman Tetrarch's court, and who brings on to the stage a real prophet out of the Bible, and all in French too! 'No, it is too much,' they say, 'we don't want to hear anything more about it, it is an outrage and an infamy.' O Happy England, land of healthy sentiment, roast beef and Bible, long may you have such men to keep guard over your morals, to point out to you the true path, and to guide your feet into the way of cant! . . .

One thing strikes one very forcibly in the treatment, the musical form of it. Again and again it seems to one that in reading one is *listening*; listening, not to the author, not to the direct unfolding of a plot, but to the tones of different instruments, suggesting, suggesting, always indirectly, till one feels that by shutting one's eyes one can best catch the suggestion. The author's personality nowhere shews itself.

The French is as much Mr. Wilde's own as is the psychological motive of the play, it is perfect in scholarship, but it takes a form new in French literature. It is a daring experiment and a complete success. The language is rich and coloured, but never precious, and shows a command of expression so full and varied that the ascetically artistic restraint of certain passages stands out in strong relief. Such a passage is the one quoted above: the conversation of the soldiers on the terrace; in which by-the-bye certain intelligent critics have discovered a re-semblance to Ollendorf, and with extraordinary shallowness and lack of artistic sensibility have waxed facetious over. O wonderful men!

Artistically speaking the play would gain nothing by performance, to my mind it would lose much. To be appreciated it must be abstracted, and to be abstracted it must be read. Let it, 'not to the sensual ear but more endeared, pipe to the spirit ditties of no tone.'

It only remains to say that the treatment of St. John the Baptist is perfectly refined and reverend.

I suppose the play is unhealthy, morbid, unwholesome, and un-English, ça va sans dire.[1] It is certainly un-English, because it is written in French, and therefore unwholesome to the average Englishman, who can't digest French. It is probably morbid and unhealthy, for there is no representation of quiet domestic life, nobody slaps anybody else on the back all through the play, and there is not a single reference to roast beef from one end of the dialogue to the other, and though it is true that

[1] That goes without saying.

there is a reference to Christianity, there are no muscular Christians. Anyone, therefore, who suffers from that most apalling and widespread of diseases which takes the form of a morbid desire for health had better avoid and flee from *Salomé*, or they will surely get a shock that it will take months of the daily papers and Charles Kingsley's novels to counteract. But the less violently and aggressively healthy, those who are healthy to live and do not live to be healthy, will find in Mr. Oscar Wilde's tragedy the beauty of a perfect work of art, a joy for ever, ambrosia to feed their souls with honey of sweet-bitter thoughts.

50. William Archer on *Salomé*

1893

Signed review, titled 'Mr. Oscar Wilde's New Play', in *Black and White* (11 May 1893), v, 290.

William Archer (1856–1924), Scottish author, critic, and translator of Ibsen's plays, which he saw as revolutionizing the English theatre, lent his support (as critic of the *World*, 1884–1905) to new developments in the theatre and vigorously opposed all forms of censorship. He was, for example, virtually the only major critic (except for Shaw) who attacked the decision of the Examiner of Plays not to license *Salomé*. Calling the Examiner 'the Great Irresponsible', Archer defended the play as 'a serious work of art' in a letter to the *Pall Mall Gazette* (1 July 1892), reprinted in *Letters of Oscar Wilde*, ed. Hart-Davis, p. 317. (See Wilde's letter of appreciation to Archer in *Letters*, p. 319.) Archer's allusion to Hilde Wangel in the following review: the young girl in Ibsen's *The Master Builder* who urges the ageing architect to climb the completed tower of his home.

. . . I have read *Salomé* twice in two hours; in other words, I have added two hours to the tale of that life within our life, which alone, in the long run, is really worth living—the life of the imagination. Hypnotised by the poet—for what is the magic of poetry but a form of hypnotism?—I have lived through what Hilde Wangel would call 'the loveliest thing in the world—a drama in the air.' A sultry, languorous Syrian night; a sinister moon gliding through the heavens, 'like a woman risen from a tomb'; Herod, 'with mole-like eyes under quivering lids,' gazing at the daughter of his brother's wife, now his own; Herodias, keeping watch on his every glance; Salomé, 'pale as the image of a white rose in a mirror of silver'. . . .

Without any scheme, and following no principle of selection, I have jotted down the high lights, as it were, of the picture left on my mind by Mr. Wilde's poem. In speaking of a picture, however, I am not sure that I use the happiest analogy. There is at least as much musical as pictorial quality in *Salomé*. It is by methods borrowed from music that Mr. Wilde, without sacrificing its suppleness, imparts to his prose the firm texture, so to speak, of verse. Borrowed from music—may I conjecture?—through the intermediation of Maeterlinck. Certain it is that the brief melodious phrases, the chiming repetitions, the fugal effects beloved by the Belgian poet, are no less characteristic of Mr. Wilde's method. I am quite willing to believe, if necessary, that the two artists invented their similar devices independently, to meet a common need; but if, as a matter of fact, the one has taken a hint from the other, I do not see that his essential originality is thereby impaired. There is far more depth and body in Mr. Wilde's work than in Maeterlinck's. His characters are men and women, not filmy shapes of mist and moonshine. His properties, so to speak, are far more various and less conventional. His palette—I recur, in spite of myself, to the pictorial analogy—is infinitely richer. Maeterlinck paints in washes of water-colour; Mr. Wilde attains the depths and brilliancy of oils. *Salomé* has all the qualities of a great historical picture—pedantry and conventionality excepted.

Its suppression by the Censor was perfectly ridiculous, and absolutely inevitable. The Censor is the official mouthpiece of Philistinism, and Philistinism would doubtless have been outraged had *Salomé* been represented on the stage. There is not a word in it which can reasonably give pain to the most sensitive Christian; but Philistinism has not yet got rid of the superstition that art is profane, especially the art of acting, and that even to name certain names—and much more to present certain persons—in the theatre, is necessarily to desecrate them. The atmosphere of the play is certainly none of the healthiest; but if an artist sets forth to paint a fever jungle, we can scarcely complain if his picture be not altogether breezy and exhilarating. As well look for a bracing sirocco or a tonic miasma. Salomé is an oriental Hedda Gabler; and who could portray such a character in the hues of radiant health? Mr. Wilde, we know, is an Irishman, but not even an Irishman can depict a contradiction in terms.

51. Unsigned notice, *Critic* [New York]

12 May 1894, xxiv (n.s. xxi), 331

The English translation (by Lord Alfred Douglas) of *Salomé* appeared on 9 February 1894.

The downward course of a certain current in English literature and art has probably not reached an end in Oscar Wilde's *Salomé*. Some one will, doubtless, arise who shall be as incoherent as Blake, as hysterical as Rossetti, as incapable of decent reserve as Swinburne, and as great a humbug as Wilde. But it is doubtful whether the latter's cleverness in patching up sham monsters can go much farther. A large part of his material he gets from the Bible, a little has once belonged to Flaubert. He borrows from Maeterlinck his trick of repeating stupid phrases until a glimpse of meaning seems almost a flash of genius. But it must be admitted that he adds something of his own, and that what he has taken bears but the same relation to what he has made of it as does the farmer's pumpkin to the small boy's bogy lantern. A single example will perhaps suffice to show the nature of his improvements. There is a vulgar simile that likens a pair of black eyes to 'burnt holes in a blanket.' This Mr. Wilde expands into:—'it is his eyes above all that are terrible. They are like *black holes burnt by torches in a tapestry of Tyre.*' The play was originally written in French, and Mr. Wilde has been so happy as to secure a noble lord as his translator into English. . . .

A WOMAN OF NO IMPORTANCE

First produced: 19 April 1893

52. William Archer on
A Woman of No Importance

1893

Signed review in the *World*, 26 April 1893; reprinted in Archer's
The Theatrical 'World' for 1893, published in 1894, pp. 105–13.
In response to Archer's praise of the play, Wilde wrote to thank
him for his 'luminous, brilliant criticism'. (*Letters*, p. 338.)

There is no such thing as 'absolute pitch' in criticism; the intervals are
everything. In other words, the critic is bound to deal in odious comparisons; it is one of the painful necessities of his calling. He must clearly
indicate the plane, so to speak, on which, in his judgment, any given
work of art is to be taken; and the value of his terms, whether of praise
or blame, must then be estimated in relation to that plane. Well, the one
essential fact about Mr Oscar Wilde's dramatic work is that it must be
taken on the very highest plane of modern English drama, and further-
more, that it stands alone on that plane. In intellectual calibre, artistic
competence—ay, and in dramatic instinct to boot—Mr Wilde has no
rival among his fellow-workers for the stage. He is a thinker and a
writer; they are more or less able, thoughtful, original playwrights.
This statement may seem needlessly emphatic, and even offensive; but
it is necessary that it should be made if we are to preserve any sense of
proportion in criticism. I am far from exalting either *Lady Windermere's
Fan* or *A Woman of No Importance* to the rank of a masterpiece; but
while we carp at this point and cavil at that, it behoves us to remember
and to avow that we are dealing with works of an altogether higher

order than others which we may very likely have praised with much less reserve.

Pray do not suppose that I am merely dazzled by Mr Wilde's pyrotechnic wit. That is one of the defects of his qualities, and a defect, I am sure, that he will one day conquer, when he begins to take himself seriously as a dramatic artist. At present, he approaches his calling as cynically as Mr George R. Sims; only it is for the higher intellects, and not the lower, among the play-going public, that Mr Wilde shows his polite contempt. He regards prose drama (so he has somewhere stated) as the lowest of the arts; and acting on this principle—the falsity of which he will discover as soon as a truly inspiring subject occurs to him —he amuses himself by lying on his back and blowing soap-bubbles for half an evening, and then pretending, during the other half, to interest himself in some story of the simple affections such as audiences, he knows, regard as dramatic. Most of the soap bubbles are exceedingly pretty, and he throws them off with astonishing ease and rapidity—

> One *mot* doth tread upon another's heels,
> So fast they follow—

but it becomes fatiguing, in the long run, to have the whole air a-shimmer, as it were, with iridescent films. Mr Wilde will one day be more sparing in the quantity and more fastidious as to the quality of his wit, and will cease to act up to Lord Illingworth's motto that 'nothing succeeds like excess.' It is not his wit, then, and still less his knack of paradox-twisting, that makes me claim for him a place apart among living English dramatists. It is the keenness of his intellect, the individuality of his point of view, the excellence of his verbal style, and, above all, the genuinely dramatic quality of his inspirations. I do not hesitate to call the scene between Lord Illingworth and Mrs Arbuthnot at the end of the second act of this play the most virile and intelligent—yes, I mean it, the most intelligent—piece of English dramatic writing of our day. It is the work of a man who knows life, and knows how to transfer it to the stage. There is no situation-hunting, no posturing. The interest of the scene arises from emotion based upon thought, thought thrilled with emotion. There is nothing conventional in it, nothing insincere. In a word, it is a piece of adult art. True, it is by far the best scene in the play, the only one in which Mr Wilde does perfect justice to his talent. But there are many details of similar, though perhaps not equal, value scattered throughout. How fine and simple in its invention, for instance, is the scene in which the mother tells her son the story of Lord

Illingworth's treachery, only to hear him defend the libertine on the ground that no 'nice girl' would have let herself be entrapped! This exquisite touch of ironic pathos is worth half a hundred 'thrilling tableaux,' like that which follows almost immediately upon it.

For it is not to be denied that in his effort to be human—I would say 'to be popular,' did I not fear some subtle and terrible vengeance on the part of the outraged author—Mr Wilde has become more than a little conventional. How different is the 'He is your father!' tableau at the end of Act III from the strong and simple conclusion of Act II—how different, and how inferior! It would be a just retribution if Mr Wilde were presently to be confronted with this tableau in all the horrors of chromolithography, on every hoarding in London, with the legend, 'Stay, Gerald! He is your father!' in crinkly letters in the corner. Then, indeed, would expatriation—or worse—be the only resource of his conscience-stricken soul. His choice would lie between Paris and prussic acid. The conventional element seems to me to come in with the character of Mrs Arbuthnot. Why does Mr Wilde make her such a terribly emphatic personage? Do ladies in her (certainly undesirable) position brood so incessantly upon their misfortune? I have no positive evidence to go upon, but I see no reason why Mrs Arbuthnot should not take a more common-sense view of the situation. That she should resent Lord Illingworth's conduct I quite understand, and I applaud the natural and dignified revenge she takes in declining to marry him. But why all this agony? Why all this hatred? Why can 'no anodyne give her sleep, no poppies forgetfulness'? With all respect for Mrs Arbuthnot, this is mere empty phrase-making. I am sure she has slept very well, say, six nights out of the seven, during these twenty years; or, if not, she has suffered from a stubborn determination to be unhappy, for which Lord Illingworth can scarcely be blamed. After all, what material has she out of which to spin twenty years of unceasing misery? She is—somehow or other—in easy circumstances; she has a model son to satisfy both her affections and her vanity; it does not even appear that she is subjected to any social slights or annoyances. A good many women have led fairly contented lives under far more trying conditions. Perhaps Mr Wilde would have us believe that she suffers from mild religious mania—that it is the gnawing thought of her unpardonable 'sin' that nor poppy nor mandragora can soothe. But she herself admits that she does not repent the 'sin' that has given her a son to love. Well then, what is all this melodrama about? Does not Mrs Arbuthnot sacrifice our interest, if not our sympathy, by her determination 'in obstinate condolement to persever'?

May we not pardonably weary a little (to adapt Lord Illingworth's saying) of 'the Unreasonable eternally lamenting the Unalterable'? Mrs Arbuthnot is simply a woman who has been through a very painful experience, who has suffered a crushing disappointment in the revelation of the unworthiness of the man she loved, but for whom life, after all, has turned out not so very intolerably. That is the rational view of her situation; and she herself might quite well take that view without the sacrifice of one scene or speech of any real value. The masterly scene at the end of the second act would remain practically intact, and so would the scene between mother and son in the third act; for the complacent cruelty of Gerald's commentary on her story could not but cause a bitter pang to any mother. It is only in the fourth act that any really important alteration would be necessary, and there it could only be for the better. The young man's crude sense of the need for some immediate and heroic action is admirably conceived, and entirely right; but how much better, how much truer, how much newer, would the scene be if the mother met his Quixotism with sad, half-smiling dignity and wisdom, instead of with passionate outcries of unreasoning horror! There is a total lack of irony, or, in other words, of commonsense, in this portion of the play. Heroics respond to heroics, until we feel inclined to beg both mother and son (and daughter-in-law, too, for that matter) to come down from their stilts and look at things a little rationally. Even Mr Wilde's writing suffers. We are treated to such noble phrases as 'I am not worthy or of her or of you,' and it would surprise no one if Master Gerald were to drop into blank verse in a friendly way. How much more telling, too, would the scene between Mrs Arbuthnot and Lord Illingworth become if she took the situation more ironically and less tragically, if she answered the man of the world in the tone of a woman of the world! How much more complete, for one thing, would be his humiliation! As it is, the vehemence of her hatred can only minister to his vanity. From the point of view of vanity, to be hated for twenty years is just as good as to be loved. It is indifference that stings. It was all very well, in the second act, for Mrs Arbuthnot to be vehement in her protest against the father's annexation of the son; in the fourth act, when that danger is past, a tone of calm superiority would be ten times as effective. In short, the play would have been a much more accomplished work of art if the character of Mrs Arbuthnot had been pitched in another key. And I am not without a suspicion that Mr Wilde's original design was something like what I have indicated. The last word spoken, 'A man of no importance' (which was doubtless the first word conceived) seems to belong to the woman I imagine rather than to the one who actually speaks it. I think, too, that the concluding situation would be more effective if some more definite indication of the unspeakable cad who lurks beneath Lord Illingworth's polished surface were vouchsafed us earlier in the play. True, his conduct towards the fair American was sufficiently objectionable; but I fear I, for my part, did not quite seriously believe in it, taking it rather as a mere *ficelle*, and not a very ingenious one, leading up to the startling picture-poster at the end of the third act. . . .

In this play, as in *Lady Windermere's Fan*, among many showy sayings, there is one really luminous and profound. 'Thought is in its essence destructive,' says Lord Illingworth. 'Nothing survives being thought of.' Nothing—not even *A Woman of No Importance*; but then it is so very, very much better worth thinking of than the average play.*

* This article (here reprinted verbatim) has been represented in more than one quarter as grossly and excessively eulogistic. *Is* it so? It does not read to me like unmixed praise. There is one sentence in the first paragraph which I would not have written a month later; but it must be remembered that Mr. Pinero still held *The Second Mrs Tanqueray* 'up his sleeve,' [Archer's note.]

53. William Archer, in defence of his praise of Wilde

1893

From a review of Arthur Pinero's *The Second Mrs Tanqueray* in the *St. James's Gazette*, 3 June 1893; reprinted in *The Theatrical 'World' for 1893*, published in 1894, pp. 140–1.
The plays alluded to by Archer in his statement are by Pinero (*The Profligate*, *Lady Bountiful*) and Henry Arthur Jones (*The Dancing Girl*, *The Crusaders*).

I have been accused of wantonly overrating Mr Oscar Wilde because I said that his two plays stood alone on the highest plane of modern English drama. That remark, I believe, was absolutely true (so far as there can be any absolute truth in criticism) at the time when it was made, more than a month ago. Now, Mr Pinero's tragedy stands alone on a still higher plane; but *Lady Windermere's Fan* and *A Woman of No Importance* surely rank as far above *The Profligate* and *Lady Bountiful*, *The Dancing Girl* and *The Crusaders*, as they rank below *The Second Mrs Tanqueray*. 'Mr Wilde's pyrotechnic wit,' I said at the same time, 'is one of the defects of his qualities—a defect which he will one day conquer when he begins to take himself seriously as a dramatic artist. At present he approaches his calling cynically;' and I went on to remark that there was only one scene in his Haymarket play in which he did his talent full justice. Is this extravagant eulogy? Is it not precisely because he has taken himself seriously as a dramatic artist that Mr Pinero has so far outstripped Mr Wilde in the present instance? It is none the less true that Mr Wilde is a writer, an *écrivain*, of the first rank. He has written things of the most exquisite quality both in verse and prose (have you read his delightful fairy-tales?), and in one or two masterly scenes and a hundred minor touches he has proved himself possessed of dramatic instinct in its highest potency. He has certainly the talent, if he has but the will, the character, to raise his work to the highest possible plane. Hitherto he has done little more than trifle gracefully with his art; but the time for trifling is past.

54. A. B. Walkley, on
A Woman of No Importance

1893

Review signed 'A.B.W.' in the *Speaker* (29 April 1893), vii, 484–5.

A dramatic critic of credit and renown made a confession to me the other day. 'I have been spending the morning,' said he, 'in trying to write my notice of Oscar's new play, and I have found it jolly tough work. It's easy enough to point out scores of faults, and one has to point them out; but, hang it all, one can't help feeling that there is more in the fellow than in all the other beggars put together.' That happens to be precisely my own experience. I feel that the 'other beggars' can, many of them, give Mr. Oscar Wilde points and a beating at the mere cat's-cradle game of dramatic intrigue-weaving, and yet in point of intellect none of them can touch him. Nine English playwrights out of ten, with all their technical skill, their knowledge of 'the sort of thing the public want, my boy,' strike one as naïve persons; they accept current commonplaces, they have no power of mental detachment, of taking up life betwixt finger and thumb, and looking at it as a queer ironic game. But Mr. Wilde is the tenth man, sceptic, cynic, sophist, as well as artist, who moves at ease amid philosophical generalisations, and is the dupe of nothing—except a well-turned phrase. This temperament is common enough among the bookmen, but among the playwrights it is exceedingly rare. And it is a temperament peculiarly sympathetic to the critic; because, when it occurs with a lower vital power, it is the very temperament which finds expression in criticism. In a play of Mr. Pinero or Mr. H. A. Jones, or one of the 'other beggars,' there is, I feel, always something fundamentally alien from my own mental processes. Under no conceivable circumstances can I fancy myself writing one of these plays. But, impudent as the assertion may seem, a play of Mr. Wilde's is just the sort of play which I am sure I could have written—had I Mr. Wilde's ability. The 'other beggars' differ from me in kind; Mr. Wilde differs from me only in degree. I am quite aware that that difference is still enormous. All I want to make clear is that the fact of Mr. Wilde's temperament being the critical temperament—raised to a higher power —prompts criticism to treat Mr. Wilde with peculiar tenderness.

For my part, I am all the more ready to forgive him, because, clever as he is, he is not so clever as to humiliate one's self-esteem. The man whom we all naturally detest is the man who says things which we are not able even to begin to think. But that is not the case with Mr. Wilde's epigrams. One may not have invented them oneself, but we easily make out the process by which they are invented; and so one hugs the flattering belief that one could have invented them—as Wordsworth believed he could have written *Hamlet*—if one only 'had the mind.' . . .

The procedure [of constructing epigrams] throughout, as you see, has been invariable. The phrase has suggested, almost automatically, the idea. No doubt, if you would expend as much patience and trouble over this phrase-making process, this game of *bouts-rimés*,[1] as Mr. Wilde, you might have said these things. But the fact remains that you have not said them, and that he has. His mistake is in saying too many of them. After half-a-dozen or so, anyone can see through the trick; and when they cease to surprise, they cease to amuse.

To tell you the whole content of my thought, I suspect that verbal antithesis is not only the secret of Mr. Wilde's dialogue, but of his dramatic action as well. What is the opposite to 'a woman of no importance'? Why, 'a man of no importance.' Has not Mr. Wilde simply set himself to write a play in which these two phrases should be the two contrasted *mots de la pièce*? I can conceive him tackling his problem something in this way. My man and woman 'of no importance' must be intimately related—obviously, by ties of love—or there will be no struggle of passion; that is, no drama. They cannot be husband and wife, because (at any rate, in the current state of stage-morality) then they could not be said to be reciprocally 'of no importance.' Nor can they be merely 'of no importance' to one another; for then, again, you have no struggle, no drama. This involves the introduction of a third person, to whom each may be of importance—clearly a child, and that child a son (otherwise the father would be 'of no importance'). And now the story begins to emerge. The man finds that he has a son by a cast-off mistress, a woman 'of no importance.' First half of the play: insist on the importance of the father to the son (easily done by making the father a peer, the son his private secretary), and upon the unimportance of the

[1] Set of rhymes for which verses are written, presumably as an exercise in ingenuity.

mother. As the son's love is the only recompense for the mother's shame, you at once have a pathetic situation.

Second half of the play: merely (as in the *mots* already analysed) the antithesis of the first half. Show the father that he is 'of no importance.' You do this by introducing an heiress ready to give the son a career more brilliant than a private secretary's (of course, you make her American, so as to bring in your puns about American 'dry goods,' 'youth,' etc. etc.). Finally, you provide a scene in which the woman may deliver at the man the second *mot de la pièce*—'a man of no importance'—after a contemptuous rejection of his tardy offer of marriage—and the trick is done.

But this, of course, is only wisdom after the event. Mr. Wilde may have conceived his play in that way or he may not. The point is, that he has worked out his ideas with true dramatic instinct, not shirking a single one of the scenes which they involve—the series of battles between man and woman, of explanations between mother and son—and giving them to us at the right moment, And the complete turning of the tables on the cynical rascal of a father makes for righteousness. I have only one serious objection to make. I should have liked the demonstration that the father is 'of no importance' to the son to have come (how? I don't know—that is the dramatist's business) from some development in the character of the son himself, not through the arbitrary and too convenient introduction of an American heiress. As it is, one feels that but for the mere accident of the heiress the father might still have had the best of the game. . . .

55. Unsigned review, *Saturday Review*

6 May 1893, lxxv, 482–3

We are somewhat late in noticing Mr. Oscar Wilde's latest play—but as to that there is a certain proverb. By dint of long persistence in a habit of whimsical eccentricity, not to mention the authorship of *Lady Windermere's Fan*, Mr. Wilde has more or less fairly earned his right to be taken seriously as a dramatist. In every line *A Woman of No Impor-*

tance betrays itself as the work of Mr. Wilde, and the two characters Lord Illingworth and Mrs. Allonby are, as a matter of dialogue, absolutely Mr. Wilde himself. The story—an extremely slight one for four acts—cannot be regarded as pleasant or satisfactory, though there is no need to attach any great importance to the reminiscences of other plays which crop up from time to time. A peer of brilliant conversational powers has just appointed as his secretary a young fellow whom a chance meeting with the mother, his former victim and mistress, reveals as his own natural son, contends with the mother for the right to control and promote the youngster's career, and finally, with no great show of feeling, offers her marriage, which she refuses. This is the story which begins somewhere in the second act, and leaves mother, son, and a young American heiress whom he is about to marry, on their way to live out their lives in a country where their pitiful, if not shameful, history is unknown. Lord Illingworth is a bad man, so bad in his talk that Mr. Henry Arthur Jones or the *London Journal* would have made him a duke at once, and mean enough in his actions to qualify as a subject for a pessimistic lady novelist. He is not quite human, and is little more than a machine for the utterance of paradox and epigram, most of them, though by no means all, wonderfully clever, but bearing upon them the hall-mark of insincerity. To make the character reasonably possible this insincerity should have been merely affected, for the man has quite enough to do to atone for his early sin. That atonement should have been made and accepted. A further reason for such an amendment may be found in the character of Mrs. Arbuthnot. There is no need to be too nicely analytical here; but, although, according to the rather strained morality of the good young American heiress, such a union might be a disgrace, Mrs. Arbuthnot's motherly instinct might have prompted her to a sacrifice which we cannot think would have been very costly either from a dramatic or a worldly point of view. Truth to tell, Gerald Arbuthnot is far from interesting, and Hester Worsley is, like him, something of a bore and a prig. Indeed, Mr. Wilde does not shine as a depictor of candour and innocence. His enthusiasms are flat and his moralizings tedious. Gerald's interest in his patron appears to be prompted by his hope of advancement, and the whole force of the strong, if not very novel, situation at the end of the third act is completely destroyed by the fact that his bold intervention, when his sweetheart has been insulted by Illingworth, follows on his mealy-mouthed comment on his mother's story.

The dialogue is brilliant, epigrammatic, paradoxical, antithetical even to a fault. Effort is too often discernible; the author is not always content to let well alone; and to work which is of his very best (and that is distinctly good) joins attempts at that kind of pseudo-paradox which is the distinguishing mark of a certain new school of machine-made humour. At the same time, it is only fair to say that the first and second acts simply bristle with 'smart' sentences to such an extent as to tempt us to forget how sadly deficient the play is in action, and how redundant in idle talk, To the dialogue in the beginning of the third act, between Illingworth and his son still unconscious of the relationship, it must be objected that talk of the kind is entirely out of place. The smoking-room is the proper theatre for such displays. An audience is necessary, and we cannot help thinking that the author has here lost an opportunity of developing or revealing the character of the father in a sympathetic way. That he can write dialogue sounding in sympathy rather than in cynicism is amply proved by his treatment of the situation in the fourth act. . . .

56. 'An Open letter to Oscar Wilde, Esq.'

1893

Signed by 'The Candid Friend' in the *Theatre* (1 June 1893), xxi n.s., 322–5.

What seems like an unrestrained attack on Wilde both as a public figure and writer gradually turns into a favourable evaluation of his talents (the writer, however, is less impressed by *A Woman of No Importance* than by *Lady Windermere's Fan*) and concludes with the hope that Wilde will take the art of playwriting seriously—a standard comment on Wilde at the time—so that he may achieve 'great' work.

Sir,—I am emboldened to take the liberty of acquainting you in this letter with my past as well as actual opinion of your personality, by the certainty that in so doing I shall give expression to the ideas of a considerable number of people, and in the hope that a timely word of counsel may have some influence in persuading you to abandon some of the methods by which you have so far been content to seek the bubble reputation. You are in yourself a paradox as strange and confusing as any which has ever flowed from your pen, presenting as you do the curious spectacle of a man of genuine and brilliant talent who has made his success, not by the worthy culture and legitimate exhibition of that talent, but by the silliest kind of trick and quackery. You persistently advertised yourself for years through the length and breadth of the English speaking world as an insipid and pretentious dullard, whose motto was 'notoriety at any price.' You were—with a very considerable difference—like the late Laureate[1] when he dreamed there would be spring no more—you plucked the thorns of public contempt and wore them like a civic crown. Such small belief in your intelligence and sanity as were abroad a year or two ago was held only by your personal acquaintances; to the world in general you were the dreariest of bores, a buffoon with one trick which had long since ceased to be amusing. That

[1] Tennyson, who died in 1892.

the spectacle of a man of talent posing as a zany was not an absolute novelty, is proved by the ancient proverb that it takes a clever man to play a fool, but if that saying had been lacking to our proverbial philosophy your career might well have inspired it. You would probably contend that the end has justified the means; but to my thinking that plea is only acceptable under serious protest. It is quite true that in the distressingly over-crowded condition of the brain-market a man of real power may find it a long and arduous business to ensure a hearing. It is true that an idle and not too cultured society will pay a readier attention to the man who can amuse, than to him who waits his hour to teach, and bides his time with the patient and scornful self-possession usually associated with real talent. The brassy voice that shouts—

> In Folly's horny tympanum
> The thing that makes the wise man dumb,

has its uses no doubt—to him who cares to use it. It must needs be listened to, applauded by the idle and foolish, and denounced as a nuisance by the thoughtful. But the vote of the first half of the community—though it is usually the bigger half—is surely not worth having. It is always a degradation to the man who gets it, and it never remains long with him, for every day Folly is justified of some new child more attractive to her devotees than any former birth; and it disgusts the thoughtful contingent altogether. The performing dog gets a bad name, and is not easily credited with the capacity of useful work among the intellectual gorse and stubble. The sterling and legitimate success you have at last made might have come much earlier had you been content to build it on a sounder and less meretricious foundation. Your pursuit of notoriety was too successful, and held you back from the attainment of fame and all the solid comforts and advantages fame brings. How much wrong it had done to your personal nature, to your instincts and breeding as a gentleman, was abundantly shown by the famous cigarette incident on the first night of *Lady Windermere's Fan*. You were, I hope, the one man alive in England capable of at once scoring so deserved a success and besmirching it by so petty an act of ill-bred braggadocio. It was not merely ill-bred, it was futile, and more than futile, as an advertisement. Had the play been a failure, the ill-considered insult to your audience might then have made a little extra talk among the silliest of their number, and so have kept about you that very dubious aureole you were so long content to wear. But it had not failed. It had posed you as one of the figures of intelligent London. Surely at such a moment you might have risen above such a mountebank trick, and have recognised that to be a successful dramatist it is not necessary to cease to be a gentleman.

The unworthy cheapening of your own personality in which you indulged has left its mark upon your work, and will, I fear, long continue to be apparent there. It is not that *Lady Windermere's Fan* was wholly, and *A Woman of No Importance* is to a great degree, languidly cynical in tone. The section of society you have chosen to observe and reproduce quite justifies your scheme of treatment. But, while one of the chief charms of the stage pictures you have drawn is their verisimilitude, it is in direct ratio with the lassitude and cynicism of the figures which people them. You have wisely refrained from attempting to depict a world wholly given over to the lusts of the flesh and of the intellect, but I cannot keep back an obtruding idea that you have done so, not because you have either a quick eye or a very ready appreciation for moral goodness; but merely and purely because one or two passably decent people are absolutely necessary in a drama intended for public performance in this latter half of the nineteenth century. But, while your *roués* and cynics, male and female, are drawn with an admirable sureness of touch and a really wonderful wealth of detail, your good people, whose office it is to furnish them their necessary relief, are, characteristically considered, mere shapes and dummies, feeble reproductions of worn out types never too well observed originally—*des poncifs faits de chic*.[1] Contrast Lord and Lady Windermere with Mrs. Erlynne, or the Arbuthnots, mother and son and Hester Worsley with Lord Illingworth. Hester Worsley is the dismallest of failures. She is not even a woman, let alone a typical woman, and certainly is not typical of any phase of womanhood known in America. She is a literal translation from the French, the bloodless, mechanical *jeune personne*[2] of Scribe and Sardou. Gerald Arbuthnot is nobody, his mother is nobody, even in the hands of Mrs. Bernard Beere, an actress of rare and galvanic capacity. Mrs. Erlynne remains by far your best character, an inspiration which may alone suffice to keep your name in the list of British dramatists for a generation or two, worthy to stand by the side of Balzac's Fœdora as a flesh and blood type of the 'Society' of her day. Her mingling of cynicism and tenderness, her affection for her child, which is strong enough to induce her to risk the failure of the only ambition she is capable of knowing, the ambition to reinstate herself in

[1] Fashionable stereotypes.
[2] Young girl.

the society which has ostracised her, and yet not sufficiently strong to make her desire her daughter's knowledge and affection, all these are indicated with the hand of a master. The crowning stroke of cynicism, her marriage with the silly old lord, was at once as true and as bold as anything this century has to show in the way of drama. What she is to *Lady Windermere's Fan*, Lord Illingworth, with a far less measure of success, attempts to be in the piece now running at the Haymarket. That he does not reach her level of characteristic excellence is certainly no fault of Mr. Tree's, for among all the striking impersonations we owe to him he has given us none more perfect in artistic quietude and truth to nature. He misses no point you enable him to make, and makes many obviously of his own conception. Nor would it be generous to reproach you with the partial failure of the character as contrasted with that of Mrs. Erlynne. Nobody is perpetually at his best, and it would be too much to expect that every drama from your pen should contain a study of character as complete and efficient as that which made the fortune of *Lady Windermere's Fan*. Lord Illingworth, though he stands on a lower level than Mrs. Erlynne, is a very respectable creation. His main fault is that he is too exclusively typical, and is very imperfectly individualised, less a cynic than a typification of cynicism. He talks vastly too much for effect, and one cannot help thinking that if the play lasted for another act he would be in grave danger of developing into a bore. He is the Mr. Barlow of immorality, the prig of conversational unconventionality. He goes to pieces woefully in the last act, where he insults Mrs. Arbuthnot, an action so at variance with his character as elaborated by you, and so dramatically futile, that one can only wonder why it is intruded. You did not know him with the absolute knowledge you brought to the construction of Mrs. Erlynne. His personality is less distinct, his story less affecting, his character less surely grasped. And as in each case the character is the play, it is easy to understand why *A Woman of No Importance* is a less satisfactory piece of work than was *Lady Windermere's Fan*.

You may find it well, before building your next play, seriously to re-consider the dramatic gospel of which you have proclaimed yourself the exponent. Simplicity of theme is an excellent thing in its way, no doubt, but there is more than a chance of your coming to wreck upon it. To dramatic excellence one of two virtues is a *sine qua non*— a strong story, or character of unusual interest and veracity. Considering the vast output of imaginative literature, both in fiction and on the stage, it is no wonder that both strong stories and strong characters are rarer than we could wish them to be. The drama which depends on mere event has long since been played out, the drama which depends entirely on character drawing has never been attempted, and could never, I believe, be a very fecund form of art, for every man's experience of his fellow men is necessarily finite, and it is impossible to go on producing new and true types of humanity by the dozen for any length of time. You will probably find it best to take the middle course trodden by the best of your predecessors and contemporaries, and increase your modicum of plot in your next drama. A real story—not a mere cleverly carpentered succession of *outré* and impossible events, but a true human story such as are happening by the thousand about us every day, a little dressed and coloured to fit it to the exigencies of the stage —is a better medium for the display of human passion than the Ibsenish baldness of theme displayed in *A Woman of No Importance*. Brilliant talk is pretty to listen to, no doubt, but one gets tired of the conversational style of the cleverest talker in time, and you have so permeated both the sets of characters you have created with your own personality that your audience has risen from each piece with the same sensation as they would feel after having a set lecture from your lips, pleased, interested, dazzled, but with that sense of repletion which is the first hint of boredom. There is such a thing as the monotony of cleverness, and it is especially likely to make itself felt by a man of your order of mind, with but little breadth or variety of method in his cleverness. In listening to both your pieces I have been strongly reminded of an utterance you put into the mouth of Lord Henry in your novel *Dorian Gray*, to the effect that 'our proverbs want re-writing.' That dictum is an exposure of the means by which a good deal of your wit is manufactured, and it would have been wise not to have published it. Paradox is a charming *hors d'œuvre*, but it is the poorest possible substitute for the bread of thought and the wine of passion, and will not long content any large section of the public. If *Lady Windermere's Fan* was anything more than a fluke you must justify its success by following it up with something better than the piece Mr. Tree and his admirable company are now playing. Face, instead of evading, the difficulties of dramatic art, take its practice seriously, respect yourself and your audience, and you have in you the capacity to do good—it may be great—work.

Believe me, Sir, yours sincerely,

THE CANDID FRIEND

June 1893, cxxxix, 706–7

After *Lady Windermere's Fan*, a well made, well written play of plot and incidents, rather than an incisive study of character, one had a right to hail in Oscar Wilde an English Sardou. Some people may see in this a reproach, for in these days of realism one is wont to sneer at Sardou, as, in the heyday of Sardou, one lustily jeered at Scribe. We call it, on the contrary, a compliment to place Mr. Oscar Wilde on the same level as Sardou, the more as no other among our playwrights equals this distinguished Frenchman either in imagination or in brilliancy of style. We prefer the more vigorous, the more direct, the more sincere methods of the Ibsen type of playwright, or even that of Emile Augier, to the indirect, we would almost say, insidious craftsmanship of Sardou; but that is our own opinion, and we do not hesitate to add that we shall never cease to admire such of his earlier works as *Les Pattes de Mouche*, *La Famille Benoîton*, and *Patrie*.

In his second play of modern life Mr. Oscar Wilde has, in our opinion, blighted some of our great expectations. We do not deny that, in a certain way, *A Woman of No Importance* is a play of distinction: its dialogue is polished; there are here and there little traits of observation which are uncommonly striking; it is full of humour, and many of the conversations are brilliant with flashes of caustic wit, qualities which, united as they are here, are all too rare in native English plays. But as a work of art we find *A Woman of No Importance* unsatisfactory. It is patched up with reminiscences of a school which is now, if not quite dead, moribund. We mean the romantic period of the days of Theodore Barrière, of Thiboust and de Leuven, when *La Voix du Sang* played such a great part in the romantic drama of France, and filled the spectators with wild delight. It is also disappointing, because the story of the woman who has been abandoned by her lover, who has borne him a child, and meets him afterwards when that son is grown up, has been often told before, and told with greater effect and more sincerity than Mr. Wilde has done. The conflict between father and son, when the father has insulted the girl of his son's choice, would be interesting if it had not been brought about by such artificial, stagey ways, and we should have felt greater sympathy for the forsaken woman if her real character had been drawn with more depth, with more feeling. In this play all the personages make on us the impression of a set of wonderfully clever people, who say wonderfully clever things, couched in a grace of language that their very distinction becomes tedious, because there is no soul, no real sentiment behind their talk. They are all *poseurs*, and in all their actions and words we do not feel the spontaneity of natural motives; but we see the author who holds the wires in his hand, pulls them at his will, and makes them speak as he would speak, as a ventriloquist who works his dolls. To listen to the bright conversation of a man like Mr. Oscar Wilde is always pleasant for a time, but when a whole play is padded out with such conversation, and when the action and the characters seem to float rudderlessly about in an ocean of words, then weariness must step in, and one cannot pronounce the play a good *drama*. This applies to the whole; in detail there is very much to admire—the character of the vicar is admirable as a parody, some of the little scenes in which society and its foibles are held up to ridicule are simply delightful—but we prefer something more substantial. We profess to be emotionalists; we go to the theatre to feel: to feel amused, to feel touched, in fine, to experience the whole gamut of sentiments. And we cannot honestly say that during the evolution of the drama in *A Woman of No Importance* we lived for one moment the life of the characters on the stage. Perhaps the interpretation on the first night, which was seriously marred by nervousness and vacillation on the part of some of the actors, was somewhat at fault, but when a play really lays hold of our entire attention the defects caused by the first night's excitement pass easily unnoticed.

58. W. B. Yeats on
A Woman of No Importance

1895

Signed review, titled 'An Excellent Talker', in the *Bookman* (March 1895), vii–viii, 182.

The occasion for this review was the publication, in book form, of *A Woman of No Importance* in October 1894. (In connection with Yeats's opening remark about Pater, see No. 25.)

Mr. Pater once said that Mr. Oscar Wilde wrote like an excellent talker, and the criticism goes to the root. All of *The Woman of no Importance* [*sic*] which might have been spoken by its author, the famous paradoxes, the rapid sketches of men and women of society, the mockery of most things under heaven, are delightful; while, on the other hand, the things which are too deliberate in their development, or too vehement and elaborate for a talker's inspiration, such as the plot, and the more tragic and emotional characters, do not rise above the general level of the stage. The witty or grotesque persons who flit about the hero and heroine, Lord Illingworth, Mrs. Allonby, Canon Daubeny, Lady Stutfield, and Mr. Kelvil, all, in fact, who can be characterised by a sentence or a paragraph, are real men and women; and the most immoral among them have enough of the morality of self-control and self-possession to be pleasant and inspiriting memories. There is something of heroism in being always master enough of oneself to be witty; and therefore the public of to-day feels with Lord Illingworth and Mrs. Allonby much as the public of yesterday felt, in a certain sense, with that traditional villain of melodrama who never laid aside his cigarette and his sardonic smile. The traditional villain had self-control. Lord Illingworth and Mrs. Allonby have self-control and intellect; and to have these things is to have wisdom, whether you obey it or not. 'The soul is born old, but grows young. That is the comedy of life. And the body is born young and grows old. That is life's tragedy.' Women 'worship successes,' and 'are the laurels to hide their baldness.' 'Children begin by loving their parents. After a time they judge them. Rarely if ever do they forgive them.' And many another epigram, too well known to quote, rings out like the voice of Lear's fool over a mad age. And yet one puts the book down with disappointment. Despite its qualities, it is not a work of art, it has no central fire, it is not dramatic in any ancient sense of the word. The reason is that the tragic and emotional people, the people who are important to the story, Mrs. Arbuthnot, Gerald Arbuthnot, and Hester Worsley, are conventions of the stage. They win our hearts with no visible virtue, and though intended to be charming and good and natural, are really either heady and undistinguished, or morbid with what Mr. Stevenson has called 'the impure passion of remorse.' The truth is, that whenever Mr. Wilde gets beyond those inspirations of an excellent talker which served him so well in *The Decay of Lying* and in the best parts of *Dorian Grey* [*sic*], he falls back upon the popular conventions, the spectres and shadows of the stage.

THE SPHINX

11 June 1894

59. Unsigned review, *Pall Mall Budget*

1894

Review in 'The City of Books' by 'The Crier', *Pall Mall Budget*, 21 June 1894, pp. 9–10.
The reviewer, prior to discussing Wilde's volume, had noted a new book titled *Marsupials and Monotremes* by Richard Lydekker: 'What a title for a volume of poems!'

What a pity Mr. Oscar Wilde has no acquaintance with marsupials and monotremes before he wrote his poem of *The Sphinx*, in which we encounter many strange beasts, but ne'er a marsupial or a monotreme. By the side of these, mere hippogriffs and basilisks, 'gryphons' and 'gilt-scaled dragons' seem commonplace monsters. He must at least introduce a monotreme in the second edition. That none of us would know what it meant matters little. Indeed, for poetical purposes, it were better not! The meaning might clash with the beautiful sound, and, at any rate, it would be as intelligible to most of us as some of the strangely named beings and things that load every rift of Mr. Wilde's curious poem with magnificence and horror. How many of us, I wonder, know the nature of 'rods of oreichalch'?—but the phrase serves none the less, but doubtless all the more, to give that sense of mysterious luxury at which Mr. Wilde is aiming. So, I am reminded, Tennyson used 'white samite,' because 'six-ply' 'shot-silk' would hardly have sounded so 'mystic, wonderful.' Few of us know the nature of 'samite,' so it remains a poetical dress-material.

Though there is a meaning underlying Mr. Wilde's poem—the keen olfactory nerves of the Nonconformist conscience would not, I fear, find it a difficult one to scent—its motive is mainly important as affording Mr. Wilde a theme for the display, in a sort of processional, of beautiful words strangely shaped and coloured, and far-sought pictures of ancient Egyptian luxury and legend. The monsters of the Egyptian room at the British Museum, half-human, half-animal, and wholly infernal, live again in his weird, sometimes repulsive, but all the same stately and impressive lines. We are introduced, as in Poe's poem, to a student sitting solitary in his room at night, and contemplating with fascinated eye a small Egyptian sphinx that gazes at him day and night from the corner of his room. Presently he falls to pondering upon the past it symbolises for him, and bids it sing to him all its memories.

O tell me were you standing by when Isis to Osiris knelt?
And did you watch the Egyptian melt her union for Antony,
And drink the jewel-drunken wine and bend her head in mimic awe
To see the huge proconsul draw the salted tunny from the brine?
And did you mark the Cyprian kiss white Adon on his catafalque?
And did you follow Amenalk, the god of Heliopolis?
And did you talk with Thoth, and did you hear the moon-horned Io weep?
And know the painted kings who sleep beneath the wedge-shaped pyramid?

Mr. Wilde proceeds to ask 'Who were your lovers? Who were they who wrestled for you in the dust?' and thereupon, like poverty, introduces us to some strange companions of his terrible goddess. Among these the least inappropriate for quotation is the fine picture of Ammon, whose fallen state is celebrated in these nobly imaginative and tenderly cadenced lines:

The god is scattered here and there: deep hidden in the windy sand,
I saw his giant granite hand still clenched in impotent despair.
And many a wandering caravan of stately negroes silken-shawled,
Crossing the desert, halts appalled before the neck that none can span.
And many a bearded Bedouin draws back his yellow striped burnous
To gaze upon the Titan thews of him who was thy paladin.
Go, seek his fragments on the moor and wash them in the evening dew,
And from their pieces make anew thy mutilated paramour!
Go, seek them where they lie alone and from their broken pieces make
Thy bruisèd bedfellow! and wake mad passions in the senseless stone!
Charm his dull ears with Syrian hymns! he loved your body! oh, be kind,
Pour spikenard on his hair, and wind soft rolls of linen round his limbs.

When asked some years ago why he did not publish this poem, which has long had a reputation in MS., Mr. Wilde replied that its publication 'would destroy domesticity in England'! Are we to infer from its publication to-day that Mr. Wilde considers the time ripe for thus dynamiting our family life? It will be interesting to watch the effect of this poem on the eminently respectable newspapers. But though Ashtaroth be his muse through the greater part of the poem, the very proper frame of mind in which he draws to a close must not be overlooked. I am afraid that Mr. Wilde's crucifix is no less an artistic property than his nenuphars and monoliths, but, all the same, he has the right to say that from a moral point of view the 'lesson' to be drawn from his poem is absolutely edifying. . . .

60. W. E. Henley on *The Sphinx*

1894

Unsigned review, titled 'The Sphinx up to Date', in the *Pall Mall Gazette*, 9 July 1894, p. 4.

William Ernest Henley (1849–1903), poet, playwright, critic, and editor of several journals, of which the *National Observer* (formerly the *Scots Observer*) was most notable for its determined opposition to Decadence in literature. Beerbohm once facetiously referred to the staff of that publication as the 'Henley Regatta', yet Henley was responsible for introducing to the public such writers as Kipling, Wells, and Yeats. The relationship between Wilde and Henley was complex. In 1888, Henley had been a sponsor of Wilde for membership in the exclusive Savile Club. Because of Henley's later attitude, Wilde directed his publisher, John Lane, not to send any of his books for review to the *National Observer* characterizing Henley as 'too coarse, too offensive, too personal, to be sent any work of mine'. (*Letters*, p. 318). Yet, with characteristic sympathy, Wilde wrote Henley a letter of condolence and encouragement on the death of his daughter in 1894 (see *Letters*, p. 352) and, when asked by William Rothenstein 1897 for a statement about Henley, Wilde wrote: 'His prose is the beautiful prose of a poet and his poetry the beautiful poetry of a prose writer. . . . He is never forgotten by his enemies, and often forgiven by his friends. . . . He has fought a good fight, and has had to face every difficulty except popularity.' (*Letters*, p. 631.)

Not to be remarked is not to live; and we are all Strug-for-Lifers now. If Hughie went forth without his coat, and walked in Piccadilly, Ernie would take off his waistcoat, and do likewise; and Bobbie and Freddie would each of them go one better than Ernie; till in due course the police must interfere. It is thus with the New Style, or Fin-de-Siècle, Minor Poet. His ancestors were modest —after their kind; they wrote and they printed, being to the manner born; but all the while they knew that in the end the Twopenny Box was theirs until the crack of doom. Their latest-born is of less abject mould. He may despair of being read; but he will be remarked, or he will die. So he goes forth into the world, year after year, as MM. Ernie and Co., into 'Piccadilly, that immortal street,' still shedding something—some rag of style or sentiment, or decent manners—as he goes; and in the end one looks to see him without his gaskins (so to speak), marching to some literary Vine-street between two brutal literary 'slops.' Not yet— we haste to add—is this the fortune of the learned and enterprising author of *The Sphinx*. He has discarded certain lendings, it is true; but he has retained enough for Mrs. Grundy and the suburbs, and the fashion of that he has retained is so deliberately frantic, its hues are of so purposeful a violence, that his end is gained, and immediate conspicuousness assured. To put his case in a figure: You mark, in front of you, under a pea-green umbrella, in a magenta chlamys, fleshings of mauve, and a yellow turban, an antic thing, whose first effect is that of a very bedlamitish bookie. You approach the creature with a view to business —when lo! you are aware that it is only Mr. Wilde's last avatar after all! Then you note that he is trading in a novel sort of fancy goods; and, vouch-safing unto him that smile of amazed amusement which it has ever been his chief ambition to win, you proceed to the examination of his wares. And wonderful wares you find they are.

What are they like? Conceive a largish quarto, bound in white and gold, and composed of some twenty leaves of fair, rough paper (many of them blank); ten designs by Mr. Charles Ricketts, all printed in a pale red-brown; thirteen initials by Mr. Charles Ricketts, all printed in a curious green; and eighty-five couplets by Mr. Oscar Wilde, all printed in small caps. and in decent black. Also, the distribution of these precious eighty-five is about as Fin-de-Siècle a business as you ever saw; for on one page there are as many as nine, and on another there are as few as one, and on another you shall count some five, and on another yet are four, or six, or two, as Providence hath willed. And the reason thereof let no man seek to know; for, if he do, the half of it shall not be told to him. This caution applies with equal force and pertinency to the couplets—they are really quatrains, as the staves of *In Memoriam*, but by a special stroke of art they are printed as something else—thus thoughtfully displayed. 'In a dim corner of my room,' the Poet starts,

> Far longer than my fancy thinks,
> A beautiful and silent Sphinx
> Has watched me through the shifting gloom.

She is something, it would seem, of a Christmas monster, is this 'lovely seneschal, so somnolent and statuesque:' having 'heavy velvet paws,' and 'claws of yellow ivory,' and 'agate breasts,' and 'flanks of polished brass;' to say nothing of 'large black satin eyes,' which have the curious property of being 'like cushions where you sink', and nothing of a 'horrible and heavy breath.' But the owner of 'my room' is not a bit afraid of her. On the contrary, he trots her out upon his hearth-rug, and after divers compliments, and a passing invitation to sing to him, he falls to cross-examining her, with great strictness and particularity, on the matter of her sexual experiences. In the course of this exercise he puts her leading questions concerning the 'ivory body' of Antinous— Antinous of the 'pomegranate mouth'; a certain 'twy-formed Bull,' whose conduct was so shocking (it appears) that it caused 'a horrid dew' to drip from 'the moaning mandragores'; a special and peculiar Chimæra; Behemoth and Leviathan; a 'Nereid wild in amber foam with curious rock-crystal breasts'; Ashtaroth; Apis; a swarthy Æthiop; 'the ivory horned Tragelaphos'; not to mention gilt-scaled dragons, giant lizards, gryphons with great metal flanks, and 'sidling' hippopotami. The Sphinx declining to own up—declining, indeed, to make him even an evasive answer—he changes his note, taxes her with improper inter-course with 'great Ammon,' and proceeds to ply her with an amount of information concerning the state, the morals, the goings-on of that deity—'his wit, his humour, his pathos, and his umbrella,' so to speak— which must prove to her, you would think, that he knows all about it, and she needn't try to come the old soldier over *him*. She does not; and he, reflecting that Ammon is dead, advises her to go back to Egypt, and see if she cannot make it up with 'dog-faced Anubis,' or 'Gaunt Memnon,' or 'Nilus with his broken horn;' or, failing these, at least to take on some 'roving lion,' some tiger 'whose amber sides are flecked with black.' The Sphinx refusing to admit the fact of his existence, he gets rather afraid of her, implores her to go for 'others more accursed, whiter with leprosies' than he is, calls her a 'hideous animal,' and urges her to leave him to his crucifix.' 'You make my creed a barren sham,' he pleads (always in small caps.).

> You wake foul dreams of sensual life,
> And Atys with his blood-stained knife
> Were better than the thing I am.

This happens in Couplet Eighty-three; and inasmuch as he is left pleading in Couplet Eighty-five, the sole inference possible is that this is no Sphinx, but a kind of cultured and undraped Mrs. Harris.

There can be no mistake about the Gamp; but, for this other, 'there never was no sich a person.' Such as she is, she is an effect of (1) an indigestion of Flaubert's *Tentation* and Gautier's *Roman de la Momie*, and (2) an heroic resolve to make 'talc' rhyme with 'orischalch.' It is fair to add that the poet's grammar is above the average; that his style is ever on a level with his description of Cleopatra's Antony as 'the huge Proconsul'; that this edition of his book is limited to two hundred copies at fifteen shillings apiece; and that the whole thing is dedicated to M. Marcel Schwob—who deserves a vastly better fate.

61. Unsigned review, *Athenaeum*

25 August 1894, civ, p. 252

If any fresh proof were needed of the cynical humour which distinguishes Mr. Wilde, it would be found in his idea of writing such a poem as *The Sphinx* in the metre of *In Memoriam*. Like its predecessor, too, the poem is written in an autobiographical form; but there the resemblance ceases. The poet imagines himself as a youth of twenty summers, and luxuriates in the licence of that callow age by limning in luscious lines the lewd imaginings suggested to him by a sphinx that has found its way into his study. The whole poem, which consists of about two hundred lines, is a catalogue (put in the form of questions) of the Sphinx's amours, which, in the words of the American humourist, would appear to have been 'frequent and free.' Not very much is known about the Sphinx, and still less about her amours, and, at any rate, no one has before brought to her charge the reckless riot of self-indulgence of which she is here accused, so that the fullest credit may be given to Mr. Wilde for the ingenious fertility of his new conception of her. And certainly the most praiseworthy industry is here displayed in the collection of possible and impossible gods and other beings represented as attempting to satisfy the Sphinx's apparently insatiable desires; while the turbid splendour in which the thoughts are clothed fully equals their Oriental profusion. Such lines, for example, as these might create astonishment elsewhere, but in the context they pass almost unobserved:

Or did you love the god of flies who plagued the Hebrews and was splashed
With wine unto the waist? or Pasht, who had green beryls for her eyes?
Or that young god, the Tyrian, who was more amorous than the dove
Of Ashtaroth? or did you love the god of the Assyrian
Whose wings, like strange transparent talc, rose high above his hawk-faced
    head,
Painted with silver and with red, and ribbed with rods of oreichalch?
Or did huge Apis from his car leap down, and lay before your feet
Big blossoms of the honey-sweet and honey-coloured nenuphar?

It really comes almost as a shock, certainly as a surprise, at the end of the poem to find that the youthful poet is quite disgusted at all these revelations, and wearies of the Sphinx's 'somnolent magnificence':

Are there not others more accursed, whiter with leprosies than I?
Are Abana and Pharpar dry, that you come here to slake your thirst?
Get hence, you loathsome mystery! hideous animal, get hence!
You wake in me each bestial sense, you make me what I would not be;

and so on for a few more lines, until the poem fitly concludes with an allusion to Christianity. Admirers of some of Mr. Oscar Wilde's previously published poems, such as 'Ave Imperatrix,' 'The Garden of Eros,' or 'The Burden of Itys,' will not welcome this poem with enthusiasm. They will miss the more restrained charm of such lines as:

And sweet to hear the cuckoo mock the spring
    While the last violet loiters by the well,
And sweet to hear the shepherd Daphnis sing
    The song of Linus through a sunny dell
Of warm Arcadia, where the corn is gold
And the slight lithe-limbed reapers dance about the wattled fold;

they will criticize the poverty of motive, disguised by the gorgeousness of diction, and will quarrel with such defects as the too frequent use of the word 'paramour' or the employment of 'curious' in a somewhat precious sense at least three times in such a short poem; but even they will not be able to deny the skilfulness with which the metre is handled, and the easy flow and sonorousness of the lines.

AN IDEAL HUSBAND

First produced: 3 January 1895

---

62. H. G. Wells on *An Ideal Husband*

1895

Unsigned review in the *Pall Mall Gazette*, 4 January 1895, p. 3. H. G. Wells (1866–1946) was at this time the drama critic on the *Pall Mall Gazette*, a post he held until May. When, on 6 November 1897, the *Academy* published a suggested list of members for an Academy of Letters—Wilde called it a list of 'Immortals'— both Shaw and Wells wrote letters proposing the addition of Wilde's name.

'Do tell me your conception of the "Ideal Husband",' said Lady Stutfield, in the *Woman of No Importance*. 'I think it would be so very, very helpful.' Mrs. Allonby, you will remember, thought there couldn't be such a thing, and wandered into objectionable flippancy. And Mr. Oscar Wilde, having, we more than suspect, a lingering sympathy with Mrs. Allonby, has written a whole play to demonstrate this impossibility. In many ways his new production is diverting, and even where the fun is not of the rarest character the play remains interesting. And, among other things, it marks an interesting phase in the dramatic development of its author. Your common man begins in innocence, in his golden youth he wears his heart upon his sleeve; but Oscar Wilde is, so to speak, working his way to innocence, as others work towards experience—is sloughing his epigrams slowly but surely, and discovering to an appreciative world, beneath the attenuated veil of his wit, that he, too, has a heart. In the end the sorely-tried Sir Robert and Lady Chiltern, amidst the applause and emotion of a crowded house, decided that love was the best of life; the engagement of Lord Goring and the altogether charming and always innocent Miss Mabel Chiltern was successfully accomplished, and the villanies of the abominable Mrs. Cheveley were—if the adjective is permissible—routed with Adelphian ignominy. . . .

So much for the play. It is not excellent; indeed, after *Lady Windermere's Fan* and *The Woman of No Importance*, it is decidedly disappointing. But worse have succeeded, and it was at least excellently received. It may be this melodramatic touch, this attempt at commonplace emotions and the falling off in epigram, may be merely a cynical or satirical concession to the public taste. Or it may be something more, an attempt to get free from the purely clever pose, that merely epigrammatic attitude, that has been vulgarized to the level of the punster. But, taking it seriously, and disregarding any possibly imaginary tendency towards a new width of treatment, the play is unquestionably very poor.

63. William Archer on *An Ideal Husband*

1895

Signed review, *Pall Mall Budget*, 10 January 1895; reprinted in *The Theatrical 'World' of 1895*, published in 1896, pp. 15–19.

Mr. Oscar Wilde might have given a second title to his highly entertaining play at the Haymarket, which we all enjoyed very nearly as much as he himself did. He might have called it *An Ideal Husband; or The Chiltern Thousands*. There were eighty-six of them—£86,000 was the price paid to Sir Robert Chiltern, then private secretary to a Cabinet Minister, for betraying to an Austrian financier the intention of the Government to purchase the Suez Canal Shares. The thousands have increased and multiplied; he is wealthy, he is respected, he is Under-Secretary for Foreign Affairs, he is married to a wife who idolises and idealises him; and, not having stolen anything more in the interim, he is inclined to agree with his wife and the world in regarding himself as the Bayard of Downing Street. The question which Mr. Wilde pro-

pounds is, 'Ought his old peccadillo to incapacitate him for public life?'
—and, while essaying to answer it in the negative, he virtually, to my
thinking, answers it in the affirmative. On the principle involved, I have
no very strong feeling. It is a black business enough; no divorce-court
scandal could possibly be so damning; but one is quite willing to believe
it possible that a sudden yielding to overwhelming temptation may
occur once in a lifetime, and may even steel the wrong-doer against all
future temptation and render him a stronger man than he would
otherwise have been. This, I repeat, is possible; but unfortunately the
first thing Mr. Wilde does is to show that Sir Robert Chiltern is not a
case in point.

Enter Mrs. Cheveley from Vienna, tawny-haired, red-cheeked,
white-shouldered. She has in her pocket the letter in which Sir Robert
let the Suez cat out of the bag; and, if he will not support in Parliament
an Argentine Canal, which he knows to be a gigantic swindle, she will
send the letter to the papers and ruin his political career. Here, then, is
an excellent opportunity for Sir Robert to show his mettle. If his
honour rooted in dishonour stands, if the boy's weakness has fortified
the man's probity, he will of course send Mrs. Cheveley to the right-
about and prepare to face the music. It will then be for the dramatist's
ingenuity to devise some means of averting the exposure, which Sir
Robert deserves to escape, for the very reason that he is man enough to
brave it rather than commit a second and greater treachery. Alas! this
is not at all Mr. Wilde's view of the matter. Sir Robert Chiltern does
not send Mrs. Cheveley to the right-about. On the contrary, he licks
the dust before her, and is quite prepared to involve his country in a
second Panama catastrophe in order to save his own precious skin. This
is giving away the whole case. It may be a mistake to hold a man disabled by his past from doing service to the State; but this man is
disabled by his present. The excellent Sir Robert proves himself one of
those gentlemen who can be honest so long as it is absolutely convenient, and no longer; and on the whole, in spite of Mr. Wilde's argument,
I am inclined to think it a wise instinct which leads us (so far as possible)
to select for our Cabinet Ministers men of less provisional probity. . . .

Upon my honour (if the creator of Sir Robert Chiltern will forgive
the Pharisaism), I had not the slightest intention when I sat down of
picking the play to pieces in this way. I don't know what possessed me.
An Ideal Husband is a very able and entertaining piece of work, charmingly written, wherever Mr. Wilde can find it in his heart to suffla-
minate his wit. There are several scenes in which the dialogue is heavily

overburdened with witticisms, not always of the best alloy. For Mr. Wilde's good things I have the keenest relish, but I wish he would imitate Beau Brummel in throwing aside his 'failures', not exposing them to the public gaze. His peculiar twist of thought sometimes produces very quaint and pleasing results. To object to it as a mere trick would be quite unreasonable. Every writer of any individuality has, so to speak, his trademark; but there are times when the output of Mr. Wilde's epigram-factory threatens to become all trademark and no substance. *An Ideal Husband*, however, does not positively lack good things, but simply suffers from a disproportionate profusion of inferior chatter. In each of Mr. Wilde's plays there has been one really profound saying, which serves to mark it in my memory. In *Lady Windermere's Fan* it was: 'There are only two tragedies in life: not getting what you want—and getting it.' In *A Woman of No Importance* it was: 'Thought is in its essence destructive; nothing survives being thought of.' In this play it is: 'Vulgarity is the behaviour of other people.' Simple as it seems, there is in this a world of observation and instruction. . . .

64. George Bernard Shaw on
An Ideal Husband

1895

Review signed 'G.B.S.' in the *Saturday Review* (12 January 1895), lxxix, 44–5; reprinted in *Our Theatres in the Nineties*, I (1932), pp. 9–12.

With characteristic wit and verve, Shaw attacks those who have attacked Wilde in a review that provides Shaw with yet another opportunity to expose his own brilliant invention—'the Englishman'. But rather startling is Shaw's comment that Wilde 'is absolutely the most sentimental dramatist of the day'. However, in view of Shaw's preference that drama serve as an instrument of political enlightenment, one may see why Shaw, for all his admiration of Wilde's wit, draws such a conclusion.

Mr Oscar Wilde's new play at the Haymarket is a dangerous subject, because he has the property of making his critics dull. They laugh angrily at his epigrams, like a child who is coaxed into being amused in the very act of setting up a yell of rage and agony. They protest that the trick is obvious, and that such epigrams can be turned out by the score by any one lightminded enough to condescend to such frivolity. As far as I can ascertain, I am the only person in London who cannot sit down and write an Oscar Wilde play at will. The fact that his plays, though apparently lucrative, remain unique under these circumstances, says much for the self-denial of our scribes. In a certain sense Mr Wilde is to me our only thorough playwright. He plays with everything: with wit, with philosophy, with drama, with actors and audience, with the whole theatre. Such a feat scandalizes the Englishman, who can no more play with wit and philosophy than he can with a football or a cricket bat. He works at both, and has the consolation, if he cannot make people laugh, of being the best cricketer and footballer in the world. Now it is the mark of the artist that he will not work. Just as people with social ambitions will practise the meanest economies in order to live expensively; so the artist will starve his way through incredible toil and discouragement sooner than go and earn a week's honest wages. Mr Wilde, an arch-artist, is so colossally lazy that he trifles even with the work by which an artist escapes work. He distils very quintessence, and gets as product plays which are so unapproachably playful that they are the delight of every playgoer with twopenn'orth of brains. The English critic, always protesting that the drama should not be didactic, and yet always complaining if the dramatist does not find sermons in stones and good in everything, will be conscious of a subtle and pervading levity in *An Ideal Husband*. All the literary dignity of the play, all the imperturbable good sense and good manners with which Mr Wilde makes his wit pleasant to his comparatively stupid audience, cannot quite overcome the fact that Ireland is of all countries the most foreign to England, and that to the Irishman (and Mr Wilde is almost as acutely Irish an Irishman as the Iron Duke of Wellington) there is nothing in the world quite so exquisitely comic as an Englishman's seriousness. It becomes tragic, perhaps, when the Englishman acts on it; but that occurs too seldom to be taken into account, a fact which intensifies the humour of the situation, the total result being the Englishman utterly unconscious of his real self, Mr Wilde keenly observant of it and playing on the self-unconsciousness with irresistible humour, and finally, of course, the Englishman annoyed with himself for being amused at his own expense, and for being unable to convict Mr Wilde of what seems an obvious misunderstanding of human nature. He is shocked, too, at the danger to the foundations of society when seriousness is publicly laughed at. And to complete the oddity of the situation, Mr Wilde, touching what he himself reverences, is absolutely the most sentimental dramatist of the day.

It is useless to describe a play which has no thesis: which is, in the purest integrity, a play and nothing less. The six worst epigrams are mere alms handed with a kind smile to the average suburban playgoer; the three best remain secrets between Mr Wilde and a few choice spirits. The modern note is struck in Sir Robert Chiltern's assertion of the individuality and courage of his wrongdoing as against the mechanical idealism of his stupidly good wife, and in his bitter criticism of a love that is only the reward of merit. It is from the philosophy on which this scene is based that the most pregnant epigrams in the play have been condensed. Indeed, this is the only philosophy that ever has produced epigrams. In contriving the stage expedients by which the action of the piece is kept going, Mr Wilde has been once or twice a little too careless of stage illusion: for example, why on earth should Mrs Cheveley, hiding in Lord Goring's room, knock down a chair? That is my sole criticism. . . .

65. Clement Scott on *An Ideal Husband*

1895

Signed review in the *Illustrated London News* (12 January 1895), cvi, 35.

The similarity between Mr. Oscar Wilde's *Ideal Husband* and Sardou's *Dora* is too marked not to be noticed. The hero, instead of being accused of stealing an important dispatch, is charged with selling a State secret. A new Zicka is introduced who blackmails the hero, instigated by another Baron Stein, who is an Austrian speculator; and instead of detection by a peculiar secret, we have a wonderful diamond bracelet, which has been stolen by the adventuress, who does not know it is a patent bracelet that cannot be unlocked except by some mysterious formula known only to one individual. But after all, these things, as I have often pointed out, concern experts far more than the general public. A play is never less interesting to the ordinary playgoer because something in it has been done before. The late Henry Pettitt, for instance, knew the whole formula of melodrama, and every effective method of treating it. In fact, he used the same incidents and series of incidents again and again with success. The critics pointed it out, but the general public were unconcerned. It is to me quite clear that the mere fact that Mr. Oscar Wilde's play suggests something else does not in the least interfere with its success—a success that is naturally increased by the author's method and trick of talk. In fact, Oscar Wilde is the fashion. His catch and whimsicality of dialogue tickle the public. Just now the whole of society is engaged in inventing Oscar Wildeisms, just as a few months ago they were employed in discovering the missing word in competitions. It is the easiest thing in the world. All you have to do is to form an obvious untruth into a false epigram. Cleverness nowadays is nothing but elaborate contradiction, and the man or woman who can say that black is white or white is black in a fanciful fashion is considered a genius. There is scarcely one Oscar Wildeism uttered in the new Haymarket play that will bear one minute's analysis, but for all that they tickle the ears of the groundlings, and are accepted as stage cleverness.

66. A. B. Walkley on *An Ideal Husband*

1895

Review signed 'A.B.W.' in *Speaker* (12 January 1895), iv, 43–4.

Two plays have been produced during the past few days with widely different fortunes at their birth. One, Mr. Oscar Wilde's *Ideal Husband*, at the Haymarket, a strepitous, polychromatic, scintillant affair, dexterous as a conjurer's trick of legerdemain, clever with a cleverness so excessive as to be almost monstrous and uncanny, was received with every token of success. The other, Mr. Henry James's *Guy Domville*, at the St. James's, laboriously wrought, pitched in a minor key, sometimes fuliginous, at others—as the Oxford Statutes put it—subfusc, maladroit, teasing to the pitch of exasperation, was so despitefully used by many of the audience that the manager virtually went down on his marrowbones and sued for pardon. Yet, of these two plays, I have not the slightest hesitation in declaring that the brilliant success is infinitely outweighed by the ostensible failure, not merely in actual achievement, but in significance, in promise for the future. Mr. Wilde's play will not help the drama forward a single inch, nor—though that is a comparatively unimportant matter—will it, in the long run, add to Mr. Wilde's reputation. . . .

On the surface, the different fates of the two plays are readily explained by the opposite qualities I have mentioned; Mr. Wilde's dexterity, his dancing rhythms, his orchestral brass; Mr. James's maladroitness, his limping and lagging, his half-inaudible reed-notes. But we must go a little deeper into the matter than this. We must look at the relations of each of the two dramatists with his silent collaborator; for every dramatist has such a collaborator—his audience, known as 'the great public', 'le vrai public', and by other fine names indicating respectful consideration. Respectfully considered by the dramatist he has to be—otherwise, instead of aiding the joint work, he hinders it at every turn, limits its range, impoverishes it, sometimes even stultifies it. And the great difference between Mr. Wilde and Mr. James is that one is on good terms with his collaborator, while the other is not. Monsieur Tout-le-Monde confronts every dramatist with this rigorous alternative; be like me—or be damned. Mr. James, failing to offer the required resemblance, has been—more or less—damned. Mr. Wilde is practically of the same mind as his audience, and gets his reward.

The statement that Mr. Wilde's strength lies in the fact that he and his public are practically of the same mind, may read, at first sight, like one of his own wilful paradoxes. What, you say, is not his most salient characteristic his unlikeness to the rest of us, is he not a notorious oddity, is not each of his 'faicts et gestes' a startling eccentricity? And it may also seem to imply that he presents the public with its own image; whereas the truth is, he is far from being a realist; actual people neither talk nor behave like his stage-personages. What I mean is this: that Mr. Wilde flatters the public, presents it with a false picture of life which it likes to fancy true, thinks its thoughts, conforms to its ideals, talks —yes, talks its talk. For—to take the last point first, because it is the most important point in any piece of Mr. Wilde's—the public talks commonplaces, and so does Mr. Wilde. It is true that his are inverted commonplaces; but the difference is immaterial, for not the nature, only the position, of a thing is altered by its being turned upside-down, These inverted commonplaces are Mr. Wilde's distinctive mark; they pullulate in all his plays, and the best that can be said for *An Ideal Husband* is that in it the output of them is considerably diminished. But there are still plenty of them, and to spare. Two specimens will suffice. 'The Seven Deadly—Virtues'; 'Nothing ages a man so quickly as—happiness.' You see the commonplaces which these invert. I do not know whether Mr. Wilde claims the credit—if credit is the right word—for the invention of this topsy-turvy process, but it is certain that he has been anticipated by M. Paul Bourget. The *Physiologie de l'Amour Moderne* dates from 1890, when Mr. Wilde had produced no play, and here is a speech made to its hero, Claude Larcher, by his friend Casal:—

Comment, vous travaillez ainsi dans la pensée. Vous n'avez donc pas remarqué combien il est facile de retourner les plus célèbres, et elles sont aussi vraies. Voulez-vous des exemples: "Le cœur vient des grandes pensées. . . . On n'a pas toujours assez de force pour supporter les maux d'autrui. . . . Le moi seul est aimable. Rien n'est vrai que le beau. . . ." Ce sont quelques célèbres maximes que je me suis amusé à mettre ainsi à l'envers, et vous voyez.[1].

I make no apology for quoting this passage at length, because it exactly explains Mr. Wilde's trick, and the cheapness of it, and its essential basis of commonplace. And we see that what in London we have learnt to call Oscarisms may long ago have been known to the Parisian public as Casalisms.

But the essential commonplace of Mr. Wilde is much more than a mere matter of language; it is the ambient air of his play; it is also its very heart and fibre. To what world does Mr. Wilde introduce us? According to the programme and the costumier, it is the world of high politics. The hero is Under-Secretary for Foreign Affairs, the heroine is the mistress of a great political salon, a minor personage is a Cabinet Minister, with the riband of the Garter. And this world, we are asked to believe, is perlustrated by fascinating adventuresses, who smoke cigarettes, wear 'too much rouge and too few clothes,' levy blackmail by means of stolen letters, and act as the secret agents of syndicates for the promotion of 'Argentine canals'. In this world, Under-Secretaries of State (who begin, in the private secretary stage, by divulging Cabinet secrets) are prepared, for private reasons, to support in Parliament measures which they have denounced at the previous debate; and refuse seats in the Cabinet because their wives bid them. When Bulwer Lytton and Disraeli wrote novels picturing politics as a drawing-room game of this kind, they only distorted, not actually falsified, the facts. But nowadays, of course, such a picture is stark, staring nonsense. Mr. Wilde might as well, while he is about it, introduce a duel between two members of the Cabinet, or send the leader of the Opposition into the street to erect barricades. But he knows his public; he knows they like this romantically absurd view of political life, and gives it them; just as the purveyors

[1] 'Why, you labour thus in thought. You have not then observed how easy it is to turn around the most celebrated thoughts, and they are also true. Do you wish some examples: "The heart comes from great thoughts. . . . One does not always have enough strength to support the evils of others. . . . The self alone is pleasing. Nothing is true except the beautiful. . . ." These are some celebrated maxims that I amused myself with by turning them inside out, and now you see.'

of penny-dreadfuls serve up to their public gigantic baronets in perpetual evening dress and betrayed damsels of low degree in white muslin. And Mr. Wilde's ideals are as commonplace as his atmosphere. Husbands as rich as Crœsus must have wives as lovely as Venus; people smack their lips with relish over 'the philosophy of power, the gospel of gold'; brutal, clamant, gaudy 'success' is the *summum bonum,* and to miss it is the tragedy of life. The great thing is not to be found out; indeed, the whole play is designed to fill us with joy over the escape of a sinner from the penalty of his sin through a trick with a diamond bracelet. And mention of this trick reminds me that the machinery of the play is as commonplace as its people and its ideals; in addition to a stolen Cabinet secret and a stolen bracelet, there are no less than two stolen letters. Even Sardou has tired of these kleptodramatics. In sum, though it has to be said that Mr. Wilde's piece, by dint of sheer cleverness, keeps one continually amused and interested; that it presents at least one pleasant and human character, everybody's friend save his own—the fact remains that Mr. Wilde's work is not only poor and sterile, but essentially vulgar.

67. Henry James, letter to William James on the 'triumphant Oscar'

1895

From a letter dated 2 February 1895, *Letters of Henry James*, vol. i, ed. Percy Lubbock (New York, 1920), p. 233.

James (1843–1916), who had met Wilde briefly in 1882 in Washington, D.C., during the latter's lecture tour of America, thought of him as merely a fatuous poseur, but later found himself overshadowed by Wilde's striking success in the theatre. On 2 February 1895, James's play *Guy Domville* closed after an unsuccessful run (it had opened on 5 January)—which James alludes to in his letter to his brother. The play that followed James's into the St James's Theatre was, of course, *The Importance of Being Earnest*, 'a great success', wrote James to his brother after it opened.

Tonight the thing will have lived the whole of its troubled little life of 31 performances, and will be 'taken off', to be followed, on Feb. 5th, by a piece by Oscar Wilde that will have probably a very different fate. On the night of the 5th, too nervous to do anything else, I had the ingenious thought of going to some other theatre and seeing some other play as a means of being coerced into quietness from 8 till 10.45. I went accordingly to the Haymarket, to a new piece by the said O.W. that had just been produced—*An Ideal Husband*. I sat through it and saw it played with every appearance (so far as the crowded house was an appearance) of complete success, and *that* gave me the most fearful apprehension. The thing seemed to me so helpless, so crude, so bad, so clumsy, feeble and vulgar, that as I walked away across St. James's Square to learn my own fate, the prosperity of what I had seen seemed to me to constitute a dreadful presumption of the shipwreck of *G.D.*, and I stopped in the middle of the Square, paralyzed by the terror of this probability— afraid to go on and learn more. 'How *can* my piece do anything with a public with whom *that* is a success?' It couldn't—but even then the full truth was, 'mercifully', not revealed to me; the truth that in a short month my piece would be whisked away to make room for the triumphant Oscar.

68. William Dean Howells on
An Ideal Husband

1895

Signed article, titled 'The Play and the Problem', in *Harper's Weekly* [New York] (30 March 1895), xxix, 294.

William Dean Howells (1837–1920), American critic and novelist, whose novel, *The Rise of Silas Lapham* (1885), is his best-known work, discusses in this article Shaw's *Arms and the Man* and Henry Arthur Jones's two plays, *The Masqueraders* and *The Case of Rebellious Susan*, in addition to Wilde's *An Ideal Husband*. Comparing the state of current fiction with that of English drama, Howells notes that in the plays he proposes to discuss 'there is distinctly a disposition on the part of the author to grapple with actualities of several kinds, and especially to wrestle with problems, and to struggle with motives. Their scene is always a recognizable semblance of the world . . .' Rather striking in this article is Howells's miscalculation as to the 'prosperity' that *Arms and the Man* will 'never achieve', despite its superiority to the other plays under discussion.

Mr. Oscar Wilde shows us a very swell world in the entourage of *An Ideal Husband*, but it is not nearly so wicked as that of *The Masqueraders*, and in spite of the author's well-known foible, it is not nearly so abandoned to paradox. In fact, I think *An Ideal Husband* is not only an excellent piece of art, but all excellent piece of sense: perhaps the two ought never to be thought of apart, but they are. The author handles in it very skilfully and very honestly the problem of a most happily married man, who in earlier life (he is still young, though an eminent parliamentary leader) sold a state secret, and got a little fortune for it. The little fortune becomes a great fortune, and just at the joyous moment when he can least bear to be confronted with his sin, a sulphurous female appears with the letter he wrote to a Viennese stock broker telling him the English government was about to buy the Suez Canal, and threatens the parliamentary leader with the exposure of this transgression of the young attaché, unless he will support her scheme of an Argentine Canal. There is money in that, too, but the husband is committed against the scheme as a piece of rascality, for being no longer dependent upon money he can afford to despise it. This often happens in life: men clean up as soon as they have the pecuniary means; but the play does not insist upon the point; nor am I going to insist upon the several points, very neatly and clearly made, by which it reaches an admirably reasoned conclusion. I was not able to convict the author of a single false step in the play (I had no great wish to do so, for I like to like things), and there are some by which he mounts to a pretty wide prospect of human nature; for instance, that where the husband upbraids the wife for idealizing him, and for not counting upon his weaknesses and his potential sins in loving him. This is very well, and it is very well where, when he has been saved from exposure, and she unwisely agrees that he must withdraw from public life, the friend of both makes her see that she is taking from him his sole chance of atonement and retrieval, and creating him a future of hatred for her and despair for himself.

In fact, Mr. Wilde manages his problem so as to come out best in the struggle. Yet the play left me with some very grave misgivings as to the usefulness of the moral problem in the drama. That is, it gave me question whether it could well be made the chief interest of a play; for there is great danger that it may be falsely solved, or else shirked, which is nearly as bad. I asked myself whether the play would not be better to be simply a picture of life, resting for its success upon incident and character, without those crucial events which in life are so rarely dramatic, but which, when they come, arrive with as little ceremony as the event of dinner or of death. I said that, after all, morality is an affair of being, rather than of doing, that the same action was not always as bad or as good at all times or for all persons; and that without more room than the drama can possibly give itself, it cannot be shown in its real relation to life, in its proportion, its value.

I might have been mistaken, and the moral problem may be the thing that the drama should concern itself with as the chief thing. But I complain that it resolves, or is apt to resolve, the leading characters to types; and that such sense of their personality as we have is not such as the author gives them, but such as the actors give them. It seems to me that the reader who has seen *The Case of Rebellious Susan* and *An Ideal Husband*, unless he is a very wrong-headed reader, will agree with me that it was the subordinate people of the plays who gave him the feeling of character, and that he cared for the heroes and heroines mainly because of what happened to them, or through them, and not because they were interesting persons except as the actors made them so. They were working out a problem, and so busy in doing it that they had no time for being.

One of the four plays I have been talking of was a mawkish melodrama, of the same value ethically and æsthetically, about, as *Camille*; but the other three were brilliant satires, and ought perhaps to be finally so considered. I think *The Case of Rebellious Susan* and *An Ideal Husband* were of a quite the same literary quality, and they were managed with about equal dexterity and grace. Mr. Jones smiled,

And lightly put the question by

in his play, and Mr. Wilde smiling faced it to the end. There was that much difference, but no such difference as separated them both from *Arms and the Man*. Was it because the affair in both was narrowed to the solution of a problem, and because in *Arms and the Man* the satire concerned the whole of civilization, that I found that so much greater? I recur to it with lasting pleasure after half a year, and the flavor of the others is faint already; yet they are both capital plays, and both enjoy a prosperity which I am afraid *Arms and the Man* will never achieve.

THE IMPORTANCE OF
BEING EARNEST

First produced: 14 February 1895

69. H. G. Wells on
The Importance of Being Earnest

1895

Unsigned review in the *Pall Mall Gazette*, 15 February 1895, p. 4.

It is, we were told last night, 'much harder to listen to nonsense than to talk it'; but not if it is good nonsense. And very good nonsense, excellent fooling, is this new play of Mr. Oscar Wilde's. It is, indeed, as new a new comedy as we have had this year. Most of the others, after the fashion of Mr. John Worthing, J.P., last night, have been simply the old comedies posing as their own imaginary youngest brothers. More humorous dealing with theatrical conventions it would be difficult to imagine. To the dramatic critic especially who leads a dismal life, it came with a flavour of rare holiday. As for the serious people who populate this city, and to whom it is addressed, how they will take it is another matter. Last night, at any rate, it was a success, and our familiar first-night audience—whose cough, by-the-bye, is much quieter—received it with delight. . . .

. . . It is all very funny, and Mr. Oscar Wilde has decorated a humour that is Gilbertian with innumerable spangles of that wit that is all his own. Of the pure and simple truth, for instance, he remarks that 'Truth is never pure and rarely simple'; and the reply, 'Yes, flowers are as common in the country as people are in London,' is particularly pretty from the artless country girl to the town-bred Gwendolen. . . .

How Serious People—the majority of the population, according to

Carlyle—how Serious People will take this Trivial Comedy written for their learning remains to be seen. No doubt seriously. One last night thought that the bag incident was a 'little far-fetched'. Moreover, he could not see how the bag and the baby got to Victoria Station (L.B. and S.C.R. station) while the manuscript and perambulator turned up 'at the summit of Primrose Hill'.Why the summit? Such difficulties, he said, rob a play of 'convincingness'. That is one serious person disposed of, at any rate.

On the last production of a play by Mr. Oscar Wilde we said it was fairly bad, and anticipated success. This time we must congratulate him unreservedly on a delightful revival of theatrical satire. *Absit omen.*[1] But we could pray for the play's success, else we fear it may prove the last struggle of its author against the growing seriousness of his dramatic style.

70. Reception of
The Importance of Being Earnest

1895

Notice signed 'H.F.' in the *New York Times*, 17 February 1895, p.1, in a front-page column of political and literary news sent from London by Hamilton Fyfe (1869–1951), drama critic and journalist on the staff of the London *Times* and the author of several books, including one on Pinero.

Oscar Wilde may be said to have at last, and by a single stroke, put his enemies under his feet. Their name is legion, but the most inveterate of them may be defied to go to St. James's Theatre and keep a straight face through the performance of *The Importance of Being Earnest*. It is a pure farce of Gilbertian parentage, but loaded with drolleries, epigrams,

---

[1] May the omen be averted.

impertinences, and bubbling comicalities that only an Irishman could have ingrafted on that respectable Saxon stock. Since *Charley's Aunt* was first brought from the provinces to London I have not heard such unrestrained, incessant laughter from all parts of the theatre, and those laughed the loudest whose approved mission it is to read Oscar long lectures in the press on his dramatic and ethical shortcomings. The thing is as slight in structure and as devoid of purpose as a paper balloon, but it is extraordinarily funny, and the universal assumption is that it will remain on the boards here for an indefinitely extended period.

71. William Archer on
The Importance of Being Earnest

1895

Signed review in the *World*, 20 February 1895; reprinted in *The Theatrical 'World' of 1895* (1896), pp. 56–60.

The dramatic critic is not only a philosopher, moralist, æsthetician, and stylist, but also a labourer working for his hire. In this last capacity he cares nothing for the classifications of Aristotle, Polonius, or any other theorist, but instinctively makes a fourfold division of the works which come within his ken. These are his categories: (1) Plays which are good to see. (2) Plays which are good to write about. (3) Plays which are both. (4) Plays which are neither. Class 4 is naturally the largest; Class 3 the smallest; and Classes 1 and 2 balance each other pretty evenly. Mr. Oscar Wilde's new comedy, *The Importance of Being Earnest*, belongs indubitably to the first class. It is delightful to see, it sends wave after wave of laughter curling and foaming round the theatre; but as a text for criticism it is barren and delusive. It is like a mirage-oasis in the desert, grateful and comforting to the weary eye—but when you come close up to it, behold! it is intangible, it eludes your grasp. What can a poor critic do with a play which raises no principle, whether of art or morals, creates its own canons and conventions, and is nothing but an absolutely wilful expression of an irrepressibly witty personality? Mr. Pater, I think (or is it some one else?), has an essay on the tendency of all art to verge towards, and merge in, the absolute art—music. He might have found an example in *The Importance of Being Earnest*, which imitates nothing, represents nothing, means nothing, is nothing, except a sort of *rondo capriccioso*, in which the artist's fingers run with crisp irresponsibility up and down the keyboard of life. Why attempt to analyse and class such a play? Its theme, in other hands, would have made a capital farce; but 'farce' is far too gross and commonplace a word to apply to such an iridescent filament of fantasy. Incidents of the same nature as Algy Moncrieffe's 'Bunburying' and John Worthing's invention and subsequent suppression of his scapegrace brother Ernest have done duty in many a French vaudeville and English adaptation; but Mr. Wilde's humour transmutes them into something entirely new and individual. Amid so much that is negative, however, criticism may find one positive remark to make. Behind all Mr. Wilde's whim and even perversity, there lurks a very geniune science, or perhaps I should rather say instinct, of the theatre. In all his plays, and certainly not least in this one, the story is excellently told and illustrated with abundance of scenic detail. Monsieur Sarcey himself (if Mr. Wilde will forgive my saying so) would 'chortle in his joy' over John Worthing's entrance in deep mourning (even down to his cane) to announce the death of his brother Ernest, when we know that Ernest in the flesh—a false but undeniable Ernest—is at that moment in the house making love to Cecily. The audience does not instantly awaken to the meaning of his inky suit, but even as he marches solemnly down the stage, and before a word is spoken, you can feel the idea kindling from row to row, until a 'sudden glory' of laughter fills the theatre. It is only the born playwright who can imagine and work up to such an effect. Not that the play is a masterpiece of construction. It seemed to me that the author's invention languished a little after the middle of the second act, and that towards the close of that act there were even one or two brief patches of something almost like tediousness. But I have often noticed that the more successful the play, the more a first-night audience is apt to be troubled by inequalities of workmanship, of which subsequent audiences are barely conscious. The most happily-inspired scenes, coming to us with the gloss of novelty upon them, give us such keen pleasure, that passages which are only reasonably amusing are apt to seem, by contrast, positively dull. Later audiences, missing the shock of surprise which gave to the master-scenes their keenest zest, are also spared our sense of disappointment in the flatter passages, and enjoy the play more evenly all through. I myself, on seeing a play a second time, have often been greatly entertained by scenes which had gone near to boring me on the first night. When I see Mr. Wilde's play again, I shall no doubt relish the last half of the second act more than I did on Thursday evening; and even then I differed from some of my colleagues who found the third act tedious. Mr. Wilde is least fortunate where he drops into Mr. Gilbert's Palace-of-Truth mannerism, as he is apt to do in the characters of Gwendolen and Cecily. Strange what a fascination this trick seems to possess for the comic playwright! Mr. Pinero, Mr. Shaw, and now Mr. Wilde, have all dabbled in it, never to their advantage. . . .

72. Unsigned review, *Truth*

21 February 1895, xxvii, 464–5

I have not the slightest intention of seriously criticising Mr. O. Wilde's new piece at the St. James's: as well might one sit down after dinner and attempt gravely to discuss the true inwardness of a *soufflé*. Nor, fortunately, is it necessary to enter into details as to its wildly farcical plot: as well might one, after a successful display of fireworks in the back garden, set to work laboriously to analsye the composition of a catherine wheel. At the same time I wish at once to admit, fairly and frankly, that *The Importance of being Earnest* amused me very much. The author has told us that he himself regards it as 'a delicate bubble of fancy'; but there is rather too much in it about babies being left in hand-bags at the cloakrooms of London termini for me to allow it is that. No, it is neither 'delicate' nor 'bubbly'; but, I repeat, it is undoubtedly amusing, and that is a quality which, in *le monde où l'on s'ennuie*,[1] is certain to meet

[1] The world where one bores oneself.

with warm approval. Whether we should have heard as much as we have about it, had anybody else written it, is doubtful; but that only shows the importance of being—Oscar.

To inquire *why* it is amusing is not, perhaps, a very edifying task, but it may not be a wholly uninteresting one. Candid friends might urge that Mr. Wilde's excellent memory has much to do with the result in question. And, indeed, his new piece is as full of echoes as Prospero's isle—echoes of Marivaux, echoes of Meilhac, echoes of Maddison Morton, echoes of William Schwenk Gilbert and of George Bernard Shaw; aye, echoes even of the 'Facetiæ' columns on the back page of the *Family Herald*! But the very fact that Mr. Wilde's inspiration can be traced to so many sources proves that he can owe very little to any of them, and I, for one, certainly do not intend to upbraid him for his eclectic taste. There are critics, too, who attribute his success to the savour of well-bred insolence which he is able to send over the footlights; and there is assuredly something not altogether displeasing to most of us in hearing other people insult one another with more or less cynical impertinence. But I have no doubt in my own mind that the chief reason why the St. James's piece proves so amusing, is because it is so completely dominated by its author. That is to say, there is no attempt in it at characterisation, but all the *dramatis personæ*, from the heroes down to their butlers, talk pure and undiluted Wildese. Whether we ought to be amused by this is quite another question; and whether we shall long continue to be amused by it is exceedingly doubtful; but, for the present, all London will flock to the St. James's; and Oscar will reap his reward. He would be wise, in my opinion, to make his hay while the sun shines. The public taste for 'Oscarisms' is not likely to be a lasting one. For once, the experiment of dressing up an old-fashioned screaming farce in the very latest and smartest verbal fashion, and then calling it 'a trival comedy', has 'caught on', but it is not at all certain that its repetition would be successful. According to Mr. Wilde, it is only mediocrities who improve. His own plays, he has assured us, 'are to each other

> as one white rose
> On one green stalk is to another one.'

In fact 'they form a perfect cycle, and in their delicate sphere complete both life and art.' Is there not a danger, then, that his future pieces may prove works of supererogation? The days of the 'Paradox *à la* Wilde' may be numbered. It may pass, as the cult of the lily has passed, and the *mode* of the green carnation. Indeed, I am not sure that Mr. Edison could not, if he gave his mind to it, design an apparatus for turning out 'Oscarisms' automatically. We might put our pennies in the slot, press a button, and draw out 'Wilde' paradoxes on tape by the yard. It would not require nearly such elaborate mechanism as the late Mr. Babbage's once famous Calculating Machine.

Surprise has been expressed that Mr. Wilde should have succeeded in catching the taste of the pit and gallery, as well as the approval of the stalls and boxes, with his new piece; but I do not think there is anything very strange in this. The people in the humbler parts of the house evidently keenly enjoyed the graphic glimpses which the dramatist gave them of the inner life of those 'higher ranks', with which, as he told an interviewer the other day, he was 'best acquainted'. They were deeply interested to note that ladies of title specially affect cucumber sandwiches at five o'clock teas, that to take sugar is now considered in smart society quite unfashionable, and that a cake is never seen on the tea-tables of really stylish families. Most thoroughly, too, did they enjoy the prolonged tussle over a plate of muffins, in which the two heroes of the piece bring the second act to so aristocratic an end. Nay, there was even something in the striking modernity of Mr. Allan Aynesworth's cuffs and the effusive loveliness of Mr. George Alexander's neckties, which could scarcely fail to be attractive. It has just occurred to me that I have said nothing about the acting—another proof of the way in which the author 'dominates his play . . .'

73. George Bernard Shaw on
The Importance of Being Earnest

1895

Review signed 'G.B.S.' in *Saturday Review* (23 February 1895), lxxix, 249–50; reprinted in *Our Theatres in the Nineties*, II, (1932), 41–4.

In a letter appended to Frank Harris's biography of Wilde (1916), Shaw expressed the idea that though Wilde's play was 'extremely funny', he thought it was 'essentially hateful'. Wilde, Shaw wrote, 'was disgusted with me because I, who had praised his first plays handsomely, had turned traitor over *The Importance of Being Earnest*. Clever as it was, it was his first really heartless play.' Shaw could not—or would not—accept a comedy of manners, however amusing, which was aloof from social and political problems.

It is somewhat surprising to find Mr Oscar Wilde, who does not usually model himself on Mr Henry Arthur Jones, giving his latest play a five-chambered title like *The Case of Rebellious Susan*. So I suggest with some confidence that *The Importance of Being Earnest* dates from a period long anterior to Susan. However it may have been retouched immediately before its production, it must certainly have been written before *Lady Windermere's Fan*. I do not suppose it to be Mr Wilde's first play: he is too susceptible to fine art to have begun otherwise than with a strenuous imitation of a great dramatic poem, Greek or Shakespearian; but it was perhaps the first which he designed for practical commercial use at the West End theatres. The evidence of this is abundant. The play has a plot—a gross anachronism; there is a scene between the two girls in the second act quite in the literary style of Mr Gilbert, and almost inhuman enough to have been conceived by him; the humour is adulterated by stock mechanical fun to an extent that absolutely scandalizes one in a play with such an author's name to it; and the punning title and several of the more farcical passages recall the

epoch of the late H. J. Byron. The whole has been varnished, and here
and there veneered, by the author of *A Woman of no Importance*; but the
general effect is that of a farcical comedy dating from the seventies, un-
played during that period because it was too clever and too decent, and
brought up to date as far as possible by Mr Wilde in his now completely formed style. Such is the impression left by the play on me. But
I find other critics, equally entitled to respect, declaring that *The
Importance of Being Earnest* is a strained effort of Mr Wilde's at ultra-
modernity, and that it could never have been written but for the opening up of entirely new paths in drama last year by *Arms and the Man*.
At which I confess to a chuckle.

I cannot say that I greatly cared for *The Importance of Being Earnest*.
It amused me, of course; but unless comedy touches me as well as
amuses me, it leaves me with a sense of having wasted my evening. I
go to the theatre to be moved to laughter, not to be tickled or bustled
into it; and that is why, though I laugh as much as anybody at a farcical
comedy, I am out of spirits before the end of the second act, and out of
temper before the end of the third, my miserable mechanical laughter
intensifying these symptoms at every outburst. If the public ever becomes intelligent enough to know when it is really enjoying itself and
when it is not, there will be an end of farcical comedy. Now in *The
Importance of Being Earnest* there is plenty of this rib-tickling: for instance,
the lies, the deceptions, the cross purposes, the sham mourning, the
christening of the two grown-up men, the muffin eating, and so forth.
These could only have been raised from the farcical plane by making
them occur to characters who had, like Don Quixote, convinced us of
their reality and obtained some hold on our sympathy. But that unfortunate moment of Gilbertism breaks our belief in the humanity of
the play. Thus we are thrown back on the force and daintiness of its
wit, brought home by an exquisitely grave, natural, and unconscious
execution on the part of the actors. . . . On the whole I must decline
to accept *The Importance of Being Earnest* as a day less than ten years old;
and I am altogether unable to perceive any uncommon excellence in its
presentations.

74. A. B. Walkley, on
The Importance of Being Earnest

1895

Review signed 'A.B.W.' in the *Speaker* 23 February 1895, iv, 212–13.
Of interest here is Walkley's attempt to analyse the source of wit in Wilde's play, one of the few attempts at the time. Walkley seems to have seen, as few other critics did, that *The Importance of Being Earnest* was the culmination of Wilde's development as a dramatist.

Believe me, it is with no ironic intention that I declare Mr. Oscar Wilde to have 'found himself', at last, as an artist in sheer nonsense. There has been good nonsense in his previous stage-work, but it failed to give unalloyed pleasure, either because it adopted serious postures or was out of harmony with an environment of seriousness. In his farce at the St. James's—Mr. Archer, I see, thinks the word 'farce' derogatory here; but why? We call *The Wasps* and *Le Médecin malgré Lui* farces—in his farce, then, *The Importance of Being Earnest*, there is no discordant note of seriousness. It is of nonsense all compact, and better nonsense, I think, our stage has not seen. This is not to be wondered at; Mr. Wilde has the advantage, an immense advantage for any artificer of the ludicrous, of being the last comer. We often hear protests raised against the view that art 'progresses'; art *is*, people say, it is a thing immovable, indeed, the only thing:—

> Tout passe. L'art robuste
> Seul a l'éternité,
> Le buste
> Survit à la cité.[1]

And we are asked how the west front of Amiens Cathedral has 'progressed' beyond the Elgin marbles, or *Hamlet* beyond the Oresteian

[1] 'All passes. Enduring art alone is eternal. The bust outlasts the city.' From Théophile Gautier's 'L'Art' in *Emaux et Camées* (1857).

trilogy. Leaving the general question undiscussed, I am quite sure one art has 'progressed', and that is the art which works in the medium of the ludicrous. Indeed, looking at a great subject in one aspect only, I think the history of civilisation is a history of gradual improvement in the quality of our laughter. To a modern, the laughter of the antique stage is cruel, or stupid, or simply incomprehensible. What a gulf there is between ancient and modern ideas on this subject may be seen from the significant little fact that, in the brief passage of the *Poetics* in which Aristotle refers to comedy (which, to be sure, was in his time only farce), he makes the ridiculous a sub-division of the ugly. Cicero—it is one of the commonplaces of the subject (or I, for one, should not be aware of the passage)—thought that bodily deformities were 'satis bella materies ad jocandum';[1] an opinion in which gutter-urchins are now your only Ciceronians. Molière's fun was ferociously cruel (*Georges Dandin*) or mere horseplay (*passim*). It is we moderns who have made Tartuffe and Shylock serious personages; beyond a doubt they were designed, in the main, to be comic. It is unnecessary to go on demonstrating the obvious. In one thing, at any rate, we surpass the great men of old and our forefathers that begat us; our laughter is of better quality.

Here is, perhaps, a general reason for the great strides made by the art of farce-writing in recent years; but there is also, I think, a special cause—the abandonment of realism for fantasy. Mr. Pinero (for we must not forget that the author of *Mrs. Tanqueray* is also the author of *The Magistrate*, *The Schoolmistress*, *Dandy Dick*, and *The Cabinet Minister*) and Mr. Gilbert were the pioneers of this movement. But enough of realism—or, at any rate, of side-reference to life—remained in their farces to mingle a little contempt with the laughter. The central idea of all Mr. Pinero's farces—the infliction of indignities on a dignitary—is not wholly joyous. As for Mr. Gilbert, he makes us laugh more often than not 'on the wrong side of our mouths.' His *Engaged*, for instance, is as grim as *The Duchess of Malfi*. Now the merit of *The Importance of Being Earnest* is that the laughter it excites is absolutely free from bitter afterthought. Mr. Wilde makes his personages ridiculous, but—you will admit the distinction?—he does not ridicule them. He introduces personages ostensibly of to-day, young men 'about town,' 'revolting' daughters, a clergyman, a prim governess, a glib valet; but he does not poke fun at them as types; he induces us to laugh at their conduct for its sheer whimsicality, not as illustrating the foibles of their class.

I say we laugh at the whimsicality of their conduct. But in what,

[1] Good enough subject for joking.

precisely, does this consist? Why, precisely, do we laugh? To answer such questions satisfactorily would involve the discussion of another question—the nature of all laughter. It is a vast subject: the gravest philosophers, from Kant to Mr. Herbert Spencer, have not yet been able to tell us why we laugh. The latest student of the psychology of laughter is M. Camille Mélinand, who puts forward some interesting views on the subject in the current number of the *Revue des Deux Mondes*. His conclusion, briefly stated, is, that the necessary condition for laughter is the simultaneous recognition of the absurd and the natural in the thing laughed at. Every mental process ultimately consists in the classification in known categories of things yet unknown. When the thing is not to be placed in any known category, it entirely escapes our thought (*e.g.* a foreign language which we cannot speak); that is the incomprehensible. When the thing is to be placed in two mutually exclusive categories, it shocks our thought (*e.g.* a quadrilateral triangle); that is the absurd. When the thing enters promptly into one category, we have the calm satisfaction of thinking, of knowing; that is the rational. When the thing is, on one side, absurd, and, on the other, falls into a familiar category, our thought is accompanied by a spasmodic shake; that is laughter. Let us see if this will help us to understand why we laugh at Mr. Wilde's personages. Take the capital situation of the farce. John Worthing, who is John in the country and (for the old reason) 'Ernest' in town, determines to kill off his imaginary brother Ernest, and arrives at his country-house clad in complete mourning. The mere sight of him in this garb sets us off laughing. For we guess at once what he is going to do; and we have just seen his bosom friend arrive at the house in the assumed character of the very Ernest who is now to be given out as dead. Why do we laugh? Because, knowing what we do, we recognise John's conduct as absurd; but, on the other hand, we recognise it, given only his knowledge, as natural. So with all the actions of the play. Two girls, believing themselves engaged to the same man, and deadly foes in consequence, show their enmity by squabbling over the division of the cake at the tea-table. A young man, about to be kicked out of the house, declines to go until he has finished the muffins. Another, finding that his sweetheart only loves him because she believes him to bear the name of Ernest, resolves to be christened 'Ernest' forthwith—and anxiously asks the parson whether he is likely to catch cold in the process, etc. A smooth valet gravely announces himself as a pessimist, and, being ironically complimented by his master, replies that 'he has always tried to give satisfaction.' A handbag

in which Worthing was left thirty years ago in a cloak-room is produced as a clue to a romantic mystery; as anti-climax, its owner, a
prim governess, remarks that 'she has been much inconvenienced by the
want of it.' I take these details at random, not with any idea of describing the piece—that, like every other good farce, is not to be described—
but as aids to the analysis of my laughter. You see that the conduct of the
people in itself is rational enough; it is exquisitely irrational in the
circumstances. Their motives, too, are quite rational in themselves;
they are only irrational as being fitted to the wrong set of actions. And
the result is that you have something like real life in detail, yet, in sum,
absolutely unlike it; the familiar materials of life shaken up, as it were,
and rearranged in a strange, unreal pattern. It is this combination of the
natural and the absurd which, according to M. Mélinand's theory,
causes our laughter. Whatever its cause, it is, to my mind, the most
delightful form of laughter. You are in a world that is real yet fantastic;
the most commonsense actions of daily life take place, with the one
important difference that the common sense has been left out; you have
fallen among amiable, gay, and witty lunatics. Of course, a root-idea of
farce like this requires an aristocratic *milieu* for due expansion, an
atmosphere of wealth and leisure; Mr. Wilde's people would be
monsters, had they not several thousands a year, handles to their names,
Grandisonian butlers, and dresses from the Rue de la Paix. And (as there
is a touch of the snob in all of us) this Persic apparatus completes the
general impression of gaiety.

75. Unsigned review, *Theatre*

1 March 1895, xxv, 169–70

The most obvious thing suggested by *The Importance of Being Earnest*
is the advantage of being frivolous, which, in a pecuniary sense, is likely
to accrue to an author who caters for the less intelligent section of the
public. Mr. Oscar Wilde has the courage of his convictions. He has
recognised that the majority of playgoers are prepared to accept him at

the value he has set upon himself, and accordingly he exhibits perfect readiness to fool them to the top of their bent. The question remains, how long is the vogue likely to last? But that, after all, is a problem of secondary consequence, for chameleon-like Mr. Wilde is always ready to change his colours. Tragedy or comedy, laughter or tears—it is all one to him. He is governed by the showman's principle—'You pays your money and you takes your choice.' His new trivial comedy is a bid for popularity in the direction of farce. Stripped of its 'Oscarisms'— regarded purely as a dramatic exercise—it is not even a good specimen of its class. The story is clumsily handled, the treatment unequal, the construction indifferent, while the elements of farce, comedy, and burlesque are jumbled together with a fine disregard for consistency. But the piece throughout bears the unmistakable impress of the author's handiwork, and that, it would appear, is sufficient for an audience un- able or unwilling to distinguish between the tinsel glitter of sham epigram and the authentic sheen of true wit. Of the success of the new comedy there can be no doubt, inasmuch as its audacity—we had almost said impertinence—will not fail to attract votaries of a society which enjoys nothing more keenly than an exhibition on the stage of its own weaknesses. To criticise the work seriously would be a measure that the author himself would probably be the first to deride. So little respect, indeed, does he show for his own piece, that in places he has not hesitated to ridicule the very creatures born of his fertile imagination; while, throughout its performance, one is constantly forced to the conclusion that his tongue must have found refuge in his cheek more frequently than not as the labour of writing progressed. . . .

76. William Archer on the loss to British drama

1895

Letter to Charles Archer, 1 May 1895, in *William Archer: Life, Work and Friendships* by Charles Archer (New Haven, 1931), pp. 215–16. Archer wrote this letter to his brother several days after Wilde's first trial began.

Really the luck is against the poor British drama—the man who has more brains in his little finger than all the rest of them in their whole body goes and commits worse than suicide in this way. However, it shows that what I hoped for in Oscar could never have come about— I thought he might get rid of his tomfoolery and affectation and do something really fine.

77. Ernest Newman on Wilde's genius for paradox

1895

Signed article, titled 'Oscar Wilde: A Literary Appreciation', in the *Free Review* (1 June 1895), iv, 193–206.

Ernest Newman (1868–1959), music critic and biographer, is best known for his *Life of Richard Wagner* (4 volumes, 1933–46). To have published this article—with its attack on the British Philistine—was daring on the part of the journal, for Wilde had just been convicted and sentenced in the previous week. (Three paragraphs, in which Newman examines the 'scientific justification of paradox', are here omitted, the omission indicated by ellipses.)

To write down a man whom everyone else is praising is one of the holiest joys that the pursuit of literature can give: but it has not quite the subtly virtuous satisfaction that comes from writing up a man whom everybody else is crying down. It is a pretty safe rule to go upon that the writer beloved of the British public is at all events not more than third-rate—Mr. Crockett and Mr. Rider Haggard for example; but this method of contraries is not always reliable. Robert Louis Stevenson seems to have a wide circle of readers, just as Gounod and Bizet have a wide circle of auditors, and nobody can question the genius of these men; though it may be doubted whether the public admires them for their best qualities or for their second-best. But the method of contraries, as we have called it, is quite reliable in the other field: if the public howls a man down or grins him down, he is certain to be possessed of genius. I am glad to say that these are not original reflections; it is very hard to say anything original about genius, and still harder to say anything original about the British public; and it would be a grievous shock to anyone if he were to discover the hitherto unknown fact that the British public is stupid and prejudiced. As it is, one grows up in the tradition, and gets hardened to the atmosphere, and so is enabled to look upon his fellow-countrymen more in equanimity than in anger.

Now if there is one thing the British Philistine cannot understand—I am not affirming, of course, that he understands anything—it is a paradox. 'The English mind is always in a rage,' said the subject of this article on one occasion. And so it is; but its rage becomes sheer madness when anyone puts a paradox before it. We pride ourselves, as an orthodox nation, on our faith, and the pride is a just one. We are the most believing nation that ever lived. The Englishman makes the primary mistake of believing in himself, and the secondary mistake of believing in other people. And so we cannot wonder that he takes a paradox seriously, and thinks the writer means every word of it to be taken as if it were a proposition in Euclid. The function of a paradox is really the same as the function of religion—not to be believed; but the Philistine takes the one as seriously as he takes the other. Let us look at the matter philosophically. Let us try to find a scientific justification of paradox—for the great value of science is the aid it gives us in supporting by argument a case which we have not the hardiness to maintain in a more courageous manner. . . .

A paradox is simply the truth of the minority, just as a commonplace is the truth of the majority. The function of paradox is to illuminate light places, to explain just those things that everyone understands. For example, everyone knows what Art is, and everyone knows what it is to be immoral; but if a thinker says 'Art is immoral', the new synthesis puzzles them, and they either call it a paradox, or say the writer is immoral. In reality, he is doing just what they cannot do; he can see round corners and the other side of things. Nay, he can do more than this; he can give to ordinary things a quality that they have not, and place them in worlds that never existed. We ordinary beings can see objects in three dimensions only; a good paradox is a view in the fourth dimension.

And no one has given more paradoxes to our literature than Mr. Oscar Wilde. To be told that art is immoral; that life imitates art; that all bad poetry springs from genuine feeling; that to be natural is to be obvious, and to be obvious is to be inartistic; that art is greater than life, and criticism greater than art; that there is no sin except stupidity; that thought is dangerous; that the three qualifications of a great critic are unfairness, insincerity, and irrationality; that it is easier to do a thing than to write about it; that life is a failure from the artistic point of view; that in the sphere of action a conscious aim is a delusion, and worse than a delusion; that sin is an essential element of progress; that all bad art comes from returning to life and nature, and elevating them into ideals; that external nature imitates art; that the remarkable increase in London fogs during the last ten years is entirely due to the impressionist painters; that the sunsets are beginning to imitate Turner's pictures; that lying, the telling of beautiful untrue things, is the proper aim of art; that the Japanese people do not exist; that nature is always behind the age; that art is our gallant attempt to teach nature her proper place; to be told all these things and many many more, is to the Philistine an insult and to Mrs. Grundy shameful. Yet there is not a single one of these paradoxes of Mr. Wilde's that does not contain—I will not say half-a-truth, for that would be a slight on any paradox— but a good truth and a half at least. To hear one of Mr. Wilde's paradoxes by itself is to be startled; to read them in their proper context is to recognise the great fact on which I have already insisted, that a paradox is a truth seen round a corner. There is not one of the paradoxes that does not argue out straightly and squarely, and we rise from the perusal of them with a self-conscious wisdom that we had not before. We become wise, and know it: and that is the only sort of wisdom worth having.

I have described the writing of a paradox as seeing round corners; to vary the metaphor a little, I might describe the reading of paradoxes as a performance in which the audience is made to dance on the tight rope, while the acrobat enjoys their unsophisticated antics. This is the explanation of the bovine rage of the Philistine when he has to read such an essay as 'The Decay of Lying', or 'The Critic as Artist', in which he is compelled literally to walk on paradoxes. He is safe enough if grounded firmly on a commonplace or on a piece of stupidity; then is he a symbol of the immovable, calling forth the admiration of the gods. But a paradox is such an unsubstantial footing! And in his rage at being compelled to dance, he calls Mr. Wilde a fool and a rogue, and gets off again, as soon as he may, to Mr. Lewis Morris and Mrs. Humphry Ward.

I have no intention of explaining any of Mr. Wilde's paradoxes, for a paradox ought no more to be explained or to need explanation, than a good joke. Anyone who cares for brilliant wit and sound judgment and a polished style will not wait to hear a paradox at second-hand, but will read 'The Decay of Lying' for himself, and rejoice that he had discovered an artist. My object in this article is rather to call attention to less-known qualities of Mr. Wilde's genius, and to show my readers, if

I can, that he is not the lackadaisical dandy they have always imagined him to be, but one of the best of contemporary critics and poets, with a style like polished agate, and a mind that combines most curiously extreme sensuousness with extreme virility of grasp and penetration. That he is a wit nobody requires to be told, and even his enemies will not dispute him the title. Unfortunately for himself, he has pushed his wit very hard in his plays, and it becomes at times so obviously forced that one feels a momentary annoyance at him. These, however, are really rare moments; and when he means to be witty he really is so, nine times out of ten. The conversations in the second act of *A Woman of No Importance* and the third act of *Lady Windermere's Fan* may have as little to do with the action of the drama as some of Congreve's scenes have; but we would be as loth to give up Mr. Wilde's wit as we would to give up Congreve's. To say that at a certain reception there were several Royal Academicians, disguised as artists, is decidedly clever, though perhaps not uniquely so; but the description of 'Robert Elsmere' as Matthew Arnold's 'Literature and Dogma' without the literature, is as good in its way as the question 'What are American dry goods'? and the answer 'American novels'. No one can be so politely rude as Mr. Wilde; no one can be so personal in so graceful a manner. When the American girl tells the Canterville Ghost that in America they have no ruins and no curiosities, the Ghost mildly ejaculates, 'No ruins! no curiosities! you have your navy and your manners'! which is funny without being vulgar. If it were for his wit alone, Mr. Oscar Wilde is decidedly worth reading. His wit has this advantage over the humor of German metaphysicians, that it is quite self-conscious and intentional.

It would be hard to say how much of Mr. Wilde's nature is paradoxical and how much normal. One would have thought that with his genius for delicate humor he would have done some work at least of this kind in verse. The curious thing is that he keeps all his humor and paradox for his prose writings, and is serious—even terribly serious—in his poetry. It is still more curious when we notice how almost inexhaustible is the fund of whimsicality in him. When he is writing prose, it seems to be really an impossibility for him to be serious throughout. His essay on 'The Truth of Masks' is perhaps his longest piece of non-paradoxical work; it is full of sound sense and happy observation; yet at the end there comes upon us, quite unexpectedly, this remark: 'Not that I agree with everything that I have said in this essay. There is much with which I entirely disagree.' The happiest example, however, of Mr.

Wilde's 'method of inversion', as we may call it, is the short story 'Lord Arthur Savile's Crime'. This is a story of a young man who, just befor his marriage, learns from a cheiromantist that he is fated to become a murderer. The narrative begins seriously enough, but after the first two chapters the tone changes to one of irony and banter, which is maintained to the end with exquisite humor. Lord Arthur feels that it is his duty to commit this murder at once, before his marriage, so that he will not be marrying Sybil Merton under false pretences, as it were; and accordingly he looks over the list of his friends and relatives to see who would be the most convenient person to sacrifice. The delicious humor of the story lies in the cool manner in which the ordinary 'murder-motive' is reversed; Lord Arthur has not the slightest compunction about doing the murder, but feels very strongly about the dishonor involved in marrying an innocent girl before the wearisome business is completed; and the moral paradox is maintained as charmingly as the intellectual paradoxes are maintained in Mr. Wilde's essays. The capacity for being humorous and ironic in the most serious manner is seen again in 'The Canterville Ghost', an amusing story of an American who buys an old English house with a ghost three centuries old, and gives the said ghost so many painful American experiences that he dies from moral shock. It would seem that Mr. Wilde is at his best when writing a story that hangs upon a paradox, for his other stories, 'The Sphinx without a Secret' and 'A Model Millionaire', have nothing noticeable about them.

But to take Mr. Wilde upon his witty side only is to do him an injustice. I do not think I am overstating the case when I say that his is one of the clearest and soundest intellects in England to-day. He made something of a sensation fifteen years ago by his volume of poems, which contained some remarkable work for a young man of twenty-five. Apparently he has not seen fit to take the course then opened out to him, for he has written singularly little poetry since then, and the 1892 edition of his poems is just a reprint of the volume of 1881. Yet it is not by his poems that he stands out so conspicuously from contemporary belletrists, but rather by his prose. This has a distinction which his verse has not; for while it is becoming easier to write passable poetry and passable music, it is becoming an increasingly difficult thing to write beautiful and original prose. Like his verse, Mr. Wilde's prose is characterised by extreme sensuousness. Yet I think that those who have attempted to satirise him—including even the brilliant author of *The Green Carnation*—have done him an injustice by representing his prose as too gorgeous and too perfume-laden. In reality it is never voluptuous at the expense of strength; it would be hard to point to a contemporary prose-style in which so luxuriant an imagination and such a feeling for beautiful words are kept as artistically subordinate to virility and ease of motion. To my mind it is a superior style to Mr. Walter Pater's, inasmuch as the latter bears upon its face, in the form of bad punctuation, the evident signs of invertebrate thinking. Mr. Pater's sentences sometimes go shambling down to their conclusion in a way that indicates clearly the looseness of the writer's thought. Mr. Wilde's prose is at once sensuous and restrained, plastic and ornate.[1] And to the distinction of beauty is added the distinction of thought. There is material enough in his scattered essays to make an excellent treatise on aesthetic. Mr. Wilde's taste is, it is safe to say, infallible. We never find him praising bad work, and never failing to praise work that is good. And better than the mere fact of praising good work, he gives just the right reason for saying it is good. To see him at his best as a critic, let us look at his passage on Browning. The flabby dilettante of the popular imagination would hardly be the man to admire Browning's tortuous and crabbed Muse; yet Mr. Wilde not only admires Browning, but admires him for exactly the right reasons. I quote the passage, as it is worth remembering:—

[quotes from 'The Critic as Artist: Part One': 'Taken as a whole, the man was great' to 'He used poetry as a medium for writing in prose'].

Could this be surpassed, either in idea or in expression?

Nor does the British public recognise the sanity there is in Mr. Wilde's paradoxes. His demonstration of the insufficiency of the emotions as aids to culture-progress is as fine a piece of psychology as we would wish to see. From the intellect alone, he says, and truly, can cosmopolitanism come.

As long as war is regarded as wicked, it will always have its fascination. When it is looked upon as vulgar, it will cease to be popular. The change will, of course, be slow, and people will not be conscious of it. They will not say 'We will not war against France because her prose is perfect', but because the prose

[1] For the sake of honesty, I must say that this does not apply to Mr. Wilde's article on 'The Soul of Man under Socialism', in the *Fortnightly Review* of February, 1891. The article itself is at once sound and brilliant, and gives one of the noblest vindications of the dignity of Art that our literature contains. But with a few exceptions, the style is as jerky and snappy as Emerson's. The epigrams keep biting at us like the blades of a pair of scissors. [Newman's note.]

of France is perfect they will not hate the land. Intellectual criticism will bind Europe together in bonds far closer than those that can be forged by shopman or sentimentalist. It will give us the peace that springs from understanding.

Mr. Wilde's doctrine of art for art's sake is too well known to need expounding here at any length. I think all artists will go with him in his contention that art, as art, has nothing to do with morality or immorality. It is the function of art to present the beauty of things, just as it is the function of science to present the truth of things; and no matter what may be the subject of the artist, he is as much above all considerations of ethics as the scientist is. He simply presents truth under a beautiful investiture. One never thinks of railing against Krafft-Ebing, for example, for diagnosing the sexual instinct in science, and no artist would think of railing against Flaubert or Maupassant for diagnosing the same instinct in art. 'One might as well speak disrespectfully of the equator.'

'Morbid,' says Mr. Wilde in 'The Soul of Man under Socialism', 'is, of course, a ridiculous word to apply to a work of art. For what is morbidity but a mood of emotion or a mode of thought that one cannot express? The public are all morbid, because the public can never find expression for anything. *The artist is never morbid. He expresses everything.* He stands outside his subject, and through its medium produces incomparable and artistic effects. To call an artist morbid because he deals with morbidity as his subject matter is as silly as if one called Shakspere mad because he wrote *King Lear*.'

The artist, equally with the scientist, sits with Spinoza's Infinite Intelligence, above the world of good and evil. The Philistine rails at many a realist for his temerity in treating of morbidity and sexuality in art. In reality the only thing to be said on the matter is that the realist is justified in taking up any subject that he can treat artistically, and that where he is offensive it is not because he is immoral, but because he is inartistic.

It goes without saying that Mr. Wilde, holding ideas like these on art, is a Hedonist in the fullest sense of the word. There are still, I believe, sombre people in the world afflicted with Nonconformist consciences and knowing it not, who look upon the Hedonist as a rather immoral creature, and preach to us, in season and out of season, the doctrine of self-sacrifice and duty. That doctrine is well enough in its way, but I think that Hedonism is better. It is not the philosophy of pleasure that is truly selfish, but the philosophy of sacrifice. The easiest form of sympathy, as Mr. Wilde has said, is sympathy with pain: the higher form of sympathy with others' joys is infinitely harder to attain to. And it is easier to sympathise with suffering, he says, than to sympathise with thought. The dreary history of human persecution would not be such sad reading if men had unlearned a little of the ethic of sacrifice and learned something of the ethic of joy; men would not try to grind each other into one universal sameness if they had less of the insanity of emotion and more of the sanity of intellect, if they knew how to sympathise with the best and strongest life of a man, his individuality as expressed in his thought:

[quotes from 'The Soul of Man Under Socialism': 'All sympathy is fine, but sympathy with suffering is the least fine mode' to 'Man will have joy in the contemplation of the joyous lives of others']

I know that words like these will not appeal to the religious public— the most morbid of all publics—who darken their narrow souls with pictures of bleeding Christs and wounded saints and emaciated Madonnas, but they will have meaning for those who believe that the time for devil-worship is past, and that it is glorious to live light in the sun.

I have left myself no space in which to speak of Mr. Wilde's poetry. The Philistine again will not like it, for it is almost entirely concerned with beauty for beauty's sake, and has nothing to say on the social question, or the rights of women, or any other modern subject. Now and again, indeed, Mr. Wilde does wander into what we may call practical spheres, as in his poems on Liberty, the Bulgarian Massacres, Louis Napoleon, and Milton, but he is scarcely successful there. To do fine work he requires the stimulus of things removed from the actual life of men. He is an artist to his finger-tips, and the Philistine disturbs the air he breathes. 'By the Ilyssus there was no Higginbotham,' said Matthew Arnold; and the artist is bound to get as far away from Higginbotham as he can. That Mr. Wilde's poems are about nothing at all but beauty, that they do not prove anything, and do not lend themselves to quotation in the hymn-books of the Independent Labor Party, can scarcely be urged as a crime against them. So many people love beauty, as so many people take up religion, for reasons quite unconnected with either, that we must needs be grateful to anyone who can love beauty for herself alone. And if it be urged that Mr. Wilde's passion is mainly for sensuous beauty, that objection also has not much weight with those who consider how rare in the modern world is a proper cultivation of the senses. Even Ibsen exhorts us occasionally to look after the joy of living, and a greater than Ibsen is here. Are we not weary of dull respectability? We would gladly go roystering in the company of Master François Villon, rogue as he was, and nearly as he escaped hanging; and sooner than breathe the atmosphere of the Conventicle we would pass by on the other side. It is fitting that the narrow-souled joyless ascetics who placed their icy hand on science should now distinguish themselves by attempting to murder art; but they will hardly succeed. The joy of living here is better than the contemplation of distant heavens which we will never live to be sarcastic at. And after all, there are more things in earth and the other place than are dreamt of in the Philistine's philosophy.

THE BALLAD OF READING GAOL

13 February 1898

---

78. Unsigned review, *Academy*

26 February 1898, liii, 236

Four brief passages, which the reviewer uses to illustrate how Wilde develops the narrative, have been omitted (indicated by ellipses).

Its subject matter is simple. A soldier is in gaol under sentence of death for murder. One of his fellow prisoners records the effect upon himself on learning the soldier's fate, his growing horror as the morning of execution draws near, the terrors of the night immediately preceding it, and the emotions that follow. The document is authentic: hence its worth. The poem is not great, is not entirely trustworthy; but in so far as it is the faithful record of experiences through which the writer —C.3.3.—has passed, it is good literature. According to its sincerity so is it valuable: where the author goes afield and becomes philosophic and self-conscious and inventive he forfeits our interests; but so long as he honestly reproduces emotion he holds it. To feel and chronicle sensations is his peculiar gift: in the present work, at any rate, he is not a thinker. Nor should he have attempted humour. Such a stanza as this is not the way in which to depict the horrors of hanging:

> It is sweet to dance to violins
> When Love and Life are fair:
> To dance to flutes, to dance to lutes,
> Is delicate and rare:
> But it is not sweet with nimble feet
> To dance upon the air!

From the 109 stanzas we would indeed like to remove some fifty; yet take it for all in all the ballad as it stands is a remarkable addition to contemporary poetry. . . .

> I never saw sad men who looked
> With such a wistful eye
> Upon that little tent of blue
> We prisoners called the sky,
> And at every happy cloud that passed
> In such strange freedom by.

That is a good stanza; but its excellence has been a snare to its author. Previously in the ballad he uses it twice with slight alterations, in both cases in describing the condemned man. Surely it is a mistake to apply the same words both to a prisoner on the bottom step of the scaffold and to his comrades just losing the terror caused by his death. This is one of the historian's occasional lapses into invention. He is not as whole-souled a battler for truth as he should be, and when he falls back on his imagination he is not well enough served. Truth (if they only knew it) is the best friend that non-creative writers have.

To continue, the description of the exercise in the yard is the occasion for these biting lines:

> The warders strutted up and down,
> And watched their herd of brutes,
> Their uniforms were spick and span,
> And they wore their Sunday suits;
> But we knew the work they had been at
> By the quicklime on their boots.

Finally, let us quote this picture of what life in prison means to a sensitive nature—one of the passages which make the poem notable:

> With midnight always in one's heart,
> And twilight in one's cell,
> We turn the crank, or tear the rope,
> Each in his separate Hell,
> And the silence is more awful far
> Than the sound of a brazen bell.

> And never a human voice comes near
> To speak a gentle word:
> And the eye that watches through the door
> Is pitiless and hard:
> And by all forgot, we rot and rot,
> With soul and body marred.

And thus we rust Life's iron chain
Degraded and alone:
And some men curse, and some men weep,
And some men make no moan:
But God's eternal Laws are kind
And break the heart of stone.

These extracts should be sufficient to assist any reader to a decision
whether to buy the book and read more or to rest content. They have
also probably recalled the author's poetical model; but if not, we might
point out that it is, of course, Hood's 'Dream of Eugene Aram'. The
intensity to which both poets—both Hood and C.3.3.—occasionally
attain proves the fitness of this metre for such a subject. Curiously
enough, the new ballad is, to some extent, supplemental of the older
one: 'The Dream of Eugene Aram' is the record of a murderer's own
emotions and impulses; *The Ballad of Reading Gaol* shows us the emotions and impulses excited in his companions by a murderer doomed to
die and dying. Hood's work is, we think, the finer of the two: it has
more concentration, its author had more nervous strength, was a more
dexterous master of words, was superior to morbidity and hysteria;
yet pruned of its extraneous stanzas the new ballad is a worthy companion to its exemplar.

79. W. E. Henley on
The Ballad of Reading Gaol

1898

Unsigned review, titled 'De Profundis', in the *Outlook* (5 March 1898), i, 146.

Henley's slashing review—with its ambiguous, tasteless final sentence—particularly distressed Wilde, who wrote to Leonard Smithers, publisher of the *Ballad*, 'I have read *Henley*—it is very coarse and vulgar, and entirely lacking in literary or gentlemanly instinct. He is so proud of having written *vers libres* on his scrofula [*In Hospital*, 1888] that he is quite jealous if a poet writes a lyric on his prison.' (*Letters*, p. 712.)

This elaborate appeal from the deeps to a vain yet reasonable world is the oddest jumble: of truth and falsehood, of sincerity and affectation, of excellence and rubbish, of stuff that moves and stuff that bores, and worse. A descant on the emotions of C. 3.3 and others on the occasion of a death by the rope in the gaol wherein they were immured, it is a piece of realism, yet it reeks with traditional phrases and effects. It states the fact with gloom, that everybody is engaged in killing the thing he loves:—

> The coward does it with a kiss,
> The brave man with a sword:

yet it seems to approve, and it pleads passionately against the penalising of such excesses in emotion. In style it reminds you now of Mr. Kipling, now of 'Eugene Aram', now of 'The Antient Mariner', now of the Border ballads, now of passionate Brompton and aesthetic Chelsea. In matter, it is a patchwork of what is and what is not. Here it is instinct and vigorous with veracity; there it is flushed and stertorous with sentimentalism. It is carefully written and elaborately designed; yet is it full fifty stanzas too long, and it is laced with such futilities as 'whisper *low*' and '*empty* space'. It is a thing of modern life, and at least a part of it

is *vécue*;[1] yet you dance to 'flutes' and you dance to 'lutes' (Ha! Old
Truepenny!), and in one stanza you make as free with Christ as Mr.
Robert Buchanan ever did, and in another:—

> The warders stripped him of his clothes
>   And gave him to the flies;
> They marked the swollen, purple throat
>   And the stark and staring eyes,
> And with laughter loud they heaped the shroud
>   In which the convict lies.

Is the detail convincing? Who reads that can think it is? Is that 'swol-
len, purple throat' observed? It does not seem so—by the sequel. And
what is a 'stark' eye? And how does the writer know that the warders
trampled down the poor devil's grave 'with laughter loud'? He wasn't
at the trampling, evidently; for he and his fellows were carefully se-
cluded till the horrid job was done:—

> But we knew the work they had been at
>   By the quicklime on their boots.

Without pretending to *expertise* in such matters, one may hazard the
presumption that quicklime, being fully as destructive of leather as it
is of flesh and bone, the warders, their work once done, would have
carefully wiped their boots; so that, in the absence of complete information, this detail is not less *suspect* than certain others.

That, in fact, is the chief defect of the Poem: you do not always
know when the Poet is 'putting it on'. Take the first stanza, and you
get a taste of unveracity which fouls your mind all through your reading of his work:—

> He did not wear his scarlet coat,
>   *For* blood and wine are red,
> And blood and wine were on his hands
>   When they found him with the dead,
> The poor dead woman whom he loved
>   And murdered in her bed.

The Convict whose passing is celebrated in these verses was, in effect,
a guardsman; but that he should not have worn his uniform *because*
blood is red, and wine is red, and his coat also was red, is surely what the
lettered Partridge called a *non sequitur*. Again, are privates in the Guards
in the habit of spreeing on burgundy and port, or even Tintara and

[1] True to life.

Cape? 'His hands were wet with beer and blood' would have made as good a line as C. 3.3 has made, and would have prepossessed the readers of C. 3.3 in the favour of C. 3.3 as a veridical person much more strongly than his own can ever do. But nobody is all at once a realist; nobody all at once can tell the truth; and, in this respect, C. 3.3 is no better gifted than the most of men. His whole description of the night before the Guardsman's execution is a proof of it. It is sentimental slush—writing for the writing's sake; stuff done on the assumption that 'He who lives more lives than one, more deaths than one must die', is not peculiar to one exceptional convict, but is common to the herd of lags in which he is merged. None who reads it can believe in any word of it. It is a blunder in taste, in sentiment, in art; for it is a misstatement of fact. If C. 3.3 had been no Minor Poet, but an Artist—!

Yet, having dissented thus, one is pleased to note that sincerity, veracity, vision even, have their part in this mixty-maxty of differences. Suppress the Poet's first stanza, for example, with its impossible welter of blood and wine and the Widow's pink, and what could be better, simpler, more natural and effective than the two that follow at its heel?—

> He walked among the Trial Men
> In a suit of shabby grey:
> A cricket cap was on his head,
> And his step seemed light and gay.
> But I never saw a man who looked
> So wistfully at the day.
>
> I never saw a man who looked
> With such a wistful eye
> Upon the little tent of blue,
> Which prisoners call the sky,
> And at every drifting cloud that went
> With sails of silver by.

Thus should the ballad have begun! Or take this stanza, which drops, as by accident, into a bog of such excited nonsense as even the *Vaillants de Mille-Huit-Cent-Trente* would have blushed to recognise in after years:—

> At last I saw the shadowed bars,
> Like a lattice wrought in lead,
> Move right across the whitewashed wall
> That faced my three-plank bed,
> And I knew that somewhere in the world
> God's awful dawn was red.

It is a little stagily expressed, perhaps. But it is observed: it has been lived; you see it as you read. And there are not a few passages in the ballad which might be quoted to much the same purpose.

But the trail of the Minor Poet is over it all. And when the Minor Poet is at rest, then wakes the Pamphleteer. What C. 3.3 has to say about our prison system is—apart from his references to Christ, and red and white roses, and 'Tannhäuser', and quicklime, and the like— worth heeding. Or would be, *if it were true*. But is it? 'Tis not for us to say. But if it be, let C. 3.3. at once proceed to sink the Minor in the Pamphleteer, and make his name honoured among men.

80. Arthur Symons on
The Ballad of Reading Gaol

1898

Signed review, *Saturday Review* (12 March 1898), lxxxv, 365–6; reprinted, in revised form, in *A Study of Oscar Wilde* (1930).

Wishing to assist Wilde after his release from prison, Symons wrote to Leonard Smithers: 'I see by your advertisement in the *Athenaeum* that you are publishing Wilde's poem. I need scarcely say that if I could do anything that would be of service to Wilde, now that he is making his first attempt to return to literature, I should be only too glad to do it' (quoted in *The Oscar Wilde Collection of John B. Stetson, Jr.*, catalogue of Mitchell Kennerly, dealer and publisher, New York, 1920). When the review appeared, Wilde, writing to Smithers, expressed his delight: '. . . it is admirably written, and most . . . artistic in its mode of approval'. (*Letters*, p. 716.)

The Ballad of Reading Gaol is written in that ballad stanza of six lines which Hood used for 'The Dream of Eugene Aram'; and the accident of two poems about a murderer having been written in the same metre has suggested comparisons which are only interesting by way of contrast. 'Eugene Aram' is a purely romantic poem; *The Ballad of Reading Gaol* aims at being a realistic poem. It may more properly be compared with Mr. Henley's 'In Hospital', where a personal experience, and personally observed surroundings, are put into verse as directly, and with as much precise detail, as possible. Taken merely as sensation recorded, this new poem is as convincing, holds you as tightly, as Mr. Henley's; and it has, in places, touches at least as finely imaginative; this, for instance:

> We have little care of prison fare,
>   For what chills and kills outright
> Is that every stone one lifts by day
>   Becomes one's heart by night.

218

But, unlike Mr. Henley's, it has not found a new form for the record of these sensations, so new to poetry; it has not entirely escaped 'poetic diction' in its language, and it has accepted what has now become the artificial structure of the ballad, without making any particular effort to use the special advantages of that structure. But then this is just because a romantic artist is working on realistic material; and the curious interest of the poem comes from the struggle between form and utterance, between personal and dramatic feeling, between a genuine human emotion and a style formed on other lines, and startled at finding itself used for such new purposes.

We see a great spectacular intellect, to which, at last, pity and terror have come in their own person, and no longer as puppets in a play. In its sight, human life has always been something acted on the stage; a comedy in which it is the wise man's part to sit aside and laugh, but in which he may also disdainfully take part, as in a carnival, under any mask. The unbiassed, scornful intellect, to which humanity has never been a burden, comes now to be unable to sit aside and laugh, and it has worn and looked behind so many masks that there is nothing left desirable in illusion. Having seen, as the artist sees, further than morality, but with so partial an eyesight as to have overlooked it on the way, it has come at length to discover morality, in the only way left possible, for itself. And, like most of those who, having 'thought themselves weary', have made the adventure of putting thought into action, it has had to discover it sorrowfully, at its own incalculable expense. And now, having so newly become acquainted with what is pitiful, and what seems most unjust, in the arrangement of mortal affairs, it has gone, not unnaturally, to an extreme, and taken, on the one hand, humanitarianism, on the other realism, at more than their just valuation in matters of art. It is that old instinct of the intellect; the necessity to carry things to their furthest point of development, to be more logical than either life or art, two very wayward and illogical things, in which conclusions do not always follow from premises.

This poem, then, is partly a plea on behalf of prison reform; and, so far as it is written with that aim, it is not art. It is also to some extent an endeavour to do in poetry what can only be done in prose; and thus such intensely impressive touches as the quicklime which the prisoners see on the boots of the warders who have been digging the hanged man's grave, the 'gardener's gloves' of the hangman, and his 'little bag', are, strictly speaking, fine prose, not poetry. But, it must not be forgotten, all these things go to the making of a piece of work, in which, beyond its purely literary quality, there is a real value of a personal kind—the value of almost raw fact, the value of the document. And here too begins to come in, in an odd, twisted way, the literary quality. For the poem is not really a ballad at all, but a sombre, angry, interrupted reverie; and it is the subcurrent of meditation, it is the asides, which count, not the story, as a story, of the drunken soldier who was hanged for killing a woman. The real drama is the drama of that one of 'the souls in pain' who tramp round the prison-yard, to whom the hanging of a man meant most,—

> For he who lives more lives than one
> More deaths than one must die.

It is because they are seen through his at once grieved and self-pitying consciousness that all those sorry details become significant,—

> We tore the tarry rope to shreds
> With blunt and bleeding nails;
> We rubbed the doors, and scrubbed the floors,
> And cleaned the shining rails:
> And, rank by rank, we soaped the plank,
> And clattered with the pails.

And the glimmerings of romance which come into these pages, like the flowers which may not grow out of the dead man's body as he lies under the asphalte of the prison-yard, are significant because they show us the persistence with which temperament will assert itself:

> It is sweet to dance to violins
> When Love and Life are fair:
> To dance to flutes, to dance to lutes,
> Is delicate and rare:
> But it is not sweet with nimble feet
> To dance upon the air!

Beauty, one sees, claiming its own in a story meant to be so sordid, so veracious, so prosaically close to fact; and having, indeed, so many of the qualities at which it aims.

And there is also something else in the poem: a central idea, half, but not more than half, a paradox,—

> And all men kill the thing they love,
> By all let this be heard,
> Some do it with a bitter look,
> Some with a flattering word,
> The coward does it with a kiss,
> The brave man with a sword!

This symbol of the obscure deaths of the heart, the unseen violence upon souls, the martyrdom of hope, trust and all the more helpless among the virtues, is what gives its unity, in a certain philosophic purpose, to a poem not otherwise quite homogeneous. Ideas were never what the writer of this poem was lacking in; but an idea so simple and so human, developed out of circumstances so actual, so close to the earth, is singularly novel. And, whatever we may think of the positive value of this very powerful piece of writing, there can be no doubt as to its relative value in a career which may now be at a turning-point.

Literature, to be of the finest quality, must come from the heart as well as the head, must be emotionally human as well as a brilliant thinking about human problems. And, for this writer, such a return, or so startling a first acquaintance with real things, was precisely what was required to bring into relation, both with life and art, an extraordinary talent, so little in relation with matters of common experience, so fantastically alone in a region of intellectual abstractions.

81. Comment, *Pall Mall Gazette*

19 March 1898, p. 4.

Comment in 'Literary Notes', signed by 'S.G.', whose identity has not been determined.

The most remarkable poem that has appeared this year is, of course, *The Ballad of Reading Gaol*. It has been much written about, but no one has commented, so far as I know, on the curious parallel between it and Mr. Kipling's 'Danny Deever', the grim lyric which stands first in *Barrack Room Ballads*. The difference is just this: 'Danny Deever'— ugly if you like, but a real poem—is a conspicuously manly piece of work; *The Ballad of Reading Gaol*, with all its feverish energy, is unmanly. The central emotion in the poem is the physical horror of death, when death comes, not as a relief or in a whirl of excitement, but as an abrupt shock to be dreaded. That the emotion is genuine admits of no doubt; but it is one very fit to be concealed. The writer's dread of anything that pains the body extends even after death; again and again he insists on the horror of burial in quicklime, the soft fibres of flesh being lapped about in 'a sheet of living flame'. If we were to judge poems by the test that Plato proposes—whether they will tend to strengthen or to enervate—we should put this poem very low indeed. Yet it has beautiful work in it, and touches of a genuine and honourable sympathy for the sorrow of weak things suffering.

82. Unsigned review, *Critic* [New York]

June 1899, xxxiv, 561–2

At the head of several reviews in the *Critic*, the author of *The Ballad of Reading Gaol* is given as 'C. 3.3 (Oscar Wilde)', but Wilde's name is avoided in the review.

If history repeats itself, so, likewise, does fable. Whatever else is to be said of this *Ballad of Reading Gaol*, it must be premised that none will fail to remark how the revisiting shade of immortal Glamour falls athwart every page of the poem under consideration. Grant that the 'Ancient Mariner,' coming off enchanted seas, in a subsequent career by land managed to get himself committed to an English prison, this is the tale of horrors wherewith he would have detained the wedding guest! No element that actual experience and accomplished art can contribute is here wanting to convey to the reader the bitterness of the situation, whether physically or spiritually considered,—the hardships and tedium to the flesh, the loathing and torment to the soul. The changing moods of pity, astonishment, infectious terror, dull apathy, that by turns lay hold of the prisoners, as they watch, day by day, the man who is doomed to 'swing' are vividly given; the quiet portraiture of the doomed man himself will not leave our mental vision:

> I never saw a man who looked
>   With such a wistful eye
> Upon that little tent of blue
>   Which prisoners call the sky.

We are made to see all the sordid details of prison drudgery in the unsparing record of the participant:

> We tore the tarry rope to shreds
>   With blunt and bleeding nails;
> We rubbed the doors, and scrubbed the floors,
>   And cleaned the shining rails;
> And, rank by rank, we soaped the plank,
>   And clattered with the pails.

Horror is added to horror in the minds of these onlookers during the three weeks that elapse before the execution of the murderer's sentence, —three weeks of a restless and terrible vigil of soul, which can have its parallel only in the realized agony of the ancient prophecy: 'In the morning thou shalt say, Would God it were even! And at even thou shalt say, Would God it were morning!' The dawn of the fatal day which fulfils the vengeance of law, brings a 'ghostly rout' of evil spirits, —the passage describing this phantomy visitation being curiously blent of 'Ancient Mariner' necromancy and of the unwinsome remnants of a faded aestheticism, which latter is fairly indicated in the stanza:

> They glided past, they glided fast,
>   Like travellers through a mist:
> They mocked the moon in a rigadoon
>   Of delicate turn and twist,
> And with formal pace and loathsome grace
>   The phantoms kept their tryst.

The reader would fain escape the realism of phrase and picture that brings before him the consummation of the death-penalty; and, likewise, much of mortuary horror following this event, he might sanely demand to be spared. But this is not to be. The iron has entered the soul of the spectator of these scenes, and, like the hapless *raconteur* in the Rime of Coleridge, nothing would seem to assuage the torments of memory save divulgation of its stern secrets. The reader who happens to possess the subconsciousness of the artist (who necessarily in greater or less degree assumes vicariously the roles he describes),—the reader alone will understand the full force of the asseveration contained in the following stanza:

And all the woe that moved him so
That he gave that bitter cry,
And the wild regrets and the bloody sweats,
None knew so well as I:
For he who lives more lives than one
More deaths than one must die.

The present reviewer has naught to do with that element of personal interest which the publishers of this volume have evidently counted upon; nor may the reviewer indulge in deductions as to the motive or the spirit in which the poem was written. The 'smoking flax' and the 'bruised reed,' never disregarded by Divine Compassion, would seem to be indicated.

And every human heart that breaks
In prison-cell or yard
Is at that broken box that gave
Its treasure to the Lord,
And filled the unclean leper's house
With the scent of costliest nard.

Nor would we question the poetic craftsmanship which everywhere characterizes the *Ballad of Reading Gaol*. Our objection should rather be based upon the unavoidable fact that the poem is a congeries of morbid descriptions, whose only wholesome purpose could possibly be to warn of 'the iron gin that waits for Sin.' We own, however, to being not a little puzzled as to the conclusion intended to be drawn in the last two stanzas. Is it, that the homicide who suffered in Reading Gaol was no more death-worthy, though with actual blood upon his hands, than are the thousands who do not thus suffer, although they (*morally* speaking) may 'kill the thing they love'?

ON THE OCCASION OF WILDE'S DEATH

30 November 1900

83. Unsigned obituary notice, *New York Times*

1 December 1900, p. 1

Unlike the relatively brief notice discreetly presented in the London *Times* in second position (Count Yorck von Wartenburg, a German army officer, precedes Wilde) under 'Obituary', the *New York Times* ran a front-page, full-length column with a major heading—'Death of Oscar Wilde'—and two sub-heads— 'He Expires at an Obscure Hotel in the Latin Quarter of Paris' and 'Is Said to Have Died from Meningitis, but There is a Rumor that He Committed Suicide'. The following excerpts evaluate Wilde as a writer. Two errors are apparent: *Dorian Gray* first appeared in 1890, not 1895; and *Intentions* appeared in 1891, not 1894.

. . . The most popular of Wilde's books was *The Picture of Dorian Gray*, which has had an immense sale, both in the United Kingdom and this country. It appeared first in *Lippincott's Magazine*, in 1895, and was afterward issued in book form, with considerable additions, by Ward, Lock and Company. After the famous trial the London publishers withdrew it from circulation, although inundated with orders for copies.

Among literary people *Intentions*, published in 1894, is regarded as Wilde's finest prose work. It is a collection of essays, and, though full of the author's favorite paradoxes, contains much art criticism which shows evidence of careful thought. Some of the essays, notably 'The

225

Decay of Lying and 'The Critic as Artist,' had previously appeared in English reviews and had attracted a good deal of attention.

Wilde's poems were first published in 1881, and a new edition was issued at the Bodley Head about ten years later. Both editions were exhausted a very short time after publication. Many isolated stanzas and lines have been quoted to show that, had he possessed the necessary perseverance and steadfastness of character, Wilde could have been one of the great poets of the nineteenth century. Many persons have also noticed the remarkable forecast of his own life which the author wrote in the dedication to this volume of verse and the passionate regret there expressed that he had not used his gifts to better purpose. . . .

After Wilde's release from prison a poem was published anonymously, entitled *A Ballad of Reading Jail* [*sic*]. It created a great deal of interest and favorable criticism, and is now known to have been written by Wilde.

Wilde was spoken of as an aspiring dramatist long before any piece signed by his name was acted. His *Salome* was cast in the dramatic form, and *Guido Ferranti*, a tragic piece briefly acted here by Lawrence Barrett, was reputed to be his work. There was a certain lyrical quality in some of its passages which credited this report. His first acknowledged play, however, was *Lady Windermere's Fan*, produced by George Alexander at the St. James's Theatre, in London, in 1893, and acted here soon afterward at Wallack's without setting the town ablaze. There was much verbal smartness in this piece, and it was no strong accusation against its merit to say that its plot was antique and its stagecraft insufficient. But its insincerity and diffusiveness were not to be denied. After the first performance in London, Wilde appeared on the stage of the St. James's smoking a cigarette, and responded to a 'call' that was not altogether friendly with imperturbable good humor and assurance. This served its purpose in giving the piece a unique advertisement.

His next play, *A Woman of No Importance*, was acted first at the London Haymarket, under Beerbohm Tree's direction, and in New York, at the Fifth Avenue Theatre, with Rose Coghlan in the principal role. It was, indeed, a play of no importance, and Miss Coghlan wisely employed her famous brother Charles to patch it up and lend it some sort of theatrical value. *The Importance of Being Earnest*, frankly a farce and full of nimble wit, on the other hand, missed a long run at the Empire Theatre because it was too dainty and fragile to suit the taste and understanding of the ordinary theatregoer, and *An Ideal Husband*, admirably acted by Daniel Frohman's company at the Lyceum, while it made no one's fortune and lacked vigorous dramatic spirit, was a clever piece of work which aroused the critical admiration of W. D. Howells. . . .

As a dramatist, Wilde was hampered by his utter lack of sincerity and his inability to master the technical side of playwriting. But his wit, his pleasing literary facility, and his droll views of life made some of his plays rather effective with a limited audience. . . .

84. Unsigned obituary notice, *The Times*

1 December 1900, p. 8

A Reuter telegram from Paris states that Oscar Wilde died there yesterday afternoon from meningitis. The melancholy end to a career which once promised so well is stated to have come in an obscure hotel of the Latin Quarter. Here the once brilliant man of letters was living, exiled from his country and from the society of his countrymen. The verdict that a jury passed upon his conduct at the Old Bailey in May 1895, destroyed for ever his reputation, and condemned him to ignoble obscurity for the remainder of his days. When he had served his sentence of two years' imprisonment, he was broken in health as well as bankrupt in fame and fortune. Death has soon ended what must have been a life of wretchedness and unavailing regret. Wilde was the son of the late Sir William Wilde, an eminent Irish surgeon. His mother was a graceful writer, both in prose and verse. He had a brilliant career at Oxford, where he took a first-class both in classical moderations and in *Lit. Hum.*, and also won the Newdigate Prize for English verse for a poem on Ravenna. Even before he left the University in 1878 Wilde had become known as one of the most affected of the professors of the aesthetic craze and for several years it was as the typical aesthete that he kept himself before the notice of the public. At the same time he was a man of far greater originality and power of mind than many of the apostles of aestheticism. As his Oxford career showed, he had undoubted talents in many directions, talents which might have been brought to fruition had it not been for his craving after notoriety. He was known as a poet of graceful diction; as an essayist of wit and distinction; later on as a playwright of skill and subtle humour. A novel of his, *The Picture of Dorian Gray*, attracted much attention, and his sayings passed from mouth to mouth as those of one of the professed wits of the age. When he became a dramatist his plays had all the characteristics of his conversation. His first piece, *Lady Windermere's Fan*, was produced in 1892. *A Woman of no Importance* followed in 1893. *An Ideal Husband* and *The Importance of Being Earnest* were both running at the time of their author's disappearance from English life. All these pieces had the same qualities—a paradoxical humour and a perverted outlook on life being the most prominent. They were packed with witty sayings, and the author's cleverness gave him at once a position in the dramatic world. The revelations of the criminal trial in 1895 naturally made them impossible for some years. Recently, however, one of them was revived, though not at a West-end theatre. After his release in 1897, Wilde published *The Ballad of Reading Gaol*, a poem of considerable but unequal power. He also appeared in print as a critic of our prison system, against the results of which he entered a passionate protest. For the last three years he has lived abroad. . . .

85. Unsigned obituary notice, *Pall Mall Gazette*

1 December 1900, p. 2

In response to the stunning miscalculation and misappraisal of
Wilde's achievement and future reputation in this unsigned notice,
the *Pall Mall Gazette* published a letter from 'A Fellow-Student'
on 5 December, p. 11, which begins: 'I am surprised to see one of
your clever young men indulging in a cheap sneer at the work of
Oscar Wilde.' After defending *Lady Windermere's Fan* and the
Ballad of Reading Gaol (which the writer of the notice had damned
with faint praise), the letter concludes: 'That the stage suffered a
loss in the tragic eclipse of this man's genius cannot be doubted.'

The tragedy of Mr. Oscar Wilde's life is ended. The labouring of moralities would be quite superfluous, but a word or two may be said upon the
sum of his achievement. Mr. Wilde led a movement in the eighties,
which, in spite of its absurdities, killed much vulgar Philistinism. He
took up the aesthetic fashion rather than made it; for its beginnings are
to be found in the paintings of Rossetti and Burne-Jones, the art work
of William Morris, and the writings of Pater. Mr. Whistler's well-
known gibe when he met Mr. Du Maurier and Mr. Wilde together,
'Which of you invented the other?' was not a historical definition
exactly. The Irishman's attacks on social conventions recalls, in other
respects, that of Disraeli the Younger, though he was a much smaller
man. He was audacious in costume, and succeeded through an elaboration of wit. 'I felt disappointed with the Atlantic' will probably remain
the most easily remembered saying of Mr. Wilde's. He made many
better jests; but they depended for their point on circumstance, and
were frequently humorous inversions of the commonplace.

Mr. Wilde had wonderful cleverness, but no substantiality. His plays
were full of bright moments, but devoid of consideration as drama. The
only one of them which showed traces of constructive capacity,
Lady Windermere's Fan, owed its central idea to Mr. Haddon Chambers.

He was content, for the most part, that his characters should sit about and talk paradoxes. Mr. Charles Brookfield's nigger-minstrel scene in 'The Poet and the Puppets' was most legitimate parody. And what can be said of *The Ballad of Reading Gaol* except that it consisted in an adroit *pastiche*? Mr. Wilde's gifts included supreme intellectual ability, but nothing that he ever wrote had strength to endure. Of his apes the less said the better. His most useful influence was as a corrective to British stolidity, but it was too diffuse to be worth much even at that.

86. Max Beerbohm on Wilde as a dramatist

1900

Comment signed 'Max', *Saturday Review* (8 December 1900), XC, 720.

Beerbohm, in one of his surveys of current London plays, here departs from usual practice by devoting a substantial portion of his article to an estimate of Wilde as a dramatist on the occasion of his friend's death, pointing out the essential limitation of Wilde's gifts—that he was not 'a born writer'. Surprisingly, Beerbohm does not grant supreme importance to Wilde's last play.

The death of Mr. Oscar Wilde extinguishes a hope that the broken series of his plays might be resumed. The hope was never, indeed, very strong. Despite the number of his books and plays, Mr. Wilde was not, I think, what one calls a born writer. His writing seemed always to be rather an overflow of intellectual and temperamental energy than an inevitable, absorbing function. That he never concentrated himself on any one form of literature is a proof that the art of writing never really took hold of him. He experimented in all forms, his natural genius winning for him, lightly, in every one of them, the success which for most men is won only by a reverent concentration. His native energy having been sapped by a long term of imprisonment, the chance that he would write again was very small. His main motive for writing was lost. He would not, as would the born writer, be likely to find consolation in his art. *The Ballad of Reading Gaol*, though it showed that he had not lost his power of writing, was no presage of industry. Obviously, it was written by him with a definite external purpose, not from mere love and necessity of writing. Still, while he lived, there was always the off-chance that he might again essay that art-form which had been the latest to attract him. Somehow, the theatre seems to be fraught with a unique fascination. Modern dramaturgy is the most difficult of the arts, and its rewards (I do not mean its really commercial rewards) seem to be proportionate to its difficulties. To it, but for his downfall, even Mr. Wilde might have devoted himself. But for his death, he might possibly have returned to it. And thus his death is, in a lesser degree than his downfall, a great loss to the drama of our day. His work was distinct from that of most other playwrights in that he was a man who had achieved success outside the theatre. He was not a mere maker of plays. Taking up dramaturgy when he was no longer a young man, taking it up as a kind of afterthought, he brought to it a knowledge of the world which the life-long playwright seldom posses-ses. But this was only one point in his advantage. He came as a thinker, a weaver of ideas, and as a wit, and as the master of a literary style. It was, I think, in respect of literary style that his plays were most remarkable. In his books this style was perhaps rather too facile, too rhetorical in its grace. Walter Pater, in one of his few book-reviews,[1] said that in Mr. Wilde's work there was always 'the quality of the good talker.' This seems to me a very acute criticism. Mr. Wilde's writing suffered by too close a likeness to the flow of speech. But it was this very likeness that gave him in dramatic dialogue as great an advantage over more careful and finer literary stylists as he had over ordinary playwrights with no pretence to style. The dialogue in his plays struck the right mean between literary style and ordinary talk. It was at once beautiful and natural, as dialogue should always be. With this and other advantages, he brought to dramaturgy as keen a sense for the theatre as was possessed by any of his rivals, except Mr. Pinero. Theatrical construction, sense of theatrical effects, were his by instinct. I notice that one of the newspapers says that his plays were 'devoid of consideration as drama,' and sug-gests that he had little or no talent for construction[2] Such criticism as

---

[1] See No. 25, Pater's review of *The Picture of Dorian Gray*.
[2] The obituary notice in the *Pall Mall Gazette* (No. 85).

this merely shows that what Ben Jonson called 'the dull ass's hoof' must have its backward fling. In point of fact, Mr. Wilde's instinct for construction was so strong as to be a disadvantage. The very ease of his manipulation tempted him to trickiness, tempted him to accept current conventions which, if he had had to puzzle things out laboriously and haltingly, he would surely have discarded, finding for himself a simpler and more honest technique. His three serious comedies were marred by staginess. In *An Ideal Husband* the staginess was most apparent, least so in *A Woman of No Importance*. In the latter play, Mr. Wilde allowed the psychological idea to work itself out almost unmolested, and the play was, in my opinion, by far the most truly dramatic of his plays. It was along these lines that we, in the early 'nineties, hoped Mr. Wilde would ultimately work. But, even if he had confined his genius to the glorification of conventional drama, we should have had much reason to be grateful to him. His conventional comedies were as superior to the conventional comedies of other men as was *The Importance of Being Earnest* to the everyday farces whose scheme was so frankly accepted in it. At the moment of Mr. Wilde's downfall, it was natural that the public sentiment should be one of repulsion. But later, when he was released from prison, they remembered that he had at least suffered the full penalty. And now that he is dead, they will realise also, fully, what was for them involved in his downfall, how lamentable the loss to dramatic literature.

87. J. T. Grein on Wilde as a dramatist

1900

Signed article in the *Sunday Special*, 9 and 16 December 1900; reprinted in *Dramatic Criticism: 1900–1*, iii, (1902), pp. 79–83.

Jacob Thomas Grein (1862–1935), Dutch-born English critic on the *Sunday Times* and other newspapers and founder, in 1891, of the Independent Theatre (modelled on the Théâtre Libre in Paris), which presented such plays as Ibsen's *Ghosts* and Shaw's *Widowers' Houses*, rejected by the commercial theatres.

With the morals of the man I have nothing to do; I have to deal with the artist who has gone, for that artist has left his mark upon literature and upon the stage. He was, not so very long ago, one of the nimblest intellects the English world could boast of.

Oscar Wilde's legacy as essayist, fanciful story-teller, poet, and novelist, will probably be dealt with by others. I say probably, for the numerous band that used to consecrate *panem et circenses*[1] to him, and was only too glad to obtain leave to hold one of the multi-coloured streamers waving from his triumphal car,—that band had dwindled down to a few stray devotees, fair friends in bad weather. The rest have shunned the artist because the man had gone under. But I wish to speak here of the dramatist who raised such great hopes, who did so much in a short space of time, and then suddenly withered like a tree struck by lightning. Oscar Wilde has contributed but four plays to our stage, *Lady Windermere's Fan*, *A Woman of no Importance*, *An Ideal Husband*, and *The Importance of being Ernest*, while a fifth, *Salomé*, which was perhaps his best, was written in French and prohibited by the censor. These four plays all run more or less on the same lines. They are what one could call society plays, pictures of fashionable life in which an unmistakable air of reality is happily wedded to playful satire. Their greatest merit is their dialogue; the plot is of secondary importance, and the characterisation is such as one would expect from an observant man who has seen much

---

[1] Bread and circuses (Juvenal, *Satire X*, line 80).

233

and read more. In other words, Oscar Wilde did not dive very deeply below the surface of human nature, but found, to a certain extent rightly, that there is more on the surface of life than is seen by the eyes of most people—he believed as much in veneer as in deep, untarnishable colour. And, as in the drama veneer is likely to please, while depth of colour is often productive of dulness, he preferred to concentrate his acumen on the language rather than on the underlying humanity of his plays. In this he proved that he knew himself, for lightness of touch, not to say a certain flippancy, was a paramount feature of his gifted nature; and when he was all gaiety, sardonism, and persiflage, as in *The Importance of being Ernest*, he was happiest. The Aristophanic vein sparkled in it, and it is scarcely an exaggeration to say that this last English play of the unfortunate author was the wittiest comedy of the nineties.

II

If there was one thing in which Oscar Wilde took himself seriously, it was his reputation as a dramatist. He was not content that his plays were called witty, well-made, and intellectually above almost all the work of his fellow playwrights. It flattered him that Archer placed him on a different plane from all other English dramatic authors, 'a plane on which he stood alone,' but even that could not satisfy him. He made it clear to me one day that he considered himself the peer of Ibsen, and when, after the production of *Lady Windermere's Fan*, I described him as an English Sardou, he said contemptuously, 'The founder of the English Théâtre Libre calls *me* an English Sardou!'—thereby indicating that henceforth his confidence in me was radically shaken; while never again did he honour the Independent Theatre with his patronage or presence.

Yet, whatever may otherwise be the shortcomings of my verdicts, for this once I know I was absolutely right. Nor did I in any way intend to belittle the merits of our writer by comparing him to his great French colleague. I was not thinking of the Sardou of *Madame Sans-Gêne*, or even of *Fedora* or *Tosca*—the Sardou who prepares pieces for exportation as a Munich brewer doctors his lager beer to suit all climates. No, I was thinking of the Sardou who, in his time, was the prince of French comedy writers, when he gave the series that began with *La Famille Bonoiton*, continued with *Nos Intimes*, and untimely concluded with

Daniel Rochat and *Odette*. For, wittingly or unwittingly, Oscar Wilde worked on precisely the same lines as Sardou, and more than once was it said that, in construction, in mechanism, even in the mould of the dialogue—when it was dramatic and not merely epigrammatic—the French master had been slavishly copied. For all that the surname of the 'English Sardou' was by no means a sobriquet—it was a compliment, and not a luke-warm one. For in those days—they seeem to lie leagues behind us now—there was a great dearth of the kind of plays called in France *Comédies de Salon*. We had the fine amiable pictures of middle class life from the pen of Mr. Pinero, the somewhat heavier drawings of Mr. H. A. Jones, the melodramatic comedies of Mr. Haddon Chambers, and here and there the pretty Dickensiana of Mr. Carton. What we had not was the play of 'high life,' aristocratic in atmosphere, in conversation, with all the foibles and graces that belong to society. Then came *Lady Windermere's Fan*, interesting by its very surroundings, pathetic in parts, but never tearful, refined to a fault, witty to the degree of being too brilliant, different withal from every kind of play of native production. It had its weak sides, particularly that air of egotism, which was all the author's own, and which culminated in his appearance before the curtain with a dyed carnation in his buttonhole and a half-smoked cigarette in his hand. The affinity between the author and his work was unmistakable. Yet to all except those who were prejudiced against Oscar Wilde and his literary work, it seemed that a fresh breeze was wafting across the footlights, and quickly the seeds of the author's wit spread themselves over the town, so that before long there arose imitators galore.

III

Oscar Wilde had no time to enjoy the ripening of his talent—he has had followers but no disciples. Before he himself had definitely tested his strength and determined his path, came the catastrophe which brought his career to a full stop. *Salome* was his last play known to fame, and to say that Sarah Bernhardt had undertaken to bring it before London is to testify to the excellence of its dramatic fibre and the felicity of its poetry. To *Salome*, which some over here have read, Oscar Wilde owed his great reputation in the French capital, where his English plays were unknown. For *Salome*, gorgeous as the woman of its title, a poem full of charm, quivering with passion, the gates of the literary stronghold of the *Mercure de France* were opened to him, and if Sarah Bernhardt had shown more courage, she might, by the production of *Salome*, have paved the way towards a rehabilitation of the author. But after the scandal the actress was ashamed to be associated with the fallen star. *Salome* was produced at the Théâtre de L'Oeuvre, and the performance was not such as to gladden the author or add to his fame; but in book form the play was an unprecedented success, and perhaps some day, when the stain on the author's character has been whitened by time, the worthy production of *Salome* will render posthumous homage to the poet.

Salome was, so far as the stage is concerned, Oscar Wilde's swan-song, the beautiful *Ballad of Reading Gaol* was his adieu to the world of literature. With the career the man was broken, and with the man his spirit. From time to time his name cropped up in connection with our theatres. It was said that he had written plays which were to be produced under another name than his own. It was rumoured that such and such successful comedy labelled with a popular name was really the work of Oscar Wilde, but there was no evidence to confirm these rumours, and unless something is found among his papers, it may be said that the recent revival of *Lady Windermere's Fan* was the last that will be heard of Oscar Wilde as a dramatist. For already in this rapidly speeding age of ours, the vitality of his plays has been sapped. We have made progress, and that brilliant epigrammatic dialogue, which at the time startled us by its freshness, has become vulgarised, overdone, and is now almost antiquated.

Still it behoves us to remember the man upon whom the friends of our drama once built their rosiest hopes; and while he has died almost in oblivion, while the Press, which derived so much inspiration and so much amusement from him, dismisses his work and his existence with a couple of small printed lines, or none at all, it has been a pleasing task to pay here a small tribute to the artist.

88. Henry-D. Davray on Wilde's career

1901

Signed notice of Wilde's death in *Mercure de France* [Paris] (February 1901), xxvii, 558–61, from which the following excerpt is taken. The translation is by the editor of this volume.

Henry-D. Davray (1873–1944), French journalist, critic, and translator of many English authors, including Wilde, was on the staff of the *Mercure de France*, where he reviewed current English publications. In 1928, he published *Oscar Wilde: La Tragédie Finale*. He was one of the few who attended Wilde's funeral.

. . . The career of Oscar Wilde was brief, but, from its beginnings, success smiled on him and he quickly achieved a triumph. Some of his verse, his essays—*Intentions*—and other still unpublished works, his poems in prose, *The House of Pomegranates*, *The Picture of Dorian Gray*, had affirmed that he was a pure artist and a great writer, for certain of his pages are as beautiful as the most beautiful in English prose. But these works were only amusements for him, and his versatile mind, so brilliant, so delicately ironic, so paradoxical, found a medium of expression which perfectly suited his uncommon gifts; it was the theatre. Oscar Wilde held particularly to his reputation as a dramatist, and this with some reason. At the time of his successes, William Archer had placed him apart and above other contemporary authors; and Wilde believed himself to be unquestionably the equal of Ibsen. When he turned to the theatre, he concerned himself with a social class which had not yet been presented on stage. Pinero had achieved notoriety with plays drawn from middle-class life and a large number of others were producing popular dramas. With a perfect sense of the theatre, Oscar Wilde took his characters from high society; he set his elegant marionnetes in motion with such mastery that his comedies can be regarded as the wittiest that have been written in a very long time. When his career was so sadly and so tragically interrupted, Oscar Wilde had given the theatre five plays: *Lady Windermere's Fan*, *A Woman of no Importance*, *An*

Ideal Husband, *The Importance of Being Earnest* and *Salome*. Of the first four, which had a success without precedent, it must be said that they are constructed with extraordinary skill; they are interesting for their settings, pathetic without ever evoking tears, witty to the point of excess, and written in a pure literary language. *Salome*, which was never presented in London, and which the Théâtre de l'Oeuvre mounted deplorably in Paris, is especially a marvellous poem which has nothing in common with the modern pieces of the author.

When, after two years of suffering, Oscar Wilde was able to escape the jail where they had severely tortured him, he published a very beautiful poem: *The Ballad of Reading Gaol*, which gave the impression that he was again going to produce works worthy of his talents. But it was his swan song. . . .

89. J. T. Grein on
The Importance of Being Earnest

1901

Signed review in *Sunday Times*, 8 December 1901; reprinted in *Dramatic Criticism: 1900–1*, iii (1902), pp. 264–7.

Grein's review appeared on the occasion of the first revival of *The Importance of Being Earnest* (at the Coronet Theatre on 2 December) following Wilde's death.

A dead man's voice has been heard again, and as we listened to it the artist himself once more stood before us. Forgotten was the history of the man, forgotten the past. The hands of the clock had moved for seven years, but the situation remained unchanged. Oscar Wilde has come to life again, and on the night of December 2, when literary and social London foregathered at the reproduction of *The Importance of Being Earnest*, there was celebrated a feast of absolution, and, to a certain extent, of rehabilitation. In the midst of our intellectual joy there sounded but two discordant notes—the one of anger, the other of sadness. It made some of us angry to read on the programme *The Importance of Being Earnest*, by the author of *Lady Windermere's Fan*, whereby was indicated that, though it was good to use the artist's work, his name was not sufficiently honourable to be given out to the public. I know full well that the publisher has erred in this direction, as well as the manager, but there is no excuse for either. The note of sadness was that so great a mind as Oscar Wilde's had prematurely come to a standstill; that matters independent of art had bereft us of the most brilliant wit of the period, and that subsequent events, instead of leading to regeneration, brought a broken career to an untimely termination.

II.

In 1895, when *The Importance of Being Earnest* saw the light at the St. James's Theatre, it was voted a perfect farce, and, but for the catastrophe it would have been played for centuries of evenings. I recall this not merely as a chronological fact, but more particularly in order to emphasise the exceeding cleverness of the play, since the duality of its fibre escaped most of the critics, and certainly the majority of the public. The practised eye discovered at once that the first and second acts and the third act were not of the same mould. They made the impression of wines of different vintages served in the same glasses. Those two acts— perfect, not only as farce, but as comedy, too, for they reflect the manners of the period, and are richly underlaid with humorous current— were written in days when the poet basked in the hot sun of popularity, when his every saying darted like an arrow through the land, when the whole of the English speaking world echoed sallies which, though they were not always Oscar Wilde's, were as *ben trovato*[1] as if they had been his. The third act was—I know it authoritatively—composed under stress of circumstances, when the web was tightening round the man, and menaces of exposure must have rendered his gaiety forced, like that of a being condemned to the stocks. Under pressure a lofty mind often does excellent work, and it is undeniable that in the third act of *The Importance of Being Earnest* there is more cleverness than in one round dozen English comedies *en bloc*. There are epigrams in it for the pater-

[1] Well invented.

239

nity of which some people would give a few years of their lives, and as a solution to a tangle well-nigh inextricable it is by no means unhappy. Yet it is not of the same quality as those other two acts, in which the real, the probable, and the impossible form a *ménage à trois*[1] of rare felicity. And as we listen to the play, what strikes us most of all is not so much the utterances of a mind which could not fail to be brilliant, but the prospect that this comedy—for I prefer to call it a comedy—will enjoy a kind of perennial youth somewhat akin to Congreve's work or that of Sheridan. It is a bold thing to say, I know, but if there is exaggeration, let it pass, for the sake of the argument that when the artist's working powers were shut off he had not yet thoroughly felt his feet, but was only just beginning to plough his furrow in a new field. *The Importance of Being Earnest* ranks high, not only on account of it gaiety —a gaiety which in many produces the smile of intimate understanding, and in the less *blasé* guffaws straight from a happy mood—but because it satirises vividly, pointedly, yet not unkindly, the mannerisms and foibles of a society which is constantly before the public eye. I need not dive into details, for the plot is, or ought to be, known to every lover of the Theatre. And I do not quote epigrams, for it is but a poor glory to feather one's own cap with another man's cleverness. Anon, when the play is revived at the St. James Theatre, when the book of an author whose name one need no longer express with bated breath, is sold by the thousand, there will be ample opportunity to refresh one's memory, and spend a joyful hour with *The Importance of Being Earnest.* . . .

[1] Household of three persons, here, of course, used metaphorically.

90. André Gide on Wilde as a stylist

1902

Excerpt from signed article in *L'Ermitage* [Paris], June 1902; reprinted as *Oscar Wilde: A Study* (1905), translated by Stuart Mason (excerpt from pp. 49–51).

Gide (1869–1951), who first met Wilde in 1891, did not regard him as a 'great' writer but a 'great *viveur*, yes, if one may use the word in the fullest sense of the French term,' reporting Wilde's famous remark: 'I have put all my genius into my life; I have put only my talent into my works.' Chiefly a study of Wilde's personality, the article contains little evaluation of Wilde's work.

The best of his writing is but a poor reflection of his brilliant conversation. Those who have heard him talk find him disappointing to read. *Dorian Gray* in its conception was a wonderful story, far superior to *La Peau de Chagrin*, and far more significant! Alas! when written, what a masterpiece spoiled. In his most delightful tales literary influence makes itself too much felt. However graceful they may be, one notices too much literary effort; affectation and delicacy of phrase conceal the beauty of the first conception of them. One feels in them, and one cannot help feeling in them, the three periods of their generation. The first idea contained in them is very beautiful, simple, profound, and certain to make itself heard; a kind of latent necessity holds the parts firmly together, but from that point the gift stops. The development of the parts is done in an artificial manner; there is a lack of arrangement about them, and when Wilde elaborates his sentences and endeavours to give them their full value, he does so by overloading them prodigiously with tiny conceits and quaint and trifling fancies. The result is that one's emotion is held at bay, and the dazzling of the surface so blinds one's eyes and mind, that the deep central emotion is lost.

DE PROFUNDIS

23 February 1905

91. Letters to Robert Ross on *De Profundis*

1905

From *Robert Ross: Friend of Friends*, ed. Margery Ross (1952). Ross, who had edited *De Profundis*, sent copies to many editors, writers, and others likely to be influential in restoring Wilde's reputation as a writer. The most notable responses are reprinted here.

(*a*) William Thomas Stead (1849–1912) became editor of the *Pall Mall Gazette* in 1885; it frequently published unfavourable reviews of Wilde's work. (Stead's letter on pp. 93–4.)

The *Review of Reviews*, Norfolk Street   Feb. 20, 1905
Dear Mr. Ross, I have been profoundly moved by *De Profundis*. We all owe you thanks for having permitted us to see the man as he really was. I think *De Profundis* will live long after all that the rest of us have written will be forgotten.

I am glad to remember when reading these profoundly touching pages that he always knew that I, at least, had never joined the herd of his assailants. I had the sad pleasure of meeting him by chance afterwards in Paris and greeted him as an old friend. We had but a few minutes' talk and then parted, to meet no more, on this plane at least. Again thanking you for the service which you have rendered all of us, I am Yours gratefully   WILLIAM T. STEAD

(*b*) Laurence Housman (1865–1959), the dramatist and brother of A. E. Housman, was particularly kind to Wilde following his release from prison. Wilde wrote to him in 1898: 'Style is certainly part of your

character: you soul has beautiful curves and colours.' (*Letters*, p.771.)
Housman's letter is on pp. 100–1.

1 Pembroke Cottages, Kensington   Feb. 25th [1905]

Dear Ross, I hoped to find you at the Gallery yesterday to thank you
rather more specially than in a mere letter for sending me the book. I
read it at once with great and almost entire admiration, and am now
reading it again. It is, for the most part, beautifully thought and written;
and is the *right* sort of book to come now in order to touch the hearts of
men made cruel by ignorance of human nature and history. Its reception seems to me remarkable,—unprophesiable five or six years ago.
Perhaps before we die a tablet will be up in Tite Street on the house
where he used to live,[1] and a Rodin statue up on the Embankment.
No—I remember you don't like Rodin,—say Gilbert then—for I
suppose you will have a voice in the matter. I hope provision is made to
publish the work complete after this generation's nerves are laid in dust.

Meanwhile, for this portion of the document, many thanks. I hope
to look in before long for the talk I missed yesterday. Always yours
sincerely   LAURENCE HOUSMAN

(*c*) Edmund Gosse (1849–1928), the poet and critic, had no great
admiration of Wilde, the man or the writer, though he did defend him
against vitriolic attacks in the Press. (Gosse's letter is on p. 101.)

17 Hanover Terrace, N.W.   26.2.05

My dear Robbie, How very kind of you. I shall prize this beautiful
volume, in which you must write my name and yours. I had already
immediately bought a common copy, which I read with the greatest
eagerness. There were many conflicting impressions in my mind when
I laid it down, but a book would hardly contain them. I should like—
and shall soon hope—to discuss them with you. The publication of so
extraordinary a document is an event in English literature, an event
which I welcome cordially. I am Always yours   EDMUND GOSSE

(*d*) Shaw published an article in the *Neue Freie Presse* (23 April 1905)—
mentioned in his letter to Ross—in which he asserts, ironically, that 'no
other Irishman had yet produced as masterful a comedy as *De Profundis*'. (Shaw's letter in on p. 111.)

10 Adelphi Terrace, W.C.   13th March, 1905

Dear Ross, I have written an article on Wilde for the *Neue Freie Presse*

---

[1] A plaque was erected at 16 Tite Street by the London County Council and unveiled
by Sir Compton Mackenzie on the centenary of Wilde's birth, 16 October 1954.

of Vienna! I am half tempted to cut into the *Saturday Review* correspondence with a letter giving the *comedic* view of *De Profundis*. It is really an extraordinary book, quite exhilarating and amusing as to Wilde himself, and quite disgraceful and shameful to his stupid tormentors. There is pain in it, inconvenience, annoyance, but no real tragedy, all comedy. The unquenchable spirit of the man is magnificent: he maintains his position and puts society squalidly in the wrong—rubs into them every insult and humiliation he endured—comes out the same man he went in—with stupendous success. The little aside in which, after writing several pages with undisguised artistic enjoyment and detachment, he remarks that they have been feeding him satisfactorily of late, is irresistible. It annoys me to have people degrading the whole affair to the level of sentimental tragedy. There is only one moment at which he shows himself subject to the common lot of mankind unconscious of its own comedy; and that is where he calls himself 'enfant de son siècle'. Of course, except in his personality, and his supermorality, he was thoroughly Irish and old fashioned, a Gautierist in 1879–1900 (!) a chivalrous romanticist (see the *Ideal Husband* etc.) in the days of Strindberg and Ibsen. The British press is as completely beaten by him *de profundis* as it was *in excelsis*. . . .

92. E. V. Lucas in *Times Literary Supplement*

24 February 1905, pp. 64–5

A review, unsigned but by Edward Verrall Lucas (1868–1938). Lucas was a director of Methuen and Company, the author of many travel books and essays, and in 1919 the editor of a collection of Wilde's reviews, *A Critic in Pall Mall*.

This is an unfailingly and now and then poignantly interesting work; it contains some beautiful prose, some confessions that cannot leave the reader unmoved and may even touch him a little with shame at his own fortunate rectitude; and a passage of theological conjecture that is most engaging in its ingenuity and of a very delicate texture. The book contains all this and more, and yet while realizing the terrible conditions under which it was written, and possessed by every wish to understand the author and feel with him in the utter wreck of his career, it is impossible, except very occasionally, to look upon his testament as more than a literary feat. Not so, we find ourselves saying, are souls laid bare. This is not sorrow, but its dexterously constructed counterfeit.

Yet when we ask ourselves in what other way we would have had Oscar Wilde's cry from the depths we are unable to reply; for the bitter truth is that he was probably unable to cry from the depths at all; perhaps, paradoxical as it may sound, was unable really to be in the depths. For this book might be held to fortify the conviction that there is an armour of egotism which no arrow of fate can pierce. How Wilde felt in the watches of the night in that squalid cell we can only conjecture; this book gives little clue. In this book he is as much as ever the bland and plausible artist in phrase, except that for the most part he is advocating a new creed of humility in place of earlier gospels. Even in prison, even at the end of everything he most valued, his artifice was too much for him; his poses were too insistent—had become too much a part of the man—to be abandoned. If the heart of a broken man shows at all in this book, it must be looked for between the lines. It is rarely in them.

That a man who had travelled by Wilde's courses to Wilde's end should write, in prison, an analysis of his temperament, and a history of his ruin, coming therein to such conclusions as are here set forth, and during his task should pen no word that bore the mark of sincerity unadorned, is in its way a considerable feat. But it vitiates the book; or rather takes the book from the category of genuine emotion and places it among the *tours de force*. But it enables us now to know absolutely—what we had perhaps before guessed—that Oscar Wilde, however he may have begun life, grew to be incapable of deliberately telling the truth about himself or anything else. Being a man of genius, he often stumbled on it; but he could not say, 'I will be truthful,' and be truthful; he lost that power. We doubt if he was truthful even to himself towards the end. But the real tragic failure of this book lies, not so much in itself and its too obviously adroit special pleading, as in the fact that its author lived for two years after it was written. It is that knowledge which will move many readers to something very like tears:—

I have lain in prison for nearly two years. Out of my nature has come wild despair; an abandonment to grief that was piteous even to look at; terrible and impotent rage; bitterness and scorn; anguish that wept aloud, misery that could find no voice, sorrow that was dumb. I have passed through every possible mood of suffering. Better than Wordsworth himself I know what Wordsworth meant when he said:—

> Suffering is permanent, obscure, and dark,
> And has the nature of infinity.

But while there were times when I rejoiced in the idea that my sufferings were to be endless, I could not bear them to be without meaning. Now I find hidden somewhere away in my nature something that tells me that nothing in the whole world is meaningless, and suffering least of all. That something hidden away in my nature, like a treasure in a field, is Humility. It is the last thing left in me, and the best; the ultimate discovery at which I have arrived, the starting point for a fresh development. It has come to me right out of myself, so I know that it has come at the proper time. It could not have come before, nor later. Had any one told me of it, I would have rejected it. Had it been brought to me I would have refused it. As I found it, I want to keep it.

There is tragedy there, if you will. To criticize coldly such a passage, written in a prison cell by the author of *The Importance of Being Earnest*, is no congenial task. But if one does so, it is because the task is forced on one by the writer.

Wilde speaks in this little book of his artistic creed, his teaching, his philosophy of life; but it is very doubtful if he had ever really formulated one and made any sustained effort to understand it and conform to it. For his genius lay in lawlessness. He was essentially lawless, and his work is of value only when the author has forgotten that he is the exponent of a system. Every writer has somewhere an intimate personal gift which distinguishes him from every other writer—although it is often so minute as to escape detection. Wilde's particular and precise gift was lawless irresponsibility—humorous inconsistency is perhaps as good a description of it. If all his work could be spread out like an extinct river bed in the Klondike, a tiny thread of gold would be seen to break out here and there fitfully and freakishly within it. That vein of gold would represent those moments in Wilde's literary career when he forgot who he was and what he thought he stood for and allowed his native self to frolic and turn somersaults amid verities and conventions. Essentially an improviser and of hand-to-mouth intellect, he allowed himself to believe himself a constructive philosopher; essentially a mocker he was weak enough to affect to be a high priest of reverence. The result is that, although he essayed almost every variety of literary expression, in none except sheer irresponsibility did he come near perfection. We have always considered *The Importance of Being Earnest* his high-water mark of completed achievement; and we should associate with it those passages in his other writings where the same mood has play. Of Wilde's other work it is conceivable that industrious disciples might have produced it with more or less—perhaps sufficient—success. In any case it does not really matter. The failure of Wilde's life and failure of his work have the same root; he could not resist temptation. We would not say that as a writer he was tempted in the same degree as a pleasure-loving man; his artistic conscience was made of better stuff than his civic conscience; but he was tempted often, and he always fell. His real destiny was to be an improviser, an inconsistent but often inspired commentator, a deviser of paradoxes, an exponent of the unfamiliar side of things; instead, he thought himself a leader of men, a prophet, a great writer of prose, a serious dramatic poet. By nature a witty and irresponsible Irishman, he grew to believe himself a responsible neo-Hellene. Born to be a lawless wit he was often something very like a pedant. Had he possessed a sense of humour he might have been saved—another illustration of the total independence of humour and wit.

Only in one part of this book does the author show his true self at all. The main part, we are convinced, is artifice; but we seem to see this most delightfully ingenious, if unscrupulous improviser of our day at work again in the essay on 'Christ as the Precursor of the Romantic Movement in Art.' Wilde introduces the fantasy by remarking that it is one of the things he had always desired to write; but we would wager he thought of it only that morning. It bears every trace of his old gift of whimsical invention and embroidery. The rest of the book is studied and overstudied; but this is fresh and spontaneous:—

[quotes from 'I see in Christ not merely the essentials of the supreme romantic type' to 'I cannot conceive a better reason for his being sent there'.]

And so on. We do not say that this is great criticism; but it is the true and the best Wilde. It is the kind of happy, swift, inverted commentary of which he had the secret and which we hold is his chief gift. And, right or wrong, it is very gay and charming, and it makes the reader think. Indeed, everything which Wilde says of Christ in this little book is worth reading and considering and reading again.

What, then, is the value of *De Profundis*? Its value is this—that it is an example of the triumph of the literary temperament over the most disadvantageous conditions; it is further documentary evidence as to one of the most artificial natures produced by the nineteenth century in England; and here and there it makes a sweet and reasonable contribution to the gospel of humanity.

93. Max Beerbohm on *De Profundis*

1905

Signed review, titled 'A Lord of Language', *Vanity Fair* (2 March 1905), cxxiii, 309.

In this perceptive review, Beerbohm grasps the complexities of Wilde's personality as it is revealed in *De Profundis:* Wilde, simultaneously the suffering victim and detached observer, aesthetically absorbed by his own tragic vision. (The allusion to an award of a farthing to Whistler for damages refers to a lawsuit he brought against Ruskin in 1878 over the latter's remark that Whistler asked 'two hundred guineas for flinging a pot of paint in the public's face'.)

There was a coincidence last week in London. An exhibition of Whistler's paintings was opened, and a book by Oscar Wilde was published; and all the critics are writing, and the gossips gossiping, very glibly, about the greatness of Whistler, and about the greatness of Oscar Wilde. Whistler during the 'seventies and 'eighties, and Oscar Wilde during the 'eighties and early 'nineties, cut very prominent figures in London; and both were by the critics and the gossips regarded merely as clever *farceurs*. Both, apart from their prominence, were doing serious work; but neither was taken at all seriously. Neither was thanked. Whistler got a farthing damages; Oscar Wilde two years' hard labour. None of the critics or gossips took exception to either verdict. Time has rolled on. Both men are dead. A subtly apocalyptic thing, for critics and gossips (especially in England), is the tomb; and praises are by envious humanity sung the more easily when there is no chance that they will gratify the subjects of them. And so, very glibly, very blandly, we are all magnifying the two men whom we so lately belittled. M. Rodin was brought over to open the Whistler exhibition. Perhaps the nation will now commission him to do a statue of Oscar Wilde. *Il ne manque que ça.*[1]

Some of the critics, wishing to reconcile present enthusiasm with past indifference, or with past obloquy, have been suggesting that *De Profundis* is quite unlike any previous work of Oscar Wilde—a quite sudden and unrelated phenomenon. Oscar Wilde, according to them, was gloriously transformed by incarceration. Their theory comprises two fallacies. The first fallacy is that Oscar Wilde had been mainly remarkable for his wit. In point of fact, wit was the least important of his gifts. Primarily, he was a poet, with a life-long passion for beauty; and a philosopher, with a life-long passion for thought. His wit, and his humour (which was of an even finer quality than his wit), sprang from a very solid basis of seriousness, as all good wit or humour must. They were not essential to his genius; and, had they happened not to have been there at all, possibly his genius would, even while he himself was flourishing, have been recognised in England, where wisdom's passport is dulness, and gaiety of manner damns. The right way of depreciating Oscar Wilde would have been to say that, beautiful and profound though his ideas were, he never was a real person in contact with realities. He created his poetry, created his philosophy: neither sprang from his own soul, or from his own experience. His ideas were for the sake of ideas, his emotions for the sake of emotions. This, I take it, is just what Mr. Robert Ross means, when, in his admirable introduction to *De Profundis* he speaks of Oscar Wilde as a man of 'highly intellectual and artificial nature.' Herein, too, I find the key to an old mystery; why Oscar Wilde, so saliently original a man, was so much influenced by the work of other writers; and why he, than who none was more fertile in invention, did sometimes stoop to plagiarism. If an idea was beautiful or profound, he cared not what it was, nor whether it was his or another's. In *De Profundis* was he, at length, expressing something that he really and truly felt? Is the book indeed a heartcry? It is pronounced so by the aforesaid critics. There we have the second fallacy.

I think no discerning reader can but regard the book as essentially the artistic essay of an artist. Nothing seemed more likely than that Oscar Wilde, smitten down from his rosy-clouded pinnacle, and dragged

[1] Only that is wanting.

through the mire, and cast among the flints, would be *diablement changé en route*.[1] Yet lo! he was unchanged. He was still precisely himself. He was still playing with ideas, playing with emotions. 'There is only one thing left for me now,' he writes, 'absolute humility.' And about humility he writes many beautiful and true things. And, doubtless, while he wrote them, he had the sensation of humility. Humble he was not. Emotion was not seeking outlet: emotion came through its own expression. The artist spoke, and the man obeyed. The attitude was struck, and the heart pulsated to it. Perhaps a Cardinal Archbishop, when he kneels to wash the feet of the beggars, is filled with humility, and revels in the experience. Such was Oscar Wilde's humility. It was the luxurious complement of pride. In *De Profundis*, for the most part, he is frankly proud—proud with the natural pride of a man so richly endowed as he, and arrogant with all his old peculiar arrogance. Even 'from the depths' he condescended. Nor merely to mankind was he condescending. He enjoyed the greater luxury of condescending to himself. Sometimes the condescension was from his present self to his old self; sometimes from his old self to his present self. Referring to the death of his mother, 'I, once a lord of language,' he says, 'have no words in which to express my anguish and my shame.' Straightway, he proceeds to revel in the survival of that lordship, and refutes in a fine passage his own dramatic plea of impotence. 'She and my father had bequeathed to me a name they had made noble and honoured. . . . I had disgraced that name eternally. I had made it a low byword among low people. I had dragged it through the very mire. I had given it to brutes that they might make it brutal, and to fools that they might turn it into folly. What I suffered then, and still suffer, is not for pen to write or paper to record.' Yet pen wrote it, and paper recorded it, even so. And sorrow was turned to joy by the 'lord of language.'

'A lord of language.' Certainly that was no idle boast. Fine as are the ideas and emotions in *De Profundis*, it is the actual writing—the mastery of prose—that most delights me. Except Ruskin in his prime, no modern writer has achieved through prose the limpid and lyrical effects that were achieved by Oscar Wilde. One does not seem to be reading a written thing. The words sing. There is nothing of that formality, that hard and cunning precision, which marks so much of the prose that we admire, and rightly admire. The meaning is artificial, but the expression is always magically natural and beautiful. The simple words seem to grow together like wild flowers. In his use of rhyme and metre, Oscar

[1] Devilishly changed on the way.

Wilde was academic—never at all decadent, by the way, as one critic has suggested. But the prose of *Intentions*, and of his plays, and of his fairy-stories, was perfect in its lively and unstudied grace. It is a joy to find in this last prose of his the old power, all unmarred by the physical and mental torments that he had suffered.

Oscar Wilde was immutable. The fineness of the book as a personal document is in the revelation of a character so strong that no force of circumstance could change it, or even modify it. In prison Oscar Wilde was still himself—still with the same artistry in words, still with the same detachment from life. We see him here as the spectator of his own tragedy. His tragedy was great. It is one of the tragedies that will live always in romantic history. And the protagonist had an artist's joy in it. Be sure that in the dock of the Old Bailey, in his cell at Reading, on 'the centre platform of Clapham Junction,' where he stood 'in convict dress, and handcuffed, for the world to look at,' even while he suffered he was consoled by the realisation of his sufferings and of the magnitude of his tragedy. Looking joyously forward to his release, 'I hope,' he says, 'to be able to recreate my creative faculty.' It is a grim loss to our literature that the creative faculty, which prison-life had not yet extinguished in him, did not long survive his liberation. But, broken as he was thereafter, and powerless, and aimless, the invincible artist in him must have had pleasure in contemplation of himself draining the last bitter dregs of the cup that Fate had thrust on him.

94. G. S. Street on *De Profundis*

1905

Signed review, titled 'Out of the Depths', in *The Outlook* (4 March 1905), xv, 294–5.

George Slythe Street (1867–1936), novelist and journalist, was associated with the counter-Decadents on the staff of the *National Observer*, which Henley edited between 1890 and 1894. His most notable work, *The Autobiography of a Boy* (1894), a satire of the Decadence, achieved considerable acclaim. Despite Street's past opposition to Decadence in literature, this moving tribute reveals his high regard for Wilde and for *De Profundis*.

Two simple impressions were left on my mind when I had read the history of his soul in prison, written by Oscar Wilde. One was that it was poignantly touching, the other that it was extraordinary and profoundly interesting. A man to whom applause was a primary need of life, acutely sensitive to beauty, impatient of any control, had fallen in squalid ruin, amidst common execration, and was condemned to two years of, perhaps, the most hideous and unlovely life ever devised by man for his fellows. How far he deserved it all is here an irrelevant consideration. It is relevant to remember that if we can put aside that for which he suffered, he was very far from being a man with whom sympathy was impossible. It is the callous, the mean, the vindictive, with whom we find it hard to sympathise. This was a humane man, generous to his friends, placable to his enemies. His books and plays had given thousands delightful moments of thought and fun. Well, such a man had to suffer such a punishment. He had to find himself again in it, some sort of tolerable relation he had to find between himself and life, some meaning in it all not utterly unbearable. Inevitably, however, being an artist, one to whom expression was necessary in a degree the average man can never understand, he had to put this meaning into words, for the world or not, at least for himself. Any record of all this must have been touching; the actual record is profoundly interesting. These, as I said, were the two simple impressions on my mind. They seemed to need no qualification. But when I heard the book discussed and read other people's opinions about it, I found that to many its interest was qualified, if not vitiated, by what they thought its insincerity. I think this criticism shallow, and it will help me to express how the book is significant to me if I explain why I think so.

It is said that the writing of the book, with its fine phrases and coloured imagery, is not that of a man who truly felt distress of soul, as apart from physical hardship. I am not thinking, of course, of writers to whom all manners of writing but their own slovenly verbiage are hateful, just as there are people who hate all speech that has not a cockney accent. To them Oscar Wilde's style is 'affected,' and there's an end of the matter. But people who heartily admire his style, so limpid and graceful, so brilliant in its unforced elegance and adornment, think that here the use of it is a token of insincerity. Surely, rather, its absence would have been. It had grown into his nature; he could not write differently without an effort. The humility of spirit he says he had gained was not needful to change his manner, if changed it could have been: his physical sufferings and privations, the reality of which, at least, no one can deny, would have done that. But it was unchangeable, and so far from finding its use insincere, I think it merely another thing to touch one—that to the setting forth of the sad doctrine now dominant in his mind he brought so naturally and instinctively the gift of his poetry and eloquence, sometimes even of his wit. Again, it is said that he lived for three years when he was free and showed no sign that the mood and determination professed in this letter *De Profundis*, persisted in him. It may have been so. It was a thousand pities, a grievous waste. Pathologically considered, it was surely inevitable. A life-long indulgence of the senses, followed by a sudden, complete, and prolonged starving of them, must have put a tax on the brain which none but the very greatest could bear. The sentence of two years' hard labour was a sentence of death to his mental energy. But how does that make *De Profundis* insincere? There is no sign in it even that he foresaw the second tragedy of failure which awaited him, or mistrusted his power to live his 'new life,' still less that he did not mean to do his best. The event was pitiable. The determination was fine and was nobly expressed, and to confuse with it the weakness of fulfilment which awaited it is shallow and unjust.

He did not determine to be a better man; that, he says characteristically, would have been 'a piece of unscientific cant.' But 'to have become a deeper man is the privilege of those who have suffered. And such I think I have become.' He wanted to live so that he might explore the 'new world' of sorrow in which he had been living. 'If I can produce only one beautiful work of art I shall be able to rob malice of its venom, and cowardice of its sneer, and to pluck out the finger of scorn by the roots.' That was a natural human resolve, and this work of art, it is clear, was to be the expression of that fuller and deeper life which sorrow had taught him. It is extraordinarily interesting. The man who all his life had been the prophet of joy, shunning all gloom and distress as a 'mode of imperfection,' was to preach the gospel of sorrow, how it is 'the ultimate type both in life and art.' Oscar Wilde had a brilliant imagination and a power of thought both subtle and at times profound, but he was no philosopher with a system impervious to logic and analysis; it was, perhaps, an unlucky vanity that made him think himself one. In the complete philosophy of this gospel of sorrow, as he sketches it, there are inconsistencies and exaggerations. It goes back to old, insoluble mysteries. But he had arrived through bitterness and tears at a truth which clearly he had realised in all its force; the truth that as men are, as the world is, only those who have known sorrow, sorrow bitter and in itself hopeless, are complete, that the most amicable natures that always have lived in the sunshine must lack tenderness and the deeper moods of love. For 'behind joy and laughter there may be a temperament coarse, hard, and callous; but behind sorrow there is always sorrow.' Oscar Wilde was not a philosopher. In his fashion he was a prophet, and prophets to be of any use in the world must be extreme. The interesting thing is that this one had preached one extreme, and was on his way to preach the opposite. Had his intellect and energy endured he might have ended by seeing some way for the hedonist and the mystic to walk together; then, indeed, he would have been a philosopher at last.

There are many fine thoughts in this book, many pieces of charming prose which I might quote. But anyone who cares to read what I think of this *De Profundis* will have read the book itself and admired, as I have, the strength of an artistic nature that moved towards beauty so inevitably, even over the most hideous obstacles—admired the bold statement and the gracious ornament, the unfailing sense of words and cadences, and such a finely-sustained study as that, daring, sometimes whimsical, but always justified by feeling, of the human Christ. Nor is it an occasion for any attempt to define Oscar Wilde's place in English literature; the book before me is too acutely personal for that. Some day, I hope, a critic fit for the task will succeed in clearing his mind from all evil associations and give us a clear and full appreciation of the written achievements. Much there is, again, in the book about which I might argue, or assert opposing opinions. But I think it would be an impertinence at the moment, and am content to have expressed my sense of the book's significance, being, as it is, the work, tragically written, of a genius whose ruin was one of the saddest tragedies in my lifetime.

95. R. B. Cunninghame Graham on *De Profundis*

1905

Signed review, titled 'Vox Clamantis', in *Saturday Review* (4 March 1905), xcix, 266–7.

Robert Bontine Cunninghame Graham (1852–1936), Scottish author and politician, was a Socialist and Member of Parliament who had been imprisoned for six weeks at Pentonville (Wilde spent approximately the same length of time there following his conviction) for his part in the Trafalgar Square riots in 1887. Cunninghame Graham gives an account of his own prison experiences in his book *Success* (1902).

I knew him and admired his gifts. Most people now recall his wit, his humour, brilliancy, his poetry, his prose, his errors, triumphs and his fall. I most remember his great kindliness. It is the greatest quality in man. Without it, all the talents, all the virtues, lack somewhat; with it all errors, even crimes, can be condoned. Few books in any language, treating of prisons and of prison life, are comparable with this. Generally (and this your doctor knows) a man in prison is sustained either by consciousness of innocence, by pride, indifference, or by the thought that on emerging from his malebolge, he has a home in which to hide himself.

He had none of these to help him as he picked the oakum, paced round and round the yard, stood in the prison chapel bawling the hymns, or worst of all sat idle in his cell in the long winter afternoons before they light the gas, or performed the dreary round of duties which only those who have performed them estimate. Some men have tamed a mouse. Others wait as a youth waits for his sweetheart, till a robin comes to the window-sill to peck at crumbs.

Nothing (to prisoners) can ever make the prison flower ridiculous, or hackneyed, in spite of sentimental books.

He had no mouse or robin, only his soul to tame, so sitting down he has depicted for us how it beat itself against the bars, until at last it fought no more, and he and it had peace. But the peace he had was not of the kind those have who throw themselves into the arms of some religion, which till then they have refused. Only the peace that comes to all men when they have learned as he did that sun and moon and stars, the seasons, tides, the equinoxes, the flowers and trees and Nature will be as much theirs even in sorrow, as they ever were in joy. So by degrees he learned to bear it all, even though from the outside world nothing but sorrow came to heap the mass of sorrow growing in his heart. His mother's death moves him to such abasement that but to read it makes oneself ashamed to be a man.

Hardly in any literature does such a great and bitter cry pierce to the heart, as does this anguish of the poor soul, dressed like a zany as he faces himself, ridiculous in grief, a clown of sorrows, as miserable as is the paint of an old woman outraged by drunkards and then scorned. Well does he say, that in most martyrdoms, to those who heaped the logs or lit the straw, the sufferer must have appeared a fool, and without dignity or style. Had Cranmer written in his cell after his great refusal, and before the fire had purified, his outpourings would surely have been akin to Wilde's. But he redeemed himself, whereas the writer of the book had no such luck. Therefore, the charitable man, if there be such in this the age of self-sufficiency, must take his book for expiation and in it find his martyrdom, and read it as a thing that might have happened to himself. This done it is a scripture for our learning. Written of course in gall, with a pen made of hyssop, but truly written and as such more valuable than all the books of all the moralists. Each man can see what he likes in it, and to some it may seem mystic, to others philosophic, and again to certain minds, a reconciliation, but to me what most attracts is that the point of view is still unchanged.

There was about the man a curious courage, rarer perhaps than that of those who rush on death (with a side-glance at glory as they run), or those who do their duty all their lives from temperament or fear. This as it seems to me is shown in every line of the whole book, and most of all when he dwells on his fits of weeping in the cell, in such a way that though one sees his weakness, at the same time you feel his strength. He has a sort of absence of what the French call 'respect humain', such as one sees in Arabs, and withal a certain dignity, like a fallen angel to whom at times celestial music echoes still, but distantly.

Surely he is right to say that punishment wipes out the offence, for, if it does not, those who punish cannot be judges, but mere torturers?

Right through the book reflections such as this must make the Philistine, whom as he rightly says is the sworn foe of all repentance, wince not a little beneath his armour of self-righteousness.

Scattered about the book are flashes of his old humour, as when he calls La Vie de Jésus a gospel by S. Thomas, or talks about an order to be founded for all those who have no faith, and this I fain would hope sustained him, for when all is lost, even to honour, it is the only stay. Perhaps it is philosophy made manifest to those brought low, and to whom consolation is denied.

No degradation seems to have killed his love of beauty for itself, and it is brave of him to say that he does not regret his previous life.

All his reflections upon Christ remind one of an educated pagan, who admired whilst not believing, but yet are true and just, so just, one wonders why one never thought them for oneself. Who but himself writing in anguish in his cell would have written 'To turn an interesting thief into a tedious honest man was not his [Christ's] aim'. And yet how true it is, for God could not deny imagination to his Son. In the letter which his faithful friend and editor prefixes to the book, the writer says that 'prison life makes me see people and things as they really are'. That is true to some extent as when he dwells upon the frank contempt of Christ for mere material success, but that the saying is but true in part he gives the proof himself. The mystical in art, in life, and nature was what he says on his re-entrance to the world shall be his goal. Now mysticism is a temperament born in a man as are his hair or eyes, no one can cultivate it, like faith it is a quality which must grow alone, and he had neither. Thus it may be by straining after what he had not, that he lost what he had, and his expression, which was everything, never returned to him.

The book is beautiful in all its misery, and worth a million of the dishonest self-revelations of the men who write about their souls as if their bodies were mere pillow-cases. One reads with indignation how he stood soaking in the rain, handcuffed and dressed in prison clothes, whilst a mob jeered him at a railway station. Had he been twice as guilty as he was and of a serious crime as cheating or the like, or cruelty, human respect should not have been thus outraged, for the man condemned by law is surely sacred, as we have taken from him all means of defence. Judges and postmen and all public servants ought to understand that whilst we pay them and place our correspondence and our property, more or less in their hands, they should execute their offices with due discretion, and not allow a letter or a soul to fall into the mud, for fools to stamp upon, for on them may be written things more sacred than themselves. With the exception perhaps of Morris and of Parnell, when he was alive, no one bulked greater in the public eye than Wilde, and when the paltry politician, even although he rest his boots upon the table of the House from the green benches of the salaried crew that forms a Government, is long forgotten, the unhonoured poet in his dishonoured grave will be remembered, and his works read by every man of taste. Reading the beautiful but miserable book, some things console one, first that he had a friend who both in evil and good repute stood by him to the last. When the poor wretch, condemned to hell before his time, records with tears how it consoled him only to have received a brief salute in passing, one thinks better of mankind, and if rewards were ever given to desert, the faithful friend has his. He who brings comfort to a soul in pain is better far than he who, himself sinless, dies without sympathy, for by that sin devils have fallen to a lower depth.

All through the book there is a vein of tenderness, not that false tenderness which sorrow sometimes gives, but real and innate. The love of flowers, of children, of the trees, the sun and moon and the stars in their courses, call to us from this crying voice, for pardon. His joy of life, and all the sufferings which to such a man those two fell years must have entailed, speak for him to us, asking us now, after his death to pardon, and when we speak of him, to call him by his name, to make no mystery of his fall, and to regard him as a star which looking at its own reflection in some dank marsh, fell down and smirched itself, and then became extinct ere it had time to soar aloft again.

96. W. B. Yeats on *Salomé*

1906

From a letter to T. Sturge Moore, dated 6 May 1906, in *W. B. Yeats and T. Sturge Moore: Their Correspondence, 1901–1937*, ed. Ursula Bridge (1953), pp. 8–9.

Thomas Sturge Moore (1870–1944), art critic, engraver, poet and dramatist, wrote the opening scene of Wilde's *A Florentine Tragedy* (which had been missing in the manuscript), when it was first produced in 1906.

As the excerpt reveals, the Literary Theatre Society with which Moore was associated, had decided to produce *Salomé* as well as The *Florentine Tragedy* in the following month.

I am sorry you have chosen *Salomé*, though *The Florentine Tragedy* will probably make all the difference between success and failure as it will bring the old audience. I think the Wilde audience is limited to a few hundred who have already been; but my real objection is that *Salomé* is thoroughly bad. The general construction is all right, is even powerful, but the dialogue is empty, sluggish and pretentious. It has nothing of drama of any kind, never working to any climax but always ending as it begun. A good play goes like this

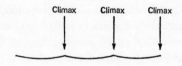

but *Salomé* is as level as a table. Wilde was not a poet but a wit and critic and could not endure his limitations. He thought he was writing beautifully when he had collected beautiful things and thrown them together in a heap. He never made anything organic while he was trying to be a poet. You will never create an audience with any liking for anything by playing his poetical works.

97. The literary position of Oscar Wilde

1906

Signed article by Wilfred M. Leadman, *Westminster Review* (August 1906), clxvi, 201–8.
Leadman's article is notable, since it pleads for a consideration of Wilde's work independent of his private life. Notable also is its announcement that the 'turning-point has been reached' in the development of Wilde's reputation as a writer, particularly since other countries were raising him to the status of first rank.

Maeterlinck has shown us in one of his admirable essays how impossible and how absurd it is to attempt to reconcile human affairs with the idea of an intelligent external justice impartially and invariably meting out good for good and evil for evil. All injustice springs originally from man himself or from what we are pleased to call Nature. The intelligence of Nature is purely mechanical; she has smiles and frowns for both moral and immoral alike without regard to character or conduct. The 'justice' or 'injustice' of man is purely arbitrary, hence its seeming inexplicability. In no sense, perhaps, is the cruelty and caprice of human justice shown more painfully than in the history of literature. Here and there, scattered over the globe, we find lonely and unrecognised geniuses whose messages have faded and remain forgotten because no one has been found to appreciate or to understand them. And too often the fault lay, not in the message or its deliverer, but in the world. On the other hand we find writers (not always so deserving) concerning whose high position the world has spoken decisively. She has placed them on lofty pedestals. And those whom she chooses for this honour are usually the writers who have made a successful appeal to some strong force in human nature. They count their followers by millions; for they have a straightforward message for plain minds. True, in distant years their names may fade for ever to make room for other names bearing similar messages, but, whatever their ultimate fate be, they have at least the satisfaction of present glory and the supreme consolation of being understood by their fellows. In the contemplation of these darlings of public opinion we feel no pain; but, when we turn to the victims of that same public opinion, we cannot but feel angered at the grotesque caprice of human justice. Among the writers so rejected by the world there are some whom she had spurned simply because she has not troubled to understand them. Prominent among this mournful group is Oscar Wilde. Around that hapless man controversy incessantly played in the past and apparently will continue to play in the future. His whole literary work (plays, poems, essays, and fiction) in vain cried out for just criticism— prejudice, misconception, and a strained sense of respectability refused it. His few admirers were dubbed a senseless clique dazzled by the showy glitter of his language. Wilde was always considered a mere 'poseur.' Fault was found with all his writings. It was said that his prose was disfigured by incongruous ornament; his poetry was a feeble echo of Keats and Swinburne. His wonderful essays— especially 'The Decay of Lying' and 'The Soul of Man'—were admired only for their peculiar brilliance; their inherent depths of philosophy was overlooked. His plays were deemed conventional in construction and overloaded with spurious wit. Great and undue stress was invariably laid on the man's eccentricities; in the public eye Wilde was only a witty fellow yearning for celebrity and capable of performing weird literary antics to attain that object. He is indeed a tragic figure. Laughed at in his youth, misunderstood in his maturity, spurned in his closing years, accused of plagiarism, blamed for his love of posture, constantly charged with artificiality, an object of unceasing attack from pulpit and press—in a word, roundly abused all his life—Wilde would seem to have small chance, in this country, at any rate, of literary fame. Long before the catastrophe of 1895 he had an extraordinary amount of prejudice against him. His downfall was the crowning condemnation. After that it looked as though he was indeed doomed to an eternal outer darkness. And yet, leaving the question of his conduct on one side, his sole fault was simply his unswerving fidelity to his own intellectual bias. He could not write about ordinary things in an ordinary way. He could not present the British public with its favourite dish of love and sport. He was incapable of moulding his maxims on traditional conceptions of virtue and vice. It was, perhaps, inevitable that the uneducated British public should turn its back on one who at almost every opportunity flaunted in its face the most unusual doctrines. For it must be confessed, Oscar Wilde enunciated doctrines utterly alien to the ingrained Puritanism and athleticism of English people. The man who runs counter to national traditions and prejudices is bound to provoke bitter hostility. The man who, in this country, places art before muscle or sets the individual will above the conventional law, seems sure sooner or later to come to grief. Yet, in spite of his unpopularity, Wilde was never discouraged. Borne up by his own motto, 'To be great is to be misunderstood,' he moved steadily forward, and made his mark. True, his influence was limited to the very few, but it existed and will expand further in the time to come. The unconventional will always thank him for his unflinching advocacy of things unconventional. The artist will remember him because he was one of the courageous few who helped to remove English theories of art from the tyranny of rigid tradition to the freedom of unfettered originality. He may have been rash, he may have been inclined to pose, his writings may show traces of plagiarism—an innocent sort of plagiarism that is almost a transformation—but there was always a thoroughness about his work which certainly deserved fairer consideration. To the average English mind his doctrines could only suggest the bizarre and the unnatural; but that was because the English mind had not learnt to appreciate an oblique point of view. Not that Wilde's outlook was always unusual. On the contrary, some of his short stories—especially 'The Happy Prince,' 'The Star-child,' and 'The Model Millionaire'—though necessarily tinted with his peculiar colouring, would satisfy the most exacting moralist by their tone of 'poetic justice.' If Wilde occasionally trampled on cherished national convictions or sometimes thrust strangely-hued flowers amongst our soberer blossoms, it was not from love of opposition; it was rather because he had to drift whither his fantastic and exuberant intellect listed.

Wilde's descent into the abyss seemed at the time to be the death-blow to what little influence he had already gained. The hasty verdict of a rather superficial morality said then that his influence must have been essentially unhealthy. From that time to the publication of *De Profundis* it was even deemed a breach of manners to allude to Wilde in any way. However, that interesting posthumous book has been the cause of a partial change of the public attitude. We are once more allowed to discuss Wilde's book without hearing a shocked 'hush,' or being suspected of loose views on moral matters. Whatever one's opinion may be as to the genuineness of the repentance shown in *De Profundis*, one may at any rate be deeply thankful for what it has undoubtedly done toward the rehabilitation of its author. He is no longer under a ban. He may eventually receive a high place in English literature. After all, his admitted writings cannot fairly be deemed unhealthy. Those who see 'an under-current of nasty suggestion' in some of his literary productions must surely be so obsessed by their knowledge of his unfortunate behaviour as to lose all power of disconnecting two absolutely independent things, namely, his art and his private life. The ludicrous charges of immorality brought against that book of painted words and lordly language, *Dorian Gray*, fall to the ground at once when it is known that the book was written solely for money. As Mr. Sherard says in his *Life of Oscar Wilde*, no author would risk the financial success of a book by filling it with immoral teachings. The marvel to me is that Wilde managed to produce such a transcendent work of art under the pressure of such a prosaic stimulus.

In the past, before his downfall, Wilde's works were only read carefully by a select few. Others, it is true, granted a certain momentary admiration to his prose, but it was the sort of admiration involuntarily and temporarily evoked by gorgeous fireworks rather than the lasting admiration felt for a permanent object of art. Now, if justice is to be done to any author's work the impersonal attitude is imperative. The intellectual reader must sink his personal predilections, he must not keep asking himself whether he agree with this or that sentiment expressed by an author. It is not very hard to do. There are minds which dislike stories packed with scenes of love, but such minds need not on that account be debarred from appreciating the almost faultless love-scenes in *Richard Feverel*. Of course, when the reader is by nature in perfect accord with the writer's sentiments, the enjoyment will be fuller and more satisfactory than when his appreciation be acquired, but in both cases the object of the writer's genius will have been attained. In the case of Wilde's works there is a real necessity for impartiality of standpoint, because only the few are by nature and inclination in tune with his work. The majority must learn to put themselves into tune. Two difficulties—broadly speaking—hamper anything like a general and intelligent recognition of Wilde's genius. The first is undoubtedly the moral obliquity or seeming moral obliquity revealed by the criminal trial of 1895. The second is the lack of effort or ability to understand Oscar Wilde's trend of thought. Would that the former might be for ever forgotten! After all, his writings are of vastly more importance to posterity than his private conduct. The stolid Englishman, however, finds it hard to differentiate between a man's private character and his books. Certain unfortunate impressions received in 1895 cloud his honest judgement in the matter of Wilde's position in literature. Now this is not the place to discuss the pathological aspect of Oscar Wilde's conduct, but I may be permitted to say that his restitution—to be permanent—must depend on a fuller knowledge of an obscure branch of morbid pathology.

This at present, for obvious reasons, is impossible. No doubt *De Profundis* with its confession of humility and its partial admission of error will impress many minds favourably, but the more matter of fact minds care little whether that book be entirely sincere or merely a huge pose intended to transform public opinion. What they do care about is a *locus standi*[1] based on sound scientific grounds. Once such a basis be generally accepted, perhaps the worst obstacle to the recognition of Wilde will have been taken away. Let is be admitted that Wilde erred greatly; then charity reminds us that there is such a thing as forgiveness of sin. Let it be granted that pathological research will explain and even excuse much of his conduct; common-sense will then bid us banish our rigid prudery and consign once and for all to oblivion what really has absolutely nothing to do with our unchecked contemplation of a great artist.

The other obstacle to an unbiassed conception of this writer's productions is not so easily defined as that just discussed, for the latter sprang into existence at a definite time, whilst this one had existed ever since Wilde published his first book of poems. From the beginning Wilde's ideas were diametrically opposed to all our eminently respectable British traditions of art. The reading world failed to grasp his meaning. And that was mainly due to what one may call our national inability to understand a creed whose keynote was the worship of beauty. We are, above all, a stolid race, in no way over-attracted by beauty; we certainly love personal cleanliness and comfort, but it is a cleanliness derived from cold water rather than from warm, and a

1 Literally, 'place to stand', i.e. a basis.

comfort obtained from blankets and brick rather than from silks and marble. We cannot see the use of any one's making a fuss of a beautiful thing simply because of its beauty. Such a proceeding savours to us of lunacy or idolatry. And when Wilde, in 1881, burst upon our sober minds with his first book of poems—saturated as it was with a lavish reckless admiration of beauty—we felt that here indeed was a strange apostle teaching a still stranger cult. Coming, as this book did, on the heels of Wilde's æsthetic campaign—after all, but as pardonable youthful extravagance, and, as, Mr. Sherard points out, completely cured by that American tour, which taught a needed practical lesson—there was, perhaps, some reason for its hostile reception. 'Here is a man,' said the critics, 'who values all glittering evanescence of a coloured bubble above morality itself.' This sweeping opinion represented the belief of many critics at that time, and, unfortunately for Wilde, later events seemed confirmatory. In one sense possibly Wilde did set beauty above morality, but it was above the conventional conception of morality— that is something arbitrary and too often uncharitable—*not* above goodness. In any case, one must not base one's conception of Wilde's attitude towards morality on anything which he has written. Some men do, indeed, project their own personalities into their books, in spite of Wilde's splendid dictum: 'To reveal art and to conceal the artist is the true aim of art. The artist can express everything.' But one may be confident that the author of *Dorian Gray* has been guilty of no such literary soul-dissecting. An intimate friend of his—a man, perhaps, more fitted to speak authoritively on this subject than any other man living—told me that Wilde only revealed *one* aspect of his own character in his books, and that not the most the most attractive aspect.

Read in the clear light of intelligent criticism, the first book of poems teaches only one thing, namely, that here is an author almost unique in his whole-hearted worship of form and colour, a worship, too, that is not casual, capricious, and superficial, but serious, terribly serious, and thoroughly healthy. Of course, all this was horribly unpractical and most Englishmen with their innate dislike of 'hollow beauty' shrugged their shoulders. Wilde, in his first as in his later efforts, wrote only for minds attuned to his. Others must take the right attitude or else pass on elsewhere.

Wilde has plainly this to his credit that he never tried to win the public, never debased the art of literature by pandering to any popular movement. Of that exquisite set of allegories *The House of Pomegranates* he finely said (in answer to some mystified critics) that 'it was intended neither for the British child nor for the British public.' Indeed, some think that much, if not all, of his work was the accidental, irresponsible, yet irresistible overflow of an ever creative intellect, and not literature written with any definite purpose. On this question, however, it is better to keep an open mind.

Wilde had an inherent horror of the commonplace, and this seems to have led him occasionally into a rather strained effort after a rather petty kind of originality. Of course his numerous enemies laid hold of that habit and made it the foundation of a great deal of silly abuse. Frivolous, frothy remarks put into the mouths of some of Wilde's characters were solemnly quoted as part of Wilde's creed. Witty repartees deliberately torn from their proper context in his plays were seriously construed as Wilde's own gospel. The words of few men have undergone such distortion and misinterpretation as have those of this genius. One can only be thankful that now at any rate there are signs of the advent of Truth, there are signs of a strong fresh breeze sweeping away those murky mists and grotesque masks that have so long hidden the real Wilde. It is at last dawning on men's minds that his writings are not so much external ornament concealing a blank void, and that his wit is often wisdom, only occasionally nonsense. Some critics say that Wilde's art may be very entertaining and very clever, but that (with the exception of De Profundis) it leads us nowhere. But is that, even if true, a sound objection to his work? For some people, at any rate, it is re- freshing to step aside from the hustle and bustle of literary missionaries and to enjoy a healthy rest with an author who does not burden his readers with any tedious lesson. As a matter of fact, whether Wilde had any fixed aim or not, his work most certainly points—and points clearly—to a definite goal. I think that there are those who will say that they have been led by this author to very fruitful regions. If some people feel that Wilde only takes them a giddy dance over tracts of glittering but useless beauty, there are others who feel that his restless flights helped them to realise the wonder of much that previously seemed common and graceless. What, pray, are many of Wilde's short stories, such as the 'Young King' and 'The Happy Prince,' but artistically embroidered pleas for social reform? Who can read Dorian Gray in- telligently without hearing the deep bass note of doom at first faint, but gradually growing louder and louder amid the brilliant cascade of frivolous treble notes till it drowns them in the final crash of just punishment for error? Can any one fail to note the stern moral lesson of Salomé? Who can study his other plays carefully without learning the superb philosophy of human life that runs through them like a silver thread amid a many-hued skein? And who can help observing the high aspirations which lift so much of his verse out of the sphere of mere decorated rhyme? The truth is, Wilde's work bristles with moral advice, but—partly owing to his own oft-repeated condemnation of stories with a moral, and partly owing to the innate obtuseness of most of his readers—it is constantly overlooked.

In the early nineties Wilde's position was almost unique; he was looked upon as a literary phenomenon defying satisfactory solution. His art bewildered, amazed, repelled; if a few here hailed him as worthy to rank with intellectual giants, a multitude there said his art was unreal, frothy, and sometimes dangerous. He was a kaleidoscope puzzle even to his own friends. This is shown by the impressions of him recorded by various personal friends; they all seemed to see a different man: none of their presentations agree. Still, Wilde kept on his way gyrating giddily onward. His art must sooner or later bear fruit and find its home; such ability could not be destined to be wasted. Then, just as he seemed on the point of grasping honour and glory, there came in his career that fatal crisis, the one bright spot in which was, perhaps, that it saved him from worse things. Prison life steadied him. It helped him to take a fuller, broader view of life, to recognise how incomplete had been his former life when it confined itself to the enjoyment of this world's splendour and refused to acknowledge or share in the world's sorrow. In the quiet of his cell he could write the pleading, passionate prose afterwards given us as De Profundis. This book has struck the public imagination. And to me, of all the puzzling problems connected with the unfortunate Oscar Wilde, none is so inexplicable as this. A book, the keynote of which is an abject almost grovelling humility, has captivated the hearts of a people whose chief characteristics are sturdiness and independence of character. It may seem a dreadful statement, but if I were asked to name any book by Wilde that was not quite healthy in tone, I should promptly mention De Profundis. At the same time, I should hasten to add that the unhealthy part of the book was the unavoidable outcome of the author's terrible position. The crushed must needs be very humble.

But, apart from that one demoralising note of excessive humility, De Profundis is a splendid progression of noble thoughts leading in very truth from the dank gutter to the gleaming stars. The price paid for its evolution by the author was awful, but, as a writer said recently in the Hibbert Journal, it may have been absolutely necessary. Both this book and *A Ballad of Reading Gaol* fill the gaps left in Oscar Wilde's earlier work—gaps which might have remained empty but for his downfall. Neither of these books is, perhaps, any real advance (from a purely literary point of view) on his former work. But because they are both serious, both more in accordance with the tastes of the 'man in the street,' they have effected a considerable change in the public attitude. It would be safe to say that Wilde's literary position was never less insecure than at the present time. The favourable reception awarded to his last two books has opened the door to a more sensible and fairer examination of all his books. And that is all we admirers of Wilde's genius demand. The rest—the eventual granting to Wilde of a niche in the temple of English literature—will follow in due course. Some of his work already smacks of 'the day before yesterday,' it is true; but much of it is imperishable, capable of standing the test of ages. Much of it represents some of the finest prose-poetry in our language. Oscar Wilde was our *one* English artist in words.

At length a turning-point has been reached. Oscar Wilde is once more on trial, but it is a trial whose result can involve no disgrace, but which may—surely will—bring him a radiant wreath of fame. It will last long, for there is a strong array of witnesses on either side, and there is much up-hill work for his advocates. The scarlet flame of his disgrace still throws a lurid light on all his literary works, but it has begun to grow paler and smaller, and ere long it may become extinct, and in its place will dazzle forth the jewelled light of his undying intellect, teaching our descendants about the eternity of beauty and joy, but bidding them never forget the temporary reign of pain and sorrow, beseeching them to sweep away the tainted refuse that hides the crystal purity below, asking them for justice. And will not these requests be granted? On the Continent, in America, the great awakening has begun; there, the genius has triumphed over the convict, the sinner has been lost in the artist. Must it be said, then, by a later generation that Britain alone never forgave the strange errors of one of her brightest thinkers, but was content to let foreign hands raise him and his from the mire? Surely no; surely we are not so rich in intellectual wealth that we can afford to pass *any* of our artists by 'on the other side.'

Anyhow, when the haze of Time has finally covered all trace of the human frailties of Oscar Wilde, his genius, now slowly forcing its way upward through many a clogging obstacle, will rise resplendent and glorious before the eyes of an understanding posterity.

98. James Joyce on
The Picture of Dorian Gray

1906

From a letter to Stanislaus Joyce, postmarked 19 August 1906, *Letters of James Joyce*, vol. II, ed. Richard Ellmann (New York, 1966), p. 150.

I have just finished *Dorian Grey* [*sic*]. Some chapters are like Huysmans, catalogued atrocities, lists of perfumes and instruments. The central idea is fantastic. Dorian is exquisitely beautiful and becomes awfully wicked: but never ages. His portrait ages. I can imagine the capital which Wilde's prosecuting counsel made out of certain parts of it. It is not very difficult to read between the lines. Wilde seems to have had some good intentions in writing it—some wish to put himself before the world—but the book is rather crowded with lies and epigrams. If he had had the courage to develop the allusions in the book it might have been better. I suspect he has done this in some privately printed books.

99. Archibald Henderson on Wilde's plays

1907

Signed article, titled 'The Dramas of Oscar Wilde', *Arena* [Boston] (August 1907), xxxviii, 134–9.

Archibald Henderson (1877–1963), American mathematician and man of letters, for many years a professor of mathematics at the University of North Carolina, was the author of Shaw's authorized biography. Despite his admiration for Wilde's plays, Henderson emphasizes their weaknesses; rather surprising is his tepid response to *The Importance of Being Earnest*, a play that 'never rises above the farcical plane'.

Nothing is easier than acquiescence in Wilde's dictum that the drama is the meeting place of art and life. And yet nowhere more clearly than in Wilde's own plays do we find the purposed divorce of art from life. It was his fundamental distinction, in the *rôle* of critic as artist, to trace with admirable clarity the line of demarcation between unimaginative realism and imaginative reality. The methods of Zola and the Naturalistic school always drew his keenest critical thrusts; and the greatest heresy, in his opinion, was the doctrine that art consists in holding up the kodak to nature. He was even so reactionary as to assert that the only real people are the people who never existed. The view of Stendhal, that fiction is *un miroir qui se promène sur la grande route*,[1] found as little favor in his eyes as the doctrine of Pinero that the dramatists are the brief and abstract chronometers of the time. The function of the artist, in his larger view, is to invent, not to chronicle; and he even went so far as to say that if a novelist is base enough to go to life for his personages, he should at least pretend that they are creations, and not boast of them as copies. To the charge that the people in his stories were 'mere catchpenny revelations of the nonexistent,' he unblushingly retorted: 'Life by its realism is always spoiling the subject matter of art. The supreme pleasure in literature is to realize the non-existent!'

---

[1] A mirror which travels on the highway.

The phenomenal popularity of Wilde's plays in an epoch of culture peculiarly marked by the *stigmata* of Naturalism is significant tribute to this rare quality of divertisement. At the time of their initial production in London, Wilde's comedies attained immediate and prolonged success; since that time they have frequently been played to captivated audiences in the United States and on the Continent. From the moment when *Salomé* was produced in Berlin by that greatest of modern actor-managers, Max Reinhard, Wilde's plays have continued to delight the theater-going public of German Europe. And the distinguished critic, Hagemann, only the other day, made so bold as to rank Wilde with Wedekind, Hoffsmannsthal, and Strindberg.

The current revival of interest in Wilde finds its source in many brochures and biographies recently published. And of those who have given competent critical testimony in regard to Wilde's work may be mentioned Carl Hagemann, Max Meyerfeld, Hedwig Lachmann, Henri de Regnier, Jean Joseph Renaud, and Arthur Symons. The plays have as yet received no adequate treatment in English; and the biography of Wilde recently published in England and America was wrongly conceived and thoroughly ill-advised. Indeed, the *raison d'être* of any critical study of Wilde is the worldwide success of his productions, viewed solely as works of art; and the only question for consideration is whether Wilde is entitled to genuine appreciation as a man of letters. There is no reason to doubt that his essays, entitled *Intentions* are subtle, brilliant, delightful, despite the fact that many of the theories propounded are whimsical, questionable and unsound. They have been translated into the principal languages of the globe, and in many countries, Italy and Austria in especial, have met with a laudation little short of panegyric. 'The Soul of Man Under Socialism' is a brilliant and subtle study, albeit profoundly radical and iconoclastic. And the fairy tales, with their delicate tracery of intent and lavish opulence of fancy, bid fair to become contemporary classics.

No such unanimity of critical opinion, however, obtains in the case of the plays. The literary claims put forward for them by German critics have so far found few if any adherents among English-speaking critics. In fact, when we pass them in review, we find that they are resplendent by reason of qualities which have no intrinsic or vital relation to dramatic art. This is particularly true of the society comedies, in which Wilde appears as the *causeur par excellence*,[1] and the clever critic of society.They rather tend to discredit the dramatist which the earlier plays proclaimed

[1] Most excellent talker.

Wilde to be. *Vera; or, The Nihilists*, written when Wilde was only twenty-two is the immature product of a romantic youth; and although it won the praise of Lawrence Barrett, should never have been published as a representative work. Modern Nihilistic Russia is the fervent background against which are silhouetted the thin profiles of Wilde's imagination; but the immaturity of its design, the pointlessness of its persiflage, and the melodrama of its plot label *Vera* a mere *Schauerstück*[1] of the weakest type. *The Duchess of Padua*, which Wilde wrote expressly for Mary Anderson who refused it, is the work of a genuine poet; and through its promise, rather than performance, gave indication of what high rank Wilde might have taken as a rival of the D'Annunzio of *Francesca da Rimini*; the Rostand of *Cyrano de Bergerac*, and the Phillips of *Paolo and Francesca*. A romantic drama of the Elizabethan model, *The Duchess of Padua* is remarkable for its tender lyricism, the romantic variations of its mood, the temperamental and passional *nuances* of its sentiment. Although the work of a 'theater poet,' like Goethe or Lessing, it possesses strong dramatic values, and would afford a worthy medium for the talent of a Julia Marlowe or an Ellen Terry.

Few plays of recent years have created more widespread discussion, appreciation and condemnation than *Salomé*, which furnished the libretto for the opera by the same name of Richard Strauss. It was originally written in French, was afterwards translated into English by Lord Alfred Douglas, and had the dubious distinction of being illustrated by that exotic artist, Aubrey Beardsley. Just as it was about to be produced in London by Sarah Bernhardt, in 1892, it was banned by the Queen's Reader of Plays; and for a time it was on the *index expurgatorius* of the German censorship. Within the last four years this play has been produced with remarkable success in the chief capitals of Europe; and Strauss' opera has been accorded a reception abroad little less remarkable. Wilde was strongly influenced by Flaubert's tale of *Hérodias*, but gave to the biblical episode a devitalizing tone of degeneracy which was not present in the French model. It is the most significant example of Maeterlinck's influence upon contemporary drama, in respect to the primitive simplicity of the dialogue, the poetry of the imagery, and the evocation of the atmosphere and imminence of doom. The coöperation of nature in intensifying the feeling of dread convicts Wilde of having carefully studied *La Princesse Maleine*; and we dimly feel the presentiment of those vast figures in the wings which

[1] Thriller.

overcloud the scene of *L'Intruse*. Much of the dialogue is remarkable for its grace and beauty; and the poetic phrasing holds at times a moon-lit radiance. But the theme itself is perverted and meretricious, with its noisome insinuations, its unveiled allusions to impure passion, its miasma of degeneracy. Little wonder that this impression gained solely from reading the play should be intensified by the instrumentalities of sight and sound to such an extent as to warrant the withdrawal of Strauss' opera from the stage of the Metropolitan Opera House.

A new, a strikingly different Wilde, next makes his *début* in the society comedy. Wilde's earlier plays brought him nothing, scarcely even notoriety, for the British public could not be persuaded to believe that any work of poetic beauty or dramatic art could emanate from a licensed jester, angler before all for the public stare. Wilde had in-contestably established his reputation as a buffoon; and once a buffoon, always a buffoon. One may truly say of Wilde, as Brandes once said of Ibsen, that at this period of his life he had a lyrical Pegasus killed under him. Like Bernard Shaw, Wilde was forced to the conclusion that the brain had ceased to be a vital organ in English life. The public, as he expressed it, used the classics as a means of checking the progress of Art, as bludgeons for preventing the free expression of Beauty in new forms. It was his aim to extend the subject-matter of art; and this was distaste-ful to the public since it was the expression of an individualism defiant of public opinion. And to Wilde, public opinion represented the will of the ignorant majority as opposed to that of the discerning few. Far from holding that the public is the patron of the artist, Wilde vigorously maintained that the artist is always the munificent patron of the public. The very bane of his existence was the popular, yet profoundly erron-eous, maxim that 'the drama's laws the drama's patrons give.' The work of art, he rightly avers, is to dominate the spectator: the spectator is not to dominate the work of art. The drama must come into being, not for the sake of the theater, but through the inner, vital necessity of the artist for self-expression. He scorned the field of popular novelism, not only because it was too ridiculously easy, but also because to meet the require-ments of the sentimental public with its half-baked conception of art, the artist would have to 'do violence to his temperament, would have to write not for the artistic joy of writing, but for the amusement of half-educated people, and so would have to suppress his individualism, forget his culture, annihilate his style, and surrender everything that is valuable to him.' In his search for a lucrative employment for his individual talents, his eye fell upon the comic stage. It dawned upon him that Tom Robertson and H. J. Byron, Sheridan and W. S. Gilbert were living factors in the English drama. While little scope was allowed the creator of the higher forms of dramatic art, in the field of burlesque and farcical comedy the artist was allowed very great freedom in England. It was under the pressure of such convictions that Wilde now sought a hazard of new fortunes.

Although as supreme an individualist as Ibsen, Wilde shows no point of contact with him as a dramatic artist; indeed, they are opposite poles in the drama of the time. Ibsen concerned himself with the tragedy of the age, Wilde with its comedy; intermediate between them stands Wedekind with his tragi-comedy. Wilde's comedies are always lightly spiced with that *grain de folie*,[1] sign-manual of Meilhac and Halévy of Gilbert and Sullivan. His comedy stems, not from the Ibsen of *Louis' Comedy* or the Hauptmann of *Der Rote Hahn* but from the Dumas *fils* of *Françillon* the Sardou of *Divorçons* and the Sheridan of *A School for Scandal*. In verve *esprit* and brilliance he is more akin to his fellow-countryman and fellow-townsman, Bernard Shaw; in both we find a defiant individualism, iconoclastic protest against conventional morality and a vein of subtle satire which gives piquant flavor to their every composition. In point of dramaturgic faculty, Wilde does not bear a moment's comparison with Ibsen, undoubtedly the supreme technician of his age. In Wilde's own opinion, his first acts are best not because, as with Shaw, they are concerned with the vigorous formulation of the dramatic problem, but because, in neglecting it, they give him free play for the irrelevant exercise of his wit. Unlike Ibsen's plays which begin many years before the opening of the first act, Wilde's comedies seldom begin until the play is half over. Wilde is even more intent upon amusement than upon instruction. To attempt analysis of Wilde's comedies were as profitless as to inquire into the composition of a *soufflée* or the manufacture of a Roman candle. It is enough that he translates us into *le monde ou l'on ne s'ennuie pas*.[2] Why carp because his theatric devices are as superficial and mechanical as those of Sardou, his sentimentality as mawkish as that of Sydney Grundy, and his moralizing as ghastly a misfit as the *Mea Culpa* of a Dowson or the confessional of a Verlaine!

Lady Windermere's Fan, the most celebrated of Wilde's comedies, is concerned with the hackneyed *donnée*[3] of the eternal triangle—the theme

---

[1] Dash of madness.
[2] The world in which one does not bore oneself.
[3] The fundamental idea.

of *Odette, Le Supplice d'Une Femme,* and countless other plays of the modern French school. Only by means of the flashing dialogue is Wilde enabled to conceal the essential conventionality and threadbare melodrama of the plot. The characters seldom impress us with their reality; and yet, by some marvelous trick of art, Wilde has succeeded in imparting to them 'the tone of the time.' In one or two places, the sparkle of the dialogue is unmatched for brilliancy in contemporary drama; and one scene at least attains a pitch of fine emotional intensity. The same sort of criticism applies to *A Woman of No Importance,* in which Wilde breaks a lance in behalf of even justice at the hands of society for men and women who have committed indiscretions. His play is the embodiment of his conviction that it was 'a burning shame that there should be one law for men and another law for women.' In answer to the complaint of the critics that *Lady Windermere's Fan* was lacking in action, Wilde wrote the first act of *A Woman of No Import-ance.* 'In the act in question,' said Wilde, 'there was absolutely no action at all. It was a perfect act!' In his plays, he always sought to throw the stress, not upon its mere technique, in which he was lamentably inept, but upon its quality of psychological interest. With Wilde, tempera-ment is the primal requisite for the artist: and the proper school to learn art in is not Life but Art. 'Nobody's else work gives me any suggestion,' he once basely prevaricated. 'It is only by entire isolation from every-thing that one can do any work. Idleness gives one the mood, isolation the conditions. Concentration on one's self recalls the new and wonder-ful world that one presents in the color and cadence of words in move-ment.' Wilde seeks to supply all deficiencies in the action by dazzling brilliancy in the dialogue. It is typical of Wilde's comedies that, whereas everything is always discussed, nothing is ever done.

It was Wilde's characteristic contention that there would never be any real drama in England until it is recognized that a play is as personal and individual a form of self-expression as a poem or a picture. Here Wilde laid his finger upon his own fundamental error. By nature and by necessity, the drama is, of all arts, the most impersonal; as Victor Hugo says, dramatic art consists in being somebody else. So supreme an individualist was Wilde that he lacked the dramatic faculty of self-detachment. He could never be anybody, but himself. To Bernard Shaw, Wilde appeared as, in a certain sense, the only thorough playwright in England, because he played with everything: with wit, with philosophy, with drama, with actors and audience, with the whole theater. The play, the play of course, is the thing; and to Wilde this meant—the play of ideas. The critics thought *An Ideal Husband* was a play about a bracelet; but Wilde maintained, not without show of reason, that they missed its entire psychology:

'the difference in the way in which a man loves a woman from that in which a woman loves a man; the passion that women have for making ideals (which is their weakness), and the weakness of a man who dares not show his imperfections to the thing he loves.'

The last of Wilde's plays—a rose-colored comedy or a fantastic farce, as you will—was *The Importance of Being Earnest*, sub-entitled *A Trivial Comedy for Serious People*. When Wilde's house in Tite Street was sacked after his conviction, the scenarios of several plays were found, in addition to a complete play entitled *The Woman Covered With Jewels*; and after his release from prison, he talked ardently of a dramatic scene about Pharoah, and of a spirited story on Judas; but all have either disappeared or never been born. *The Importance of Being Earnest*, a light, impossible farce in the French style, is based on the absurd complications arising from the employment of *aliases*. It is extravaganza such as only Wilde could write, and never rises above the farcical plane because its characters are endowed with every grace save the saving grace of reality. Wilde is reported to have said that 'the first act is ingenius, the second beautiful, the third abominably clever.' *The Importance of Being Earnest*, indeed, all of Wilde's comedies, indubitably testify, in the language of *Truth*, to the importance of being Oscar!

'To be free,' wrote a celebrity, 'one must not conform.' Wilde secured freedom in the drama through refusing to conform to the laws of dramatic art. He claimed the privileges without shouldering the responsibilities of the dramatist. He imported the methods of the *causerie* into the domain of the drama, and turned the theater into a house of mirth. Whether or no his destination was the palace of truth, certain it is that he always stopped at the half-way house. Art was the dominant note of his literary life; but it was not the art of drama, but the art of conversation. He made many delightful, many pertinent observations upon English life, and upon life in general; but they had no special relation to the dramatic theme he happened for the moment to have in mind. His plays live in and for the sake of the moment, neither enlarging the mental horizon nor dilating the heart. Wilde was too self-centered an individualist ever to come into any real or vital relation with life. It was his primal distinction as artist to be consumed with a passionate love of Art. It was his primal deficiency as artist to have no genuine sympathy with humanity. And although he imaged life with clearness and distinction, certain it is that he never saw life steadily, nor even saw it whole.

100. R. A. Scott-James on *De Profundis*

1908

From Chapter VI, titled 'The Decadents', in *Modernism and Romance* (1908), pp. 71–5.

Rolfe Arnold Scott-James (1878–1959), journalist, critic, and editor of the *London Mercury*, writes in his chapter on the Decadents that they are egoists who create 'their own standards of pleasure' and morality. Immediately preceding the discussion of Wilde, he writes of the typical Decadent: 'All that is ugly, base and jarring will be used for the purposes of background to the picture. His aim is to find new raw material for sensations, and new arts with which to incarnate them.'

To take the case of the late Oscar Wilde is, no doubt, to taken an extreme instance. But suppose we consider that one of his works which seemed to show him in his most sincere mood, at a time when, as many have asserted, he repented his life and turned to the deep contemplation of religion. Suddenly in *De Profundis* we find him declaring: 'I need not tell you that to me reformations in morals are as meaningless and vulgar as Reformations in theology.' This is only one of many sentences in his prison utterance which show that it was too hastily judged by many of the newspaper critics. Most of them, recalling the tragedy of his death and his return from prison to an unreformed life, wondered how these melodious confessions of regret, this intimate talk about Christ and the Gospels, could be reconciled with so shameful an ending. They affected to see in this little book something like a death-bed repentance, the expression of poignant regret for a moral suicide, the finding of consolation in religion and the celebration, as it were, of the rites of Supreme Unction. But for my part I cannot find in those confessions the last utterances of a fallen tragic hero, with the well-proportioned tragedy marred only by a sordid ending. Nor does it seem necessary to regard these pages as a deliberate deceit, as one of the intentional poses of a man who had lived always before the footlights. 'It is a very un-imaginative nature,' he says himself, 'which only cares for people on their pedestals.' Perhaps this fine writing, with its Epicurean philosophy, is not so incompatible with the dismal after-act as many have supposed.

To be fair to the book, there are not many sentences which strike a false note or suggest a resonant appeal to the balcony. The studied phrase, the seeking after the just effect of words, the delicate poise of thought and feeling, these indeed are to be found, but are they not the very art of which Wilde, 'once a lord of language,' as he proudly calls himself, was always a consummate master? In the moments of anguish in his prison he felt the need of expressing his mood and his feelings about life as he, by nature an artist, had always felt it. 'Expression,' he cries—and why should the use of a fine simile be a token of insincerity? —'expression is as necessary to me as leaf and blossoms are to the black branches of the trees that show themselves above the prison walls and are so restless in the wind.' What Wilde felt, meant and knew in Reading gaol he has written down truthfully, and to me it seems perfectly consistent with his brilliant literary career and his contemptible philosophy.

After all, when he began to write this book, he had passed through the period of tears and bitter complaint, of self-reproach and mortifica-tion, and now he had begun again to 'possess his soul,' to 'feel more regret for the people who laughed than for myself,' to accept proudly and turn to account this period of suffering. The book is not a confession of sin; it is a challenge and a vindication of the life of universal experi-ence. He boldly reviews himself as 'a man who stood in symbolic relations to the art and culture' of his age. Suddenly he finds that his crime has turned 'a sort of eternity of fame to an eternity of infamy,' and in the degradation of his prison cell he for the first time learns the full meaning of 'sorrow.' But he refuses to be crushed by it; he is not fundamentally ashamed at his own 'perversity'; he is much more concerned to learn the meaning of this strange experience—sorrow— one of the few great emotions he had never understood.

I don't regret for a single moment having lived for pleasure. I did it to the full, as one should do everything that one does. There was no pleasure I did not experience. I threw the pearl of my soul into a cup of wine. I went down the primrose path to the sound of flutes. I lived on honeycomb. But to have continued the same life would have been wrong, because it would have been limiting. I had to pass on. The other half of the garden had its secrets for me also.

This is not the note of repentance. Surely it is nearer to exultation. If now he is prepared to accept sorrow and the 'treasure' of humility, it is not because he regrets, but because, having exhausted one field of emotion, he seeks a new range of life, where the feeling may be more intense and the outlook of a deeper and more vivid hue. His very degradation is to be an influence in 'spiritualising the soul.' 'I want to get to the point when I shall be able to say quite simply, and without affectation, that the two great turning-points in my life were when my father sent me to Oxford, and when society sent me to prison.'

And then there are those intimate, unfamiliar passages about Christ and the Gospels. Here is no spectacle of a sinner turning for comfort to the broad charity of the Christian religion. It is in no humble spirit of surrender that he approaches the study of Christ the individual. Rather there is a touch of proud defiance, of self-confidence and inalienable egotism, the utmost that the Greeks meant by ὕβρις[1] in the manner in which he reads nineteenth century aestheticism into the personality of Christ. He speaks of 'Christ as the precursor of the romantic movement in life'; as one who saw that 'to be unpractical was to be a great thing'; who 'through some divine instinct in him seems to have always loved the sinner as being the nearest possible approach to the perfection of man.' 'That is the charm about Christ,' he says, as if he were speaking of a picture; his whole life 'is really an idyll'; there is an 'intimate and immediate connection between the true life of Christ and the true life of the artist.' His place, he says with later Renaissance blitheness, 'is with the poets'; and thus the greatest spiritual influence in the western world is rhythmically and insolently relegated to the exclusive poetical coterie of Shelley and Sophocles and Oscar Wilde!

Surely in the whole history of literature no 'confessions' ever contained so proud and wilful a self-justification as this attempt to justify an unordered epicureanism—the decadent philosophy of Wilde—by an appeal to the spirit of the Gospels! With its clear, rhythmic language, its union of thought and feeling, its direct appeal to the sense of the

---

[1] Hubris, the characteristic response of the Greek tragic hero to the gods.

beautiful, *De Profundis* may possibly have attained a lasting place in literature. But its author is one whom Plato would have sent on crowned and garlanded to another city. He has proclaimed that the undisciplined life was good. He writes in no chastened spirit of submission, but with a cry of self-approval and triumph. Not content to say, 'Evil, be thou my good,' he has the daring to make even the gods his accomplices.

---

101. St John Hankin on Wilde's collected plays

1908

Signed article, titled 'The Collected Plays of Oscar Wilde', *Fortnightly Review* (1 May 1908), lxxxiii, n.s., 791–802.

St John Hankin (1869–1909), critic and playwright, who was an admirer of Ibsen, here offers several startling observations, the first being that *The Importance of Being Earnest* is Wilde's 'most serious' and 'most sincere' play—'the very greatest of English comedies'—a departure from previous critical estimates, but Hankin's remark that it was a movement toward 'more naturalistic methods of the newer schools' is equally startling—and certainly untrue—for the 'curtains' that he discusses are less significant than the dandiacal element that dominates the play. The climax of startling moments occurs towards the close of Hankin's article, where *Salomé* is declared Wilde's 'greatest play'. (In the penultimate paragraph of his article, Hankin asks whether the original four-act script of Wilde's *Importance* still exists. A quarter of the manuscript is in the British Museum; the remainder, including the deleted act, is in the Arents Collection, The New York Public Library. The four-act version was reconstructed and edited by Vyvyan Holland for publication in 1957.)

The complete edition of the works of Oscar Wilde, which Messrs. Methuen are now issuing under the editorship of Mr. Robert Ross, has a special interest for the student of the English drama of the latter part of the nineteenth century. For the first six volumes of it are devoted to the plays, and by their appearance one is now enabled for the first time to consider their author's dramatic work as a whole. Hitherto this has been impossible, since the early plays, *Vera, or The Nihilists* and *The Duchess of Padua*, and also the fragment of *A Florentine Tragedy*—which belongs in style to the early period though it was actually written comparatively late in his career—have never hitherto been either published or publicly performed in this country. *The Duchess of Padua* was originally produced in the United States, and has also been played, in a prose translation, in Germany, and both it and *Vera* have been printed in pirated editions in America and elsewhere. But seeing that the pirated edition of *Vera* was a careless and inaccurate reprint from a prompt copy, and that of *The Duchess of Padua* a prose translation of the German version—Wilde's play is in blank verse—it will be understood that not much help could be got from them by anyone who desired to form a critical estimate of the plays, even if he were prepared to go to the trouble and expense of smuggling them.

This unsatisfactory state of things is now at an end. All the plays are now published in an authorised and unmutilated form, and though one cannot pretend that any of the three now printed for the first time are on a level with their author's best work, they have their importance for anyone who wishes to understand Wilde as a dramatist and to estimate his powers and his limitations. On the whole, they certainly illustrate the limitations rather than the powers. Mr. Ross, in a characteristic dedicatory letter prefixed to *The Duchess of Padua*, acknowledges with engaging frankness that the play is artistically of small account, and that its author at the end of his life recognised the fact. In doing so, I think Mr. Ross has acted wisely. Honesty is the first essential in an editor, and nothing is to be gained by pretending that bad work is good—especially as in this case the pretence could take nobody in.

There will be some people, perhaps, who will urge that if a play is poor it is hardly worth exhuming after so many years, and that Wilde's reputation can only suffer by its publication. But this, I think, is a mistaken view. Writers of real distinction stand or fall by the best they produced, not by the worst. Byron and Wordsworth wrote plenty of inferior verse, which is duly entombed in the collected editions of their works. But no sane person pretends to think the less of their genius on that account. If *Vera* and *The Duchess of Padua* were far worse plays than they are—*Vera* could hardly be that, by the way—it would still be desirable that they should be published. Wilde is a writer of quite sufficient power and accomplishment to deserve the compliment of a complete edition. Moreover, the early work of great writers has an interest for intelligent people out of all proportion to its intrinsic merit. Ibsen's early plays are frankly bad for the most part and no one can pretend that the actual artistic loss to the world would have been great if they had vanished as completely as the lost plays of Aeschylus. But they are interesting for the indications they contain of certain tendencies in his genius, and of the lines on which that genius was to develop, and for this reason the critic would regret their disappearance, though he cannot pretend that there is any particular aesthetic pleasure to be derived from their perusal.

From this point of view, it must be confessed, the early plays of Wilde are less illuminating, for there is far less of Wilde in the early Wilde plays than there is of Ibsen in the early Ibsens. *Lady Inger of Osträt* is a poor play with an elaborate intrigue constructed on absurd Scribe lines—and not very well constructed. For, whereas Scribe's construction is always clear and workmanlike, *Lady Inger*'s is involved and tenebrous. Mysterious strangers pop in and out of dimly-lighted chambers, and nobody, either on the stage or in the auditorium, is allowed to know who they are or what they are about. When the Stage Society performed the play a season or two ago in London only a small fraction of the audience succeeded in disentangling the plot. This is quite remarkable in a play by the man who was to evolve the superb technique of the 'social dramas.' But though *Lady Inger* is a preposterous play, the eye of faith can see in it something of the Ibsen that was to come. There is an austerity and simplicity in the dialogue, an absence of mere rhetoric for its own sake, and a relative naturalness in the character drawing and the incidents which differentiate it from the work of his predecessors, and herald, faintly but surely, the rising of a new school of drama. Wilde's early work is less prophetic. There are moments in *Vera* and *The Duchess of Padua* when the dialogue or the characterisation gives a foretaste of the later comedies. The talk between the Russian Cabinet Councillors in *Vera* reads rather like a parody of the talk between the men in Lord Darlington's rooms in *Lady Windermere's Fan*, while Padua's Duke is a sort of blank-verse Lord Illingworth. And there is the same faculty for working up an exciting theatrical scene, the same fatal tendency to rely upon rhetoric instead of simplicity in emotional scenes, which made—and marred—the author's plays almost to the end. But except for this, the early drama give no hint of the later work. The reason, of course, is simple enough. Wilde as a playwright was always an imitator rather than an original artist. In him, in fact, the faculty of imitation was carried to a point that was almost genius. He had an extraordinarily keen sense of literary style. If he had had ambitions in that direction he might have become a literary forger of the first distinction worthy to rank with Chatterton or Simonides. And, as was natural, this imitative faculty of his had the fullest play in his earliest work. Every artist begins by imitating someone. Even the greatest genius does not spring full-born from the head of Zeus. After a time he 'finds himself,' and ceases to be an echo, but in the beginning he models himself on others.

The difficulty about Wilde as a playwright was that he never quite got through the imitative phase. *The Importance of Being Earnest* is the nearest approach to absolute originality that he attained. In that play, for the first time, he seemed to be tearing himself away from tradition and to be evolving a dramatic form of his own. Unhappily it was the last play he was to write, and so the promise in it was never fulfilled. Had his career not been cut short at this moment, it is possible that this might have proved the starting-point of a whole series of 'Trivial Comedies for Serious People,' and that thenceforward Wilde would have definitely discarded the machine-made construction of the Scribe-Sardou theatre which had held him too long and begun to use the drama as an artist should, for the expression of his own personality, not the manufacture of clever *pastiches*. It would then have become possible to take him seriously as a dramatist. For, paradoxical as it may sound in the case of so merry and light-hearted a play, *The Importance of Being Earnest* is artistically the most serious work that Wilde produced for the theatre. Not only is it by far the most brilliant of his plays considered as literature. It is also the most sincere. With all its absurdity, its psychology is truer, its criticism of life subtler and more profound, than that of the other plays. And even in its technique it shows, in certain details, a breaking away from the conventional well-made play of the 'seventies and 'eighties in favour of the looser construction and more naturalistic methods of the newer school.

Consider its 'curtains' for a moment and compare them with those of the conventional farce or comedy of their day or of Wilde's other plays. In the other plays Wilde clung tenaciously to the old-fashioned 'strong' curtain, and I am bound to say he used it with great cleverness, though the cleverness seems to me deplorably wasted. The curtain of the third act of *Lady Windermere's Fan*, when Mrs. Erlynne suddenly emerges from Lord Darlington's inner room, and Lady Windermere, taking advantage of the confusion, glides from her hiding-place in the window and makes her escape unseen, is theatrically extremely effective. So is that of the third act of *An Ideal Husband*, when Mrs. Chieveley triumphantly carries off Lady Chiltern's letter under the very eyes of Lord Goring, who cannot forcibly stop her because his servant enters at that moment in answer to her ring. It is a purely theatrical device only worthy of a popular melodrama. But it produces the requisite thrill in the theatre. On the analogy of these plays one would expect to find in *The Importance of Being Earnest* the traditional 'curtains' of well-made farce, each act ending in what used to be called a 'tableau' of comic bewilderment or terror or indignation. Instead of this we have really no 'curtains' at all. Acts I. and II. end in the casual, go-as-you-please fashion of the ultra-naturalistic school. They might be the work of Mr. Granville Barker. Of course, there is nothing really go-as-you-please about them save in form. They are as carefully thought out, as ingenious in the best sense, as the strong 'curtain' could possibly be. But this will not appear to the superficial observer, who will probably believe that these acts 'end anyhow'. Here is the end of Act I.:—

ALGERNON Oh, I'm a little anxious about poor Bunbury, that is all.

JACK If you don't take care, your friend Bunbury will get you into a serious scrape some day.

ALGERNON I love scrapes. They are the only things that are never serious.

JACK Oh, that's nonsense, Algy. You never talk anything but nonsense.

ALGERNON Nobody ever does.

(Curtain)

This may seem an easy, slap-dash method of ending an act, and one which anybody can accomplish, but it is very far from being so easy as it looks. To make it effective in the theatre—and in *The Importance of Being Earnest* it is enormously effective—requires at least as much art as the more elaborate devices of the earlier comedies. Only in this case it is the art which conceals art which is required, not the art which obtrudes it.

In *The Importance of Being Earnest*, in fact, Wilde really invented a new type of play, and that type was the only quite original thing he contributed to the English stage. In form it is farce, but in spirit and in treatment it is comedy. Yet it is not farcical comedy. Farcical comedy is a perfectly well recognised class of drama and a fundamentally different one. There are only two other plays which I can think of which belong to the same type—*Arms and the Man* and *The Philanderer*. *Arms and the Man*, like *The Importance of Being Earnest*, is psychological farce, the farce of ideas. In it Mr. Shaw, like Wilde, has taken the traditional farcical form—the last acts of both plays are quite on traditional lines in their mechanism—and breathed into it a new spirit. Similarly, *The Philanderer* is psychological farce, though here there is less farce and more psychology. Unluckily, the Court performances of this play were marked by a dismal slowness and a portentous solemnity by which its freakish humour and irresponsibility were hidden away out of sight, and its true character completely obscured. Properly played, it would prove, I believe, one of the most amusing and delightful things in Mr. Shaw's theatre.

Having spoken of the most original of Wilde's plays, let me turn now to the least original, to the one in which his imitative faculty finds its fullest expression, *The Duchess of Padua*. *The Duchess of Padua* is a really remarkable example of this faculty. I may add that it is also an extremely amusing one, though the humour is, I suspect, wholly unconscious. It is a tragedy planned on the most ambitious Elizabethan lines, though a certain concession to Mid-Victorian theatrical conventions is made in the way of 'strong' curtains. In all other ways it follows its models with touching fidelity. Here you have the swelling rhetoric, the gorgeous imagery, the piling up of the agony, of Webster himself. There is the magniloquent verse for the nobles and the homely prose for the populace to which Shakespeare has accustomed us. First and Second Citizen speak with all the traditional imbecility. The croaking raven bellows for revenge. His name in this case is Moranzone. There is a Court scene in the manner of *The Merchant of Venice*. In fact, there is everything which one might count on finding in the play of a genuine Elizabethan—except originality. That, unluckily, is absent. *The Duchess of Padua*, in fact, is an exercise, a study in style, not an authentic work of art. Indeed, there are moments when it is not merely a study but something dangerously like a parody. Here is an example. It comes from the opening scene of the fourth act:—

MORANZONE Is the Duke dead?
SECOND CITIZEN He has a knife in his heart, which they say is not healthy for any man.
MORANZONE Who is accused of having killed him?
SECOND CITIZEN Why, the prisoner, sir.
MORANZONE But who is the prisoner?
SECOND CITIZEN Why, he that is accused of the Duke's murder.
MORANZONE I mean, what is his name?
SECOND CITIZEN Faith, the same which his godfathers gave him: what else should it be!

This kind of thing is quite amusing as a skit, but it is a little out of place in a serious tragedy.

And some of the blank verse passages are equally funny with their elaborate reproduction of the best Elizabethan manner, though here the humour is subtler:—

GUIDO	Let me find mercy when I go at night
	And do foul murder.
DUCHESS	Murder did you say?

Murder is hungry, and still cries for more,
And Death, his brother, is not satisfied,
But walks the house, and will not go away,
Unless he has a comrade! Tarry, Death,
For I will give thee a most faithful lackey
To travel with thee! Murder, call no more,
For thou shalt eat thy fill. There is a storm
Will break upon this house before the morning
So horrible, that the white moon already
Turns grey and sick with terror, the low wind
Goes moaning round the house, and the high stars
Run madly through the vaulted firmament,
As though the night wept tears of liquid fire
For what the day shall look upon. O weep
Thou lamentable heaven! Weep thy fill!
Though sorrow like a cataract drench the fields,
And make the earth one bitter lake of tears,
It would not be enough.   (*A peal of thunder*)
                    Do you not hear?
There is artillery in the Heavens to-night.
Vengeance is wakened up, and has unloosed
His dogs upon the world, and in this matter
Which lies between us two let him who draws
The thunder on his head beware the ruin
Which the forked flame brings after.

GUIDO	Away! Away!

Would Webster or Cyril Tourneur do it differently? Or any better for that matter? I think not. *The Duchess of Padua* is a school exercise, a set of Latin verses, as it were, constructed after the best Ovidian models, but it is the exercise of a very exceptional schoolboy. And though all of it is imitative and some of it is absurd, it has from the theatrical stand-point very real merits. It is not great drama in any sense, but it would be very effective on the stage—which, after all, is what plays are meant to be. It has a good harrowing plot, plenty of 'thrills,' plenty of declamation, and plenty of impassioned love-making, everything, in fact, which makes for success with the romantic playgoer. The principal characters, too, except the Duke, who is frankly ridiculous, are well drawn after their kind. Not subtly drawn, of course—subtlety would be thrown away in work of this kind—but drawn clearly and boldly. Some of the verse is really fine, and none of it sinks below a respectable level. Altogether, as the work of quite a young man it is creditable enough. If all the blank verse dramas which have graced the English stage during the past ten years had been half as good, the discerning critic would have had less to complain of.

The Duchess of Padua, in fact, is quite good second-rate work. But as soon as you compare it with first-rate work the poverty of its texture at once becomes obvious. Browning, in A Soul's Tragedy—I think his best, because his most characteristic and individual, play—took a subject belonging to much the same period as The Duchess of Padua. His scene also is mediaeval Italy where cities groan under the tyranny of their rulers and worldly ecclesiastics pull the strings of government. But where Wilde could only turn out a clever copy of other men's work, Browning produced an entirely original type of drama, which bears in every line the impress of his own personality, which nobody else could have written. It is a real reconstruction of the life of its period as Browning saw it, not as he believed Shakespeare or Webster would have seen it. It has its alternation of blank verse and homely prose, but here too Browning is no mere imitator. He does not simply borrow a trick from the Elizabethans. His first, second and third citizens talk their prose and make their simple jokes in it, but their speeches never for a moment read like a parody of the gravediggers in Hamlet. And it is not only the citizens who talk prose. The Papal Legate talks prose too—because he thinks prose. So do the romantic characters, Chiappino and the rest, when they have come down from the romantic heights and have to face a commonplace, practical issue. Browning himself, it will be remembered, divides the play into two parts, 'Act I., being what was called the poetry of Chiappino's life, and Act II., its prose,' and he writes the first act in verse and the second in prose to carry out the idea. This is to give a fresh significance to the traditional blending of verse and prose in tragedy, and put fresh life into what had become an obsolete convention. If The Duchess of Padua had been written with the artistic sincerity of A Soul's Tragedy—Wilde, by the way, admired that play very highly—Mr. Ross would not have had to write so deprecatingly of it in his dedicatory letter.

The same imitative quality which prevents one from taking *The Duchess of Padua* seriously as a work of art mars the comedies also. As far as plot and construction are concerned they are frankly modelled on the 'well-made play' of their period. Indeed, they were already old-fashioned in technique when they were written. The long soliloquy which opens the third act of *Lady Windermere's Fan* with such appalling staginess, and sends a cold shiver down one's back at each successive revival, was almost equally out of date on the first night. Ibsen had already sent that kind of thing to the right-about for all persons who aspired to serious consideration as dramatists. Luckily the fame of Wilde's comedies does not rest on his plots or his construction. It rests on his gifts of characterisation and of brilliant and effective dialogue. Both these gifts he possessed in a pre-eminent degree, but in both of them one has to recognise grave limitations. His minor characters are generally first-rate, but he never quite succeeded with his full-length figures. He is like an artist who can produce marvellously life-like studies or sketches, but fails when he attempts to elaborate a portrait. Windermere and Lady Windermere, Sir Robert and Lady Chiltern, none of them is really human, none of them quite alive. As for the principal people in *A Woman of No Importance*, Lord Illingworth himself, Mrs. Arbuthnot and her son, Hester Worsley, they are all dolls. The sawdust leaks out of them at every pore. That is the central weakness of the play, that and its preposterous plot. But when you turn to the minor characters, to Lady Hunstanton and Lady Caroline Pontefract and Sir John and the Archdeacon, how admirably they are drawn! Did anybody ever draw foolish or pompous or domineering old ladies better than Wilde? Think of Lady Hunstanton's deliciously idiotic reply to poor Miss Worsley when that American young lady, with impassioned fervour, has just been proclaiming to the assembled company the domestic virtues of her countrymen who are 'trying to build up something that will last longer than brick or stone.' 'What is that, dear?' asks Lady Hunstanton with perfect simplicity. 'Ah yes, an Iron Exhibition, is it not, at that place which has the curious name?' How it sets before us in a flash the whole character of the speaker, her gentleness, her stupidity, her admirable good breeding as contrasted with Miss Worsley's crude provincialism! Or again, think of that other reply of hers when Mrs. Allonby tells her that in the Hunstanton conservatories there is an orchid that is 'as beautiful as the Seven Deadly Sins.' 'My dear, I hope there is nothing of the kind. I will certainly speak to the gardener.'

Lady Caroline is equally well drawn, with her sharp tongue and her shrewd masculine common sense. She also has a brief encounter with Miss Worsley, in which the latter is again put to rout, but by quite different means. Lady Hunstanton conquered by sheer gentle futility. Lady Caroline administers a deliberate snub, all the more crushing because it is given with a deadly semblance of unconsciousness. Here is the scene:—

HESTER Lord Henry Weston! I remember him, Lady Hunstanton. A man with a hideous smile and a hideous past. He is asked everywhere. No dinner-party is complete without him. What of those whose ruin is due to him? They are outcasts. They are nameless. If you met them in the street you would turn your head away. I don't complain of their punishment. Let all women who have sinned be punished.

LADY HUNSTANTON My dear young lady!

HESTER It is right that they should be punished, but don't let them be the only ones to suffer. If a man and a woman have sinned, let them both go forth into the desert to love or loathe each other there. Let them both be branded. Set a mark, if you wish, on each, but don't punish the one and let the other go free. Don't have one law for men and another for women. You are unjust to women in England. And till you count what is a shame in a woman to be an infamy in a man, you will always be unjust, and Right, that pillar of fire, and Wrong, that pillar of cloud, will be made dim to your eyes, or be not seen at all, or if seen, not regarded.

LADY CAROLINE *Might I, dear Miss Worsley, as you are standing up, ask you for my cotton that is just behind you? Thank you.*

It must be admitted that in order to get his effect, Wilde has exaggerated the rhetoric of Miss Worsley's speech to an unfair degree, thereby 'loading the dice' against her in the encounter. But the effect is so admirable in the theatre that one forgives the means.

When I say that it was only in his 'minor characters' that Wilde was completely successful, I do not mean unimportant characters, or characters who only make brief appearances in his plays, such as the walking ladies and gentlemen in his evening parties, or the impassive men-servants who wait upon Lord Goring and Mr. Algernon Moncrieff. I include under the description all the people who are not emotionally of prime importance to the plot. Lady Bracknell and the Duchess of Berwick are very important parts in the plays in which they appear, and Wilde obviously took an immense amount of trouble

with them, but they are not emotionally important as Lady Windermere is or Mrs. Erlynne. In that sense they are minor characters. It is
in the drawing of such characters that Wilde is seen absolutely at his
best. Who can ever forget Lady Bracknell's superb scene with Mr.
Worthing in *The Importance of Being Earnest*, when she puts that
gentleman through a series of questions as he is 'not on her list of
eligible bachelors, though she has the same list as the dear Duchess of
Bolton'? Who can forget the inimitable speech in which she sums up
the sorrows of the modern landowner?—

What between the duties expected of one during one's lifetime, and the duties
exacted from one after one's death, land has ceased to be either a profit or a
pleasure. It gives one position, and prevents one from keeping it up. That is all
that can be said about land.

Yes, Lady Bracknell is an immortal creation. She is in some ways
the greatest achievement of the Wilde theatre, the fine flower of his
genius. It is impossible to read any of her scenes—indeed, it is impossible
to read almost any scene whatever in *The Importance of Being Earnest*—
without recognising that for brilliancy of wit this play may fairly be
ranked with the very greatest of English comedies. But though Lady
Bracknell is wonderfully drawn, she is not profoundly drawn. As a
character in so very light a comedy, there is, of course, no reason why
she should be. I merely mention the fact lest she should be claimed as an
exception to the statement that Wilde's more elaborate portraits are all
failures. Lady Bracknell is brilliantly done, but she is a brilliant surface
only. She has no depth and no subtlety. Wilde has seen her with
absolute clearness, but he has seen her, as it were, in two dimensions
only, not in the round. That is the weak point of all Wilde's character
drawing. It lacks solidity. No one can hit off people's external mani-
festations, their whims and mannerisms, their social insincerities, more
vividly or more agreeably than he. But he never shows you their souls.
And when it is necessary that he should do so, if you are really to understand and to sympathise with them, as it is in the case of Mrs. Arbuthnot, for example, or Lady Chiltern, he fails.

Why he failed I do not know. Possibly it was from mere indolence,
because he was not sufficiently interested. Possibly he could not have
succeeded if he tried. To analyse character to the depths requires
imaginative sympathy of a very special kind, and I am not sure whether
Wilde possessed this, or at least possessed it in the requisite degree of
intensity. He had a quick eye for the foibles of mankind and a rough

working hypothesis as to their passions and weaknesses. Beyond that he does not seem to me to have gone, and I doubt it ever occurred to him to examine the springs of action of even his most important characters with any thoroughness. So long as what they did and the reasons assigned for their doing it would pass muster in the average English theatre with the average English audience, he was content. That is not the spirit in which the great characters of dramatic literature have been conceived.

The fact is, Wilde despised the theatre. He was a born dramatist in the sense that he was naturally equipped with certain very valuable gifts for writing for the stage. But he was not a dramatist from conviction in the sense that Ibsen was or that Mr. Shaw is. Ibsen wrote plays, not because play-writing seemed a particularly promising or remunerative calling in the Norway of his day. It did not. He wrote plays because the dramatic form irresistibly attracted him. Mr. Shaw writes plays because he believes in the stage as an influence, as the most powerful and the most far-reaching of pulpits. Wilde's attitude towards the theatre was utterly different from either of these. He wrote plays frankly for the market and because play-writing was lucrative. Of course, he put a certain amount of himself into them. No artist can help doing that. But no artist of Wilde's power and originality ever did it less. His plays were frankly manufactured to meet a demand and to earn money. There is, of course, no reason why an artist should not work for money. Indeed, all artists do so more or less. They have to live like their neighbours. Unhappily, Wilde wanted a great deal of money, and he wanted it quickly. He loved luxury, and luxury cannot be had for nothing. And if an artist wants a large income and wants it at once, he generally has to condescend a good deal to get it. Wilde condescended. He looked around him at the kind of stuff which other playwrights were making money by, examined it with contemptuous acumen, saw how it was done—and went and did likewise. The only one of his plays which seems to me to be written with conviction, because he had something to express and because the dramatic form seemed to him the right one in which to express it, is *Salome*—and *Salome* was not written for the theatre. When Wilde wrote it he had no idea of its ever being acted. But when Madame Bernhardt one day asked him in jest why he had never written her a play, he replied, equally in jest, 'I have,' and sent her *Salome*. She read it, and, as we know, would have produced it in London if the Censor of Plays had not intervened. But when Wilde wrote it, it was not with a view to its ever being performed, and so his genius had free scope. He was writing to please himself, not to please a manager, and the result is that *Salome* is his best play. *The Importance of Being Earnest* is written with conviction, in a sense. That is to say, it is the expression of the author's own temperament and his attitude towards life, not an insincere re-statement of conventional theatrical ideas. But *The Importance of Being Earnest* is only a joke, though an amazingly brilliant one, and Wilde seems to have looked upon it with the same amused contempt with which he looked on its predecessors. Perhaps he did not realise how good it was. At least he treated it with scant respect, for the original script was in four acts, and these were boiled down into three and the loose ends joined up in perfunctory fashion for purposes of representation. I wonder whether there is any copy of that four-act version still in existence, by the way? It is just possible that a copy is to be found at the Lord Chamberlain's office, for it may have been submitted for license in its original form. If so, I hope Mr. Ross will obtain permission to copy it with a view to its publication. If the deleted act is half as delightful as the three that survive, every playgoer will long to read it. But that a man of Wilde's theatrical skill and experience should have written a play which required this drastic 'cutting'—or should have allowed it to be so cut if it did not require it—is an eloquent proof of his contempt for play-writing as an art.

Yes, Wilde despised the drama, and the drama avenged itself. With his gifts for dialogue and characterisation, his very remarkable 'sense of the theatre,' he might have been a great dramatist if he had been willing to take his art seriously. But he was not willing. The result was that in the age of Ibsen and of Hauptmann, of Strindberg and Brieux, he was content to construct like Sardou and think like Dumas *fils*. Had there been a National Theatre in this country in his day, or any theatre of dignity and influence to which a dramatist might look to produce plays for their artistic value, not solely for their value to the box office, Wilde might, I believe, have done really fine work for it. But there was not. And Wilde loved glitter and success. It would not have amused him to write 'uncommercial' masterpieces to be produced for half a dozen *matinées* at a Boxers' Hall. His ambition—if he can be said to have had any 'ambition' at all where the theatre was concerned—did not lie in that direction. So he took the stage as he found it, and wrote 'pot-boilers.' It is not the least of the crimes of the English theatre of the end of the nineteenth century that it could find nothing to do with a fine talent such as Wilde's save to degrade and waste it.

102. Arthur Symons on Wilde as 'a prodigious entertainer'

1908

Unsigned review, *Athenaeum*, 16 May 1908, pp. 598–600.

Symons's sane evaluation of Wilde's achievement did not entirely please Vernon Horace Rendall, editor of the *Athenaeum*, for in a letter dated 12 June 1908, he wrote to Robert Ross: 'I thought myself our reviewer was a little hard on Wilde, in particular under-rating his work on the Aesthetic movement, which did away with early Victorian horrors.' (From *Robert Ross: Friend of Friends*, ed. Margery Ross, pp. 149–50.)

Oscar Wilde was a prodigious entertainer, and now that his complete works are brought together—eleven volumes of them, with another or two to come, in white and pale gold covers, fine paper, print, and margins, each volume separate, so that they can be arranged in what order you like—they have the aspect of a kind of *Thousand and One Nights*, so vari-coloured are they. The whole pageant is decorative, and passes swiftly; blood streams harmlessly across stages where a sphinx sits, with and without a secret, repeating clanging verse and mysterious prose, and where Sicilian shepherds and young girls on English lawns pass and return, and everywhere paradox-puppets turn somersaults like agile acrobats to the sound of a faint music which sometimes rises to a wild clamour. Verse and prose are spoken by carefully directed marionettes; songs, dialogues, and dramas are presented, with changing scenery and bewildering lights. At times the showman comes before the curtain, and, cutting a caper, argues, expostulates, and calls the attention of the audience to the perfection of the mechanism by which his effects are produced, and his own skill in the handling of the wires. Scene follows scene, without rest or interval, until suddenly the lights go out, and the play is over.

Such an artificial world Wilde created, and it is only now beginning to settle down into any sort of known order. In Germany he is the writer of *Salome*, in France a poet and critic, in England the writer of *The Ballad of Reading Gaol*, or perhaps of *De Profundis*. Nowhere is there any agreement as to the question of relative merit; in fact, nowhere is there any due acknowledgment of what that merit really is. There is, indeed, so much variety in Wilde's work, he has made so many experiments in so many directions, that it is only now, with this almost complete edition before us, that we can trace the curious movement, forward and backward, of a mind never fully certain of its direction. It was a long time before Wilde discovered that he was above all a wit, and that it was through the medium of the comic stage that he could best express his essential talent. His desire was to write tragedies, above all romantic tragedies in verse. His failure in the attempt was hopeless, because he had got hold of the wrong material and the wrong manner.

The earliest thing that he wrote was a play in prose, now printed for the first time, called *Vera; or, the Nihilists*, written for the most part in excited language of this kind: 'Peace! ye gorged adders, peace!' The plot is melodramatic, and the whole action altogether futile; it is amusing to read now and discover the first ineffectual attempts to be witty. Prince Paul says to the Marquis de Poivraro: 'Ah! Marquis. I trust Madame la Marquise is well.' The Marquis answers: 'You ought to know better than I do, Prince Paul; you see more of her.' Whereat the Prince, bowing, replies: 'Perhaps I see more *in* her, Marquis.' Soon after *Vera* comes *The Duchess of Padua*. This and the fragment of *The Florentine Tragedy* are also published for the first time, and we see in them an attempt to write romantic drama. The end of *The Florentine Tragedy* is done on almost the same method as the end of the third act of *Lady Windermere's Fan*. It is meant to be a great climax, and it is really only a bad epigram. The merchant-husband, Simone, who is hated by his wife Bianca, kills her lover (to whom she has cried: 'Kill him!') under her eyes. The stage direction instructs us:—

He dies—Simone rises and looks at Bianca. She comes towards him as one dazed with wonder and with outstretched arms.

BIANCA   Why
Did you not tell me you were so strong?
SIMONE   Why
Did you not tell me you were beautiful?

Then the curtain falls, and we are fed with a fruitless epigram. Now turn to that scene which ends the third act of *Lady Windermere's Fan*. The appearance of Mrs. Erlynne from Door R is a great climax, because it is psychologically right and theatrically right. Her words, which seem to say nothing, are tragic, because they are the expression of a concealed heroism. The curtain falls on a suspense which leaves us breathless.

The Duchess of Padua is meant to be an imitation of Webster or Marston, a macabre tragedy of blood. It is meant to be passionate and heroic, and splendid in versification. The passion is mere ice; the speech, hackneyed, far-fetched, and cheap-bought, is offered at second hand. The murderous Duchess would go beyond Lady Macbeth, and wash, not only her hands, but also her soul. 'Can I not wash my hands? Ay, but my soul?' she exclaims. Her moods and her lover's toss to and fro from one to the other a dozen times in less than twenty minutes in a corridor at the top of a staircase where the murder has just been committed. The time is past when lovers can say to one another:—

DUCHESS   And Passion sets a seal upon the lips.
GUIDO   Oh, with mine own life let me break that seal!

Still less can we listen to one of the same lovers, at their first meeting, when he elaborates on the spur of the moment this series of figures of speech:—

> Nay, sweet, lift up your head,
> Let me unlock those little scarlet doors
> That shut in music, let me dive for coral
> In your red lips, and I'll bear back a prize
> Richer than all the gold the Griffin guards
> In rude Armenia.

'These are but words, words, words,' as the Duchess comments on another occasion. Even the frenzied speech in which the two lovers squabble with one another on the edge of death has no natural heat, no appropriate anguish.

Wilde's last attempt at romantic drama is, if not successful, filled with a strange fascination, not easy to define. *Salome*, which in Germany is regarded as great work, is difficult for us to dissociate from Beardsley's illustrations, in which what is icily perverse in the dialogue (it cannot be designated drama) becomes in the ironical designs pictorial, a series of poses. On the stage these poses are less decorative than on the page, though they have an effect of their own, not fine, but languid, and horrible, and frozen. To Wilde passion was a thing to talk about with elaborate and colored words. Salomé is a doll, as many have imagined her, soulless, set in motion by some pitiless destiny, personified momentarily by her mother; Herod is a nodding mandarin in a Chinese grotesque. So *The Sphinx* offers no subtlety, no heat of an Egyptian desert, no thrill in anything but the words and cadences; the poem, like *Salome*, is a sort of celebration of dark rites.

Wilde was not in the highest sense a poet, though his verse has occasionally a technical singularity, as in *The Sphinx*, which can delude the mind through the ears to listen, when the lines are read out, to a flow of loud and bright words which are as meaningless as the monotonous Eastern music of drum and gong is to the Western ear. One or two lyrics and *The Ballad of Reading Gaol* come near to being poetry, but there is nothing else, in the blank-verse plays or the idylls, and elegies, and sonnets of the volume of 1881, which is anything but imitation of some good poet, but dangerous model.

Where Wilde comes nearest to poetry is in the prose stories (now contained in one volume) of *A House of Pomegranates* and *The Happy Prince*. Wilde's sense of beauty was uncertain, his technique came and went; yet, in these stories for children, what was artificial in him, and vulgar, and foolish (as in the earlier sensational and burlesque experiments) took on lovely new draperies, which suggested at times the beating of a real heart under them. Every narrative is an allegory, and is filled with delicate suggestions; its scene is a dream-world, made for the pleasure of children; it is something between a fairy-tale and an 'Imaginary Portrait.' The style has quieted; the teller of the tale is hardly discernible. Here are parables, decked out for young minds— moral tales, one might call them; somehow as real in their imaginary world as the impossible credible people in the modern comedies. The same ingenuity is seen at play, here for children, there for too acutely grown-up people. Each has its own atmosphere, form, and locality.

But when we turn from this almost faultless book to the *Poems in Prose* of a later date, we find an attempt to be Biblical and remotely imaginative, and a specious symbolism creeps in, no longer sincere or significant. It is a shallow pool, trying to look as if it had some deep meaning.

Here we may begin to consider what Wilde really understood by beauty, a word which recurs persistently throughout his work. In an enumeration of his gifts ('the gods have given me almost everything'), Wilde said with confidence: 'Whatever I touched I made beautiful in a new mode of beauty.' His expression of what he conceived by beauty is developed from many models, and has no new ideas in it; one can trace it, almost verbally, to Pater, Flaubert, Gautier, Baudelaire, and other writers from whom he drew sustenance. Throughout a large part of his work he is seen deliberately imitating the effects that these and other writers have achieved before him. All through the *Intentions* there is a far-off echo of Pater; in *Salome* melodrama is mixed with recollections of *Pelléas et Mélisande* and of *La Tentation de Saint Antoine*. *The Picture of Dorian Gray* owes much, I think, to the work of Huysmans. Of the writers named, all but the last had their own sense of beauty, their own imaginative world where they were at home, and could speak its language naturally. Wilde's style is constantly changing, as made things do when one alters them, and it is only at intervals that it ceases to be artificial, imitative, or pretentious. The attempt to write constantly in a beautiful way leads to a vast amount of grandiloquence, which is never convincing because it is evidently not sincere. In a sense, every writer is sincere, for he has only himself to work with. But Wilde was artificial; he looked on art as 'the supreme reality,' and life as 'a mere mode of fiction.' Hence the attempt to combine words and epithets in a striking and unusual way, the frequent incapacity to distinguish between pure gold and alloy, the preference, indeed, of tinsel to plain cloth; the uncertainty, in short, as to what was real and what was false beauty. That sense, never instinctive, goes off gradually in the course of his career, ending in the conscious sonority of such passages in *De Profundis* as this: 'or to move with sufficient stateliness of music through the purple pageant of my incommunicable woes'. Here words have ceased to become capable of expressing what may have been a sincere feeling.

From the first, one of Wilde's limitations had been his egoism, his self-absorption, his self-admiration. This is one of the qualities which have marred the delightful genius of the Irish nation, and it can be traced in the three other Irishmen who may be said to have formed, with Wilde, a group apart in the literature of our time. It is not needful to name them: one is a dramatist, one a novelist, one a poet.[1] All have remarkable qualities, each a completely different individuality, and the desire of each is, as Wilde admits, to 'make people wonder.' In each there is something not human, which is either the cause or the outcome of an ambition too continually conscious of itself. The great man is indifferent to his greatness; it is an accident if he is so much as conscious of it.

There is a passage in *De Profundis* in which Wilde brags of his greatness with incredible *naïveté*. It is now well known. It begins: 'I was a

[1] An allusion, probably, to Shaw, George Moore, and Yeats.

man who stood in symbolic relations to the art and culture of my age'; and it continues: 'Byron was a symbolic figure, but his relations were to the passion of his age and its weariness of passion. Mine were to something more noble, more permanent, of more vital issue, of larger scope.' Now Wilde, with his critical sense, must have been aware that the words *noble, permanent,* and *vital* were precisely the negatives of whatever reasonable praise could be given to him. The only moment of nobility which can be found in the whole of his work is in those two terrible, unforgettable, no doubt useless letters, written to a daily paper on the atrocities committed legally in English prisons;[1] and they were wrung from him through the personal suffering which had forced upon him a consciousness of the evil that was being done to others more helpless than himself. Those letters should have put all England in revolt against its permitted ignorance of cruelty, and it is well that they should have been reprinted at the end of *De Profundis*. Beyond this one outburst, where shall we find in Wilde's work anything noble, permanent, or vital? Byron, with all his defects, had these qualities in the highest degree. He too was an egoist, but his egoism was justified, and he took his greatness lightly. He did not, like Wilde, pose admiringly before the reflection of himself in a flattering mirror.

Wilde was a maker of idols, of painted idols, Salomé and the Sphinx. He bowed down before the pagan gods who were never actual to him. He did often good service for what seemed to him, and often was, the cause of art against the Philistines. But his manner of attacking them was not always adequate, and many of the stones in his sling rebounded upon him from the forehead of Goliath.

To alter the minds of men is to possess a vast magnetic and irrefutable mind filled by a conviction which may seem irrational, as the forces of nature seem to our ignorance. Wilde was never concerned with fundamental ideas, except perhaps in 'The Soul of Man under Socialism,' which contains his best and sanest and most valuable thinking, yet is almost as entertaining as *Intentions*.

Disobedience, in the eyes of any one who has read history, is man's original virtue. . . . In a word, it comes (the use of the word 'unhealthy') from that monstrous and ignorant thing that is called Public Opinion, which, bad and well-meaning as it is when it tries to control action, is infamous and of evil meaning when it tries to control thought of Art. . . . One who is an Emperor and King may stoop down to pick up a brush for a painter, but when the demo-

---

[1] Two letters to the *Daily Chronicle*, reprinted in *Letters*, ed. Hart-Davis, pp. 568–74 and pp. 722–6.

cracy stoops down it is merely to throw mud. . . . It is impossible for the artist
to live with the People. All despots bribe. The people bribe and brutalise.

All that has been laughed at; but it is indeed a fine and severe form
of wit, in which the truths are hardly so much as paradoxes.

Intentions is the most amusing book of criticism in English. It has
nothing to say that has not been proved or disproved already, but never
was such boyish disrespect for ideas, such gaiety of paradox. Its flaw is
that it tries to be Paterish and pagan and Renaissance and Greek, and to
be clothed in Tyrian robes, and to tread 'with tired feet the purple
white-starred fields of asphodel.' But it is possible to forget the serious,
exasperating pages in a lazy delight in so much pleasant wit. 'Utterance,'
the Irishman's need of talk and invariable talent for it: that is there,
scattering itself casually like fireworks, but on its way to become a
steady illumination.

Wilde's last and greatest discovery was when, about the year 1891,
the idea came to him that the abounding wit, which he had kept till
then chiefly for the entertainment of his friends, could be turned quite
naturally into a new kind of play. Sheridan was the best model at hand
to learn from, and there were qualities of stage speech and action in
which he could surpass him. Then might not Alfred de Musset show
him some of the secrets of fine comedy? He had, to start with, a wit
that was typically Irish in its promptness and spontaneity. His only rival
in talk was Whistler, whose wit was unpleasantly bitter. The word
sprang from Wilde's lips, some unsought nonsense, a flying paradox;
Whistler's was a sharper shaft, but it flew less readily. And now this
inventiveness of speech found itself at home in the creation of a form of
play which, in *Lady Windermere's Fan*, begins by being seriously and
tragically comic, and ends in *The Importance of Being Earnest*, which is
a sort of sublime farce, meaningless and delightful.

Lady Windermere's Fan has been imitated since by popular playwrights, and Wilde was justified in saying:—

I took the drama, the most objective form known to art, and made it as personal
a mode of expression as the lyric or sonnet; at the same time I widened its range
and enriched its characterisation.

One begins by admiring its wit; one ends by being convinced by its
drama. What other dramatist of our age has concealed such ingenuity
of plot under such ready wit; has presented life jesting so gaily on the
edge of a precipice, over which no one quite falls? A temperament is
expressed in an epigram, and the speech comes naturally in its place. In

A Woman of No Importance the epigrams almost obliterate the action until the end of the third act, almost every sentence being a separate piece of wit. Many of the epigrams are celebrated, almost classic ('The Book of Life begins with a man and a woman in a garden. It ends with Revelations.' 'The English country gentleman galloping after a fox—the unspeakable in full pursuit of the uneatable'), yet the click, click of them is after a time almost tedious. Even the stupid people never say stupid things.

A Woman of No Importance is scarcely so good, dramatically, as *Lady Windermere's Fan*, and *An Ideal Husband* is not so good as either, while *The Importance of Being Earnest* is by far the most perfect of the four. It is, however, really the least witty, and too serious in its parade of the circumstances, which are as winding and difficult as a maze. All are experimental, all have some ingenious difference, though the actual stage tricks do not vary much in method. There is always a fan, or a glove, or a letter, or a handbag by which somebody is incriminated or identified. Dramatically Lady Windermere's fan is more significant and more natural than Ibsen's 'vine-leaves in the hair,' which is a bad symbol; and as for the hand-bag in *The Importance of Being Earnest*, it is an unparalleled invention of its kind. That perfect play is nothing but delirious nonsense. 'Delightful work may be produced under burlesque and farcical conditions,' Wilde had written, a few years before he wrote the play, and he added: 'And in work of this kind the artist in England is allowed very great freedom.' It is a great freedom that he takes in making a work of art in the act of merely amusing us. The matter has been questioned, quite unnecessarily. A great wit who can condense that volatile essence into a permanent savour, perfume, or tonic, has his place among artists. Wilde had many failures; they have been taken for masterpieces; but if, as it has been said by the just, generous, and scrupulous editor of his works, 'in his last years he was the severest critic of his own achievements,' it is not unlikely that he would have been content to survive, in men's memories and in his own printed pages, as the most brilliant and entertaining wit of his time.

103. Harold Child on Wilde's
Collected Works

1908

Unsigned review in the *Times Literary Supplement*, 18 June 1908, p. 193.
Harold Child (1869–1945), poet, Shakespearian scholar, and drama critic of *The Times* and later of the *Observer*, was a founder and major contributor to the *Times Literary Supplement*. Child's assessment of Wilde is admirably balanced, though there are the usual comments on Wilde's insincerity.

We have before us twelve volumes bound in a white cover which is clearly the design of a good artist, printed in bold and handsome type on hand-made paper with deckled edges, and published by Messrs. Methuen at 12s. 6d. net each. There is no title to the set; but these are the collected works of Oscar Wilde. The collected works of Lord Acton or of Samuel Johnson give, in their very different way, as unsatisfactory an account of their authors as do these beautiful white volumes. The real works of Oscar Wilde lie partly in the delight in art and letters, the joy in things of beauty of all kinds, experienced to-day by people who perhaps never suspect that to him they owe the impulse to seek their pleasure in such things; partly in the echoes of old laughter, the recollection of sallies that used to set the table in a roar, or of brilliant flashes of capricious wisdom struck out, as it seemed, almost by accident; Hamlet's melancholy and yet inspiring thoughts of Yorick. Wilde's chief influence was a personal influence. Through his personality and his poses he did more than any one to spread abroad the not too abstruse elements of the aesthetic doctrines excogitated by wiser and more silent men than himself, and to give minds and men of middle class something, at least, of the benefit of a movement which we have not so completely absorbed into our daily lives that we forget what our culture owes to it. Through his personality, again, and his reckless Irish wit, he became the delight of dinner-tables, where he prodigally scattered the best of his genius. The spoken, not the written, word was his proper vehicle; and no one ever so lacked a Boswell.

Yet to speak of his personality is to broach the very reason why the abiding taste left in the mind by the reading of these twelve beautiful volumes is the taste of disappointment and disillusion. Superficially, no one was more introspective than Wilde. His gaze was constantly fixed on himself; yet not on himself, but on his reflection in the looking-glass. There is a vast difference between honest introspection, in which a man turns his eyes inward to search for what is there that he may develop and improve it, and the actor's pose before his mirror to see that his make-up, his disguise, his semblance, is becoming and effective. Wilde never got further than that; he stopped short at Peter Pan's 'Oh, the cleverness of me!' and the Neronic 'Qualis artifex pereo!'[1] which is the real text of his apologia De Profundis. Introspection of the genuine kind he never achieved. Probably he was never compelled to learn the art. A brilliant youth, and the astonishing success of his early poses, relieved him of the necessity and unfitted him for the exercise; and it is only when we come to read his collected works that we see how he paid for it in the end. Never being forced to search in himself for himself and develop what he found there into the firm basis of his life's work, he continued to pose, to imitate, to build on sand. How long will it be before the sand covers all his building? With a mind not a jot less keen than Whistler's, he had none of the conviction, the high faith, for which Whistler found it worth while to defy the crowd. Wilde had poses to attract the crowd. And the difference was this, that while Whistler was a prophet who liked to play Pierrot, Wilde grew into a Pierrot who liked to play the prophet.

The prophetic period with him was not unimportant, and it produced some of his most amusing work. It is permissible to have done very shortly with the romantic plays, which are the first stage in his development. The Duchess of Padua is a charming piece of verbal imitation; Vera rings no truer; by the time of the Florentine Tragedy the author had outgrown the grosser methods of imitation, but wrote to little better purpose. Of Salomé we find it difficult to speak. What devil of mischief prompted some blunderer to have the English translation illustrated by Beardsley? To have read the play in the light of Beardsley's deadly irony is to be unable to give it independent judgment. The book becomes an amusing duel. 'This is tremendous!' says the author; 'This is humbug!' says the artist. He turns Salomé into a drama of powder-

[1] Nero's final words: 'What an artist I die!'

puff and grease-paint. Acted with profound seriousness, in Germany, it is, we are told, impressive; in the study, even the French original is a piece of soulless craftsmanship in the style of modern Indian silver.

The prophetic books, this is to say *Intentions* and 'The Soul of Man under Socialism,' are far above mere verbal imitation. The author has mastered his material sufficiently to be able to give it a form of his own. And here will be found some of his wittiest, keenest prose, some of his most delightful reading. Here, too, are some of his happiest ideas. The essay on 'The Critic as Artist' must have opened the eyes of hundreds to facts about literature and art which might have escaped them in the less brilliant, dashing statements of Wilde's authorities. Dare we suggest that, if Wilde had been less witty and less arrogant, he would have made an admirable University extension lecturer? His classes at summer meetings would have been crowded, while he explained in alluring and not too difficult lectures the chief systems of philosophy, the periods of history, the tendencies and schools of literature. He could be trusted for his facts, for he knew what he was writing about; but more than knowledge is required if a man is to be a philosopher, a critic, or an historian of weight. And even 'The Soul of Man under Socialism,' in which occur some of the most thoughtful, most illuminating things in all his written works, suffers from the lack of that conviction, that deeper personality, without which a man must be content to go on saying what other people have said before him. It was all play to Pierrot, and he soon tired of the game. We look for some satisfactory statement of the nature of this 'beauty', the name of which is so constantly on his lips; and find that, if it means anything more than the momentary gratification of the senses with light, form, or colour, it means not, as it had meant to his models, the sublimation of nature by art, but that dangerous avoidance of the natural world, almost a negation of reality, which puts the intellect at the mercy of the senses. Contrast his case with Pater's. The development of the genuine philosopher can be traced from 'The Renaissance' to the lecture on Lacedaemon; no philosophic development was possible from so much of the doctrine of 'The Renaissance' as Wilde chose to master.

It is not in mere loyalty to our conception of him that we find the same fault with his poems—with all except one, to which we shall come later. The lack of conviction and the ease with which his brilliant mind could play any game it liked lie at the root of the dissatisfaction with which we close a volume so full of clever craftsmanship. Its numerous errors of taste are the natural result of playing at passion, the inevitable lapses of a mind with no serious poetic purpose. The impulse to 'go one better' than his models, which led to some delicious things in the essays, seems in the poems to land him only in mawkishness or offence when his models are Keats, or Rossetti, or Matthew Arnold. In their uncertainty, their annoying mixture of fine intention and phrase with extravagance and counterfeit, the poems make the most disappointing of all these volumes.

The best of this side of Wilde, that is the side of the clever craftsman at play, is nowhere more delightful than in the little stories in *A House of Pomegranates*. Here we are in Pierrot's own country, the land of fantasy, and he is quite at home there. We turn again and again to these delicious little things, to enjoy their dewy freshness, their tenderness, and their laughing wit, no less than the perfection of their form. They would never have been written but for Hans Anderson; but the game of writing them was one which the author seems thoroughly to enjoy, one in which for the moment he forgets himself and the looking-glass and delights merely in what he is producing. Wilde was an admirable story-teller, with the pen no less than with the tongue. 'Lord Arthur Savile's Crime,' one of the wittiest of modern tales, belongs really to the same category, and is a forerunner of the single masterpiece which crowned Wilde's literary career. And only three years after this story came *The Picture of Dorian Gray*—a withering comment on the lack of conviction and of a standard in art and life in one who would teach, or even amuse, his fellows. In that horrible book all the imagination, the power, the ingenuity of the short stories, are perverted to deplorable uses.

The time came when necessity drove Pierrot to the theatre; and there, as men often do when they obey necessity, he found his proper field. He had played at poetry and criticism and philosophy, with astonishing skill; he was to do more than play at comedy. Not all at once, however. His plays have been so often discussed that we need not repeat at length the common finding that the first three comedies are founded on the dramatic stock in trade of the day. But even here, it must be remembered, he was not playing at comedy, as he played at poetry and criticism, so much as playing with it. The ground-work remained what it had been; the surface was completely changed. From a dull and dingy expanse it became sparkling and exquisite. The epigram, which had been useful enough in forcing something of the profounder truths of criticism on the public, acquired in the theatre a new dignity and a new importance. That much of it was machine-made, a mere verbal jingle—like 'the unspeakable in pursuit of the uneatable,'[1] as a description, and surely a very feeble one, of fox-hunting—and that some of it consisted solely in turning accepted phrases upside down, cannot detract from its value as an element in Wilde's comedy, setting the very atmosphere of his plays. There are living writers who have founded serious reputations on the dregs of his achievement in this field of epigram. And the time came at last, if all too late, when Pierrot had the courage to dispense with all models, to walk through (if we may put it so) his looking-glass instead of posturing before it, and to come back with a fragment of the life of his own fantastic, irresponsible world, which lay on the other side. In *The Importance of Being Earnest* he perfected the vein he had first attempted in 'Lord Arthur Savile's Crime.' He became at last, what he had always pathetically claimed to be, a creator; and in tossing off a trifle he conquered a kingdom.

There was one other occasion when he spoke with sincerity. It is not a pleasant occasion to refer to, but to omit mention of it would be unfair to him as author. We refer to the *Ballad of Reading Gaol*. Pierrot, the gay creature of summer nights and Chinese lanterns, was shocked, infuriated, frightened. And there was wrung from him a scream of pain and terror which it still turns one cold to recall. The ballad is not free from his besetting sin of word-hunting. The much-quoted recurring stanza which begins 'Yet each man kills the thing he loves,' will not stand examination. But the poem as a whole gathers up nearly every characteristic of Wilde's mind—its brilliance, its gift of epigram, its preoccupation with the loathly beauties of vice, its arrogance, its mastery of vivid expression, and its penetrating force—and flings them passionately at the head of his friend turned foe, the world. We wish that we could find the same sincerity in that other work of the same period, *De Profundis*, which is now issued with matter not published in the previous editions. There is a looking-glass, it seems, even in the depths; and one may pose before it as beautifully there as in the sunshine.

Qualis artifex pereo! It is the thought which recurs, which sums up the contents of these twelve beautiful volumes. What intellectual force, what infectious joy in fine craftsmanship, his own or another's! To have the twelve beautiful volumes on one's shelves is to be certain of inspiriting mental recreation. It is to keep a private jester of amazing shrewdness, a genius for perfect impromptu, infinite wit, audacity, and gaiety. The very affectations of your Dagonet are enjoyable—if you happen to be in the mood for them. And whether you deplore it as a

---

[1] From Act One of *A Woman of No Importance*.

tragedy, or accept it as another jest, that one who began by aiming so high and persistently claimed to have achieved his aim should come to be summed up as a jester will depend upon which you value the higher, philosophers or fools. The combination is at least piquant and unique. And while you are under the spell of the jester's charm there is no need to worry about the necessity of conviction, the whole-hearted devotion to truth, a truth, any truth, which is demanded of one who would be something higher than a craftsman, would be an artist.

104. Lord Alfred Douglas on Wilde's collected works

1908

Review signed 'A.D.', titled 'The Genius of Oscar Wilde', *Academy* (11 July 1908), lxxv, 35.

One of the oddities of this review is the contention that Wilde's plays were 'almost without any exception . . . received with mockery, ridicule, and rudeness'—clearly a statement in excess of the facts. However, Douglas's conclusion that 'from the purely literary point of view [Wilde] was unquestionably the greatest figure of the nineteenth century' leaves one breathless. (For an indication of Douglas's change of heart, see No. 116.)

The publication in twelve volumes by Messrs. Methuen of the complete works of Oscar Wilde marks, in a striking way, the complete literary rehabilitation which this author has achieved. When one considers that at the time of Oscar Wilde's downfall the whole of his copyrights could have been purchased for about £100, one cannot help entertaining grave suspicions as to the value of criticism in England. It must be remembered that the contempt with which Mr. Wilde's work was greeted by the general mass of contemporary criticism was not confined to the period after his condemnation. A reference to the files of the newspapers containing the criticisms of his plays as they came out would reveal the fact that almost without any exception they were received with mockery, ridicule, and rudeness.

It is intensely amusing to read the comments in the daily papers at the present juncture on the same subject. Oscar Wilde is referred to, as a matter of course, as a great genius and a great wit, and takes his place, in the eyes of those who write these articles, if not with Shakespeare, at any rate with the other highest exponents of English dramatic art. This, of course, is as it should be, but we wonder what the gentlemen who write these glowing accounts of Mr. Wilde's genius were doing at the time when those works of genius were being poured out, and why it should have been necessary for him in order to obtain recognition to undergo the processes of disgrace and death. With the exception of the *Ballad of Reading Gaol* and *De Profundis* every work of Oscar Wilde's was written before his downfall. If these works are brilliant works of genius now, they were so before, and the failure of contemporary criticism to appreciate this fact is a lasting slur upon the intelligence of the country.

If any one wishes to see a fair sample of the sort of criticism that used to be meted out to Oscar Wilde, let him turn to the dramatic criticism in *Truth* which appeared on the production of *Lady Windermere's Fan*.[1] The article was, we believe, written by the late unlamented Clement Scott, and at this time of day, of course, Clement Scott's dramatic criticism is not taken seriously; but at the time it was taken quite seriously, and it is astounding to think that such a criticism should have passed absolutely unresented by anybody of importance, with the obvious exception of Oscar Wilde himself. Nowadays if a critic were to write such an article about a playwright of anything approaching the status of Oscar Wilde he would be refused admission to every theatre in London.

This state of affairs must give pause to those good people who have decided that the late W. E. Henley was a 'great editor' and a 'great critic.' If Henley had been anything approaching either of these two things he would have seen and appreciated the value of Oscar Wilde; and if we refer to any of the much-lauded and much-regretted reviews or journals which were conducted by Henley, we find that so far from

---

[1] The anonymous reviewer in *Truth* (25 February 1892, p. 385) referred to the play as 'twaddle that has been patted on the back with sublime condescension by the newest of the dramatists and the oldest of the society clowns'.

appreciating Oscar Wilde it was he who led the attack against him, an attack which was conducted with the utmost malevolence and violence, and which was, moreover, distinguished by a brainlessness which is almost incredible in a man who, like Henley (overrated as he is), was not without great talents of his own. That Henley was a great poet or a great writer of prose we have never believed, and the recent publication of his collected works by Messrs. Nutt does not give us any reason to alter our opinion.

The subject of the first great attack made by Henley on Oscar Wilde was *The Picture of Dorian Gray*. Henley affected to think this was an immoral work, and denounced it as such.[1] Now, anybody who having read *Dorian Gray* can honestly maintain that it is not one of the greatest moral books ever written, is an ass. It is, briefly, the story of a man who destroys his own conscience. The visible symbol of that conscience takes the form of a picture, the presentment of perfect youth and perfect beauty, which bears on its changing surface the burden of the sins of its prototype. It is one of the greatest and most terrible moral lessons that an unworthy world has had the privilege of receiving at the hands of a great writer.

It is characteristic of what we may call the 'Henleyean School' of criticism to confuse the life of a man with his art. It would be idle to deny that Oscar Wilde was an immoral man (as idle as it would be to contend that Henley was a moral one); but it is a remarkable thing that while Oscar Wilde's life was immoral his art was always moral. At the time when the attack by Henley was made there was a confused idea going about London that Oscar Wilde was a wicked man, and this was quite enough for Henley and the group of second-rate intelligences which clustered round him to jump to the conclusion that anything he wrote must also necessarily be wicked.

The crowning meanness of which Henley was guilty with regard to Oscar Wilde was his signed review of the *Ballad of Reading Gaol*.[2] Henley was always an envious man; his attack on the memory of Stevenson is sufficient to show that; but he certainly surpassed himself when he wrote that disgraceful article. Surely a man possessing the smallest nobility of soul would have refrained at that juncture from attacking an old enemy—if, indeed, Wilde could properly be called an enemy of Henley's. Henley chose to make an unprovoked attack upon

---

[1] Henley did not review Wilde's novel, nor did he take part in the ensuing controversy that followed in the pages of the *Scots Observer* (see No. 19).

[2] Henley's review was not signed (see No. 79).

Wilde, from whom, as a matter of fact, he had received many benefits and kindnesses, but Wilde never retaliated in an ungenerous way, although his enormous intellectual superiority would have rendered it an easy task for him to pulverise Henley. It was always Wilde's way to take adverse criticism contemptuously, and, to the last, he never spoke of Henley with anything but good humour, albeit with some deserved disdain. The slow revenge of time has in this particular case bestirred itself to some purpose, and if we cannot say with justice 'Who now reads Henley?' we can at any rate state very positively that for every reader that he has, Oscar Wilde has twenty. The reason is not far to seek. Wilde, putting aside his moral delinquencies, which have as much and as little to do with his works as the colour of his hair, was a great artist, a man who passionately loved his art. He was so great an artist that, in spite of himself, he was always on the side of the angels. We believe that the greatest art is always on the side of the angels, to doubt it would be to doubt the existence of God, and all the Henleys and all the Bernard Shaws that the world could produce would not make us change our opinion. It was all very well for Wilde to play with life, as he did exquisitely, and to preach the philosophy of pleasure, and pluck-ing the passing hour; but the moment he sat down to write he became different. He saw things as they really were; he knew the falsity and the deadliness of his own creed; he knew that 'the end of these things is Death;' and he wrote in his own inimitable way the words of Wisdom and Life. Like all great men, he had his disciples, and a great many of them (more than a fair share) turned out to be Iscariots; but it is his glory that he founded no school, no silly gang of catchword repeaters; he created no 'journalistic tradition,' and he was not referred to by ridiculous bumpkins occupying subordinate positions in the offices of third-rate Jewish publishing-houses as 'dear old Wilde.' Those who knew and loved him as a man and as a writer were men who had their own individualities and were neither his shadows nor his imitators. If they achieved any greatness they did it because they had greatness in them, and not because they aped 'the master.' Henley has his school of 'Henley's young men,' of whom we do not hear much nowadays. Wilde has his school of young men in those who copy what was least admirable in him, but from a literary point of view he has no school. He stands alone, a phenomenon in literature. From the purely literary point of view he was unquestionably the greatest figure of the nine-teenth century. We unhesitatingly say that his influence on the literature of Europe has been greater than that of any man since Byron died, and, unlike Byron's, it has been all for good. The evil that he did, inasmuch as he did a tithe of the things imputed to him, was interred with his bones, the good (how much the greater part of this great man!) lives after him and will live for ever.

105. G. K. Chesterton on Wilde as a great artist and charlatan

1909

Signed review, *Daily News*, 19 October 1909, p. 3; reprinted in a slightly different version in *A Handful of Authors*, edited by Dorothy Collins (New York, 1953), pp. 143–6.

Chesterton (1874–1936) offers an interesting contrast between Wilde and Shaw, whom he characterizes as a 'demagogue of wit', concluding that Wilde had 'a much deeper and more spiritual nature' than Shaw.

The full edition of the works of Oscar Wilde which Messrs. Methuen have recently published appears at a time very appropriate for some sound considerations of them. The time has certainly come when this extraordinary man, Oscar Wilde, may be considered merely as a man of letters. And for this purpose the new Methuen edition is very valuable. It contains two poems that have never been published and many that have never been read and one can really now read them all without prejudice, as if they came from a new genius. He sometimes pretended that art was more important than morality, but that was mere play-acting. Morality or immorality was more important than art to him and everyone else. But the very cloud of tragedy that rested on his career makes it easier to treat him as a mere artist now. His was a complete life, in that awful sense in which your life and mine are incomplete; since we have not yet paid for our sins. In that sense one might call it a perfect life, as one speaks of a perfect equation; it cancels out. On the one hand we have the healthy horror of the evil; on the other the healthy horror of the punishment. We have it all the more because both sin and punishment were highly civilized; that is, nameless and secret. Some have said that Wilde was sacrificed; let it be enough for us to insist on the literal meaning of the world. Any ox that is really sacrificed is made sacred.

But the very fact that monstrous wrong and monstrous revenge cancel each other, actually does leave this individual artist in that very airy detachment which he professed to desire. We can really consider him solely as a man of letters.

About Oscar Wilde, as about other wits, Disraeli or Bernard Shaw, men wage a war of words, some calling him a great artist and others a mere charlatan. But this controversy misses the really extraordinary thing about Wilde: the thing that appears rather in the plays than the poems. He was a great artist. He also was really a charlatan. I mean by a charlatan one sufficiently dignified to despise the tricks that he employs. A vulgar demagogue is not a charlatan; he is as coarse as his crowd. He may be lying in every word, but he is sincere in his style. Style (as Wilde might have said) is only another name for spirit. Again, a man like Mr. Bernard Shaw is not a charlatan. I can understand people thinking his remarks hurried or shallow or senselessly perverse, or blasphemous, or merely narrow. But I cannot understand anyone failing to feel that Mr. Shaw is being as suggestive as he can, is giving his brightest and boldest speculations to the rabble, is offering something which he honestly thinks valuable. Now Wilde often uttered remarks which he must have known to be literally valueless. Shaw may be high or low, but he never talks down to the audience. Wilde did talk down, sometimes very far down.

Wilde and his school professed to stand as solitary artistic souls apart from the public. They professed to scorn the middle class, and declared that the artist must not work for the bourgeois. The truth is that no artist so really great ever worked so much for the bourgeois as Oscar Wilde. No man, so capable of thinking about truth and beauty, ever thought so constantly about his own effect on the middle classes. He studied the Surbiton school-mistress with exquisite attention, and knew exactly how to shock and how to please her. Mr. Shaw often gets above her in seraphic indignation, and often below her in sterile and materialistic explanations. He disgusts her with new truths or he bores her with old truths; but they are always living truths to Bernard Shaw. Wilde knew how to say the precise thing which, whether true or false, is irresistible. As, for example, 'I can resist everything but temptation.'

But he sometimes sank lower, sank into the lowest gorges and chasms of Surbiton. One might go through his swift and sparkling plays with a red and blue pencil marking two kinds of epigrams; the real epigram which he wrote to please his own wild intellect, and the sham epigram which he wrote to thrill the very tamest part of our tame civilization. This is what I mean by saying that he was strictly a charlatan—among other things. He descended below himself to be on top of others. He became purposely stupider than Oscar Wilde that he might seem cleverer than the nearest curate. He lowered himself to superiority; he stooped to conquer.

One might easily take examples of the phrase meant to lightly touch the truth and the phrase meant only to bluff the bourgeoisie. For instance, in *A Woman of No Importance*, he makes his chief philosopher say that all thought is immoral, being essentially destructive; 'Nothing survives being thought of.' That is nonsense, but nonsense of the nobler sort; there is an idea in it. It is, like most professedly modern ideas, a death-dealing idea not a life-giving one; but it is an idea. There is truly a sense in which all definition is deletion. Turn a few pages of the same play and you will find somebody asking, 'What is an immoral woman?' The philosopher answers, 'The kind of woman a man never gets tired of.' Now that is not nonsense, but rather rubbish. It is without value of any sort of kind. It is not symbolically true; it is not fantastically true; it is not true at all.

Anyone with the mildest knowledge of the world knows that nobody can be such a consuming bore as a certain kind of immoral woman. That vice never tires men, might be a tenable and entertaining lie; that the individual instrument of vice never tires them is not, even as a lie, tenable enough to be entertaining. Here the great wit was playing the cheap dandy to the incredibly innocent; as much as if he had put on paper cuffs and collars. He is simply shocking a tame curate; and he must be rather a specially tame curate even to be shocked. This irritating duplication of real brilliancy with snobbish bluff runs through all his three comedies. 'Life is much too important to be taken seriously'; that is the true humorist. 'A well-tied tie is the first serious step in life'; that is the charlatan. 'Man can believe the impossible, but man can never believe the improbable'; that is said by a fine philosopher. 'Nothing is so fatal to a personality as the keeping of promises, unless it be telling the truth'; that is said by a tired quack. 'A man can be happy with any woman so long as he does not love her'; that is wild truth. 'Good intentions are invariably ungrammatical'; that is tame trash.

But while he had a strain of humbug in him, which there is not in the demagogues of wit like Bernard Shaw, he had, in his own strange way, a much deeper and more spiritual nature than they. Queerly enough, it was the very multitude of his falsities that prevented him from being entirely false. Like a many-coloured humming top, he was at once a bewilderment and a balance. He was so fond of being many-sided that among his sides he even admitted the right side. He loved so much to multiply his souls that he had among them one soul at least that was saved. He desired all beautiful things—even God.

His frightful fallacy was that he would not see that there is reason in everything, even in religion and morality. Universality is a contradiction in terms. You cannot be everything if you are anything. If you wish to be white all over, you must austerely resist the temptation to have green spots or yellow stripes. If you wish to be good all over, you must resist the spots of sin or the stripes of servitude. It may be great fun to be many-sided; but however many sides one has there cannot be one of them which is complete and rounded innocence. A polygon can have an infinite number of sides; but no one of its sides can be a circle.

106. T. Sturge Moore on Wilde's place in English literature

1909

Letter to Robert Ross, dated 2 December 1909, in *Robert Ross: Friend of Friends*, ed. Margery Ross (1952), pp. 172–3.

St. James's Square, Holland Park W. 2.12.09

My dear Ross, . . . Life has lately been an orgy of Oscar Wilde's prose. When I read some of it 15 years ago I believed in English literature. An exploded myth! Alas! Outside Shakespeare and Milton there is very little that can rank as art and not too much that has any vital interest. Oscar will certainly count with Landor, Ruskin and Pater if

not before them. He is indiscriminately brilliant, perhaps, and no doubt
lost his head, but as you say he is the most variously gifted, the most
capable prose writer of the 19th century.

My brother says that in Italy he is believed to be still alive, and has
been seen by sundry positive people. They explain that he wanted to
disappear and so had a corpse smuggled into his lodging and duly
buried. I gather that this is widely credited there. How very beautiful,
if a hermit near the Trasimenian lake had been fulfilling the promise of
Wilde's powers all these years! He deserves such a legend in any case.
. . . Yours very sincerely

T. S. MOORE

107. Edmund Gosse, letter to André Gide on Wilde's mediocrity

1910

From a letter dated 7 March 1910, *The Correspondence of André
Gide and Edmund Gosse*, 1904–28, ed. Linette Brugmans (New
York, 1959), p. 53.
Gosse wrote to Gide on the occasion of the latter's *Oscar Wilde:
In Memoriam*, which had just appeared.

There has been a great deal of folly written about Wilde. I like the
complete sanity of your picture. Of course he was not a 'great writer.'
A languid romancier, a bad poet, a good (but not superlatively good)
dramatist,—his works, taken without his life, present to a sane criticism,
a mediocre figure.

108. Lewis Piaget Shanks on Wilde's place in literature

1910

Signed article, titled 'Oscar Wilde's Place in Literature', in *Dial* [Chicago] (16 April 1910), xlviii, 261–3.

Lewis Piaget Shanks (1878–1935), American professor of romance languages at the University of Tennessee at the time this article appeared (later professor at Johns Hopkins University) and author of books on Flaubert, Anatole France, and Baudelaire. In judging Wilde's works, Shanks is bedevilled by his use of the critical concept of 'sincerity', hence his high regard for *De Profundis* and for little else.

After a decade of noisy oblivion, the writings of Oscar Wilde have received the recognition of a definitive edition, worthy as to form and complete in contents. No longer need we contend with the pornographic stock-broker at the book-auction, or shake our heads over the excessive prices of items listed in the catalogues under the dreadful caption of *Oscariana*. However, no one but the collector will complain that Wilde is no longer a rarity. Now at last we can fight in the light: we may 'adopt an attitude,' to use a phrase of Wilde's own, toward a definitely presented literary talent; and even the apologists who plead that Villon was a rascal and Shakespeare a poacher, may judge whether or not we shall forget that the 'apostle of the English Renaissance' was an improper person.

Will Wilde survive? The answer lies in these substantial volumes; the evidence is all in, though it may be over-early to discuss it. What strikes one first is the range of the writings: there are plays, novels, poems, essays, art-criticism, book-reviews, and autobiography; nothing is lacking but history and the 'miscellaneous divinity' of the old-book stores! Wilde preferred making history to writing it (we are still trying to forget the lily!); and if he worshipped Pater's style, he did not care in the least for patristic literature. Here, therefore, we must content ourselves with the Pre-Raphaelite lyrics, filled with aesthetic religiosity as the poems of Dante Gabriel Rossetti: charming decorative pieces surely, but insincere in spirit as most of our modern cathedral glass. Mediaeval feeling, after all, can hardly be reproduced in a copy of a copy.

Rossetti is but one of Wilde's literary models; every great poet of the Victorian age finds a second immortality in his verses. They pass before us in 'The Garden of Eros'—Keats, Shelley, Swinburne, Morris, and the poet-painter himself. But if we add to these self-confessed mentors most of the other great English poets, and to these Homer and the Greeks, and Dante, and a few of the lyrists of France, we shall get a better idea of the range of his reading and the strength of his memory. No academic ear is needed to detect this; echo follows echo as in a musical comedy. 'The true artist is known,' said Wilde in one of his reviews, 'by the use he makes of what he annexes; and he annexes everything.' So our poet modestly lived up to his maxim, aware that in literature at least there is no Monroe Doctrine. Had not Molière said, before him, 'Je prends mon bien où je le trouve'?[1] Like Molière, we are all plagiarists—though hardly, perhaps, with such an excuse; and some Elysian day, when all but the scholars have ceased to read the classics, judicious plagiarism may become a literary virtue, supported by a socialistic culture and justified by the pedagogic theories of Rousseau.

So perhaps might Wilde have justified his imitations. But his plagiarism was of the old-fashioned sturdier sort, like Shakespeare's or Molière's. He copied from other poets, hoping, as all plagiarists hope, that in the course of time others might copy him. He copied himself, to show that he was not unworthy of the compliment. Did not Homer repeat his adjectives, his similes? So in these books the best refuses to be hidden, and telling epithets, aphorisms, and puns reappear like comets in the cosmic life. Over a score of the epigrams in *A Woman of No Importance* are taken from *Dorian Gray*. Like the bird in Browning's verses, Wilde

> Sings each song twice over,
> Lest you should think he never could recapture
> The first fine careless rapture.

One cannot see how much of the early verse can survive. We soon tire of hydromel, and a Keats devoid of genius becomes the most dread-

[1] See No. 14, note 1.

ful of literary diets. Alas for Wilde! he feasted too long on ambrosia, and drank too deeply of his 'poppy-seeded wine.' To read his verse at all is cloying, and to read much of it is like a literary debauch. The best things are the Sonnets, in which the imagery is definitely limited by the form: there at least the reader is sure of one thought for every fourteen lines. Next to these come, not the 'Pagan' verses, far too morbidly romantic to be Greek, but the pastel-like pictures inspired by Gautier, some of which have all the delicate impressionism of *Emaux et Camées*. What could be better in its way than this:

[quotes 'La Fuite de la Lune']

No minor poet in England ever attained a more thorough mastery of technique than Wilde: we see it in the sonnets, as nearly perfect in construction as the study of Milton could make them; we see it pushed to the extreme of *l'art pour l'art* in that bit of Byzantine mosaic, *The Sphinx*. Yet of these early poems none are to be found in the anthologies save 'Ave Imperatrix,' which alone catches a breath of national feeling in an adequate chord. Most of them, to be sure, are esoteric; when we read them we wonder what is the matter, but when we have read them we conclude that there isn't any. Never did Wilde conform more closely to his maxim, 'Youth is rarely original.'

The Ballad of Reading Gaol was written fifteen years later. We all remember how it was received; we remember—alas!—how it was compared to 'The Ancient Mariner.' Such judgments show the evils of literary journalism: they indicate that the critic has had no time to read Coleridge since his college days. *Reading Gaol* has more limp-leather editions to its credit in the department stores,—but where in Wilde's ballad do we find anything like the conception, the imaginative power, and the classic simplicity of 'The Ancient Mariner,' whose every sentence is as full of meaning as the etcher's line? *Reading Gaol* does recall Coleridge, as 'Charmides' recalls something of Keats; but the first poem is too brutal, the second too delicately indelicate, to carry out the comparison invited by occasional imitative lines. No realism, however poignant, can match the serene imaginative reality of the earlier poem; we want no paradoxes in the ballad, we want no ballad so artistic as to be artificial. And, after all, Wilde never forgets that the important thing in his poem is the manner.

The tyranny of technique is Wilde's real prison-wall. If art is not able to efface itself—*ars est celare artem*[1]—better to write without regard

[1] 'Art is to conceal art', Quintilian, *De institutione oratoria*, I.

for style than use the diction of *The Decay of Lying*. Such prose makes one think that it is possible for an artist to be too articulate. 'The world was created,' said Stéphane Mallarmé, 'in order to lead up to a fine book.' For Wilde, apparently, the cosmic processes led up to the paradox. 'Pen, Pencil, and Poison' was built around an epigram, and 'The Model Millionaire' was written for the sake of a pun. 'Paradoxy is my doxy' is the basis of his artistic creed; and the principle of his method is simple contrariety. For example:

After the death of her third husband her hair turned quite gold from grief.
We live in an age that reads too much to be wise, and thinks too much to be beautiful.

What could be simpler than the *modus operandi*? Yet each of these phrases occurs three times in the volumes before us, with many another gem of rare and recurrent wit. Surely Wilde knew that the best of paradoxes will scarce bear repetition, and that the wittiest of epigrams loses its flavor when it becomes a refrain.

The least affected of Wilde's prose is to be found in the journalistic criticism which fills a volume and a half of the collected works; book-reviews of purely ephemeral interest, yet written with sprightly grace and wit, and full of literary judgments which will be turned against their author—when our would-be doctors fall upon the difference between Wilde's preaching and his practice! And to reward their labors, they will find some charming 'purple patches'; the best of these were afterwards worked into the pages of *Intentions*. Wilde might have become a critic of importance, had it been given him to out-grow his paradoxes and to chasten his style. He had a nice appreciation of all the arts, and a sense of the melodic possibilities of language that puts his best work beside that of Pater; and, unlike Pater, he never falls from music to mosaic. Truly, *Intentions* is a delightful book,—but how far below Pater, if we consider it as a collection of essays! How far below Landor in its management of the dialogue form! Wilde's adversary is always the man of straw; there is none of the play of personality, the contrast of opposite standpoints, that we find in such books as Mallock's *New Republic*.[1] Wilde could not project himself into the intellectual life of another.

This is the fault of all his work. The very types in his plays, excepting those that call for a mere surface characterization, are at

---

[1] The satirical novel, published in 1877, by W. H. Mallock (1849–1923), in which various contemporary figures, including Pater, appear in fictional disguise.

heart merely dramatic phrases of the moods or poses of their author. He gives them emotions, but not minds or characters; he makes them real by their repartee. They are puppets animated by puns; they bedazzle our judgment with a pyrotechnic shower of epigrams. We are carried away by it all, but we are left nothing which we can carry away. The aesthetic *Katharsis* of his dramatic theories is lost sight of; we must purge our souls with paradoxes, and in improper situations make them clean. After all, the characters of these plays are not characters, for all they have the tone of good society. They are sometimes society men and women, but more often only marionettes with manners.

Marionettes, too, are the men and women of *Dorian Gray*. Lord Henry Wotton, brilliant, autobiographic, the monocled Mephisto of an ineffectual Faust, may alone be said to live, and at times the reader finds him more lively than alive. Dorian simply doesn't exist; he has sold his conscience for an eternal youth,—and what man can exist without a conscience? Sybil Vane is a shadow, and the painter Hallward the shadow of a shade. He is never so living as when he is slain, and his corpse sits sprawling in the dreadful attic. Only a few of the minor characters, sketched in, like the unctuous Jew of the theatre, with broad realistic touches, may be said to live even as properties. No, *Dorian Gray* is a good subject spoiled. One can imagine how Flaubert would have told the story, how Balzac would have filled it with fiery-colored life. Yet some have compared this novel to *La Peau de Chagrin!*

The shorter stories need not detain us; they are less real than the fairy-tales. We turn with pleasure to *The Happy Prince* and *The House of Pomegranates*,—for the luxuriance that cloys in the poems becomes delightful when submitted to the partial restraint of a poetic prose. No one, of course, would go to Oscar Wilde for the trenchant simplicity of the German folk-tale. His are merely artistic apologues, touching life with the light satire of the drawing-room. One forgets their author, excepting when he is sticking pins into his puppets to create an artistic pathos; only then do we rebel. However, Wilde did not take his heroes seriously, nor need we. Let us be thankful that he does not, that he drags in no pompous moral, for without it these fables have all the honesty of the frankly artificial, and in their very slightness of texture lies the secret of their charm.

The case is the same with the plays. The best of the comedies have a sort of frivolous unity; they are often terribly affected, but they never affect a moral. Sincerity makes Wilde inconsistent with his art; he becomes impossible when he assumes a purpose, and intolerable when he has a paradox to prove. Could anything be worse than the essay on Socialism? But no problems spoil his plays, and when we find that the least serious of them is incomparably the best, the inference is easy. He felt too much the charm of his material; he found it easier to play with constructions than to construct a play. As a follower of *l'art pour l'art*, a purpose would spoil him, and he admitted sincerity only in his attitude toward aesthetics. Yet the value of a fundamental seriousness is nowhere more apparent than in the superiority of his art-lectures to such work as 'Pen, Pencil, and Poison.'

The final necessity of subduing style and spirit in a deeper unity is shown in *De Profundis*. Reading Gaol, and not Oxford, gave us the final development of Wilde's prose. It is said that prisons make men liars; but it was none the less a prison that made *De Profundis* sincere. Here first his art attains its final unity,—a unity of spirit and form which puts certain pages of his confession almost beyond criticism. All of his early work, in comparison, seems little more than a promise; for here alone he attains the simplicity of great art.

When we add to this its value as a 'document,' we cannot doubt that *De Profundis* will survive. It is a pity that this is all we can be sure of. But *The Ballad of Reading Gaol* contains too much alloy; if it becomes a classic our classics will have lived. The art-criticism, the aesthetic 'philosophy,' will be stolen and rewritten, as it was originally stolen and rewritten by Wilde. The life of the plays is limited by the life of their paradoxes, as we can see from the puns in Shakespeare; and even the fairy tales need more human nature to keep them alive. Wilde's place in literature, in so far as he concerns us, is that of a precursor: he prepared the way for Shaw's paradoxes, and the success of Chesterton is to be laid at his door. He revealed to us a certain kind of wit, but he has made some of our critics tremendously trifling. Everything considered, Wilde's literary executors would have done better to give us a selection from his works—a careful selection, with all the cheapest epigrams expunged. Not even a reviewer can read a dozen volumes of this sort with impunity!

109. T. W. H. Crosland on *De Profundis* as a disgrace to humanity

1912

'Foreword' to *The First Stone: On Reading the Unpublished Portions of Oscar Wilde's 'De Profundis'* (1912), pp. 5–7.

Thomas William Hodgson Crosland (1865–1924), journalist and founder of several unsuccessful periodicals, met Lord Alfred Douglas around 1905 and joined the staff of the *Academy* when Douglas purchased it in 1907. A hater of Wilde—one of his 'psychopathically conceived enmities', as Rupert Croft-Cooke states in his biography of Douglas, *Bosie* (1963)—Crosland composed a free verse diatribe, the 'Foreword' to which is included here. *The First Stone* begins:

> Thou,
> The complete mountebank,
> The scented posturer,
> The flabby Pharisee,
> The King of Life,
> The Lord of Language,
> With the bad teeth;
> The whining convict
> And Prince of Hypocrites,
> That slouchest
> Out of the shameless slime,
> Shamelessly . . .

De Profundis is everybody's book. One's opinion of it does not alter the fact that it is read and admired by people who have nothing but loathing for *The Picture of Dorian Gray*, and little but amused contempt for *Intentions*. It was put before the world as an 'explanation' and accepted more or less as an expression of contrition. With the exception of a very occasional row of periods, there is nothing about it to indicate that it is a fragmentary or incomplete work, or that it has been edited into its present form by the simple process of omitting quite half of what the author really wrote. In his preface Mr. Robert Ross, Wilde's literary executor, says, 'I have only to record that it was written by my friend during the last months of his imprisonment, that it was the only work he wrote while in prison, and the last work he ever wrote.' The parts which have been printed are supposed in the main to be creditable to Oscar Wilde. Of the parts cut out it is charity to say that they are sufficiently discreditable to render the whole ignominious. Posterity can arrive at no other view. The blame, if any, must attach to Wilde rather than to his friends or publishers, who, as they tell us, have acted upon his clear wishes.

My justification for printing the following pages will be more than apparent when *De Profundis* sees the light of day, complete and un-expurgated. We are told that the complete work is not 'for this genera-tion.' Until the race of men get rid of the last vestige of moral sense it ought not to be for any generation. I have read every word of it and shuddered as I read. A blacker, fiercer, falser, craftier, more grovelling or more abominable piece of writing never fell from mortal pen. It may be held shameful in me that I rake it up at all. I admit that in ordinary circumstances common decency would have prevented me. Wilde is dead; let his crowning devilry die with him—yes, Mr. Robert Ross, I say, devilry!

But the *De Profundis* we know passes for a work of edification. Its introducer ventured to hope that it would 'give many readers a different impression of the witty and delightful author.' Nobody with his eyes open can doubt that this wish is being abundantly realised. The 'revul-sion of feeling' for which Wilde's friends have laboured with such tender assiduity is actually occurring, and *De Profundis* has helped it on mightily. Oscar Wilde is nowadays to figure among the 'improving' authors whom he affected so to despise! Roughly speaking we are in-vited to say of him, 'Thy sins which were many are forgiven thee; because at the end thou madest a "beautiful," tearful book for the Sunday Schools.' The criticism of the time, which is always a few lengths ahead of the public sentiment or prejudice, commends us even to a more perilous and preposterous complaisance.

Is it not time that somebody with a trifle of power over printer's ink spoke out? I think it is, and, accordingly, I seem to have said my say. I shall be told to remember that Wilde was a man of genius, and that he is dead. In view of what is happening under our noses, I refuse to forget that he is fearfully alive, that his genius belonged essentially to the stews, and that he spent his last literary strength on the deliberate production of a work which is disgraceful to humanity.

110. Charles Ricketts on Wilde
as talker and writer

1912

From the postscript of a letter to William Anthony Pye in *Self-Portrait*, ed. Cecil Lewis (1939), consisting of Ricketts's letters and journals, pp. 177–9.

Charles Ricketts (1866–1931), artist and book designer, was co-editor (with Charles Shannon) of a privately printed magazine titled the *Dial* (1889–97). Almost all of Wilde's books were designed by either Ricketts or Shannon.

I agree with you, *Dorian Gray* is a dreadful book, and, had Wilde lived to do his work, it would have been forgotten as a poor, early, money-making effort. At the most it contains the subject for a small story such as Poe's 'William Wilson' or Gautier's 'Fortunio,' neither of which is good. Wilde wrote during five years only; it is only in the very last things, *The Soul of Man*, *Poems in Prose* and *Salomé*, and in *The Importance of Being Earnest*, that he has given a hint at the power of thought, sardonic insight, and wit which characterized the man himself. Les Goncourt say that nothing published by Gautier showed the power, originality, and beauty of his conversation. Nothing written by Wilde hints at the richness of his conversation. He at once summarized a period, in all its faults, but was also the *enfant terrible* of that period. His fall was an accident, a miscalculation, and the result of a conspiracy. He impressed me as at once the kindliest and most generous of men I ever met and the most richly endowed in intellect. At that time I was a very young man and did not credit him with the powers he had, and which were latent more than actual; I was conscious of his quite extraordinary vitality and also of his bad taste and occasional triviality. I now believe we lost in him the possibilities of one of those strange, complex blends in character such as Heine, for instance, whose influence is incalculable. Heine was a cynic and a sentimentalist, often a rare genius. What would Wilde have been? Would he have been a great critic, would he have

324

revived the art of artificial comedy—by that I mean criticism of manners and character instead of our modern comedy of adultery and brutal pathos? I am unable to say! Believe me, there was something in him which had the power to charm or fascinate the rarer type of man, since he won friends in France among people of very different range and character, and at that time he was a mental and physical wreck, under the influence of drink and the threat of illness. That no one among the greater Englishmen of his time should have befriended him at the time of his fall, has left with me an incurable distrust of them; it has altered my estimate of their intellect and work, and left an element of hostility towards England itself.

111. Holbrook Jackson on Wilde as dandy and artist

1913

'Oscar Wilde: The Last Phase', chapter iv of *The Eighteen Nineties* (1913), pp. 72–90.
Holbrook Jackson (1874–1948), literary historian, editor, and biographer of Shaw and Morris, here presents an admirably balanced assessment of Wilde, whose personality, he states, 'is not only dominant but essential' to an estimate of his art. Jackson's incisive observations on the relationship of Wilde's life to his art were a major influence on later critics.

The singularity of Oscar Wilde has puzzled writers since his death quite as much as it puzzled the public during the startled years of his wonderful visit to the glimpses of Philistia; for after all that has been written about him we are no nearer a convincing interpretation of his character than we were during the great silence which immediately followed his trial and imprisonment. Robert H. Sherard's *Oscar Wilde: The Story of an Unhappy Friendship* throws the clear light of sincerity and eloquence upon his own and his subject's capacity for friendship, but little more than that; André Gide has created a delightful, literary miniature which must always hang on the line in any gallery of studies of Oscar Wilde, but his work is portraiture rather than interpretation. For the rest, we have to be content with such indications of character as may be obtained from the numerous critical essays which have been published during the last few years, notable among them being Arthur Ransome's fine study, and the always wise commentations of Wilde's literary executor and editor, Robert Ross, and the notes and collectanea of Stuart Mason. But whatever ultimate definition his character may assume in future biography, and however difficult such definition may be, it is not so hard to define Oscar Wilde's position and influence during the last decade of the nineteenth century, and what proved to be as well the last decade of his own life.

In the year 1889 Oscar Wilde might have passed away without creating any further comment than that which is accorded an eccentric poet who has succeeded in drawing attention to himself and his work by certain audacities of costume and opinion. His first phase was over, and he had become an out-moded apostle of an aestheticism which had already taken the place of a whimsically remembered fad, a fad which, even then, almost retained only its significance through the medium of Gilbert and Sullivan's satirical opera, *Patience*. He was the man who had evoked merriment by announcing a desire to live up to his blue-and-white china; he was the man who had created a sort of good-humoured indignation by expressing displeasure with the Atlantic Ocean; 'I am not exactly pleased with the Atlantic,' he had confessed. 'It is not so majestic as I expected'; and whose later dissatisfaction with Niagara Falls convinced the United States of America of his flippancy: 'I was disappointed with Niagara. Most people must be disappointed with Niagara. Every American bride is taken there, and the sight of the stupendous waterfall must be one of the earliest if not the keenest disappointments in American married life.' These sayings were beginning to be remembered dimly, along with the picturesque memories of a plum-coloured velveteen knickerbocker suit and a famous stroll down Bond Street as a form of aesthetic propaganda by example. This memory also was aided by W. S. Gilbert:

If you walk down Piccadilly
With a poppy or a lily
In your mediaeval hand. . . .

But certain encounters with Whistler, in which Oscar Wilde felt the sting of the Butterfly, were remembered more distinctly and with more satisfaction, with the result that, besides being outmoded, he became soiled by the charge of plagiarism. 'I wish I had said that,' he remarked once, approving of one of Whistler's witticisms. 'You will, Oscar; you will!' was the reply. And still more emphatic, the great painter had said on another occasion: 'Oscar has the courage of the opinions . . . of others!' The fact was that the brilliant Oxford graduate had not yet fulfilled the promise of his youth, of his first book, and of his own witty audacity. He had achieved notoriety without fame, and literary reputation without a sufficient means of livelihood, and so small was his position in letters that, from 1887 to 1889, we find him eking out a living by editing *The Woman's World* for Messrs Cassell & Co.

His successes during this period were chiefly in the realms of friendship, and of this the public knew nothing. Publicly he was treated with amiable contempt: he was a social jester, an intellectual buffoon, a *poseur*; food for the self-righteous laughter of the Philistines; fair quarry for the wits of *Punch*, who did not miss their chance. Yet during the very years he was controlling editorial destinies which were more than foreign to his genius, he was taking the final preparatory steps towards the attractive and sometimes splendid literary output of his last decade. During 1885 and 1890 his unripe genius was feeling its way ever surer and surer towards that mastery of technique and increasing thoughtfulness which afterwards displayed themselves. This was a period of transition and co-ordination. Oscar Wilde was evolving out of one *bizarrerie* and passing into another. And in this evolution he was not only shedding plumes borrowed from Walter Pater, Swinburne and Whistler, he was retaining such of them as suited his needs and making them definitely his own. But, further than that, he was shedding his purely British masters and allowing himself to fall more directly under the influence of a new set of masters in France, where he was always at home, and where he had played the 'sedulous ape' to Balzac some years earlier. From time to time during these years he had polished and engraved and added to the luxuriant imagery of that masterpiece of ornate poetry, *The Sphinx*, which was published in 1894 in a beautiful format with decorations by Charles Ricketts. Essays like 'The Truth of Masks' and 'Shakespeare and Stage Costume' appeared in the pages of *The Nineteenth Century* in 1885; in other publications appeared such stories as 'The Sphinx without a Secret,' 'The Canterville Ghost' and

'Lord Arthur Savile's Crime,' and in 1888 he issued *The Happy Prince and Other Tales*. 'Pen, Pencil and Poison' appeared in *The Fortnightly Review* in 1889, and in the same year *The Nineteenth Century* published the first of his two great colloquies, *The Decay of Lying*. In all of these stories and essays his style was conquering its weaknesses and achieving the undeniable distinction which made him the chief force of the renaissance of the early Nineties. In 1890 his finest colloquy, 'The Critic as Artist,' appeared in *The Nineteenth Century*. Several of the above-named essays and tales went to the making of two of his most important books, *The House of Pomegranates* and *Intentions*, both of which appeared in the first year of the Nineties, and in the same year he published in book form the complete version of *The Picture of Dorian Gray*, thirteen chapters of which had appeared serially in *Lippincott's Monthly Magazine* in the previous year.

Thus, with the dawn of the Eighteen Nineties, Oscar Wilde came into his own. *The House of Pomegranates* alone was sufficient to establish his reputation as an artist, but the insouciant attitude of the paradoxical philosopher revealed in *The Picture of Dorian Gray* and *Intentions* stung waning interest in the whilom apostle of beauty to renewed activity. Shaking off the astonishing reputation which had won him early notoriety as the posturing advertiser of himself by means of the ideas of others, he arose co-ordinate and resplendent, an individual and an influence. He translated himself out of a subject for anecdote into a subject for discussion. And whilst not entirely abandoning that art of personality which had brought him notoriety as a conversationalist and dandy in *salon* and drawing-room and at the dinner-table, he transmuted the personality thus cultivated into the more enduring art of literature, and that brought him fame of which notoriety is but the base metal. For many years he had looked to the theatre as a further means of expression and financial gain, and he had tried his 'prentice hand on the drama with *Vera: or the Nihilists* in 1882, which was produced unsuccessfully in America in 1883, and with *The Duchess of Padua*, written for Mary Anderson and rejected by her about the same time, and produced without encouraging results in New York in 1891. There were also two other early plays, *A Florentine Tragedy*, a fragment only of which remains, and *The Woman Covered with Jewels*, which seems to have been entirely lost. The failure of these works to make any sort of appeal involves no reflection on the public, as they are the veriest stuff of the amateur and imitator; echoes of Sardou and Scribe; romantic costume plays inspired by the theatre rather than by life, and possessing none of the signs of that skilled craftsmanship upon which the merely stage-carpentered play must necessarily depend. But with that change in the whole bent of his genius which heralded the first year of the Nineties came a change also in his skill as a playwright. In 1891 he wrote *Salomé* in French, afterwards translated into English by Lord Alfred Douglas and published by the Bodley Head, with illustrations by Aubrey Beardsley, in 1894. This play would have been produced at the Palace Theatre in 1892 with Madame Sarah Bernhardt in the cast, had not the censor intervened. Oscar Wilde achieved his first dramatic success with *Lady Windermere's Fan*, produced by George Alexander at the St James's Theatre, on 20th February 1892. The success was immediate. Next year Herbert Beerbohm Tree produced *A Woman of No Importance* at the Haymarket Theatre to even more enthusiastic audiences. In 1895 *An Ideal Husband* was produced at the same theatre in January, and, in February, *The Importance of Being Earnest* was produced at the St. James's.

Oscar Wilde had now reached the age of forty-one and the height of his fame and power. 'The man who can dominate a London dinner-table can dominate the world,' he had said. He had dominated many a London dinner-table; he now dominated the London stage. He was a monarch in his own sphere, rich, famous, popular; looked up to as a master by the younger generation, courted by the fashionable world, loaded with commissions by theatrical managers, interviewed, paragraphed and pictured by the Press, and envied by the envious and the impotent. All the flattery and luxury of success were his, and his luxuriant and applause-loving nature appeared to revel in the glittering surf of conquest like a joyous bather in a sunny sea. But it was only a partial victory. The apparent capitulation of the upper and middle classes was illusory, and even the man in the street who heard about him and wondered was moved by an uneasy suspicion that all was not well. For, in spite of the flattery and the amusement, Oscar Wilde never succeeded in winning popular respect. His intellectual playfulness destroyed popular faith in his sincerity, and the British people have still to learn that one can be as serious in one's play with ideas as in one's play with a football. The danger of his position was all the more serious because those who were ready to laugh with him were never tired of laughing at him. This showed that lack of confidence which is the most fertile ground of suspicion, and Wilde was always suspected in this country even before the rumours which culminated in his trial and imprisonment began to filter through the higher strata of society to the lower. It sufficed that he was strange and clever and seemingly happy and indifferent to public opinion. This popular suspicion is summarised clearly, and with the sort of disrespect from which he never escaped even in his hour of triumph, in an article in *Pearson's Weekly* for 27th May 1893, written immediately after the success of *Lady Windermere's Fan* and *A Woman of No Importance*:

Where he does excel is in affectation. His mode of life, his manner of speech, his dress, his views, his work, are all masses of affectation. Affectation has become a second nature to him, and it would probably now be utterly impossible for him to revert to the original Oscar that lies beneath it all. In fact, probably none of his friends have ever had an opportunity of finding out what manner of man the real Oscar is. . . . So long as he remains an amiable eccentricity and the producer of amusing trifles, however, one cannot be seriously angry with him. So far, it has never occurred to any reasonable person to take him seriously, and the storms of ridicule to which he has exposed himself have prevented his becoming a real nuisance. For the present, however, we may content ourselves with the reflection that there is no serious danger to be apprehended to the State from the vagaries of a butterfly.

The above may be taken as a fair example of the attitude of the popular Press towards Oscar Wilde, and the same sentiments were expressed, varying only in degrees of literary polish, in many directions, even at a time when the new spirit of comedy he had introduced into the British theatre was giving unbounded delight to a vast throng of fashionable playgoers; for these plays had not to create audiences for themselves, like the plays of Bernard Shaw; they were immediately acclaimed, and Wilde at once took rank with popular playwrights like Sidney Grundy and Pinero.

There were of course many who admired him; and he always inspired friendship among his intimates. All who have written of him during his earlier period and during the early days of his triumph refer to his joyous and resplendent personality, his fine scholarship, his splendid manners and conversational gifts, his good humour and his lavish generosity. André Gide gives us many glimpses of Wilde both before and after his downfall, one of which reveals him as table-talker;

I had heard him talked about at Stephane Mallarmé's house, where he was described as a brilliant conversationalist, and I expressed a wish to know him, little hoping that I should ever do so. A happy chance, or rather a friend, gave me the opportunity, and to him I made known my desire. Wilde was invited to dinner. It was at a restaurant. We were a party of four, but three of us were content to listen. Wilde did not converse—he told tales. During the whole meal he hardly stopped. He spoke in a slow, musical tone, and his very voice was wonderful. He knew French almost perfectly, but pretended, now and then, to hesitate for a word to which he wanted to call our attention. He had scarcely any accent, at least only what it pleased him to affect when it might give a somewhat new or strange appearance to a word—for instance, he used purposely to pronounce *scepticisme* as *skepticisme*. The stories he told us without a break that evening were not of his best. Uncertain of his audience, he was testing us, for, in his wisdom, or perhaps in his folly, he never betrayed himself into saying anything which he thought would not be to the taste of his hearers; so he doled out food to each according to his appetite. Those who expected nothing from him got nothing, or only a little light froth, and as at first he used to give himself up to the task of amusing, many of those who thought they knew him will have known him only as the amuser.

With the progress of his triumph as a successful playwright, his friends observed a coarsening of his appearance and character, and he lost his powers of conversation. Robert H. Sherard met him during the Christmas season of 1894 and described his appearance as bloated. His face seemed to have lost its spiritual beauty, and he was oozing with material prosperity. At this time serious rumours about his private life and habits became more persistent in both London and Paris, and countenance was lent to them by the publication of *The Green Carnation*, which, although making no direct charge, hinted at strange sins. Oscar Wilde knew that his conduct must lead to catastrophe, although many of his friends believed in his innocence to the end. André Gide met him in Algiers just before the catastrophe happened. Wilde explained that he was fleeing from art:

He spoke of returning to London, as a well-known peer was insulting him, challenging him, and taunting him with running away.

'But if you go back what will happen?' I asked him. 'Do you know the risk you are running?'

'It is best never to know,' he answered. 'My friends are extraordinary—they beg me to be careful. Careful? But how can I be careful? That would be a backward step. I must go on as far as possible. I cannot go much further. Something is bound to happen . . . something else.'

Here he broke off, and the next day he left for England.

Almost immediately after his arrival he brought an action for criminal libel against the Marquis of Queensberry and, upon losing the case, was arrested, and charged under the 11th Section of the Criminal Law Amendment Act, and sentenced to two years' penal servitude.

During his imprisonment he wrote *De Profundis*, in the form of a long letter to his friend, Robert Ross, a part of which was published in book form in 1905, and after his release he wrote *The Ballad of Reading Gaol*, published, under a pseudonym, 'C. 3. 3.' (his prison number), by Leonard Smithers, and he contributed two letters on the conditions of prison life, 'The Cruelties of Prison Life,' and 'Don't Read this if you Want to be Happy To-day,' to *The Daily Chronicle* on 28th May 1897 and 24th March 1898. These were his last writings.

After leaving prison he lived for a while, under the assumed name of 'Sebastian Melmoth,' at the Hôtel de la Plage, and later at the Villa Bourget, Berneval-sur-Mer, near Dieppe, where he wrote *The Ballad of Reading Gaol*, and the prison letters, and where he contemplated writing a play called *Ahab and Jezebel*. This play he hoped would be his passport to the world again. But a new restlessness overcame him, and all his good resolutions turned to dust. For a while he travelled, visiting Italy, the south of France and Switzerland, eventually settling in Paris, where he died, in poverty and a penitent Catholic, on 30th November 1900. He was buried in the Bagneux Cemetery, but on 20th July 1909 his remains were removed to Père Lachaise.

It is too soon, perhaps, even now, to set a final value upon the work of Oscar Wilde. Time although not an infallible critic, is already winnowing the chaff from the grain, and almost with the passing of each year we are better able to recognise the more permanent essences of his literary remains. It is inevitable in his case, where the glamour of personality added so significantly to the character of his work, that Time should insist upon being something more than a casual arbiter. In proof of this the recollection of so much futile criticism of Wilde cannot be overlooked. Both the man and his work have suffered depreciations which amount to defamation, and appraisals which can only be described as silly. But finally he would seem in many instances to have suffered more at the hands of his friends than his enemies. There have been, to be sure, several wise estimations of his genius, even in this country, notably those of Arthur Ransome and the not altogether unprovocative essays of Arthur Symons, entitled 'An Artist in Attitudes'; and the various prefaces and notes contributed by Robert Ross to certain of the volumes in the complete edition of the works are, of course, of great value. But, as the incidents associated with the life and times of Wilde recede further into the background of the mental picture which inevitably forms itself about any judgment of his work, we shall be able to obtain a less biased view. Even then, our perspective may be wrong, for this difficulty of personality is not only dominant, but it may be essential.

The personality of Oscar Wilde, luxuriant, piquant and insolent as it was, is sufficiently emphatic to compel attention so long as interest in his ideas or his works survives. Indeed, it may never be quite possible to separate such a man from such work. It is certainly impossible to do so now. With many writers, perhaps the majority, it requires no effort to forget the author in the book, because literature has effectually absorbed personality, or all that was distinctive of the author's personality. With Oscar Wilde it is otherwise. His books can never be the abstract and brief chronicles of himself; for, admittedly on his part, and recognisably on the part of others, he put even more distinction into his life than he did into his art. Not always the worthier part of himself; for that often, and more often in his last phase, was reserved for his books. But there is little doubt that the complete Oscar Wilde was the living and bewildering personality which rounded itself off and blotted itself out in a tragedy which was all the more nihilistic because of its abortive attempt at recuperation—an attempt which immortalised itself in the repentant sincerity of *De Profundis*, but almost immediately fell forward into an anticlimax of tragedy more pitiful than the first.

So far as we are able to judge, and with the aid of winnowing Time, it is already possible to single out the small contribution made by Oscar Wilde to poetry. The bulk of his poetry is negligible. It represents little more than the ardent outpourings of a young man still deeply indebted to his masters. One or two lyrics will of a surety survive in the anthologies of the future, but if Wilde were dependent upon his verses for future acceptance his place would be among the minor poets. There is, however, a reservation to be made even here, as there is in almost every generalisation about this elusive personality; he wrote three poems, two towards the close of his earlier period, *The Harlot's House* and *The Sphinx*, and one near the close of his life, *The Ballad of Reading Gaol*, which bear every indication of permanence. The two former will appeal to those who respond to strange and exotic emotions, the other to those who are moved by the broader current of average human feeling. His last poem, and last work, does not reveal merely Oscar Wilde's acceptance of a realistic attitude, it reveals what might have been, had he lived to pursue the matter further, conversion to a natural and human acceptation of life. The sense of simplicity in art which previously he had been content to use as a refuge for the consciously complex, as a sort of intensive culture for modern bewilderment, is now used with even greater effect in the cause of the most obvious of human emotions—pity:

> I never saw a man who looked
> With such a wistful eye
> Upon that little tent of blue
> Which prisoners call the sky,
> And at every drifting cloud that went
> With sails of silver by.
>
> I walked, with other souls in pain,
> Within another ring,
> And was wondering if the man had done
> A great or little thing,
> When a voice behind me whispered low,
> *'That fellow's got to swing.'*

There is none of the old earnest insincerity in this poem, and only occasionally does the poet fall back into the old *bizarrerie*. Had *The Ballad of Reading Goal* been written a hundred years ago, it would have been printed as a broadside and sold in the streets by the balladmongers; it is so common as that, and so great as that. But there is nothing common, and nothing great, in the universal sense, about the two earlier poems. These are distinguished only as the expressions of unusual vision and unusual mood; they are decadent in so far as they express emotions that are sterile and perverse. They are decadent in the sense that Baudelaire was decadent, from whom they inherit almost everything save the English in which they are framed. But few will doubt their claim to a place in a curious artistic niche. *The Sphinx*, a masterly fantasy of bemused artificiality, is really a poetic design, an arabesque depending for effect upon hidden rhymes and upon strange fancies, expressing sensations which have hitherto been enshrined in art rather than in life:

> Your eyes are like fantastic moons that shiver in some stagnant lake,
> Your tongue is like some scarlet snake that dances to fantastic tunes,
>
> Your pulse makes poisonous melodies, and your black throat is like the hole
> Left by some torch or burning coal on Saracenic tapestries.

Similarly, 'The Harlot's House' interprets a mood that is so sinister and impish and unusual as to express disease rather than health:

> Sometimes a horrible marionette
> Came out, and smoked its cigarette
> Upon the steps like a live thing.

Then turning to my love, I said,
'The dead are dancing with the dead,
The dust is whirling with the dust.'

But she—she heard the violin,
And left my side, and entered in:
Love passed into the house of lust.

Wilde developed this abnormal attitude towards life in *The Picture of Dorian Gray* and in *Salomé*, and in each of these prose works he endeavours, often with success, to stimulate feelings that are usually suppressed, by means of what is strange and rare in art and luxury. It is not the plot that you think about whilst reading *Salomé*, but the hidden desire of the author to tune the senses and the mind to a preposterous key:

[quotes Herod's speech from 'I have jewels hidden in this place' to 'I will give thee the veil of the sanctuary']

The mere naming of jewels and treasures in a highly wrought prose-poem might in itself be as innocent as one of Walt Whitman's catalogues of implements, but even removed from its context there is something unusual and even sinister about Herod's offering to Salomé. The whole work is coloured by a hunger for sensation that is negative with excess of civilisation.

In the essays collected under the title *Intentions*, Oscar Wilde has let us into the secret which produced these works. That secret is involved in an attempt to push Gautier's idea of art for art's sake, and Whistler's idea of art as Nature's exemplar, to their logical conclusions. He out-does his masters with the obvious intention of going one better. Throughout the whole of his life he was filled with a boyish enthusiasm which took the form of self-delight. 'His attitude was dramatic,' says Arthur Symons, 'and the whole man was not so much a personality as an attitude. Without being a sage, he maintained the attitude of a sage; without being a poet, he maintained the attitude of a poet; without being an artist he maintained the attitude of an artist.' It is certainly true that his intellect was dramatic, and it is equally true that he was fond of adopting attitudes, but it is far from true to name three of his favourite attitudes and to say that these began and ended in the mere posture. For Oscar Wilde was both poet and sage and artist. He may not have been a great poet, he may not have been a great sage, he may not, which is more doubtful, have been a great artist, but the fact remains that the attitudes representing those faculties and adopted by him, were the symbols of demonstrable phases of his genius. Whilst always longing to express himself in literary forms, and knowing himself to be capable of doing so, he found it easier to express himself through the living personality. Writing bored him, and those who knew him are agreed that he did not put the best of himself into his work. 'It is personalities,' he said, 'not principles, that move the age.'

Throughout the whole of his life he tried to live up, not to his blue-and-white china, but to an idea of personality; and the whole of his philosophy is concerned with an attempt to prove that personality, even though it destroy itself, should be the final work of art. Indeed, in his opinion, art itself was nothing but the medium of personality. His attitudes thus become details in the art of personality. If they had no basis in fact, Oscar Wilde would have been no more than an actor playing a part in a work of art, but although he played, played at intellectual dandy, much as a boy will play at pirates, he was playing a part in the drama of life; and he adopted the attitude of dandy in response to as real an emotion at least as that which inspires a boy to adopt the attitude of pirate. What he seemed to be doing all the time was translating life into art through himself. His books were but incidents in this process. He always valued life more than art, and only appreciated the latter when its reflex action contributed something to his sensations; but because he had thought himself into the position of one who transmutes life into art, he fell into the error of imagining art to be more important than life. And art for him was not only those formal and plastic things which we call the fine arts; it embraced all luxurious artificialities. 'All art is quite useless,' he said. Such an attitude was in itself artificial; but with Oscar Wilde this artificialism lacked any progressive element: it was sufficient in itself; in short, it ended in itself, and not in any addition to personal power. Oscar Wilde never, for instance, dreamt of evolving into a god; he dreamt of evolving into a master of sensation, a harp responding luxuriously to every impression. This he became, or rather, this he always was, and it explained the many quite consistent charges of plagiarism that were always being brought against him, and it may explain his insensate plunge into forbidden sin, his conversion and his relapse. He lived for the mood, but whatever that mood brought him, whether it was the ideas of others or the perversities of what is impish in life, he made them his own. What he stole from Whistler, Pater, Balzac, Gautier and Baudelaire, whilst remaining recognisably derivative, had added unto them something which their originals did not possess. He mixed pure wines, as it were, and created a new complex beverage, not perhaps for quaffing, but rather a liqueur, with a piquant and quite original flavour which still acknowledged the flavours of its constituents.

This, then, was in reality an attitude towards life, and not an empty pose. I do not think that Oscar Wilde had any hope of finding anything absolute; he was born far too late in the nineteenth century for that. He had no purpose in life save play. He was the playboy of the Nineties; and, like the hero of John Millington Synge's drama, he was subject to the intimidation of flattery. Naturally inclined to go one better than his master, he was also inclined to please his admirers and astonish his enemies by going one better than himself, and as this one better generally meant in his later life one more extravagance, one further abandonment, it resulted, from the point of view of convention, in his going always one worse. Repetition of this whim turned perversity into a habit, and the growing taunt of those who knew or suspected his serious perversions drove him into the final perversion of deliberately courting tragedy, much as the mouse is charmed back into the clutches of the cat after it has apparently been given a loophole of retreat. It would not have been cowardice if Oscar Wilde had escaped while he had the chance, and it was not bravery that made him blind to that chance; he was bemused by his own attitude. Afterwards, he learnt the meaning of pain, and he arrived at a conclusion similar to that of Nietzsche. But it was not until afterwards. And although he found consolation in Christian mysticism whilst in prison, and again on his deathbed, we shall never know with what subtle joy he permitted his own destruction during the intervening period. Looked at from such a point of view, his books help in explaining the man. The best of them, *Intentions*, *The House of Pomegranates*, *The Importance of Being Earnest*, *The Soul of Man*, *The Ballad of Reading Gaol*, *De Profundis*, and a handful of epigrams and short parables which he called *Prose Poems*, must, it seems to me, take a definite place in English literature as the expression and explanation of the type Wilde represented.

This type was not created by Oscar Wilde: it was very general throughout Europe at the close of the last century, and he represented only one version of it. Probably to himself he imagined himself to approximate somewhat to the cynical idlers of his plays: Lord Goring in *An Ideal Husband*, Lord Darlington in *Lady Windermere's Fan*, Lord Illingworth in *A Woman of No Importance* and Algernon Moncrieff in *The Importance of Being Earnest* may be partial portraits of the sort of personal impression their author imagined he was creating in the

337

fashionable world. But he drew fuller portraits of himself in his novel. Lord Henry Wotton and Dorian Gray represent two sides of Oscar Wilde; they are both experimenters in life, both epicureans and both seeking salvation by testing life to destruction. *The Picture of Dorian Gray* is really a moral tale, and that also is characteristic of the genius of Oscar Wilde, for at no period of his life had he the courage of his amorality. He was always haunted by the still small voice which broke bounds and expressed itself freely in *De Profundis*. And whilst reading his books, or listening to his plays, one cannot help feeling that their very playfulness is but the cloak of tragedy. The decadent, weary with known joys and yearning for new sensations, perpetually being rebuked by the clammy hand of exhausted desire, must needs laugh. Oscar Wilde laughed, and made us laugh, not by his wit so much as by his humour, that humour which dances over his plays and epigrams with the flutter of sheet lightning, compelling response where response is possible, but always inconsequent and always defying analysis. It reached its height in *The Importance of Being Earnest*, a comedy so novel, so irresistibly amusing and so perfect in its way that discussion of it ends in futility, like an attempt to explain the bouquet of old Cognac or the iridescence of opals. It is the moonshine of genius. The still small voice in him, of which his lambent humour is the mask, lurks also in 'The Soul of Man' and *The Ballad of Reading Gaol*, and it is quite possible that had he lived the even life that he began to live on the bleak coast of Normandy after his release from prison, this underlying strain in his character would have turned him into a social reformer. His harrowing letters on prison conditions point to that when associated with his philosophic dash into the realm of Socialism. As it was, such humanitarian zeal as he had ended on the one side in pity and on the other in the dream of a Utopia for dandies.

Dandy of intellect, dandy of manners, dandy of dress, Oscar Wilde strutted through the first half of the Nineties and staggered through the last. So pleased was he with himself, so interested was he in the pageant of life, that he devoted his genius, in so far as it could be public, to telling people all about it. His genius expressed itself best in stories and conversation, and he was always the centre of each. The best things in his plays are the conversations, the flippancies of dandies and the garrulities of delightful shameless dowagers. His best essays are colloquies; those that are not depend for effect upon epigrams and aphorisms, originally dropped by himself in the dining-rooms and *salons* of London and Paris. When he was not conversing he was telling stories,

and these stories perhaps, the *Prose Poems, The House of Pomegranates*
and *The Happy Prince,* will outlive even his wittiest paradox. *Salomé* is
more a story, a 'prose-poem,' than a play, and it is more, to use for once
the method of inversion in which he delighted, an epigram than a story.
One can imagine the glee with which Oscar Wilde worked up to the
anti-climax, to the moment after Salomé has kissed the dead mouth of
Jokanaan, and Herod has turned round and said: 'Kill that woman.'
One can taste his own delight whilst writing the final stage instruction:
'The soldiers run forward and crush beneath their shields Salomé,
daughter of Herodias, Princess of Judaea.' But more easily still can one
imagine this remarkable man for ever telling himself an eternal tale in
which he himself is hero.

112. Ernst Bendz on Wilde's literary reputation

1914

Excerpt from 'Introductory', *The Influence of Pater and Matthew
Arnold in the Prose Writings of Oscar Wilde* (Gothenburg and
London, 1914), pp. 5–9.
Ernst Bendz (1880–1966), Swedish critic, wrote extensively on
Wilde in three languages. Like many Continental critics, Bendz
places Wilde among 'the most brilliantly gifted literary men that
England ever produced'. (For another estimate by Bendz, see
No. 116.)

It is noteworthy and, to some, an unpalatable fact that for ten years or
more the literary renown of Oscar Wilde has been steadily spreading,
the true character of his personality and work revealing itself more and
more clearly to ever-widening circles of appreciative students. It is
beginning to be realized, it seems, that Wilde's contributions to English

Letters are, perhaps, the most remarkable furnished by any writer of his generation, with the possible exception of Stevenson, and that he was one of the most brilliantly gifted literary men that England ever produced. No change in the general attitude of men's minds regarding matters of literature can explain this away. On the contrary, the 'Aesthetic Movement,' with which Wilde was identified at the outset of his career, has long ceased to be a thing of actual interest; and so, almost, in its turn has that 'Decadent School,' whose great literary figure he was to become. Things in him that struck his contemporaries as audaciously 'advanced,' and were so no doubt, may now seem a little false and faded. To us of a later generation who take an interest in his writings, this interest is neither a personal one, nor one largely bound up with considerations of 'schools' or 'movements.' It is an aesthetic interest. In other words, we are beginning to see his work in its true perspective, to form an artistic judgment on it, to apply to it what Matthew Arnold called 'the real estimate' of literature, in contradistinction to the 'personal' and the 'historic' estimate. We are no longer impassioned against the man by the sensational incidents of his life. His crime against Society need only occupy our attention in so far as it influenced his artistic nature. Indeed, hardly anybody now, save those who have cultivated an over-delicacy of sentiment, would care to take offence at the tolerant conceit implied in such terms as a 'chronological error' or an 'anachronism,' in dealing with one whose fantasy led him to imagine himself living in the Italy of the Renaissance, or in Greece at the time of Socrates. The long years that already separate us from his death have helped to throw into the background all that was ephemeral and unessential in him; and with each year that passes, the essential fact about him stands out more clearly and prominently: that he was a man of supreme literary talent, who wrote wonderful and extraordinary things, and who exercised, and still exercises, and will no doubt continue to exercise for a long time to come, an important intellectual and artistic influence, both in his own country and abroad. Ten years ago, Sir Richard Garnett and Edmund Gosse, in their history of *English Literature* (vol. IV, 1903,) had not a word for Oscar Wilde. Even as late as 1907, another well-known compiler of literary history, either from personal rancour or for some equally cogent reason, could affect a sort of semi-official ignorance of the man who wrote *De Profundis* and *The Ballad of Reading Gaol*. Perhaps the time-limit was reached in 1912 when Andrew Lang, in his *History of English Literature*, a book of nearly 700 pp., still felt justified in ignoring Wilde. This attitude is no longer possible. Ill-will and prejudice have had their day, even among the professional distributors of praise and blame in matters literary. Nobody who would now set forth however bare an outline of the English literature of the last few decades can pretend to know nothing of a man who so effectively summed up and impersonated, in his life and in his writings, some of the vital tendencies of an epoch. Even into the popular manuals of literary history Oscar Wilde, so long excluded and so rigorously tabooed, is forcing his way at last. Thousands of ordinary readers who were taught to look upon Wilde as merely the infamous central figure in some fearful scandal, will now learn to associate his name with many choice works of art, made accessible to them in cheap editions. It is a significant fact that in one of the latest and most concise of these handbooks, Compton-Rickett's admirable little *History of English Literature*, Pater and Arnold (as critic and prose-writer) are dismissed in six lines each, whereas Wilde alone occupies twenty-six.

The most obvious proof that Wilde's writings are steadily and firmly gaining ground, in and out of England, and are at length receiving their due meed of attention, if not always of competent criticism, is of course the very considerable number of books, pamphlets, and articles published about him within the last ten years or so, in almost every European language. All these productions are utterly heterogeneous in character and value. Most of them are either mere biographical records, or approach the subject in a general and popular sort of way. Only a few are founded on personal recollections. A small number of treatises or magazine articles contain fairly minute analyses of some of his writings, or treat of these from some special or technical point of view. Mr. Sherard's books are universally known and need no further mention here. His great *Life of Oscar Wilde* (1906), though it may not quite satisfy us on all points, still remains our chief source of information concerning the external facts of the poet's life. Stuart Mason's craftsmanlike bibliography of the poems (1907) and his other collectanea are equally well-known to all students. Mr. Robert Ross's Introductions to some of the volumes in Methuen's editions of the works,—those, for instance, in the volumes entitled *Miscellanies* and *Reviews* in the library edition,—include some important matter and will afford highly suggestive reading. Mr. Arthur Ransome's *Oscar Wilde* (1912), which gave rise to the Douglas libel action, is the one really critical and comprehensive monograph on Wilde that exists, and is simply beyond praise. A brief study of Mr. Arthur Symons, which I know in a French translation only (*Portraits Anglais*, Bruges, 1907), though not very sympathetic in tone, is noteworthy for its delicate analysis of character and well-balanced estimate. Mention should be made also of Mr. Walter Hamilton's *The Aesthetic Movement in England* (3rd ed. 1882), which devotes a whole chapter to Wilde,—probably the first appreciative study of him that appeared in print. Some other books on Wilde published during the last few years in England are mostly made up of a few trifling anecdotes or scraps of personal reminiscences, and offer little of interest beyond what is already generally known. The articles or essays by André Gide, Ernest La Jeunesse, and Henri de Régnier (partly reprinted in book-form) are all most interesting, being from the pens of distinguished writers who had some personal acquaintance with the poet. As for the Germans, it is well known that, in true accordance with their fine spirit of intellectual hospitality, they were practically the first to recognize Wilde's genius, his writings finding generous acceptance among them, and this at a time when in his own country but few ventured to manifest an interest in his works. On the other hand, the Germans would, perhaps, seem temperamentally not over-well capacitated for a really intimate and subtle valuation of a writer of such an extravagant type. Most German books or pamphlets on Wilde, will, in fact, be found deficient in the finer shades of sympathy and intuition, and, lacking any literary qualities of their own, have not much in them to attract foreign readers. However, there are exceptions. A study by Carl Hagemann, *Oscar Wilde: Studien zur modernen Weltliteratur* (1904), is decidedly good, and so is an article by Helene Richter in *Englische Studien* (1912), 'Oscar Wildes künstlerische Persönlichkeit.' Dr. Bock's treatise, *Walter Pater's Einfluss auf Oscar Wilde* (1913), too, must be called a clever and painstaking piece of work. . . .

113. James Gibbons Huneker on
Wilde as an imitator

1914

Signed article, under title 'The Seven Arts', *Puck* [New York] (28 November 1914), lxxvi, 17; reprinted in *Unicorns* (New York, 1924).

James Gibbons Huneker (1860–1921), American 'critic of the seven arts', was music and drama critic for several newspapers and periodicals and the author of books on Chopin, Liszt, and other figures. Huneker's incapacity to see Wilde as anything but a clever, superior journalist who imitated greater artists reveals the limitations of Huneker rather than of Wilde. His reference to Swinburne's remark that Wilde was a 'harmless young nobody' is misleading, for the remark was made in a letter to the American poet E. C. Stedman in April 1882, when Wilde was in America on a lecture tour, designed to advertise himself. Swinburne made no such judgments in the 1890s, when Wilde had reached the summit of his literary career.

It is an enormous advertisement nowadays to win a reputation as a martyr—whether to an idea, a vice, or a scolding wife. You have a label by which a careless public is able to identify you. Oscar Wilde was a born advertiser. From the sunflower days to Holloway Gaol, and from the gaol to the Virgins of Dieppe, he kept himself in the public eye. Since his death the number of volumes dealing with his glittering personality, negligible verse and more or less insincere prose, have been steadily accumulating; why, I'm at a loss to understand. If he was a victim to British 'middle-class morality,' then have done with it, while regretting the affair. If he was not, all the more reason to maintain silence. But no, the clamour increases, with the result that there are many young people who believe that Oscar was a great man, a great writer, when in reality he was neither. . . . For copiousness, sustained wit, and verbal brilliancy the man had few equals. It was amazing, his

343

conversation. I met him when he came here, and once again much later. Possibly that is why I care so little for his verse, a pasticcio of Swinburne—(in the wholly admirable biography of this poet by Mr. Gosse, reference is made to O. W. by the irascible hermit of Putney: 'I thought he seemed a harmless young nobody. . . . I should think you in America must be as tired of his name as we are in London of Mr. Barnum's and his Jumbos')—Milton, Tennyson, or for his prose, a dilution of Walter Pater and Flaubert. His *Dorian Gray*, apart from the inversion element, is poor Huysmans's—just look into that masterpiece, 'A Rebours;' not to mention Poe's tale, 'The Oval Portrait;' while Salomé is Flaubert in operetta form—his gorgeous Herodias watered down for uncritical public consumption. It is safe to say the piece—which limps dramatically—would never have been seriously considered if not for the Richard Strauss musical setting. As for the vaunted essay on Socialism, I may only call attention to one fact, *i.e.*, it does not deal with Socialism at all, but with philosophical anarchism; besides, it is not remarkable in any particular. His *Intentions* is his best, because his most 'spoken' prose. The fairy-tales are graceful exercises by a versatile writer, with an excellent memory, but if I had children I'd give them the *Alice in Wonderland* books, through which sweeps a bracing air, and not the hothouse atmosphere of Wilde. The plays are fascinating as fireworks, and as remote from human interest. Perhaps I'm in error, yet, after reading Pater, Swinburne, Rossetti, Huysmans, I prefer them to the Wilde imitations, strained as they are through his very gay fancy.

. . . I have read in cold type that Pater was a 'forerunner' of Wilde; that Wilde is a second Jesus Christ—which latter statement stuns one. (The Whitmaniacs are fond of claiming the same for Walt, who is not unlike that silly and sinister monster described by Rabelais as quite overshadowing the earth with its gigantic wings, and after dropping vast quantities of mustard-seed on the embattled hosts below flew away yawping: 'Carnival, Carnival, Carnival!') For me, he simply turned into superior 'journalism' the ideas of Swinburne, Pater, Flaubert, Huysmans, De Quincey, and others. If his readers would only take the trouble to study the originals there might be less talk of his 'originality.' I say all this without any disparagements of his genuine gifts; he was a born newspaper man. Henry James calls attention to the fact that the so-called aesthetic movement in England never flowered into anything so artistically perfect as the novels of Gabriel d'Annunzio. Which is true; but he could have joined to the name of the Italian poet and play-wright that of Aubrey Beardsley, the one 'genius' of the 'Eighteen-

Nineties.' Beardsley gave us something distinctly individual. Wilde, a veritable *cabotin* did not—nothing but his astounding conversation, and that, alas! is a fast fading memory.

114. Alice Wood on Wilde as a critic

1915

'Oscar Wilde as a Critic', *North American Review* (December 1915), ccii, 899–909.
Alice I. Perry Wood (1872–1967), for many years a professor of English literature at Wellesley College in Massachusetts, here approaches, as Miss Wood calls Wilde, 'a *flâneur*, one who trifled with and abused life', with a seriousness of purpose in evaluating Wilde's contribution to literary theory.

In Oscar Wilde as a late growth of that later Renaissance which was seen in part in the Pre-Raphaelite Movement, there is an increasing interest. And indeed, now that more than a decade has passed since his death, it is easier to see where he stands, and to estimate his contribution to his age.

In his *De Profundis* Wilde says of himself, in his self-analytic, self-conscious way: 'I was a man who stood in symbolic relations to the art and culture of my age. I had realized this for myself at the very dawn of my manhood, and had forced my age to realize it afterwards. Few men hold such a position in their own life-time, and have it so acknowledged. It is usually discerned, if discerned at all, by the historian, or the critic, long after both the man and his age have passed away. With me it was different. I felt it myself, and made others feel it. Byron was a symbolic figure, but his relations were to the passion of his age and its weariness of passion. Mine were to something more noble, more permanent, of more vital issue, of larger scope.' In another passage he says: 'I am a born antinomian.' It was his wish to be considered an anomaly, unique,

345

always different. Thus, 'When people agree with me I always feel that I must be wrong.' Perhaps it was his love of paradox which caused Wilde to believe that, by virtue of his antinomianism, he held this symbolic relation to his age,—that thus he separated and made apparent the subconscious strains in English thought and feeling. That England should recognize itself when thus brought face to face with aestheticism is not a necessity, according to Wilde's idea of the relation of the critic to his age; rather it added to his satisfaction, as an antinomian, to *épater le bourgeois;* it kept in emphasis that symbolic relation by the forced attention which he demanded.

It is this phase that is particularly interesting in Wilde's position in the criticism of his day, especially in his work in what he calls 'the art-literature of the nineteenth century,' and it is in this connection that Wilde may be allied with the tendencies in English art, and with that development of the Pre-Raphaelite doctrine and usage, that showed itself especially in the work of Walter Pater. This later connection, noted by many, was not entirely grateful to Pater; he was a little amazed, it appears, by the rather emphatic discipleship of Wilde, and, as one biographer says, 'both disgusted and appalled' by the reckless-ness with which his fatherhood was claimed for the extravagances of certain of his followers. And it must be confessed that the student of Pater's aesthetic theory is perhaps in somewhat the same state of mind. Wilde, with his sunflowers and aestheticism, is apt, at times, to dodge behind these theories like a ridiculous or evil imp, or, if you will, a kind of Frankenstein, an embodied *reductio ad absurdum*, a caricature of some of the most passionate, most severely chastened and ordered of Pater's work.

To the constant assertion that, in his aesthetic excesses, Wilde was but carrying out Pater's ideas expressed in the Conclusion to the *Renaissance,* an answer is found in a comparison of *Dorian Gray* with *Marius the Epicurean,* with its high, ethical purpose and spiritual reach. But that Wilde gave but partial or contorted interpretation to Pater's ideas is not a sufficient explanation to account for so keen a critic and so eager a disciple, and so signal a failure. In these self-confessions there is a note of fatefulness, of the recognition of weakness of will against the very temptations presented by his alertness and intellectual curiosity, a consciousness of organic and native limitations, which are later shown in *De Profundis.* But more than this, there is also a real disparity, and a conscious departure on the part of Wilde from the position of Pater. Nowhere is this better seen than in their critical theories. It is in this connection that I wish to consider Wilde especially, to show his derivation through Pater, from the most notable art-theory of the later nineteenth century, and his subsequent development into a theory of criticism quite at variance with this, but into a type of criticism which is still felt in our art-theory of to-day, and is concomitant with later Impressionism. Wilde is the expression in criticism of this, as truly as was Ruskin of Pre-Raphaelitism. And his life, in its self-centred interests and energy, its disregard of anything alien to the satisfaction of those interests, its insistence upon the value of 'doing nothing,' its constant eagerness for exploring the world of subjective experience, its aloofness and disinterestedness shown constantly in love of paradox in thought and of eccentricity in action, is a background for this art-theory which is truly expressive of it.

Comparing, them, their ideas of criticism, we may take the Preface to *The Renaissance* as a conclusive summing up of Pater's critical theory.

The æsthetic critic . . . regards all the objects with which he has to do, all works of art, and the fairer forms of nature and human life, as powers or forces producing pleasurable sensations, each of a more or less peculiar or unique kind. This influence he feels and wishes to explain, analysing it, and reducing it to its elements. To him, the picture, the landscape, the engaging personality in life or in a book, *La Gioconda*, the hills of Carrara, Pico of Mirandola, are valuable for their virtues, as we say, in speaking of a herb, a wine, a gem; for the property each has of affecting one with a special, a unique, impression of pleasure. . . . And the function of the aesthetic critic is to distinguish, analyse, and separate from its adjuncts, the virtue by which a picture, a landscape, a fair personality in life or in a book, produces this special impression of beauty or pleasure, to indicate what the source of that impression is, and under what conditions it is experienced. His end is reached when he has disengaged that virtue, and noted it, as a chemist notes some natural element, for himself and others. . . .

What is important, then, is not that the critic should possess a correct abstract definition of beauty for the intellect, but a certain kind of temperament, the power of being deeply moved by the presence of beautiful objects. He will remember always that beauty exists in many forms. To him all periods, types, schools of taste, are in themselves equal. . . . The question he asks is always: In whom did the stir, the genius, the sentiment of the period find itself?

This theory, as we find here and in repeated criticism, rests upon the idea of beauty as *expressiveness*, and is connected with the theory of style that gives as the ultimate problem the finding of the unique word. The critic's chief qualification is susceptibility to beauty, and the critic's aim is the disengaging of the particular phase of beauty, or the *virtue* of a work of art, that he may show in whom 'the stir, the genius, the sentiment of the period' found itself. It is to this aspect of criticism that Oscar Wilde was introduced both by the lectures of Ruskin and by the teaching of Pater, the two chief influences of his Oxford days. In Wilde's criticism, as in Pater's declaration in his Preface, all criticism is based upon the susceptibility of the critic. Thus his statement that 'Temperament is the primary requisite for the critic—a temperament exquisitely susceptible to beauty, and to the various impressions that beauty gives us,' corresponds to the requirement that Pater makes, of 'a certain kind of temperament, the power of being deeply moved by the presence of beautiful objects.'

When we turn to Wilde's explanation of what the aesthetic experience consists in, we find the typical term to be *satisfying*. Thus, in the Envoi to *Rose-Leaf and Apple-Leaf* by Rennell Rodd (one of Wilde's most complete critical essays) we see that he defines 'joy in art' as that "incommunicable element of artistic delight which, in poetry, for instance, comes from what Keats called the 'sensuous life of verse,' the element of song in the singing, made so pleasurable to us by that wonder of motion which often has its origin in mere musical impulse, and in painting is to be sought for, from subject never, but from the pictorial charm only— the scheme and symphony of color, the satisfying beauty of design." Again, in speaking of modern painting, he declares that the quality 'comes from the mere inventive and creative handling of line and color, from a certain form and choice of beautiful workmanship, which, rejecting all literary reminiscence and all metaphysical idea, is in itself entirely satisfying to the aesthetic sense, is, as the Greeks would say, an end in itself.' Pater's idea of the aesthetic experience is only vaguely given as 'pleasurable sensations,' but we may fill out this phrase from his utterances in the Conclusions to *The Renaissance*, where the life of aesthetic appreciation is described as the power 'to burn always with this hard, gemlike flame, to maintain this ecstasy'; and as marked by a 'quickened sense of life,' by a 'quickened, multiplied consciousness,'— expressions not so different from those of Wilde, but rather involving closer analysis. The difference, as Pater showed plainly in a later essay, lay in the scope of satisfaction.

But while Pater insists on the susceptibility of the critic, and upon the end of the aesthetic experience as 'quickened, multiplied consciousness,' and declares that art gives 'the highest quality to your moments as they pass, and simply for those moments' sake,' yet in his criticism, in the attitude which he takes toward those 'moments' of 'poetic passion,' the end he proposes for his 'quickened, multiplied consciousness,' is entirely different from that of Wilde. The requirements for the critic are fundamentally the same, the experience in each case is 'enthusiastic activity'; but it is the view taken of the value of the experience, or, in other words, of the function of the critic and of criticism, that differentiates them.

Pater, by the very use of the word *virtue*, suggests, to a certain degree, an objective, a *social* conception of criticism that Wilde's theory entirely lacks. The Conclusion to *The Renaissance* must be interpreted in the light of his practise. One needs only to compare Pater's essay on Botticelli, or on Wordsworth, with Wilde's on Rennell Rodd, to see the entirely different attitude suggested in the words *virtue* or *expressiveness* by the one, and *impression* and *satisfying* by the other. Pater uses this susceptibility as a revelatory agent, as a solvent which shall bring to crystallization the ments that elemake for the significance or the appeal of a work of art, which may indicate the line of possible sympathy between the artist or author and the observer or reader. This is seen in Pater's description of the ideal method of procedure for the aesthetic critic, in the Preface to *The Renaissance*, where, after defining the 'unique, incommunicable faculty' of Wordsworth, he says, 'Well! that is the *virtue*, the active principle, in Wordsworth's poetry; and then the function of the critic of Wordsworth is to follow up that active principle, to disengage it, to mark the degree in which it penetrates his verse.' And in his essay on Wordsworth, Pater carefully shows that 'the writings of Wordsworth are the central and elementary expression' of that which is 'a large element in the complexion of modern poetry.' In other words, the work of the critic is not accomplished in the mere noting or entering pleasurably into the quality of a work of art, but must also include its identification with some larger entity.

Wilde uses this susceptibility to gain impressions, as of value in themselves, for he says of the critic: 'The sole aim is to cherish his own impressions.' Again, 'That is what the highest criticism really is, the record of one's own soul,' for it 'is in its essence purely subjective, and seeks to reveal its own secret and not the secret of another.' His justification for this view of criticism rests in the facts of the development of art, for 'the ultimate expression of our artistic movement in painting has been, not in the spiritual visions of the Pre-Raphaelites, for all their marvel of Greek legend and their mystery of Italian song, but in the work of such men as Whistler and Albert Moore, who have raised design and color to the ideal level of poetry and music.' He continues:

349

'Now, this increased sense of the absolutely satisfying value of beautiful workmanship, this recognition of the primary importance of the sensuous element in art, this love of art for art's sake, is the point in which we of the younger school have made a departure from the teaching of Mr. Ruskin—a departure definite and different and decisive.' What had in the work of Pater constituted a basis for a definition of beauty, and could, therefore, be justly called an aesthetic,—an aesthetic with its basis in the idea of expressiveness,—is here denied as being the foundation of the critic's search. With Wilde, the critic's ultimate duty is to record the perception of beauty—not by way of analysis, rather in effusion. The eloquent passages of the essay on Rennell Rodd or the fantastic utterances of 'The Critic as Artist,' placed beside Pater's thoughtful building up of a consistent and unforgettable portrayal in 'Botticelli' or 'Pico della Mirandola,' show such a difference.

Beginning with the statement that 'The highest criticism deals with art not as expressive but as impressive purely,' Wilde leads on to the conclusion that 'to the critic the work of art is simply a suggestion for a new work of his own, that need not necessarily bear any obvious resemblance to the thing it criticises.' Further, he says, 'Criticism is no more to be judged by any low standard of imitation or resemblance than is the work of poet or sculptor.' And again, 'No ignoble considerations of probability, that cowardly concession to the tedious repetitions of domestic or public life, affect it ever.' He admits that 'the primary aim of the critic is to see the thing as in itself it really is not.' Thus the work of art may be inferior or unusual; it is all one to the impressionist in criticism, or, as he phrases it, in criticism as 'a creative art.' And later he states, 'The one characteristic of a beautiful form is that one can put into it whatever one chooses to see.' He adds that the critic will turn 'to such works as make him brood and dream and fancy, to works that possess the subtle quality of suggestion.' He states this theory more precisely in the following paragraph:

The sculptor gladly surrenders imitative colour, and the painter the actual dimensions of form, because by such renunciations they are able to avoid too definite a presentation of the Ideal, which would be too purely intellectual. It is through its very incompleteness that Art becomes complete in beauty, and so addresses itself, not to the faculty of recognition nor to the faculty of reason, but to the aesthetic sense alone, which, while accepting both reason and recognition as stages of apprehension, subordinates them both to a pure synthetic impression of the work of art as a whole, and, taking whatever alien emotional elements the work may possess, uses their very complexity as a means by which a richer unity may be added to the ultimate impression itself. You see, then, how it is that the aesthetic critic rejects those obvious modes of art that have but one message to deliver, and having delivered it become dumb and sterile, and seeks rather for such modes as suggest reverie and mood, and by their imaginative beauty make all interpretations true, and no interpretation final. Some resemblance, no doubt, the creative work of the critic will have to the work that has stirred him to creation, but it will be such resemblance as exists, not between Nature and the mirror that the painter of landscape or figure may be supposed to hold up to her, but between Nature and the work of the decorative artist. . . . The critic reproduces the work that he criticises in a mode that is never imitative, and part of whose charm may really consist in the rejection of resemblance, and shows us in this way not merely the meaning but also the mystery of Beauty, and, by transforming each art into literature, solves once for all the problem of art's unity.

We find the same difference in the practise of Pater and of Wilde. Pater, in his self-analysis in *The Child in the House*, says: 'For him, everywhere, that sensible vehicle or occasion became, perhaps only too surely, the necessary concomitant of any perception of things, real enough to be of any weight or reckoning, in his house of thought. There were times when he could think of the necessity he was under of associating all thoughts to touch and sight, . . . a protest in favor of real men and women against mere gray, unreal abstractions. . . . But certainly, he came more and more to be unable to care for or think of soul but as in actual body, or of any world but that wherein are water and trees, and where men and women look, so or so, and press actual hands.' For Pater, the 'imaginative reality' *resides* in line and color and pose, and can never be felt completely except through these 'sensible attachments,' as he calls them. Wilde speaks of the 'fine contempt for Nature,' the 'dim, dull abyss of facts'; and again, 'The best that one can say of most modern creative art is that it is just a little less vulgar than reality, and so the critic, with his fine sense of distinction and sure instinct of delicate refinement, will prefer to look into the silver mirror or through the woven veil, and will turn his eyes away from the chaos and clamour of actual existence, though the mirror be tarnished, and the veil be torn.' With such a theory, the object criticised necessarily falls from view, and the experience of the soul in the presence of the object of art takes its place. Every reader or beholder is a creator even as it is that creation which forms the material of the critical product. Thus Wilde insists that criticism is creation; Pater calls it appreciation. In departing from Pater's position with such a result, Wilde is brought to the characteristic attitude of those French artists and writers with whom we find him in sympathetic intercourse during his residence in Paris, namely, the Impressionists and the Symbolists. These had undoubtedly exercised a strong influence upon him, an influence which is perhaps most directly seen in Wilde's poems and in his drama, *Salomé*. In this, as in the work of the Symbolists, we have effects gained through a kind of refrain-like repetition, significant silences, indefinite persons, absorbing moods, and a constant appeal to sound. And in their general theory we find the Symbolists aiming at 'a pure synthetic impression,' depending much upon the association of ideas, preferring the indefinite and suggestive rather than the precise, and in every case emphasizing the subjective and individual nature of literary production. The most fruitful of their speculations, as their critics have pointed out, has resulted in an exposition of the creative function of the reader. This, it is seen, corresponds closely to the ultimate conclusion of Wilde's criticism.

One can, of course, find in Pater not only the essential basis of creative criticism, but, as well, an example of it in the famous La Giaconda passage from the essay on Leonardo da Vinci; but such a passage, it has been recognized by critics, is almost unique in its extremely associative appeal, and certainly cannot be paralleled in the more mature work of Pater. In *Appreciations*, for instance, we have a similar disparity between Pater's later work and the passage mentioned, as between the theory of Pater and that of his enthusiastic disciple, Oscar Wilde. And this passage is the one from Pater's work that Wilde quotes as illustrating his idea of creative criticism, and as being most in opposition to that other theory which gives its aim as 'to see the object as in itself it really is.'

In the dictum that art must not imitate,—for art must not say anything,—lies not only his connection with the Symbolists, but, according to his own confession, his point of departure from the so-called Impressionists. 'I am very fond of the work of many of the Impressionist painters of Paris and London. Subtlety and distinction have not yet left the school. . . . Their white keynote, with its variations in lilac, was an era in color. . . . Yet they will insist on treating painting as if it were a mode of autobiography invented for the use of the illiterate, and are always prating to us on their coarse, gritty canvases of their unnecessary selves and their unnecessary opinions, and spoiling by a vulgar over-emphasis that fine contempt of Nature which is the best and only modest thing about them. One tires, at the end, of the work of individuals whose individuality is always noisy, and generally uninteresting.' He prefers 'that newer school at Paris, the *Archaicistes*, as they call themselves, who, . . . rejecting the tedious realism of those who merely paint what they see, try to see something worth seeing, and to see it not merely with actual and physical vision, but with that nobler vision of the soul which is as far wider in spiritual scope as it is far more splendid in artistic purpose.' Further he says, 'Still, the art that is frankly decorative is the art to live with. It is, of all our visible arts, the one art that creates in us both mood and temperament. Mere color, unspoiled by meaning, and unallied with definite form, can speak to the soul in a thousand different ways. . . . By its deliberate rejection of Nature as the ideal of beauty, as well as of the imitative method of the ordinary painter, decorative art not merely prepares the soul for the reception of true imaginative work, but develops in it that sense of form which is the basis of creative no less than of critical achievement. . . . To be natural is to be obvious, and to be obvious is to be inartistic.' And as Wilde departed from the Impressionists in his ideas, so he approaches the theory voiced by the later school of artists, the Neo-Impressionists or Post-Impressionists.

A sympathetic critic of the work of the Post-Impressionists at the Grafton Gallery in 1911, Mr. Roger Fry, speaks of these artists as 'freed from the incubus of complete representation,' and says further, 'Post-Impressionist artists have discovered empirically that to make allusion to a natural object of any kind vivid to the imagination, it is not only not necessary to give it illusive likeness, but that such illusion of actuality really spoils its imaginative reality.'

Perhaps it is not unfair to take the utterances of the later exponents of this school to show the tendency of their theory of art. Thus in a recent book called *Cubism*, by Albert Gleizes and Jean Metzanger, we read: 'Let the picture imitate nothing; let it nakedly present its motive, and we shall indeed be ungrateful were we to deplore the absence of all those things—flowers, or landscape, or faces—whose mere reflection it might have been. Nevertheless, let us admit that the reminiscence of natural forms cannot be absolutely banished; as yet, at all events. An art cannot be raised to the level of a pure effusion at the first step.' And 'We seek the essential, but we seek it in our personality, and not in a sort of eternity, laboriously divided by mathematicians and philosophers.' And Cubism, I believe, may be taken here not in any restricted sense, but as synonymous for the art that dates from Cézanne and includes the present school of 'profound realism' (to use their own term) as distinguished from the 'superficial realism' of the Impressionists.

I have given Wilde's theory thus in detail, in its relation to Pater's idea of criticism, because it is in this relation that its peculiar interest lies,—in its fundamental agreement with it, and its ultimately wide departure from it. We see here an interesting parallel in the case of Wilde and Pater to the advance of the art-theory in the last half of the nineteenth century. In Pater, we may trace the theory of criticism as it runs parallel to the art-theory of the Pre-Raphaelites; in Wilde, we come to a later kind of criticism which, in the creative field, is paralleled by the appearance of paintings illustrating a view of art that, while it derives from the Pre-Raphaelite theory of expressiveness as the basis of beauty, puts the emphasis upon the subjective experience of the artist rather than upon the attempt to communicate and share those experiences. As we noted, one is inevitably impressed by Wilde's close alliance with the Post-Impressionists. But between him and our present Post-Impressionists there is the same difference as between the Pre-Raphaelites and the earlier Impressionists, that is, in the choice of subjects; the present-day artists keeping close to the life about them, Wilde dealing still with the remote and strange as most fit to set up the train of pleasurable associations.

The tendency of this 'new' aestheticism, the possible value of it, is not unlike that which we hope to derive from the art of the Post-Impressionists and their successors. The most unsympathetic may feel, I believe, that while the newest art seems perverse in choice of subject, and goes to such extremes (as the writers upon Cubism themselves confess) as 'juxtaposing the six faces of a cube or the two ears of a model seen in profile,' yet it does attempt to widen the field of art by dealing subjectively and sometimes profoundly with the volatile and subtle notions of depth, motion, etc., and by weighing and appreciating interrelations that are often overlooked. The value that may come from this new aesthetic criticism lies in the same direction of individual dealing with experience, which has already been claimed for the Symbolists, and has given rise to the modern and valuable conception of what we mean by *creative* reading, or *creative* observation. It is in this direction that the criticism of Wilde, deriving from that of Pater, tends.

The value of this new aesthetic criticism, however, is certainly limited by its strongly individualistic and subjective nature, which, on the one hand, does not give us any psychological analysis of the aesthetic experience (the ideal process being, as we see, effusion), nor on the other hand any social conception of the function of the critic such as one gets from the earlier aesthetic criticism of Walter Pater,—who in England, at least, is the point of departure for this later theory.

This scant review of Wilde's critical theory brings out his symbolic relation to his age. He is touched by the modern spirit in many ways, he suggests in his work many phases of recent thought upon art and literature. Because of this, even a *flâneur*, one who trifled with and abused life, is worthy of study by those who would observe the modern spirit in its growth.

115. John Cowper Powys on Wilde as a symbolic figure

1916

Essay in *Suspended Judgments* (New York, 1916), pp. 401–22. John Cowper Powys (1872–1963), novelist, poet, and critic, portrays Wilde as victim of middle-class brutality, elaborately defending him and attacking the Philistines in yet another affirmation of the mythology of Aestheticism.

The words he once used about himself—'I am a symbolic figure'—remain to this day the most significant thing that can be said of Oscar Wilde.

It is given to very few men of talent, this peculiar privilege—this privilege of being greater in what might be called the *shadow of their personality* than in any actual literary or artistic achievement—and Wilde possesses it in a degree second to none.

'My genius is in my life,' he said on another occasion, and the words are literally and most fatally true.

In the confused controversies of the present age it is difficult to disentangle the main issues; but it seems certain that side by side with political and economic divisions, there is a gulf growing wider and wider every day between the adherents of what might be called the

Hellenic Renaissance and the inert, suspicious, unintelligent mob; that mob the mud of whose heavy traditions is capable of breeding, at one and the same time, the most crafty hypocrisy and the most stupid brutality.

It would be hardly a true statement to say that the Renaissance referred to—this modern Renaissance, not less formidable than the historic revolt which bears that name—is an insurrection of free spirits against Christianity. It is much rather a reversion to a humane and classic reasonableness as opposed to mob-stupidity and middle-class philistinism—things which only the blundering of centuries of popular misapprehension could associate with the sublime and the imaginative figure of Christ.

It is altogether a mistake to assume that in De Profundis Wilde retracted his classic protest and bowed his head once more in the house of Rimmon.

What he did was to salute, in the name of the aesthetic freedom he represented, those enduring elements of human loveliness and beauty in that figure which three hundred years of hypocritical puritanism have proved unable to tarnish. What creates the peculiar savagery of hatred which his name has still the power to conjure up among the enemies of civilisation has little to do with the ambiguous causes of his final downfall. These, of course, gave him up, bound hand and foot, into their hands. But these, though the overt excuse of their rancour, are far from being its real motive-force. To reach that we must look to the nature, of the formidable weapon which it was his habit, in season and out of season, to use against this mob-rule—I mean his sense of humour.

The stupid middle-class obscurantism, so alien to all humane reasonableness, which, in our Anglo-Saxon communities, masquerades under the cloak of a passionate and imaginative religion, is more sensitive to ridicule than to any other form of attack, and Wilde attacked it mercilessly with a ridicule that cut to the bone.

They are not by any means of equal value, these epigrams of his, with which he defended intelligence against stupidity and classical light against Gothic darkness.

They are not as humorous as Voltaire's. They are not as philosophical as Goethe's. Compared with the aphorisms of these masters they are light and frivolous. But for this very reason perhaps, they serve the great cause—the cause of humane and enlightened civilisation—better in our age of vulgar mob-rule than more recondite 'logoi.'

They pierce the hide of the thickest and dullest; they startle and bewilder the brains of the most crass and the most insensitive. And it is just because they do this that Wilde is so cordially feared and hated. It was, one cannot help feeling, the presence in him of a shrewd vein of sheer boyish bravado, mingled—one might go even as far as that—with a dash of incorrigible worldliness in his own temper, that made his hits so effective and wounding.

It is interesting, with this in mind, to compare Wilde's witticisms with those of Matthew Arnold or Bernard Shaw. The reason that Wilde's lash cuts deeper than either of these other champions of rational humanism, is that he goes, with more classical clearness, straight to the root of the matter.

The author of 'Thyrsis' was not himself free from a certain melancholy hankering after 'categorical imperatives,' and beneath the cap and bells of his theological fooling, Shaw is, of course, as gravely moralistic as any puritan could wish.

Neither of these—neither the ironical school-master nor the farcical clown of our Renaissance of intelligence—could exchange ideas with Pericles, say, or Caesar, without betraying a puritanical fussiness that would grievously bewilder the lucid minds of those great men.

The philosophy of Wilde's aesthetic revolt against our degraded mob-ridden conscience was borrowed from Walter Pater, but whereas that shy and subtle spirit moved darkly and mysteriously aside from all contact with the vulgar herd, Wilde, full of gay and wanton pride in his sacred mission, lost no opportunity of flaunting his classic orthodoxy in the face of the heretical mob.

Since the death of Wilde, the brunt of the battle for the spiritual liberties of the race has been borne by the sterner and more formidable figure of Nietzsche; but the vein of high and terrible imagination in this great poet of the Superman sets him much closer to the company of the saints and mystics than to that of the instinctive children of the pagan ideal.

Oscar Wilde's name has become a sort of rallying cry to all those writers and artists who suffer, in one degree or another, from the persecution of the mob—of the mob goaded on to blind brutality by the crafty incentives of those conspirators of reaction whose interest lies in keeping the people enslaved. This has come about, in a large measure, as much by the renown of his defects as by reason of his fine quality.

The majority of men of talent lack the spirit and the gall to defy the enemy on equal terms. But Wilde while possessing nobler faculties had

357

an undeniable vein in him of sheer youthful insolence. To the impertinence of society he could oppose the impertinence of the artist, and to the effrontery of the world he could offer the effrontery of genius.

The power of personality, transcending any actual literary achievement, is what remains in the mind when one has done reading him, and this very faculty—of communicating to us, who never saw him or heard him speak, the vivid impact of his overbearing presence—is itself evidence of a rare kind of genius. It is even a little ironical that he, above all men the punctilious and precious literary craftsman, should ultimately dominate us not so much by the magic of his art as by the spell of his wilful and wanton individuality, and the situation is heightened still further by the extraordinary variety of his works and their amazing perfection in their different spheres.

One might easily conceive an artist capable of producing so clean-cut and crystalline a comedy as *The Importance of Being Earnest*, and so finished and flawless a tragedy as *Salome*, disappearing quite out of sight, in the manner so commended by Flaubert, behind the shining objectivity of his flawless creations. But so far from disappearing, Oscar Wilde manages to emphasise himself and his imposing presence only the more startlingly and flagrantly, the more the gem-like images he projects harden and glitter.

Astoundingly versatile as he was—capable of producing in *Reading Gaol* the best tragic ballad since 'The Ancient Mariner,' and in *Intentions* one of the best critical expositions of the open secret of art ever written at all—he never permits us for a second to lose touch with the wayward and resplendent figure, so full, for all its bravado, of a certain disarming childishness, of his own defiant personality.

And the fact remains that, perfect in their various kinds though these works of his are, they would never appeal to us as they do, and Oscar Wilde would never be to us what he is, if it were not for the predominance of this personal touch.

I sometimes catch myself wondering what my own feeling would be as to the value of these things—of the 'Soul of Man,' for instance, or *Intentions*, or the Comedies, or the Poems—if the unthinkable thing could be done, and the emergence of this irresistible figure from behind it all could be drastically eliminated. I find myself conscious, at these times, of a faint disturbing doubt; as though after all, in spite of their jewel-like perfection, these wonderful and varied achievements were not quite the real thing, were not altogether in the 'supreme manner.' There seems to me—at the moments when this doubt arises—something too self-consciously (how shall I put it?) *artistic* about these performances, something strained and forced and far-fetched, which separates them from the large inevitable utterances of classic genius.

I am ready to confess that I am not sure that this feeling is a matter of personal predilection or whether it has the larger and graver weight behind it of the traditional instincts of humanity, instincts out of which spring our only permanent judgments. What I feel at any rate is this: that there is an absence in Wilde's writings of that large cool spaciousness, produced by the magical influence of earth and sky and sea, of which one is always conscious in the greater masters.

'No gentleman,' he is said to have remarked once, 'ever looks out of the window'; and it is precisely this 'never looking out of the window' that produces his most serious limitations.

In one respect I must acknowledge myself grateful to Wilde, even for this very avoidance of what might be called the 'magical' element in things. His clear-cut palpable images, carved, as one so often feels, in ebony or ivory or gold, offer an admirable relief, like the laying of one's hand upon pieces of Hellenic statuary, after wandering among the vague mists and 'beachéd margents.'

Certainly if all that one saw when one 'looked out of the window' were Irish fairies with dim hair drifting down pallid rivers, there would be some reason for drawing the curtains close and toying in the lamp-light with cameo-carved profiles of Antinous and Cleopatra!

But nature has more to give us than the elfish fantasies, charming as these may be, of Celtic legend—more to give us than those 'brown fauns' and 'hoofed Centaurs' and milk-white peacocks, which Wilde loves to paint with his Tiepolo-like brush. The dew of the morning does not fall less lightly because real autumns bring it, nor does the 'wide aerial landscape' of our human wayfaring show less fair, or its ancient antagonist the 'salt estranging sea' less terrible, because these require no legendary art to endow them with mystery.

Plausible and full of significance as these honeyed arguments in *Intentions* are—and fruitful as they are in affording us weapons wherewith to defend ourselves from the mob—it is still well, it is still necessary, to place against them the great Da Vinci saying, 'Nature is the Mistress of the higher intelligences.'

Wilde must be held responsible—along with others of his epoch— for the encouragement of that deplorable modern heresy which finds in bric-a-brac and what are called 'objets d'art' a disproportionate monopoly of the beauty and wonder of the world. One turns a little wearily at last from the silver mirrors and purple masks. One turns to the great winds that issue forth out of the caverns of the night. One turns to the sun and to the rain, which fall upon the common grass.

However! It is not a wise procedure to demand from a writer virtues and qualities completely out of his rôle. In our particular race there is far more danger of the beauty and significance of art—together with all its subtler and less normal symbols—perishing under crude and sentimental Nature-worship, than of their being granted too large a place in our crowded house of thought.

After all, the art which Wilde assures us adds so richly to Nature, 'is an art which Nature makes.' They are not lovers of what is rarest and finest in our human civilisation who would suppress everything which deviates from the common track.

Who has given these people—these middle-class minds with their dull intelligences—the right to decide what is natural or unnatural in the presence of the vast tumultuous forces, wonderful and terrible, of the life-stream which surrounds us?

The mad smouldering lust which gives a sort of under-song of surging passion to the sophisticated sensuality of *Salome* is as much an evocation of Nature as the sad sweet wisdom of that sentence in *De Profundis*—'Behind joy and laughter there may be a temperament, coarse hard and callous. But behind sorrow there is always sorrow.'

What, beneath all his bravado and his paradoxes, Wilde really sought, was the enjoyment of passionate and absorbing emotion, and no one who hungers and thirsts after this—be he 'as sensual as the brutish sting itself'—can fail in the end to touch, if only fleetingly with his lips, the waters of that river of passion which, by a miracle of faith if not by a supreme creation of art, Humanity has caused to issue forth from the wounded flesh of the ideal.

It is in his 'Soul of Man'—perhaps the wisest and most eloquent revolutionary tract every written—that Wilde frees himself most completely from the superficial eccentricities of his aesthetic pose, and indicates his recognition of a beauty in life, far transcending Tyrian dyes and carved cameos and frankincense and satin-wood and moon-stones and 'Silks from Samarcand.'

It is impossible to read this noble defence of the natural distinction and high dignity of our human days when freed from the slavery of what is called 'working for a living', without feeling that the boyish bravado of his insolent wit is based upon a deep and universal emotion. What we note here is an affiliation in revolt between the artist and the masses. And this affiliation indicates that the hideousness of our industrial system is far more offensive than any ancient despotism or slave-owning tyranny to the natural passion for light and air and leisure and freedom in the heart of man.

That Oscar Wilde, the most extreme of individualists, the most unscrupulous of self-asserters, the pampered darling of every kind of sophisticated luxury, should thus lift up his voice on behalf of the wage-earners, is an indication that a state of society which seems proper and inevitable to dull and narrow minds is, when confronted, not with any mere abstract theory of Justice or Political rights, but with the natural human craving for life and beauty, found to be an outrage and an insult.

Oscar Wilde by pointing his derisive finger at what the gross intelligence of our commercial mob calls the 'honourableness of work' has done more to clear our minds of cant than many revolutionary speeches. . . .

Oscar Wilde must be forgiven everything in his gay impertinence which may jar upon our more sensitive moments, when one considers what he has done in dragging this great issue into the light and making it clear. He shows that what we have against us is not so much a system of society or a set of laws, as a definite and contemptible type of human character. . . .

After all, it is not on the strength of his opinions, wise and sound as these may be, that Wilde's reputation rests. It rests on the beauty, in its own way never equalled, of the style in which he wrote. His style, as he himself points out, is one which seems to compel its readers to utter its syllables aloud. Of that deeper and more recondite charm which lies, in a sense, outside the sphere of vocal articulation, of that rhythm of the very movements of thought itself which lovers of Water Pater catch, or dream they catch, in those elaborate delicately modulated sentences, Wilde has little or nothing.

What he achieves is a certain crystalline lucidity, clear and pure as the ring of glass upon glass, and with a mellifluous after-tone or echo of vibration, which dies away upon the ear in a lingering fall—melancholy and voluptuous, or light and tender as the hour and the moment lead.

He is at his best, or at any rate his style shows itself at its best, not in the utterances of those golden epigrams, the gold of which, as days pass, comes in certain cases to look lamentably like gilt, but in his use of those far-descended legendary images gathered up into poetry and art again and again till they have acquired the very tone of time itself, and a lovely magic, sudden, swift and arresting, like the odour of 'myrrh, aloes, and cassia.'

The style of Wilde is one of the simplest in existence, but its simplicity is the very apex and consummation of the artificial. He uses Biblical language with that self-conscious preciosity—like the movements of a person walking on tip-toe in the presence of the dead—which is so different from the sturdy directness of Bunyan or the restrained rhetoric of the Church of England prayers. There come moments when this premeditated innocence of tone—this lisping in liturgical monosyllables—irritates and annoys one. At such times the delicate unction of his naïveté strikes one, in despite of its gravity, as something a little comic; as though some very sophisticated and experienced person suddenly joined in a children's game and began singing in a plaintive tenderly pitched voice—

> This is the way we wash our hands, wash our hands,
>   wash our hands—
> This is the way we wash our hands,
>   On a cold and frosty morning!

But it were absurd to press this point too far. Sophisticated though the simplicity of Wilde is, it does actually spring with all its ritualistic tip-toeing straight out of his natural character. He was born artificial, and he was born with more childishness than the great majority of children.

I like to picture him as a great Uranian baby, full of querulousness and peevishness, and eating greedily, with a sort of guileless wonder that anyone should scold him for it, every species of forbidden fruit that grows in the garden of life! How infantile really, when one thinks of it, and how humorously solemn the man's inordinate gravity over the touch of soft fabrics and the odour of rare perfumes! One seems to see him, a languid-limbed 'revenant,' with heavy-lidded drowsy eyes and voluptuous lips, emerging all swathed and wrapped in costly cerements out of the tomb of some Babylonian king.

After all, it remains a tremendous triumph of personality, the manner in which this portly modern Antinous has taken captive our imagination. His influence is everywhere, like an odour, like an atmosphere, like a diffused flame. We cannot escape from him.

In those ridiculous wit-contests with Whistler, from which he always emerged defeated, how much more generous and careless and noble he appears than the wasp-like artist who could rap out so smartly the appropriate retort! He seems like a great lazy king, at such times, caught off his guard by some skipping and clever knave of his spoilt retinue. Perhaps even now no small a portion of the amused and astonished wonder he excites is due to the fact that he really had, what so few of us have, a veritable passion for precious stuffs and woven fabrics and ivory and cedar wood and beads of amber and orchid-petals and pearl-tinted shells and lapis-lazuli and attar of roses.

It is open to doubt whether even among artists, there are many who share Wilde's Hellenic ecstasy in these things. This at any rate was no pose. He posed as a man of the world. He posed as an immoralist. He posed as a paradoxist. He posed in a thousand perverse directions. But when it comes to the colour and texture and odour and shape of beautiful and rare things—there, in his voluptuous delight in these, he was undeniably sincere.

He was of course no learned virtuoso. But what does that matter? The real artist is seldom a patient collector or an encyclopedic authority. That is the role of Museum people and of compilers of hand-books. Many thoroughly uninteresting minds know more about Assyrian pottery and Chinese pictures than Oscar Wilde knew about wild flowers.

Knowledge, as he teaches us himself, and it is one of the profoundest of his doctrines, is nothing. Knowledge is external and incidental. The important thing is that one's senses should be passionately alive and one's imagination fearlessly far-reaching.

We can embrace all the treasures of the Herods and all the riches of the Caesars as we lay our fingers upon a little silver coin, if the divine flame is within us, and, if not, we may excavate a thousand buried cities and return learned and lean and empty. Well, people must make their own choice and go their own way. The world is wide, and Nature has at least this in common with Heaven, that it has many mansions.

The feverish passion for fair things which obsessed Oscar Wilde and carried him so far is not for all the sons of men; nor even, in every hour of their lives, for those who most ardently answer to it. That feverishness burns itself out; that smouldering fire turns to cold ashes. Life flows on, though Salome, daugher of Herodias, lies crushed under the piled-up shields, and though in all the prisons of the world 'the damned grotesques make arabesques, like the wind upon the sand.'

Life flows on, and the quips and merry jests of Oscar Wilde, his artful artlessness, his insolence, his self-pity, his loyalty and fickleness, his sensuality and tenderness, only fill after all a small space in the heart's chamber of those who read him and stare at his plays and let him go.

But there are a few for whom the tragic wantonness of that strange countenance, with the heavy eyelids and pouting mouth, means something not easily forgotten, not easily put by.

To have seen Oscar Wilde and talked with him gives to such persons a strange significance, an almost religious value. One looks long at them, as if to catch some far-off reflection from the wit of the dead man. They do not seem to us quite like the rest. They have seen Oscar Wilde, and 'They know what they have seen.' For when all has been said against him that can be said it remains that Oscar Wilde, for good and for evil, in innocence and in excess, in orthodoxy and in rebellion, is a 'symbolic figure.'

It is indeed easy enough, when one is under the spell of the golden gaiety of his wit, to forget the essential and irresistible truth of so many of his utterances.

That profound association between the 'Sorrow that endureth forever' and the 'Pleasure that abideth for a moment,' which he symbolises under the parable of the Image of Bronze, has its place throughout all his work.

It is a mistake to regard *De Profundis* as a recantation. It is a fulfilment, a completion, a rounding off. Like a black and a scarlet thread running through the whole tapestry of his tragic story are the two parallel 'motifs,' the passion of the beauty which leads to destruction and the passion of the beauty which leads to life.

It matters little whether he was or was not received into the Church before he died. In the larger sense he was always within those unexcluding walls, those spacious courts of the Ecclesia of humanity. There was no trace in him, for all his caprices of, that puritanism of denial which breaks the altars and shatters the idols at the bidding of scientific iconoclasm.

What the anonymous instinct of humanity has rendered beautiful by building into it the golden monuments of forlorn hopes and washing it with the salt tears of desperate chances remained beautiful to him. From the narcissus-flowers growing on the marble ledges of Parnassus, where Apollo still weeps for the death of Hyacinth and Pan still mourns the vanishing of Syrinx, to the passion-flowers growing on the slopes of Calvary, he, this lover of eidola and images, worships the white feet of the bearers of dead beauty, and finds in the tears of all the lovers of all the lost a revivifying rain that even in the midst of the dust of our degeneracy makes bloom once more, full of freshness and promise, the mystical red rose of the world's desire.

The wit of his 'Golden lads and girls' in those superb comedies may soon fall a little faint and thin upon our ears. To the next generation it may seem as faded and old-fashioned as the wit of Congreve or Sheridan. Fashions of humour change more quickly than the fashions of manner or of dress. The only thing that gives immortality to human writing is the 'eternal bronze' of a noble and imaginative style. Out of such divine material, with all his petulances and perversities, Oscar Wilde's style was hammered and beaten. For there is only one quarry of this most precious metal, and the same hand that shapes from it the 'Sorrow that endureth forever' must shape from it the 'Pleasure that abideth for a moment,' and the identity of these two with that immortal bronze is the symbol of the mystery of our life.

The senses that are quickened by the knowledge of this mystery are not far from the ultimate secret. As with the thing sculptured, so with the sculptor.

Oscar Wilde is a symbolic figure.

116. Ernst Bendz: a defence of Wilde against the attack by Lord Alfred Douglas

1916

Excerpts from signed article, titled 'Lord Alfred Douglas's Apologia', *Englische Studien* [Leipzig] (April 1916), xlix, 377–402; reprinted in *Oscar Wilde: A Retrospect* (Vienna, 1921).

At the beginning of his article, Bendz explains the circumstances leading to the attack on Wilde in Douglas's *Oscar Wilde and Myself* (1914).

In April 1913, Lord Alfred Douglas having brought an action against Mr. Arthur Ransome, the author of a well-known monograph on Wilde, and claiming damages in respect of certain statements contained therein, Mr. Ross, acting on behalf of the defendant, caused parts of the unpublished portion of *De Profundis* to be read out in court, to prove that the incriminating passages, if libellous at all, were in every way justified by the actual facts. Full reports of this trial, which roused considerable interest, appeared at the time in the London press, and so we may be said to have anticipated to some extent the sensations that were to have been reserved for the curious of a future generation. That part of Wilde's letter which has still been withheld from publication, may be characterized briefly, in so far as it bears on Lord Alfred Douglas, as a vicious attack on the latter, in his capacity of friend and man of letters. But of the real character of this work, commenced as a letter to Lord Alfred Douglas and bearing his address, Lord Alfred himself states that he had no knowledge whatever up to the moment the unpublished MSS. were produced against him in court,—although a copy of it is alleged to have been sent him by post on its completion. And it does not seem an unreasonable deduction, in view of what is now known, for him to describe the expurgated *De Profundis* as 'a collection of elegant extracts' affording no faithful picture of the author's frame of mind at the time of writing, nor of the trend and spirit of the work as a whole. However, Lord Alfred, esteeming that never was fouler deed of defamation and backbiting perpetrated by a false friend upon an honourable and innocent man, and failing, moreover, to obtain a verdict in his libel action, set to work upon a volume that was to be, not merely a thorough and final refutation of the charges brought against him by Wilde, but also an impartial estimate of the latter, of his personality and writings, and of his influence on the thought and letters of his age. All his life, he says, from his twentieth year, had been 'overshadowed and filled with scandal and grief' through his association with Wilde;—he wished to be done with it all, to silence at a blow and forever the thousand tongues set wagging with all manner of preposterous rumours and filthy slander. As for his competence to judge Wilde as a literary man, he frankly gives it as his opinion that 'there is no man living who can put Oscar Wilde into his true relation to the life and literature of his time more accurately.'

[In the excerpts that follow, Bendz defends Wilde as a writer against Douglas's judgments. (For earlier estimates of Wilde by Douglas, see Nos. 49 and 104).]

We have seen that, in his position of the once intimate associate of Wilde, Lord Alfred puts forward the claim to be considered the one and only authority. Just as on the moral side it was his aim to establish, on the strength of his own evidence, that Wilde was a scoundrel, an evil liver, and a vituperative slanderer, so he tries to make out a case against him as an author, on the plea that his works have been immensely over-estimated and have exerted a disastrous influence on the literature and the journalism of the age. Or let us have it in his own words:—
'With the passing of the years and a more serious and mature outlook on the facts of life and on the responsibilities of those who seek the suffrages or merely the ears of the general reader, I had arrived at the conclusion that Oscar Wilde's writings were ridiculously over-rated, that he was never either a great poet or a great writer of prose, and that the harm he had caused to the whole body of English literature, and the pernicious effect he had exercised on the literary movements and the journalism of the period immediately succeeding his own, very much more than counterbalanced the credit of any legitimate success he may have achieved.'
Here, however, difficulties arose. It was no longer for the author to say:—'Such and such a thing happened, you may take my word for it.' . . . You cannot argue with a man about a matter of his own sole experience, there is no impugning a statement that admits of no verifica-

tion. But the estimate of any public man, say, a prominent writer, is not to be monopolized by his personal friends, or, for that matter, by his enemies. Of this, Lord Alfred was well aware. He knew there were two essential facts about Wilde,—his genius and his influence,—that could not possibly be ignored, and which had to be discounted in order to justify the volume now under review. He admits, p. 17:— 'That he had what passed for genius nobody will, I think, nowadays dispute . . .' But, as we shall see, this acknowledgment, not of genius, mark you, but of 'what passed for genius,' is very far from being borne out by what follows. Similarly with regard to Wilde's literary fame. Wilde undeniably 'has come into a sort of artificial kingdom of his own, on the Continent and in America just as in England.' But 'it is a kingdom based on rottenness,' amounting to no more nor less than 'one of the most scandalous movements that has (*sic*) ever excited and betrayed mankind.'

Wilde's intellectual equipment,—if we are to believe his quondam friend and pupil,—was not suggestive of any unusual brilliancy. His was 'a shallow and comparatively feeble mind, incapable of grasping unaided with even moderately profound things, and disposed to fribble and antic with old thoughts for lack of power to evolve new ones.' He knew himself for a shallow and oblique thinker, and it was no secret to him that, 'when it came to serious things he was always considered more or less of a dabbler.' This seems rather hard upon a man who, if not a thinker in the abstract, had undoubtedly traced out for himself a scheme of life on purely intellectual lines, and many of whose sayings and philosophizings, no matter on what topic, or to what effect, if put to the test of experience and common sense will emerge victoriously, I think, despite their apparent affectedness and flippancy. The fact is, that the statements quoted contain one side of the truth, and one only, while, if meant as a comprehensive description and general estimate of Wilde's intellect, they are grossly unjust. Wilde, of course, was not strictly speaking an originator of ideas,—a man of speculative mind. He sought his expression, not in principles, but in prose; his creative power actualized itself, not in the abstract sphere of thought, but in the concrete sphere of language. He was essentially and primarily an artist in words. Now, no poetry, no literary work, will survive on its mere melody or music, on its outward perfection alone, or has any chance of enduring unless it bears some relation to the moral conscience of its age, or of all ages, or affords, at the same time, some sort of intellectual stimulus. Will the life-work of Oscar Wilde be found wanting in spiritual calibre, in substance? It has every distinction of polite scholarship; in its exquisite union of fluency and finish, of natural ease and conscious endeavour, it certainly excels all other attempts at artistic prose writing made in the English tongue within the last three decades or so. But has it a true inwardness? Does it serve any purpose of the intellect? Can it be said to embody a peculiar, a unique conception of the universe, of man, of anything? Or was it a 'shallow and comparatively feeble mind' that conceived *De Profundis*, the essays of *Intentions*, the *Poems in Prose*? Is it true that the cultivated people whom Wilde entertains 'place no value upon his opinions?' . . . Wilde certainly will never be mentioned among the greatest. But this is not the point. The point is, whether his work has stamina enough to preserve it amid the fluctuations of taste and fashion, and to assure it of permanence and life, beyond the limits of duration which its mere outward excellence seems likely to set upon it. No doubt but that, taken all in all, Wilde was not what is called a great man. There was nothing grand about him, either as a character or as a writer. Not even in its purest or its most exalted moments, does his life present an ideal aspect of humanity triumphant or suffering. His work, considered from no matter what angle, exhibits no essential or appreciable furtherance of the spiritual development of mankind, and, if accepted at all, his teachings and influence must be taken with a wide allowance for their exceptionality and fallacies.

And yet, all this duly admitted, will any unprejudiced mind fail to realize that there was in everything he wrote a curious fitness, a perfect and subtle equipoise, of soul and matter, of means and purpose? In his personality and writings he sums up, more truly and strikingly than any other man of letters of his day, the distinctive features of a remarkable, though brief, period in English Letters. There is true insight and but plain justice to himself, in his saying that he was 'a man who stood in symbolic relations to the art and culture' of his age: the English 'Decadent' movement of the nineties will be always associated, as with its most expressive label, with the name of Oscar Wilde. In every leadership, in every position of some eminence, there enters of necessity an element of intellectual superiority. That this was so in Wilde's case, is clear. It was not merely as a writer of perfect prose, still less as a skilled versifier, that he came to find himself at the head of those 'decadent' writers that filled the closing years of the XIX century with their fevered and high-strung activity. If among those writers Wilde outtopped all the rest and alone attained to real prominence, it was because he asserted himself as the dominant personality, the genius. For in all his really inspired work,—from some of the early poems down to the *Ballad* and *De Profundis*, including his best comedies, his best essays, and a few other things,—we surely recognize that very ardour and keenness of spiritual fire, that extraordinary clearness and buoyancy of the intellectual life that we know as genius.

Wilde no doubt had his moods of flippancy and shallowness, of stereotyped emotions and cheap paradox-mongering, and what with laziness of mind and exuberant facility, he committed some work of a fairly trivial nature. Who, some ten years hence, will care greatly for 'The Canterville Ghost,' 'London Models,' and other elegant trifles of their class? . . . It is also true that some of his imaginative writing seems curiously void of intellectual motive. That weirdly artificial thing, 'The Fisherman and his Soul,'—the most striking example of this manner or attitude,—whatever may be its moral or its hidden symbolism, impresses one as having been written with no other purpose than the realization, through the medium of pictorial language, of some huge and intricate scheme of decorative beauty.

But there was another Wilde, as we all know. There was the man who, under the incitement of the work of Matthew Arnold, cultivated a 'spirit of disinterested curiosity,'—that rare 'flower of the intellectual life,'—though, as transplanted in the hothouse beds of *Intentions*, some may have failed to recognize it among its neighbours of more exotic growth;—the Wilde to whom, amid the allurements and distractions of a dissipated existence, the contemplative mode of life never quite lost its charm of a distant promise, an ideal possibility, the complete realization of which, however, he felt he was never to achieve. Wilde, one tells us with tedious insistence, 'had no serious views or intentions about anything, and he considered that the art of life lay in flippancy.' But who has gauged, who will ever gauge, those depths of irony and insight of which we get such strange fitful glimpses, and that render the study of his character, no less than that of his writings, so intensely fascinating? Would a shallow-minded and obvious writer, however able in other respects, have attracted such a number of students and critics as those many who for years have been trying,—with small success hitherto, in most cases, because prejudiced for or against,—to interpret the personality of Wilde, and to explain the baffling duality of his nature? Remembering the shrewdness and subtlety of so many of Wilde's aphorisms and reasonings on innumerable topics of high and serious import, remembering, also, the introspective and meditative character of much of his later work, Lord Alfred's views of Wilde's mental capacity seem to me, not only untenable, but preposterous.

Take Art, of all subjects for speculation and debate the one nearest to his heart, the predominant interest of his life: both in his disquisitions upon the essence of aesthetic criticism, on style, on the conditions and principles of dramatic representation, and on a dozen kindred matters, and in countless appreciations of individual writers, he displayed remarkable keenness of insight and fine critical discernment, as well as taste and learning.

Or take his essay on 'The Soul of Man,' where, in as coherent and methodical a way as he ever cared to set forth his thoughts, he offered his views on Society,—as it is, and as it should be,—from the individualist and aesthetic stand-point. This paper, according to Lord Alfred, would never have been written unless Wilde had known Mr. Shaw; and this may be true, though hardly in any more emphatic sense than that some writing of the latter's may have served him as a stimulus or a starting-point. The fact remains that, whereas most of the Fabian tracts fall flat by sheer drudgery and deadweight of detail, by their complete lack of imaginative sympathy and ridiculous pretence to science, Wilde's little work, amid much that will bear no serious examination, or that touches a harsh note, will be found to contain some of the truest and most trenchant things ever uttered on the actual state of civilized humanity, and on the means of escape from it. I can do no better here than cite a passage from Mr. Ross's 'Note of Explanation' to a late edition of 'The Soul of Man' published by Mr. A. L. Humphreys. 'The Soul of Man,' he says, 'is unique in English literature. At least there is no more comprehensive essay with which I am acquainted. Without being in the least desultory, it touches, though ever so slightly, almost every subject on which educated people think when they think at all. And every subject is illuminated by a phrase which haunts the memory.' Lord Alfred is very far from sharing this favourable opinion of Wilde's opuscule. 'Like pretty well everything else that Wilde wrote,' he declares, it 'fails entirely when you come to look into it,' being, to quote his own homely metaphor, 'neither fish, flesh, fowl nor good red herring.' On purpose to lay bare the futility of Wilde's reasoning, Lord Alfred accuses him of being 'always a rebel in his heart,' a man of subversive principles, and as such unable to realize that altruism, and altruism alone, remains the only true foundation of Society. But this is merely turning things upside down. What Wilde wished to point out in 'The Soul of Man' was precisely that, in place of that organized altruism which is the basis of the existing social order, and which has merely succeeded in making man utterly miserable, and in smothering him under a burden of intolerable and meaningless obligations, there should be substituted a refined and carefully studied egoism, a new individualism, having for its sole aim the evolution of self, and which, by allowing each man to cultivate freely what he feels to be the one thing wherein he differs from every other being, might in the end make life at least endurable to the majority of us . . . Did Wilde set up for a practical reformer? Did he propound his scheme of social improvement with an eye to its feasibility and acceptableness, or even because he believed in its ultimate coming true? Assuredly not. He simply sketched out the configuration of a Utopia, as he sighted it dimly beyond the measureless ocean of Time. 'And when Humanity lands there, it looks out, and, seeing a better country, sets sail. Progress is the realisation of Utopias.' But this essential character of the work Lord Alfred has chosen to ignore, just as he will not recognize that writing of this kind may evince as much experience, penetration, and thoughtfulness as any positive scheme towards the amelioration of the conditions of life within the limits of the present system. But I fancy there is just a chance that, when all the unexhilarating lucubrations of a hundred well-meaning Sidney Webbs are long dead and forgotten, 'The Soul of Man' will still be remembered and read, not for its magic of words only, but because, after another century or two has completed its course, poor incorrigible Humanity will be still as hopefully yearning for and struggling towards those fortunate shores that Wilde has presented to our vision with intuitive and ideal truth.

Or finally let us consider for a moment what lessons concerning his mental scope, his depth of judgment and character, might be gathered from that of his prose works which is regarded by many as his finest,— De Profundis. The extracts published with that title by Mr. Ross, on their appearance in 1905 caused some perplexity among reviewers, as will be remembered,—very different opinions being then put forward as to what should be the right mode of approaching the work, and interpreting its message,—and for anything that I know to the contrary, this may be the case still. What Lord Alfred's views are in this regard, we have seen already; whether they are at all likely to be accepted as the the last word on the question, is for readers of his book to judge. The objection commonly raised, with more or less of irritation, against De Profundis was, that it is so 'insincere,'—that it is far too fine writing to be equally valuable as a purely human 'document.' And, in fact, the exquisite finish of its style at first sight would seem to detract from the weight of its confessional evidence. The agonies of despair that the writer says he has suffered, the awful temptations he has fought through, surely these should have left some traces in the outward form of the work? That stately sequence of word-waves, gliding along so tunefully-cadenced, so delicately-curved, churned into foam by no sudden convulsion of passion, unruffled even by any passing peevishness,—why pry into their shallow deeps (it seemed natural to ask) for any clash and turmoil of feelings that could not be there, for any realities of profound spiritual life? But this, as I have pointed out elsewhere, is to misconceive Wilde's nature entirely. Wilde was too much of an artist to be able to write anything that had not style, that was not beautified with some touches, at least, of artistic invention. That is why, as I once put it, he simply 'could not set to work upon that martyrology of his "solitudes and sufferings" until . . . there had at last come into his mind the tranquillity and clarity requisite for the inception of a true work of art.'

Let us, then, take *De Profundis* for what it is, and professes to be: an account of certain mental struggles and speculations, the truth of which is not impaired by the fact that the book is, at the same time, a piece of choice writing. What species of mind, what disposition, do these meditations reveal to us? If much in Wilde's earlier work would seem to bear out the charges of superficiality so often brought against him, in *De Profundis* I see nothing that justifies such an accusation. Here Wilde puts to himself the old question that every human being will have to face some day: 'How am I to find a meaning in my life?' We all know his answer. It may be summed up thus: Humility, Pity, Love. Are these fine words merely, with no seriousness or substance behind them? Was his yearning after 'the Mystical in Art, the Mystical in Life, the Mystical in Nature,' mere pretence or self-delusion? . . . Surely no man in prison, even were he a person of abandoned life and a monstrous blasphemer, would sit down in cold blood to caricature his own sufferings, or to simulate a state of mind to which he was a stranger. The literary charm and beauty of the work may deceive us as to its truth, and so may its gentle dignity of attitude. But there is, in the very circumstances of its origin, an evidence of sincerity not easily to be refuted. To me the book stands for the sincere utterance of a man not wholly unattentive to life's bitter teachings, and in whom there had awakened a new sense of responsibility towards himself and his fellow-creatures,—a man who, while pondering his own fate, so sadly suggestive and so curiously emblematic, had realized how, on even the slightest of our actions, may depend the greatest and most momentous issues. Like 'The Soul of Man' before it, though in a more ideal manner, and with an impassioned simplicity of thought rarely equalled in modern literature, *De Profundis* epitomizes some of the central problems of life as reflected in a sensitive and highly complex soul. . . .

In two consecutive chapters (XVI and XVII), Lord Alfred offers a fairly detailed account of Wilde's poetry and of his plays and prose works. It is pleasant to note, for once, that he gives full and ungrudging recognition to the last-completed and perhaps best known of Wilde's works,—*The Ballad of Reading Gaol*,—and praises it in excellent and apt terms. After pointing out the evident influence of Hood's 'Eugene Aram' and of Coleridge's 'Ancient Mariner,' of which latter, however, 'in certain ultimate qualities it falls far short,' he goes on to explain that in Wilde's Ballad 'we have a sustained poem of sublimated actuality and of a breadth and sweep and poignancy such as had never before been attained in this line.' Or as he puts it elsewhere:— 'It is a work which stands out head and shoulders above any other of Wilde's performances by virtue of its human appeal and its relative freedom from defects which render the bulk of Wilde's poetry practically unreadable.' It is, in his view, 'the only poem of Wilde's which is likely to endure,' and on it alone 'his reputation among posterity will stand.'—Very likely he will be backed here by many critics. Mr. G. K. Chesterton, for instance, resolutely names it 'the one real thing' Wilde ever wrote. Yet who can help feeling that its note of horror and suspense becomes almost unbearable at times, and that there are moments when this masterly poem sets us a-trembling, not with the exquisite thrill of high and pure art, but with the shiver of crude facts? Wilde himself was not blind to this blemish in the work. He was well aware that, in spite of the enormous labour he spent on making his poem artistically perfect, he had not perhaps quite succeeded in merging reality and art. In a letter to his publisher, Smithers, of Nov. 16, 1897,—quoted in Stuart Mason's *Bibliography of Oscar Wilde,* 1914, p. 412,—he alludes to it, with obvious exaggeration of phrase, as to 'a poem, whose subject is all wrong and whose treatment too personal.'

With regard to Wilde's poetry generally, Lord Alfred is not by any means equally laudative. I cannot admit that his estimate of Wilde the poet, though in some ways it may seem legitimate, is on the whole a fair one. The fact that all of Wilde's poetry was, to a certain extent, of derivative inspiration and, like his other work, carries the suggestion of his wide and various reading, may be easily over-emphasized. Lord Alfred's assertion that, 'leaving out *The Ballad of Reading Gaol* and, up to a point, *The Sphinx*, Wilde's poetical work consists of clever, and occasionally, perhaps, brilliant imitations,' as a general criticism of that work, is neither worse nor better than several others that have appeared on the subject. It gives but half the truth, and imperfectly; for while recognizing the poet's brilliancy and cleverness, it strangely omits to mention that, for all his echoing of other poets, he remains, in some subtle way, individual and original, and that, amid much that is spurious, his poems convey a note of peculiar and marked novelty in tone and treatment. It would be an easy thing in most of these poems to point out a fair number of lines or entire stanzas that 'can be pronounced to be pure Wilde,' and are traceable, in no one point of either thought or phrasing, to any of those masters of contemporary or earlier poetry by whom he was mainly influenced. . . .

No more generous is the author's estimate of another famous poem of Wilde's, *The Sphinx*,—not, I mean, in respect of its theme, for that, no doubt, we must call, with a certain virtuous critic, 'frankly bestial,' and well fit to stir 'certain resorts in the neighbourhood of Piccadilly Circus to their foundations,' but in its quality of by far the most purely artistic poem he ever wrote of any considerable length or sustained inspiration. 'There is an undoubted pomp and swing about some of the stanzas; there are pictures well visualised,' he owns, 'and put on the canvas with a fine eye for colour; and the element of curiousness or weirdness is well sustained.' This sounds liberal enough. Yet all that follows is merely, as it were, to limit the value of these admissions, and practically deprives them of all importance. 'He has succeeded only,' we read, 'in establishing a sort of Wardour Street receptacle for old, tarnished and too-vividly-coloured lots.' Lord Alfred further objects to the 'uneasy effect' of the metre. But he will be at some difficulty to explain wherein it consists, unless it were in the fact that the stanzas are meant to be printed in two lines, an arrangement adopted simply for the sake of avoiding the more obvious aspect of a four-lined double-rhymed stanza (abba), and the 'uneasy effect' of which will be unnoticed by most readers. Lord Alfred's just-quoted remarks in commendation of the style of the poem, though apposite, hardly convey a full idea of its incomparable splendour of workmanship, of its 'firm, lava-like verse,' to borrow a suggestive phrase from Mr. Arthur Ransome. Let me quote just one stanza, than which I can call to mind none more lovely in the whole body of Wilde's poetry,—

Inviolate and immobile she does not rise she does not stir
For silver moons are naught to her and naught to her the suns that reel.

I do not give these lines as an adequate specimen of the certainly astounding craftsmanship displayed in this poem, or as in the least characteristic of the peculiar mood in which it originated, their delicate and simple grandeur placing them, as I think, considerably above its general level. But I give them as a fair sample of Wilde's poetic diction, when at its loftiest and purest. If we want to capture the same inimitable accent again, we must turn to his last work in prose, which alone among all his writings has that 'clear note of lyrical beauty' he so warmly praised in Arnold,—to one of those admirable little passages in rhythmic prose whose sweetly attuned cadences and splendour of imagery make us forget for a moment that, after all, they merely state certain scientific eventualities, or utter a commonplace reflection, as in—'When one has weighed the sun in the balance, and measured the steps of the moon, and mapped out the seven heavens star by star, there still remains one-self.'

It is a significant fact that, in his examination of Wilde's prose works in their literary aspect, Lord Alfred omits every mention of *De Profundis*,—esteeming, possibly, that, having denounced it as a 'farrago of hysterical abuse,' and shown up the irrelevant and misleading character of the work as now published, it matters little whether such despicable and dubious substance is couched in perfect prose, or not. This view may be quite legitimate. Only, as every artist has a right to be judged, in the last instance, by his best work, and as, in the opinion of most good judges, Wilde never rose higher as a master of prose than in these pages, one looks for an acknowledgment of the fact, beyond the vague admission that Wilde 'did, at times, write accomplished prose,'—if indeed this is meant to allude to the work in question. Failing to hit upon a single criticism that might be adduced in disparagement of the artistic quality of *De Profundis*, the author prefers to keep silent about it,—that is how most readers will be bound to interpret his attitude.

Nor is there much left of Wilde's other prose writings after our author has been at work on them in his characteristic way for a dozen or so pages. Those peculiar excellencies with which they are now generally credited, and which, one might innocently fancy, would have explained their considerable and still growing vogue, simply do not exist, save in the sickly brains of such as let themselves be taken in by the brazen puffings of the 'Ross-Ransome faction.' The writer has formed the ingenious device of now and then citing Wilde himself in support of his views and verdicts, with the obvious aim of making these appear the more impugnable. Thus he would like his readers to believe that Wilde 'never made any great fuss about his prose writings other than the plays. He regarded—and very properly regarded—the essays in *Intentions*, together with the fairy tales and his other stories (excepting, of course, *The Picture of Dorian Gray*), as so much donkey work, and pretty well on the level with his lectures, which were written for the pure purpose of getting money and with no eye to "supreme artistry".' To these assertions, whether based on fact or not, too much importance should not be attached. I am told on unimpeachable authority that, after his inprisonment, Wilde thoroughly disliked most of his writings, as being 'inadequate expressions of his genius.' On the other hand, I have it on the same authority that, in the years preceding the catastrophe, he 'constantly said that all his works were technically perfect and equally so.' Nor do the terms in which, in *De Profundis*, Wilde refers to certain of his works,—among them one of the dialogues in *Intentions*,—point to the conclusion that he held such a low opinion of the bulk of his prose writings as Lord Alfred insinuates. Even had he done so, it would merely go to prove that Wilde was quite incapable of appreciating his own work at its true value.

Lord Alfred complacently echoes the rather hackneyed charges of plagiarism brought against Wilde by another famous artist, whose irascible and arrogant temper rendered him invidious of emulation,— Whistler. Wilde 'knew that "The Decay of Lying," "The Critic as Artist" and "The Truth of Masks" were, in a large measure, cribbed from Whistler . . .' Let me quote, on this often contested point, some pertinent remarks of Mr. R. B. Glaenzer in the 'Introduction' to his edition of Wilde's lecture on *Decorative Art in America* (New York, Brentano's, 1906):— 'In many respects, Wilde was in accord with Whistler as regards the conditions of art. He has even been accused of borrowing his ideas from Whistler. That is absurd. It would be easier, if anything, to prove the reverse. In point of time, the exposition of Wilde's doctrines takes precedence over that of the painter.' Mr. Ross advocates the same view in his Preface to Wilde's *Essays and Lectures* (Lo. Methuen, 1909), where this question of plagiarism is considered so explicitly that any comments of mine are superfluous. 'That Wilde derived a great deal from the older man goes without saying, just as he derived so much in a greater degree from Pater, Ruskin, Arnold and Burne-Jones. Yet the tedious attempt to recognise in every jest of his some original by Whistler induces the criticism that it seems a pity the great painter did not get them off on the public before he was forestalled.'

The author further attempts to convince us that Wilde 'knew' that the pages entitled 'Pen, Pencil and Poison' was 'the merest review article, and neither better nor worse than the average stodginess which the public of his day accepted from their somnolent monthlies.' The palpable injustice of the criticism implied in these lines is no more amazing than is the suggestion that Wilde himself might have expressed his adhesion to it. It is an unfortunate thing that Wilde is not in a position to defend himself against this sort of gratuitous imputations. There is, however, no doubt that, were it obtainable, his evidence in the present case as in a great many others would prove damaging to our belief in Lord Alfred Douglas as the sole receptacle of Wilde's most intimate thoughts concerning himself and his literary work. 'Pen, Pencil and Poison' stands unique among Wilde's essays, in so far as it is devoted to the delineation of an individual life and to the estimate of a single man's work, presenting thus, in the words of Mr. Ransome, 'some of the angular outlines of the set article on book or public character.' But if less characteristic of its writer in plan and structure, the essay is the more so in the choice of its subject,—Thomas Wainewright, that man of terrible and exquisite accomplishments, between whose personality and Wilde's own we may trace some obvious analogies, and whose tragic fate offers such a strange prefiguration to that of the latter. Taking it for what it is, a biographical sketch, this paper certainly does not fall short, either in literary merit or in intellectual brightness, of Wilde's other essays.

After stating it as his conviction that the doctrine in *Intentions* (or more correctly: 'The Decay of Lying' and 'The Critic as Artist') 'will not bear examination,'—a view it would carry us too far to refute in this place,—the author concludes his appreciation of that book with a few remarks to the effect that even in artistry and style it is far from unassailable. Wilde, he says, in common with Mr. Gilbert Chesterton and Mr. Frank Harris (thus deliberately bracketing him with two inferior writers), is 'killed by the exuberance' of his facility . . . 'They have the pen of the ready writer and they fall accordingly.' There is of course a measure of truth in this, as in the statement that Wilde is 'prone to the over-sugared and over-gilded passage.' But the same reproach might be levelled at some of the greatest masters of English prose, without detracting from their merit. To say that his split infinitives are 'a standing disgrace to him,' is making a mountain out of a mole-hill. The divided infinitive, despite the authority of Lord Alfred Douglas, seems moreover to have come to stay, nor has the condemnation of the professed grammarians succeeded in banishing it. . . .

117. Edgar Saltus on Wilde's literary ability

1917

From Edgar Saltus's *Oscar Wilde: An Idler's Impression* (Chicago, 1917), pp. 24–6.

Wilde was a third rate poet who occasionally rose to the second class but not once to the first. Prose is more difficult than verse and in it he is rather sloppy. In spite of which, or perhaps precisely on that account, he called himself lord of language. Well, why not, if he wanted to? Besides, in his talk he was lord and more—sultan, pontifex maximus. Hook, Jerrold, Smith, Sheridan, rolled into one, could not have been as brilliant. In talk he blinded and it is the subsiding wonder of it that his plays contain.

In the old maps, on the vague places, early geographers used to put: Hic sunt leones—Here are lions. On any catalogue of Wilde's plays there should be written: Here lions might have been. For assuming his madness, one must also admit his genius and the uninterrupted conjunction of the two might have produced brilliancies such as few bookshelves display.

Therein is the tragedy of letters. Renan said that morality is the supreme illusion. The diagnosis may or may not be exact. Yet it is on illusions that we all subsist. We live on lies by day and dreams at night. From the standpoint of the higher mathematics, morality may be an illusion. But it is very sustaining. Formerly it was also inspirational. In post-pagan days it created a new conception of beauty. Apart from that, it had nothing whatever to do with the arts, except the art of never displeasing, which, in itself, is the whole secret of mediocrity.

Oscar Wilde lacked that art, and I can think of no better epitaph for him.

118. H. L. Mencken on Wilde as Puritan and aesthete

1918

Signed introduction to *A House of Pomegranates* (New York, 1918), i–viii.

Henry Louis Mencken (1880–1956), American journalist, author, and editor of the *Smart Set* and the *American Mercury*, emphasizes Wilde's underlying Puritanism, in Mencken's sense of the term, and the innocence of the aesthetic response, corrupted by Wilde's 'inheritance' of Puritanical dishonesty. *A House of Pomegranates*, Mencken concludes, is Wilde's best work, for only here was he completely the artist.

A House of Pomegranates was done almost exactly at the middle point of Wilde's career as an author, and in the days, coincidently, of his soundest and least perturbed celebrity. His poems, his posturings and his high services to W. S. Gilbert and to *Punch* were beginning to recede; ahead of him were *Salomé*, the four West End comedies, and catastrophe. Relatively placid waters surrounded him, shining in the sun. He had been married, and had got over it. There was a pleasant jingle of gold, or, at all events, of silver in his pocket. The foremost reviews of the day were open to him. He was not only a popular success, a figure in the public eye; he was, more importantly, beginning to get the attention of men of sense, to be taken with growing seriousness, to feel firm ground under him. And in age he was thirty-six, with the gas of youth oozed out and the stiffening of the climacteric not yet set in.

So situated, pleasantly becalmed between two storms, he wrote *A House of Pomegranates*, and into it, I have always believed, he put the most accurate and, on the whole, the most ingratiating revelation of his essential ideas that was ever to get upon paper. And without, of course, stating them at all—not a hint of exposition, of persuasion, of pedagogy is in the book. But that is precisely what gives them, there, their clarity and validity; they are not spoken for, they speak for them-

380

selves—and this is always the way a man sets forth the faith that is in him most honestly and most illuminatingly, not by arguing for it like some tin-pot evangelist, but by exhibiting it like an artist. Here we have the authentic Wilde, the Wilde who explains and dignifies all the lesser and more self-conscious Wildes. He is simply one who stands ecstatic before a vision of prodigious and almost intolerable beauty, a man haunted by ineffable magnificences of color, light, mass and line, a rapt and garrulous drunkard of the eye. Hs is one who apprehended loveliness in the world, not as sound, not as idea, not as order, not as syllogism, above all, not as law, but as picture pure and simple—as an ocular image leaping with life, gorgeous in its variety, infinite in its significances. And in the face of that enchanting picture, standing spellbound before its eloquent and narcotic forms, responding with all senses to its charming and intricate details, he appears before us as the type of all that the men of his race and time were not—as a rebel almost colossal in the profound artlessness of his denial. What he denied was the whole moral order of the world—the fundamental assumption of the Anglo-Saxon peoples. What he set up was a theory of the world as purely aesthetic spectacle, superb in its beauty, sufficiently its own cause and motive, ordered only by its own inner laws, and as innocent of all ethical import and utility as the precession of the equinoxes.

In this denial, of course, there was a challenge, and in that challenge was Wilde's undoing. To see him merely as a commonplace and ignoble misdemeanant, taken accidentally in some secret swinishness and condemned to a routine doom for that swinishness alone, is to accept a view of him that is impossibly journalistic and idiotic. He stood in the dock charged with a good deal more than private viciousness, and the punishment he got was a good deal more than private viciousness ever provokes, even from agents of the law who seek acquittal of themselves in their flogging of the criminal. What he was intrinsically accused of, and what he was so barbarously punished for, was a flouting of the premises upon which the whole civilization of his time was standing—a blasphemous attempt upon the gods that all docile and well-disposed men believed in, even in the midst of disservice—an heretical preaching of predicates and valuations that threatened to make a new generation see the world in a new way, to the unendurable confusion of the old one. In brief, his true trial was in the character of a heretic, and the case before the actual jury was no more than a symbol of a quite medieval summoning of the secular arm. What the secular arm thought of it I have often wondered —so astoundingly vast a hub-bub over an affair of everyday! Surely fish of precisely the same spots were coming into the net constantly, and in the sea of London there were many more, and some much larger to the eye. But Wilde, in truth, was the largest of them all. He had been marked for a long while, and delicately pursued. Lines had been cast for him; watchers had waited; there was a sort of affrighted and unspoken vow to dispose of him. And so, when he was hauled in at last, it was a good deal more than the mere taking of another spotted fish.

Thus I see the whole transaction, so obscenely wallowed in by the indignant and unintelligent, and thus I see Wilde himself—as one who cried up too impudently, too eloquently, and, above all, too persuasively a philosophy that was out of its time. As formidably ardent and potent upon the other side, I haven't the slightest doubt that his pathological sportings in the mire might have gone unchallenged, or at all events unwhooped. One hears of such things in Y.M.C.A.'s often enough, but in whispers; the very newspapers show discretion; surely no great state trials ensue. But here was a man who had done a great deal more than bring a passing stench into the synagogue. Here was one who had brought a scarlet woman there, and paraded her up and down, and shoved the croaking Iokanaan back into his rain-barrel, and invited the young men to consider the dignity and preciousness of beauty, and fluttered even the old ones with his Byzantine tales. Here, in brief, was one to be put down in swift dudgeon if disaster was to be avoided—if the concept of life as a bondage to implacable law was to stand unshaken—if the moral order of the world, or, at least, of that little corner of it, was to hold out against a stealthy and abominable paganism. Wilde was the first unmistakable anti-Puritan, the first uncompromising enemy of the essential Puritan character—the fear of beauty. He was destroyed, on the one hand, because he was getting power. He was destroyed, on the other hand, because he was fundamentally weak.

That weakness resided, in part, in a childish vanity, an empty desire for superficial consideration, that was peculiar to the man, but the rest of it, and perhaps the larger part, had deeper roots. It belonged to his race, to the ineradicable Scotticism of the North of Ireland Protestant; one perceives the same quality, lavishly displayed, in George Bernard Shaw—a congenital Puritanism beneath the surface layer of anti-Puritanism, a sort of moral revolt against the moral axiom, a civil war with fortunes that vary curiously, and often astonishingly. Wilde, as a youth, went to Greece with Mahaffy, and came home a professed Greek, but underneath there were always Northern reservations, a

Northern habit of conscience, a Northern incapacity for Mediterranean innocence. One gets here, it seems to me, an explanation of many things —his squeamishness in certain little ways (all his work, in phrase, is as 'clean' as Walter Pater's or Leonardo's); his defective grasp of the concept of honor, as opposed to that of morals; the strange limits set upon his aesthetic reactions (*e.g.*, his anesthesia to music); his touches of grossness; his inability to distinguish between aristocracy and mere social consideration; most of all, that irrepressible inner reminder which led him constantly to stand aghast, so to speak, before his own heresies— that pressing and ineradicable sense of their diabolism. In a word, the man was quite unable to throw off his inheritance entirely. It dogged him in the midst of his prosperity. It corrupted his sincerity. It sent doubts to tease him, and flung him into hollow extravagances of self-assertion. And when, in the end, he faced a tremendous and inexorable issue, he met it in an almost typically Puritanical manner—that is, timorously, evasively, dishonestly, with an eye upon the crowd, almost morally—as you will find set forth at length, if you are interested, in Frank Harris' capital biography.

In a word, Wilde was, at bottom, a second-rate man, and so inferior to his cause that he came near ditching it. One gets, from the accounts of those who were in close relations with him, a feeling of repugnance like that bred by the familiar 'good man'; he was, on his plane, as insufferable as a Methodist is on his. But there was in him something that is surely not in the Methodist, and that was a capacity for giving his ideas a dignity not in himself—a talent as artist which, at its best, was almost enough to conceal his limitations as a man. What he did with words was a rare and lovely thing. Himself well-nigh tone-deaf, he got into them a sonorous and majestic music. Himself hideous, he fashioned them into complex and brilliant arabesques of beauty. Himself essentially shallow and even bogus, he gave them thunderous eloquence, an austere dignity almost Biblical, the appearance of high sincerity that goes with all satisfying art. In these stories, I believe, he is at his best. His mere flashiness is reduced to very little; his ideas, often hollow, are submerged in feelings; he seems to forget his followers, his place, his celebrity, and to devote himself wholly to his work; he is the artist emancipated, for the moment, from the other things that he was, and the worse things that he tried to be. I know of no modern English that projects color and warmth and form more brilliantly, or that serves more nobly the high purposes of beauty, or that stands further from the flaccid manner and uses of everyday stupidity. There are faults in it, true enough. At times it grows self-conscious, labored, almost sing-song. But in the main it is genuinely distinguished—in the main it is signal work.

119. George Moore on Wilde as a writer in the 'third or fourth class'

1918

Letter to Frank Harris in *Pearson's Magazine* [New York] (March 1918), xxxviii, 386.

Moore (1852–1933) had been invited by Harris, who was then editing the American edition of *Pearson's Magazine*, to comment on the latter's biography of Wilde, between whom and Moore there had been mutual antipathy. The final paragraphs of the letter, which mention Shaw ('Shaw and I had nothing in common') and Anglo-Saxon attitudes toward pornography, have been omitted. (See No. 120 for Vincent O'Sullivan's response to Moore's letter.)

My dear Harris: I have just received your letter and my memories of pleasant hours I spent with you in conversation when we were both young men compel me to reply to your letter at once, though I am afraid my answers to your questions will not be those that you would care to receive or that will be of use to you. You know that I came into the world under bonds to speak the truth, I mean what appears to me truth about art, and, however much I might like to write you a letter that would be of use to you I can only write the letter which the post will put into your hands in ten or a dozen days if the vessel that carried it escapes a torpedo.

The first thing you ask is for me to write to you about Oscar Wilde, and this I can do easily, but I am afraid that my opinions regarding him

384

will not please you, for they are not the opinions you hold. You would put him in the first class as a writer and I should put him in the third or fourth. It is not a long time since I read a book of his called *Intentions*, and it seems to me very thin and casual, without depth, therefore, unoriginal; no man is original in the surface of his mind; to be original we must go deep, right down to the roots, and Oscar Wilde's talent seems to me essentially rootless; something growing in a glass in a little water. I was struck by his lack of style; by style, I mean rhythm. It is all quite clear and correct but his sentences do not sway. There is no current and I return to glass for an image, it is all very glassy. He had a certain dramatic gift, he moves his characters deftly and his dialogue is not without grace. It is often to the point. He had a pretty ingenious drawing-room wit, and these qualities enabled him to write plays that are not intolerable to a man of letters, and superficial enough to attract audiences. If I understand your letter rightly you seem to think that Wilde's abnormal impulses mark him out as an interesting subject for literary study. It might be so if Wilde were a great writer.[1] He is that in your opinion, but in my opinion, as I have already said, he is in the third or fourth class and, therefore, not worth troubling about, and I do not think that anybody would have troubled about him if the Marquis of Queensbury had not written him a post card; had it not been for that unlucky post card Wilde and his literature would be sleeping comfortably in the dust at the bottom of an almost forgotten drawer in company with Frank Miles' drawings. I never had any other opinions about Wilde than those I am expressing in this letter, and as time has confirmed me in my opinions regarding him, you will understand that I am more unfitted than perhaps anybody else to write an article on your biography. . . .

Very sincerely yours,

GEORGE MOORE

[1] *The Ballad of Reading Gaol* will live longer than anything written in England from 1875 to 1900.—FRANK HARRIS

120. Vincent O'Sullivan replies to Moore

1918

Letter to Frank Harris in *Pearson's Magazine* [New York] (April 1918), xxxviii, 441.
Vincent O'Sullivan (1868–1940), American poet and novelist, who lived most of his life in France and whose friendship with Wilde resulted in his *Aspects of Wilde* (1936), wrote the following letter in defence of Wilde against George Moore's depreciation, which appeared in a previous issue of *Pearson's Magazine* (See No. 119). Paul Souday's article on Wilde, which O'Sullivan refers to in his letter, appeared in *Le Temps* (with the title 'L'Esthétique d'Oscar Wilde') in 1912; reprinted in *Les Livres du temps*, i (1913), pp. 384–402, in which Souday states: 'It is probably as an esthetician that Oscar Wilde has the greatest chance of maintaining a place in literary history.'

To the Editor of *Pearson's Magazine*

Sir: It would be a pity to let Mr. George Moore have the last word about Oscar Wilde. I once asked Wilde if he had read *Evelyn Innes*. He replied: 'I hear it has to be played on the piano.'

This may be 'very glassy,' but nobody can deny that it is, to use another of Mr. Moore's phrases, 'to the point.'

The depreciation of Wilde is going on at such a pace lately that people who have never read Wilde, or who take their opinions from the high-class reviews, will begin to believe he was a nobody. Every few weeks some solemn little pedantic ass, wandering in the pastures of the *New Republic* or elsewhere, says pompously in an academic voice: 'Wilde was really fourth-rate.' That ought to settle it, of course; but somehow it does not for some of us. Mr. Moore thinks that all Wilde's fame comes from his trial and imprisonment. He forgets that not a few writers have been before the courts, and even in gaol, and neither they nor their writings are any better known for it. The Dreyfus case was much more celebrated and important than the Wilde case; Dreyfus wrote a book; but who thinks of Dreyfus himself now-a-days? Wilde went to gaol, but he had it in him to draw *De Profundis* and *The Ballad* out of the gaol. There is the difference.

So far from Wilde's sexual aberration adding to the interest of his writings, as Mr. Moore seems to think, it did him infinite harm, not only temporal harm, but harm as an artist. Owing to this, his writings are placed in a special light. People come to them hardly ever with the same impartiality with which they consider, say, Charles Lamb or Goldsmith. Further, to it may be ascribed, no doubt, in some measure, his indolence. It did to him what opium did to Coleridge.

Wilde's indolence, from whatever cause it arose, is the one thing that prevented his being one of the greatest figures of the nineteenth century. Nobody who was even a little in his company could doubt that he was an extraordinary man. He was not only an author. If he had gone into the House of Commons, he would have been remarkable in politics; and he is about the only English writer of his time of whom this can be said. One has the impression that he never put out more than half of his strength in his books. If he had only had a tithe of the industry of Mr. George Moore, what books and plays he might have written! But he would only do the thing which could be got over quickly. He was afraid if he stayed long at a work that the first thing he met in the street would distract him from it. I suppose he never spent longer than six weeks over anything he ever wrote. *Salome*, he told me, was written between luncheon and twelve o'clock at night.

Of course a man must be judged, not by what he was capable of doing, but by what he actually did. Wilde was a great writer; he had it in him, if he had taken thought and time to purge himself of certain vulgarities, to be much greater. At his worst he is never so vulgar as some I could name who are at present in much esteem. Mr. Moore says Wilde's sentences do not sway. I don't know what that means. He also says that Wilde's sentences lack rhythm. Let anybody put pages of the *Fairy Tales* or of *Intentions* beside pages of *Sister Teresa* and *Modern Painting*, and read them aloud. It will surprise me if any reader unprejudiced against Wilde, who judges Wilde as he might Coleridge or De Quincy, will thereupon say that the rhythm is on the side of George Moore.

I am only writing this letter for the sake of the anecdote at the beginning. Still I would add a word. Mr. Moore and others seem to think that Wilde had no foundation. The one essay on Wilde I know which treats him seriously as a thinker and philosopher, and not as a mere amuser, is by Mr. Paul Souday, the critic of the Paris *Temps*. If anybody wants to see just how much new and original there was in Wilde, he should read that.

Mr. Moore is like Dr. Johnson. 'Nothing strange lasts,' said Dr. Johnson; 'the man Sterne did not last.' But the man Sterne *has* lasted, in spite of criticisms not unlike those of Moore on Wilde. And the truth is that Wilde's vitality in literature is due to reasons which are in literature itself, and hardly at all today to the accidents of his career. He did that extremely rare thing in literature: he produced a form, an accent, quite new. Whether you like or dislike it, whether you think it is trivial or not, of whatever materials he composed it, there it is—it is Oscar Wilde. Any schoolgirl somewhat practised in literature, upon hearing a page of *Intentions* or of *De Profundis* read, would recognize it at once. Of how many can this be said? George Moore, for instance, is considered by many to be a great writer; he is certainly a very painstaking writer. His novels are always interesting; but to anybody who knows Flaubert, and the Goncourts, and Zola, and Huysmans, they do not come as new. Only to those who reach Moore before arriving at the Frenchmen, do they come as new. There has never been any circulation of Mr. Moore's books among the French, because he has taken their form and can bring them nothing that they want in return. *The Mummer's Wife* was translated into French, but it interested nobody but Mr. Moore's personal friends. With Wilde it is different. The other day I was looking through a French catalogue of his books. Most of them are in the tenth or twelfth edition. *Salomé* has been translated into all European languages, and even into Hebrew, according to the bibliography in Mr. Robert Ross's edition. These things do not happen to a man without originality. Mr. Moore, in his letter to you, says that to be original you must go down to the roots, and that Wilde was only on the surface. The original man is not always the man who makes a fuss about it— who takes off his coat and sweats, digging down, as Mr. Moore says, to the roots. Industry cannot very well be genius, or many people would be geniuses who decidedly are not.

VINCENT O'SULLIVAN

121. Upton Sinclair on Wilde as an overrated writer

1918

Letter to Frank Harris in *Pearson's Magazine* [New York] (July 1918), xxxix, 167–9.

Upton Sinclair (1878–1968), American novelist and Socialist, whose novel, *The Jungle* (1906), an exposé of corruption in the Chicago stockyards, brought him fame, was the author of some eighty books and an ardent supporter of Socialist causes. Harris invited Sinclair (as he did George Moore—see No. 119) to comment on his biography of Wilde, which had just been reprinted in the United States. Sinclair's narrow Socialist bias in judging Wilde's *The Importance of Being Earnest* ('Just plain stupid!') is sufficient to disqualify him as a serious literary critic, but his letter to Harris—though concerned primarily with the latter's biography—is here given in full, for it reveals a critical orientation shared by many less—and more—gifted than Sinclair.

My dear Frank Harris

I have been sitting up nights with your Oscar Wilde. It is assuredly one of the most interesting books in English; it is one of our great biographies. You had a moving, tragic story to tell, and you have told it plainly and honestly, with no concealments, no nonsense. You have trusted to our intelligence—and we appreciate it. Would to God that all biographers might have that generous faith! What would I not give, for example, to read such a biography of John Ruskin! He had some dark shadow in his life, which colored all his work; but I, one of his soul's children, am forbidden to know about it—because, forsooth, a solemn British jack-ass, the official biographer, has stuck his long ears as a screen between us.

So much for the book's right to be. You ask me to go on and tell all I think about the work, 'the truth, the whole truth, and nothing but the truth.' I hesitate to do this—any man might hesitate to criticize a book, the subject of which is so complex, involving as it does, not merely the sins and virtues of a mere man, but the sins of a man of genius, and the more important subject of the layman's attitude toward genius and the sins of genius. With such a complicated subject you have done so well that any adverse criticism might seem an impertinence. But I will do the best I can, and will strike out by saying that it seems to me that you, as commentator upon the life of Oscar, reveal a certain amount of confusion in your point of view. You follow the wise old advice to hate the sin and love the sinner, and we love you for that; but unfortunately, you have not been able to love the enemies of the sinner. Your abhorrence of the leading British virtues is almost as great as your abhorrence of Oscar's sins; so you are like the rebel Milton, portraying Satan; you are seduced into making him a hero in spite of logic. It is true that you give us the facts, so that, if we have the brains, we can judge for ourselves; but alas, not all men have brains—you will agree with that profound critical dictum, I am sure.

For the most part you see your protagonist quite clearly as the pitiful victim of his own will-less nature; but when the tragedy of this nature begins to work itself out, your pity for the sinner, combined with your abhorrence of his enemies, tempts you to offer him to us in a new rôle, that of persecuted hero and martyred genius. Now, the question is complicated, hardly to be covered by a formula; but weighing the various factors as carefully as I can, I find myself at this conclusion—that the reason Oscar Wilde was sent to prison was not because of his vices, nor yet because of his genius, but because he had attacked, in a particularly conspicuous and aggravating way, a member of the hallowed ruling caste of the country.

You will say that I am interpreting your tragic drama in a way to make it serve as a Socialist pamphlet; you might have foreseen that, when you asked me to give you my views! Jesting aside, I consider that a man cannot interpret any case of persecution unless he sees its economic implications; unless he has studied its relation to whatever class-struggle may at that time be prevailing. I should say that if you had been a thoroughly conscious social revolutionist, your book would have been more powerful and convincing, because you would have been less tempted to blame individuals for evils which are social in their origin. You would have given us an economic interpretation of Oscar, the spoiled darling of a putrescent leisure class, thrown overboard, like Jonah, as a sacrifice in a middle-class hurricane of virtue. Will you pardon me if I add that if you had that revolutionary view-

point, you would be personally a less bitter man, and yet more dangerous to your enemies. For to have analyzed by the methods of exact
science the economic forces driving our world, and to know where
and how they are driving—that is the only way I know to confront the
horrors of our time and keep one's complete self-possession.

To come back to Oscar, I will say that I think you overrate his
genius. You praise his comedies as imperishable classics; you may be
shocked to hear that there is one man they bore. I saw *The Importance
of Being Earnest* in New York many years ago; I never saw anything I
thought more stupid. Just plain stupid! The trick of taking the simple
common-sense of mankind, the moral heritage of the race for countless
ages, and making epigrams by proclaiming the opposite—any one can
learn that trick. If I had nothing else to do, I could go round jotting down
'epigrams' of that sort on my cuff, and very soon have enough to fill
four acts of a 'society' play.

A man who is absorbed in useful work, and therefore has few impulses to depravity, can encounter such Wildeness with nothing more
than indifference; but the average man, who is never sure of his own
self-control, and who, besides, has sons and daughters to train in as
much decency as he can, is made frantic by such perversity, such deliberate bedeviling of the wits of our blind and struggling humanity. There
are 'epigrams' of Oscar Wilde's which are like the snapping of a whip-
lash in the face of men's everyday moral sensibility; and the storm of
execration which burst upon him was simply the turning back of this
whip-lash. You realize it quite clearly, and point it out in places, but
you seem in other places to lose sight of it—because of your intense
aversion to hypocrisy, the use of the common moral sentiments as a
cloak for class-oppressions. In order to see the Oscar Wilde tragedy in its
true perspective, we have to make an effort to put ourselves in the
position of the average man of the time—a man having no knowledge
of the inside circumstances, but merely seeing a writer of smart plays
trip jauntily into the limelight and bring a libel suit against a father for
trying to save his son from sodomy. Of the fact that the father was a
bad one, and the son worse, and that the courts were being used to
maintain a knavish ruling class—of these things the average man could
have no knowledge. He will never have it—until there is a Socialist
daily press in England, with the right to tell the truth about the ruling
class.

There is another place where your heart has an impulse to run away
with your head—when you are dealing with your hero's imprison-

ment. You hate prisons so intensely that before you have done with
them you have overlooked the significant fact, to which you yourself
gave testimony, that Wilde's incarceration was of positive benefit to
him. (I refer, of course, to the period after you had got him better food
and the right to have his books.) During one of your visits to him in
prison you saw plainly a 'spiritual deepening' in him, which, so you
admit, was due to the rigid disciplining of his selfish nature; you never
saw him so well, or so in possession of his mental faculties, as when he
came out; but then he went back to his vomit, and ate and drank and
loafed himself to death, according to the customs prevailing in the
putrescent leisure class to which he belonged; and yet you are led by
your pity and your hatred of British cant to declare that the prison
system killed Oscar Wilde! Is not the true conclusion to be drawn
from your book that decadent poets should be sent to prison and kept
there permanently? Anything to save them from smart society!
While Oscar was at large, the spoiled darling of that society, he idled and
wrote futile plays; but when he was locked up, he forgot himself and
his poses, and wrote the greatest ballad in English, a supremely eloquent and noble poem!

Seriously, perhaps we might agree upon prison sentences for will-
less men, if we could have the right kind of prison, the kind towards
which Thomas Mott Osborne is groping his way; places where such
unhappy men might have as much self-government as they could use,
together with plain wholesome food, moderate work outdoors, and
enforced abstinence from alcohol and tobacco and drugs. Having set
up such prisons, we might agree to send to them, not merely thieves
and highwaymen and esthetes, but men of fashion, princes and dukes,
bishops, stockbrokers and fat persons.

There is an essay of Wilde's which is extensively circulated in
pamphlet form—'The Soul of Man Under Socialism.' You do not
mention it. We ought to know about it. Was it a youthful aberration?
It is so utterly out of key with the rest of his early work. I, of course,
would like to believe that it was an expression of his true self, before
leisure-class society corrupted him. I hope you can let me believe that!

You give us a long letter of Wilde to Alfred Douglas, which you
tell us was 'read out in court.' Under what circumstances? You ought
to tell us about the incident. The fact that this atrocious little animal
escaped sharing Wilde's prison sentence is one of the most significant
points in your book. If the all-sacred British law, which so carefully
protects its noble lords while punishing its men of genius, ever slipped

up sufficiently to permit Lord Alfred to be caused any humiliation or discomfort—we surely want the satisfaction of hearing about it! And, by the way, I think you have slipped up in your Note 2, page 554. Oscar is not implying that his lordship has any 'want of education;' on the contrary, he is crediting him with all the ornamental education there is, but saying that he lacked 'the very sweetest wisdom'—and, assuredly, he did lack that.

Now, I have spent several paragraphs in disagreeing with you. But the splendors of your book make me unwilling to close on that note. These splendors are triumphant. Your style flows like a beautiful, clear stream, your sincerity is convincing, your humanity touches our hearts, your authority compels our judgment. I only wish you could print your book on thinner paper, bind it in one volume, and sell it at a moderate price. You would then achieve a best seller, and enrich the world, as well as Frank Harris. It might be the means of leading our critics to pay more attention to your other books: your Shakespeare, for example, which is one of the finest books in English, and *The Bomb*, which is one of the world's great revolutionary novels. For I consider Frank Harris a greater writer and a far more interesting personality than Oscar Wilde.

Again I thank you for a great book. It has increased my knowledge of life. If it could be widely read, it would increase the virtue of mankind, the dread of self-indulgence and cynicism, and also the hatred of luxury and parasitism.

Sincerely,
UPTON SINCLAIR

122. John Middleton Murry on Wilde's literary achievement

1920

Excerpt from signed review, titled 'Oscar Wilde as a Tragic Hero', in *Athenaeum*, 24 September, 1920, pp. 401-3.

John Middleton Murry (1889-1957), critic, biographer, and editor of the *Athenaeum* from 1919 to 1923, when he founded the *Adelphi*, with which he was associated until 1948. In 1913, he married Katherine Mansfield, later editing her journals and co-authoring her biography. In his lengthy review of Frank Harris's *Oscar Wilde: His Life and Confessions* (New York, 1918), from which the following excerpt is taken, Murry concludes that it is 'one of the most masterly biographies in the English language'.

. . . It is not easy for us to accept Wilde as a man of commanding genius. This does not imply that Mr. Harris believes that he was—he has himself too firm a grip on the reality of the relation between art and life really to believe this—but in some degree the significance of Mr. Harris's book as a work of art depends upon his compelling us to believe it. And at times, as in duty bound, he does most powerfully suggest it. He speaks, for instance, of *The Ballad of Reading Gaol* as 'incomparably the greatest ballad in the English language'—a statement which, unless it is safeguarded by some quibble on the word 'English,' seems extravagant praise of a poem which, for all its fine theme and great emotional power, is nevertheless marred by the whole of the unnecessary and 'aesthetic' fifth movement ('Out of his mouth a red, red rose, Out of his heart a white'). It is Wilde's greatest, perhaps his only poem; but it is certainly not the greatest ballad in English. At least a half-dozen old ballads—one of them *Sir Patrick Spens*—are finer; and of the modern, 'The Ancient Mariner' is indubitably greater. We bring this forward not for the doubtful pleasure of challenging Mr. Harris's critical opinion, but because, as we have said, the impression made by the book as a presentation of a spiritual tragedy must largely depend on the case made out for Wilde as a man of genius.

When, however, Mr. Harris says that Wilde has a place with Congreve as a dramatist, we advance with him willingly on to surer ground. In the comedy of manners he has his certain position; and more than this, his criticism has in it some elements of permanent value. *Intentions* is an extravagant and paradoxical book, it is true; it is also true that the central idea in the essay 'On the Decay of Lying' and much of its working out are lifted without acknowledgment from Sainte-Beuve's masterly essay on Balzac. Nevertheless, in 'The Critic as Artist' there is plenty of original thinking and acute insight and, though the passages of jewelled writing are tedious enough, one has the satisfaction of feeling that Wilde wrote them with his tongue either wholly in his cheek or half-way there. (Mr. Harris, by the way, has been taken in by one piece of paste, when he quotes Wilde as seriously speaking of 'a mad, scarlet thing by Dvorak.' The grin is peculiarly obvious in that passage of *Intentions*.) But when we sum up Wilde's artistic achievement in the drama and the critical essay, and add to it the unconvincing *De Profundis*, and add to that the half-successful *Ballad of Reading Gaol* and *The Sphinx* (to which the late James Elroy Flecker and others through him have owed not a little), what have we? Something considerable, no doubt, but nothing unique. It was Wilde's hard fate that he should have been beaten in his own field by his own contemporaries. We are told that as a talker he could not hold his own with Whistler; we know for ourselves that he was no match for him as a controversialist. We can see, moreover, that in the comedy of manners he has been equalled, if not surpassed by Mr. Shaw, with whom as a writer of English prose he cannot even be compared.

The personal magnetism of a man dies with him; his solid achievement as an artist alone has substance in the eyes of posterity; and we, who are posterity for Wilde, must confess that he is rather a pale ghost as an artist. . . .

123. W. B. Yeats on *The Happy Prince and Other Tales*

1923

Signed introduction to Volume iii, *The Complete Works of Oscar Wilde* (New York, 1923), ix–xvi.

When I was lecturing in Boston a little before the War an Arab refugee told me that Oscar Wilde's works had been translated into Arabian and that his *Happy Prince and Other Tales* had been the most popular:— 'They are our own literature,' he said. I had already heard that 'The Soul of Man under Socialism' was much read in the Young China party; and for long after I found myself meditating upon the strange destiny of certain books. My mind went back to the late eighties when I was but just arrived in London with the manuscript of my first book of poems, and when nothing of Wilde's had been published except his poems and *The Happy Prince*. I remember the reviews were generally very hostile to his work, for Wilde's aesthetic movement was a recent event and London journalists were still in a rage with his knee breeches, his pose—and it may be with his bitter speeches about themselves; while men of letters saw nothing in his prose but imitations of Walter Pater or in his verse but imitations of Swinburne and Rossetti. Never did any man seem to write more deliberately for the smallest possible audience or in a style more artificial, and that audience contained nobody it seemed but a few women of fashion who invited guests to listen to his conversation and two or three young painters who continued the tradition of Rossetti. And then in the midst of my meditation it was as though I heard him saying with that slow precise, rhythmical elocution of his, 'I have a vast public in Samarkand.' Perhaps they do not speak Arabian in Samarkand, but whatever name he had chosen he would have chosen it for its sound and for its suggestion of romance. His vogue in China would have touched him even more nearly, and I can almost hear his voice speaking of jade and powdered lacquer. Indeed, when I remember him with pleasure it is always the talker I remember, either as I have heard him at W. E. Henley's or in his own house or in some passage in a play, where there is some stroke of wit which had first come to him in conversation or might so have come. He was certainly the greatest talker of his time. 'We Irish', he had said to me, 'are too poetical to be poets, we are a nation of brilliant failures, but we are the greatest talkers since the Greeks.' He talked as good Irish talkers always do—though with a manner and music that he had learnt from Pater or Flaubert—and as no good English talker has ever talked. He had no practical interest, no cause to defend, no information to give, nor was he the gay jester whose very practical purpose is our pleasure. Behind his words was the whole power of his intellect, but that intellect had given itself to pure contemplation. I know two or three such men in Ireland to-day, and one of them is an unknown man who lurched into my carriage in a Wicklow train two or three years ago:—'First class carriage, third class ticket, do it on principle,' he began, and then, speaking of a friend of his killed in the war, burst out with, 'Why are so many dead that should be alive and so many alive that should be dead?' For twenty minutes of drunken speech he talked as Shakespeare's people talked, never turning away for a moment from the fundamental and insoluble; and he told me one story that Wilde would have told with delight. Then too I think of a doctor and of a priest with whom I have talked in many places, but especially on a remote Connemara sea coast where, day after day, their minds, more learned in all the poetry of the world than mine, and vehement with phantasy, played with the fundamental and the insoluble.

The further Wilde goes in his writings from the method of speech, from improvisation, from sympathy with some especial audience the less original he is, the less accomplished. I think 'The Soul of Man under Socialism' is sometimes profound because there are so many quotations in it from his conversation; and that *The Happy Prince and Other Tales* is charming and amusing because he told its stories, (his children were still young at that time) and that *A House of Pomegranates* is over-decorated and seldom amusing because he wrote its stories; and because when he wrote, except when he wrote for actors, he no longer thought of a special audience. In 'The Happy Prince' or 'The Selfish Giant' or 'The Remarkable Rocket' there is nothing that does not help the story, nothing indeed that is not story; but in 'The Birthday of the Infanta' there is hardly any story worth the telling. 'The Fisherman and his Soul', from the same book, has indeed so good a story that I am certain that he told it many times; and, that I may enjoy it, I try to imagine it as it must have been when he spoke it, half consciously watching that he might not bore by a repeated effect or an unnecessary description, some child or some little company of young painters or writers. Only when I so imagine it do I discover that the incident of the young fisherman's dissatisfaction with his mermaid mistress, upon hearing a description of a girl dancing with bare feet was witty, charming and characteristic. The young fisherman had resisted many great temptations, but never before had he seen so plainly that she had no feet. In the written story that incident is so lost in decorations that we let it pass unnoticed at a first reading, yet it is the crisis of the tale. To enjoy it I must hear his voice once more, and listen once more to that incomparable talker.

I arrived in London after a long visit to Ireland a few months before his great disaster and said to some friend of his, 'What is Wilde doing?' 'Oh,' said his friend, 'he is very melancholy, he gets up about two in the afternoon, for he tries to sleep away as much of life as possible, and he has made up a story which he calls the best story in the world and says that he repeats it to himself after every meal and upon going to bed at night.' He then told me the story and I believe I can trust my memory to recall his very words:—'Christ came over a white plain to a purple city, and, as He went through a street, He heard voices above His head. He looked up and saw a young man lying drunk upon a window-sill. Christ said, "Why do you waste your soul in drunkenness" and the young man answered, "Lord, I was a leper and you healed me. What else can I do?" A little further on He saw a young man following a harlot with glittering eyes, and said "Why do you dissolve your soul in debauchery?" and the young man answered, "Lord, I was blind and you healed me. What else can I do?" In the middle of the city He found an old man crouched upon the ground weeping and said, "Why do you weep?" and the old man answered, "Lord, I was dead and you raised me into life—what else can I do but weep?"' I, too, think that is one of the best stories in the world, though I do not like, and did not like when I first heard it, 'white plain' 'purple city', 'glittering eyes.' It has definiteness, the simplicity of great sculpture, it adds something new to the imagination of the world, it suddenly confronts the mind—as does all great art—with the fundamental and the insoluble. It puts into almost as few as possible words a melancholy that comes upon a man at the moment of triumph, the only moment when a man without dreading some secret bias, envy, disappointment, jealousy, can ask himself what is the value of life. Wilde, when I knew him first, was almost a poor man. 'People think I am successful', he said, or some such words, 'but at this moment I do not know how to earn even a few shillings.' And now he had three plays running at once, had earned it was said ten thousand pounds in a year: 'Lord, I was dead and you raised me into life, what else can I do but weep?'

The other day I found at the end of one of his volumes, in a section called 'Poems in Prose', that very story expanded to fifty or sixty lines, and by such description as 'Fair pillars of marble', 'the loud noise of many lutes', 'the hall of calcedony and the hall of jasper', 'torches of cedar', 'One whose face and raiment were painted and whose feet were shod with pearls.' The influence of painting upon English literature which began with the poetry of Keats had now reached its climax, because all educated England was overshadowed by Whistler, by Burne Jones, by Rossetti; and Wilde—a provincial like myself—found in that influence something of the mystery, something of the excitement, of a religious cult and of a cult that promised an impossible distinction. It was precisely because he was not of it by birth and by early association that he caught up phrases and adjectives for their own sake, and not because they were a natural part of his design, and spoke them to others as though it were his duty to pass on some password, sign or counter-sign. When his downfall came he had discovered his natural style in *The Importance of Being Earnest*, constrained to that discovery by the rigourous technique of the stage, and was about to give to the English theatre comedies which would have been to our own age what the comedies of Goldsmith and of Sheridan were to theirs. He had already but one rival—Mr. Bernard Shaw—whose provincialism led him not to Walter Pater but to Karl Marx, and who, for all his longer life and his greater imaginative energy, has never cast off completely the accidental and the soluble.

124. A. B. Walkley on Wilde's comedies

1923

Signed introduction to Volume vii, *The Complete Works of Oscar Wilde* (New York, 1923), ix–xiv.

Walkley's introduction advances the interesting notion that Wilde at his best, as in *The Importance of Being Earnest*, was sincere in his insincerity. In so doing, Walkley disposes of the many judgments of 'insincerity' (as a measure of failure) which plagued Wilde in his own lifetime.

'In matters of grave importance,' says a young lady in the blithest and most brilliant of Oscar Wilde's comedies, 'style, not sincerity, is the vital thing.' She must have been thinking of her author's plays. Superficially, these are all style and no sincerity. But we must distinguish. Without sincerity there can be no style: only flatulence, stereotypes, empty verbiage, what in Paris they call *le poncif*. Without, that is to say, the artist's sincerity of presentation, the true expression of his intuitions. You cannot have perfect form without genuine feeling. Wilde was a dramatic artist who had a keen feeling on the dramatic virtues of insincerity—the sudden surprise of its paradoxes, its inverted commonplaces, its pouring of old wine into old bottles—and he sincerely presented it in a delightful style, terse, tense, witty, urbane. And so, when all his personages are insincere, as all are in *The Importance of Being Earnest*, he is most sincere, his style is at his best, and the result is a comedy worthy of the same shelf as *Marriage à la Mode* or *The Way of the World*. Nor am I 'dragging in' Dryden and Congreve. For not only in the happy, easy elegance of his form is Wilde in the direct line of these masters of style; he is of their lineage, too, in his triumphantly sincere expression of insincerity.

Conversely, there is such a thing as the insincere presentation of sincerity. Wilde, it is clear enough, was much under the influence of two great Frenchmen, Augier and the younger Dumas, whose authority in the theatre, though on the wane, was even then scarcely to be ignored. From Augier he took his 'natural' sons who unwittingly raise an arm against their father, and his 'adventuresses' vainly attempting to force the portals of 'society'; from Dumas *fils* he took what no English dramatist can afford even to touch, the *tirade*. Both these men were serious at heart, where Wilde never was; both did sincerely present sincerity, which Wilde never could. Both, in short, were romantic, with the perfervid emotionalism of the romantic tradition; and it was with an eye on its tendency to degenerate into the mere simulation of emotion that Sainte-Beuve said, *l'écueil particulier du genre romantique, c'est le faux*.[1] You will find *le faux* in Wilde so soon as you turn to any of his presentations of the sincere. The husband and wife in *Lady Windermere's Fan* are mere mechanical dolls, who are none the more human for behaving like lunatics. The mother and son and the Puritan maidens in *A Woman of No Importance* discredit virtue and seriousness by their hopeless inferiority in interest to the vicious and frivolous of the company. The Puritan maiden delivers a Dumasian tirade against English society, with variations by Wilde ('It lives like a leper in purple. It sits like a dead thing smeared with gold') which is not only rhetoric, but 'twopence coloured' rhetoric. For mark the peculiar penalty of insincerity: it not merely makes a nonentity of the author's personage, but ruins his style!

Take those two other insincere presentations of sincerity, Sir Robert and Lady Chiltern in *An Ideal Husband*. Wilde was never tired of railing at the newspapers. By a kind of Nemesis, his own Sir Robert always talks the most pompous journalism. Thirty years ago, at any rate, this was not the lingo of an English cabinet minister. As for Lady Chiltern, she is not, at a domestic crisis, above borrowing the favourite literary *cliché* of the kitchen. 'Don't touch me!' Such were the misadventures of Wilde's fine culture, and fastidious taste, when sincerity failed him!

Style *with* sincerity, then 'is the vital thing,' and, when all is said, Wilde had enough of it to keep his work alive. His conversations of the frivolous are inimitable. They out-Chamfort Chamfort. Many of his epigrams have become legendary. 'The Book of Life begins with a man and a woman in a garden; it ends with Revelations.' Women are 'Sphinxes without secrets.' 'I can resist everything, except temptation.' 'To be intelligible is to be found out.' 'The English country gentleman galloping after a fox—the unspeakable in full pursuit of the uneatable.' These are sheer wit. But others are wisdom, too. As, 'In this world there are only two tragedies. One is not getting what one wants, and

[1] The particular danger of the romantic style is falsehood.

the other is getting it.' And: 'All thought is immoral. Its very essence is destruction. Nothing survives being thought of.' Evidently the author of *obiter dicta* such as these could do something more than manufacture epigrams by the mechanical process of turning commonplaces upside down or inside out. But he was sometimes reduced to that extremity, because, at all costs, epigrams he must have. He believed, you see, like a true artist, in unity of tone; but unity of tone, when artificially prolonged, is called monotony.

His plots are as artificial as his weaker epigrams; almost as artificial, indeed, as the plots of Congreve. His stage situations are striking rather than inevitable, or even plausible. There is no real reason for Lord Windermere's persistence in bringing Mrs. Erlynne into his wife's drawing-room. General Arbuthnot's desire to inflict the death-penalty, on the spot, on Lord Illingworth is somewhat excessive—and is really created by the author's sore need for a situation wherein the relationship of the two men shall be strikingly divulged. The story of *An Ideal Husband* is a mere list of articles of stolen property—letters, Cabinet secrets, bracelets, more letters. In plot, as in characterisation, when Wilde tried to be serious he succeeded only in being artificial.

In the single comedy without a blemish of seriousness, *The Importance of Being Earnest,* the situations are not only striking in themselves, but naturally contrived. I would almost go so far as to say that the situation on Worthing's entrance in Act II is the most *visually* comic thing in the English drama. Worthing has come to announce the death of his (wholly fictitious) brother, and is ignorant of the fact that his mischievous friend Moncrieff, personating that brother, has preceded him. Worthing is in deep mourning, and, before a word is spoken, the whole situation is revealed to the eye. This is a supreme example of that rare thing, wit in action. On the first night at the St. James's the house shook with laughter and, as often as Worthing stalks in solemn black on the stage, the world will laugh again. The story of Miss Prism and the travelling bag is natural, too—natural, that is, in the make-up atmosphere, the 'high fantastical' plane of the play. If the three earlier comedies are less comedies than tissues of epigrams stretched, and stretched something too thin, over a framework of conventional romance, we must cry at any rate over *The Importance of Being Earnest* what they cried over *Les Précieuses Ridicules* to Molière, *Voilà enfin de la vraie comédie!*[1]

[1] That is, at last, a true comedy.

125. John Drinkwater on
The Importance of Being Earnest

1923

Signed introduction to Volume viii, *The Complete Works of Oscar Wilde* (New York, 1923), ix–xiv; reprinted in *The Muse in Council* (1925).

John Drinkwater (1882–1937), critic, biographer, novelist, poet, and dramatist, whose play *Abraham Lincoln* (1918) brought him fame, judges Wilde's play as a masterpiece of the same rank as Congreve's and, like A. B. Walkley (see No. 124), regards the play as the supreme expression of Wilde's sincerity.

It may sound wilful to say of a man who, more perhaps than any other of his generation, attacked the bourgeoisie with great if rather fantastic courage that his chief defect as an artist was want of taste. And yet, considering his work as a whole, that seems to be the truth about Oscar Wilde. He cared very much about art and said many brave and challenging things for it. He was preoccupied always with it, and as an artist himself he tried honourably to deal with an experience of life which, although it was turgid and forlorn, was real enough. Mere reality of experience, however, is not enough. Before he can create largely the artist must not only have his personal vitality of experience, but he must love that experience passionately, however dark its mood may be. In reading most of Wilde's poetry, all his plays but one, and his critical studies, one feels, while all the time admiring a very rare executive gift, that here is a man who, for the most part, instead of standing bravely by his experience was trying to escape from it. This is not at all to suggest that he was a man lacking in common courage; few men have met disaster of fortune and temperament with so gallant a bearing. It is in a way easy for the protagonist in one of the great tragic movements of nature to meet fate fearlessly. But there is little enough of exaltation for the man who is destroyed not by passion but a merely trivial wasting of his own character. But, while Wilde did not lack courage of that

403

kind, he was deficient in that other courage which makes the artist loyal to himself at whatever cost. If the artist cannot approach universal beauty surely through the channels of his own emotional life, he is certain to fall into cynicism or sentimentality or both, and this is what Wilde did in most of his work. He was sensitive enough to the profound normal beauty of life, free play of character, charity, understanding, and the mystery of sacrifice. But he saw it all afar off, pathetically, as something which he cared for devotedly, but could not himself quite be out of the resources of his own nature. And so passion is replaced by mere wistfulness, and the tragic realisation at which he aimed is continually sentimentalised. And at moments when the artist's awareness of this defect in himself left him with nothing but a forlorn sense that the beauty of which he knew so well was never quite truly his own, cynicism became his inevitable refuge. It is fair to say that this with Wilde did not happen often. As in the conduct of his own unhappy life, so in his art he did strive with courage towards what he knew to be the better reason. But the final issue remains that his work taken as a whole in its brilliance and pathos misses the profounder qualities of humour and passion, and it must be remembered that this was not by deliberate intention.

Once, however, Wilde's own nature, with all its limitations, worked clearly in delight of itself, and achieved what is in its own province a perfect work of art. *The Importance of Being Earnest* is not really a comedy of manners in the sense of being primarily a criticism of the follies into which a society is betrayed by its conventions, and a tearing off of the masks. Nor is it primarily a comedy of wit, sure and sustained as the wit is. Attempts have been made to derive the play in some measure from the Restoration masters, but without much conviction, and while the manner employed by Wilde has clearly influenced some later writers notably St. John Hankin, *The Importance of Being Earnest* really forms a class in English drama by itself. It is in mere simplicity that one says that it seems to be the only one of Wilde's works that really has its roots in passion. Every device of gaiety and even seeming nonsense is employed to keep the passion far back out of sight, and, if it were otherwise, the play would not be the masterpiece it is. But the passion is there. That is to say that the play is directly an expression of that part of Wilde's own experience which was least uncontaminated and in which he could take most delight. And this meant that all his great gifts as a craftsman were for once employed in work where, with insincerity almost as the theme, there was more sincerity than in anything else he did. Plays like *Salomé* and *The Florentine Tragedy* are at best little more than virtuosity, while *The Woman of no Importance, Lady Windermere's Fan* and *The Ideal Husband*, although they may have many of the qualities that mark Wilde's one great achievement, are on the whole frank surrenders to a fashion of the theatre which Wilde had too good a brain not to despise. But in *The Importance of Being Earnest* there is neither virtuosity nor concession. It is a superb and original piece of construction, with several moments of stage mastery which can hardly be excelled in comedy, and packed throughout with a perfect understanding of dramatic speech. One has only to recall any scene in the play and place it beside almost any of the successful comedies that one sees in the ordinary run of theatre production, to see how definitely apart that greatness is set which comes of having not three words in seven dramatically right but seven in seven. But when art comes to this excellence of form it can only mean excellence of life at the springs, and flowing through *The Importance of Being Earnest* is the surest and clearest part of Wilde's life. There was much, perhaps everything, in the more profoundly moving story of man that Wilde saw always imperfectly or not at all. But he did see, with a subtlety that can hardly be matched in our dramatic literature, that the common intrigues of daily life are not really the moralist's province at all, but interesting only for the sheer amusement that can be got out of them. Shakespeare gave to the English stage a comedy as full of poetic passion as great tragic art, Ben Jonson the comedy of humours, and Congreve and his fellows the true comedy of manners, but Wilde in his one masterpiece brought into the same company of excellence the comedy of pure fun.

126. Edward Shanks on Wilde's literary reputation

1924

Signed article, 'Oscar Wilde', *London Mercury* (July 1924), x, 278–87; reprinted in *Second Essays on Literature* (1927).

Edward Shanks (1892–1953), journalist, poet, critic, playwright, and assistant editor of the *London Mercury* (1919–22), examines possible reasons for Wilde's extraordinary reputation on the Continent, concluding that the personality rather than the works has absorbed the imagination of Wilde's admirers. Shanks grants that *The Importance of Being Earnest* will 'probably' outlive the other plays, but his judgment is restrained. In discussing the other works, Shanks sees only what Wilde borrowed, but sees little of the transmutations. In short, Shanks concludes, 'Wilde was not so much a writer as a museum'—but obviously, it should be added, one much visited.

A little while ago, by way of celebrating the centenary of Byron's death, nearly every critic in England felt himself in honour bound to attempt to explain why that poet holds a higher place in Continental, than in English, estimation. It is a matter that has been canvassed again and again, and in the course of innumerable discussions some light, I think, has been thrown on the problem, which is one of the prettiest in all the theory of international literature. Byron was a great, and above all a typical figure: he did not so much invent Byronism as give it a name, and that because he was the first to isolate it in large and recognisable quantities from the confused emotional material of the age. His career was spectacular, and his end both spectacular and heroic. Moreover, what now makes us rank him somewhat lower than do Continental readers is something which is more apparent to us than to them, something which hides more from us than from them his none the less real virtues. The intolerable roughness and even shoddiness of his style are facts which do, for us, fight against his strength and originality: for foreigners, reading him whether in translation or in the original, they are necessarily facts of less weight.

Now the position of Oscar Wilde, here and abroad, has many points of similarity to this. We tend here more and more to look on him as a writer decidedly of the second rate. His influence, never very strong with the mature, grows less and less even with the young; and under-graduates are ceasing to quote his epigrams in their essays. The time is perhaps coming when it will no longer be a hopeful enterprise to revive his plays. It would not be easy to find any critic of literature who would be likely to refer to him as a considerable writer. Nevertheless, even with us, his name conveys a vague sense as of something important, and abroad it does much more than that. In Germany, certainly, most critics would name Shakespeare, Byron and Wilde as the three writers whom England has given to the world.

Those who say this may make themselves seem a little absurd to us; but what they state is a fact and not an opinion. In literature the persons whom a nation gives to the world are those whom the world consents to accept from her. We may continue to offer Shelley, Keats and Wordsworth as alternatives, but it is Byron that is chosen. We may offer as an alternative either George Meredith or Mr. Hardy, if we please, but it is Wilde that is chosen. This is a fact and, instead of look-ing at it as though it were an inexplicable curiosity of nature, we shall do well to ask ourselves whether it does not spring from a fact of even greater interest, whether we must not in view of it apply to Wilde standards rather different from those applicable to writers who are ours alone, whether we should not attempt to see in him something more than simply an author of English prose and verse.

At first sight, the parallel with Byron does not appear likely to be very fruitful. Byron's virtues, we have said, are to some extent ob-scured from us by the roughness of his style. But, though Wilde may not have been—and I do not think that it can be maintained that he was —in the first rank of English prose-writers, yet smoothness, brilliance and glitter of style are among the chief of his qualities. For the rest, a certain similarity of fate is obvious enough; but Wilde's downfall and his wretched death in Paris make but a sordid caricature of Byron's mysterious exile from England and his heroic death in Greece.

When we consider Wilde, of course, the imagination is stirred by that sudden and disastrous reversal of fortune, by fate's evident rebuke to good luck too great and too insolently borne. He set out at an early period to make himself, with apparently small materials, a conspicuous figure, and when he fell, it was, for apparently small reason, in a blaze of conspicuousness. But such things do not happen quite accidentally, and their causes must be sought.

Let us, once and for all, be frank about his offence. It was a squalid and disgusting business, with every circumstance of vulgarity and some of madness. But the crime for which he was sentenced was not a great crime. It was one which goes oftener known and unpunished than any other; and Wilde was not a great sinner, no Nero or Heliogabalus or Caesar Borgia.

Yet he and the public at large were for the first time at one in holding that he was a great sinner. The crowds which howled savagely outside the Old Bailey after he had been found guilty, he himself writing De Profundis in Reading Gaol agreed that he was an enemy of society whom society had crushed. He says:

Of course I know that from one point of view things will be made different for me than for others; must indeed, by the very nature of the case, be made so. The poor thieves and outcasts who are imprisoned here with me are in many respects more fortunate than I am. The little way in grey city or green field that saw their sin is small; to find those who know nothing of what they have done they need go no further than a bird might fly between the twilight and the dawn; but for me the world is shrivelled to a handsbreadth, and everywhere I turn my name is written on the rocks in lead. For I have come, not from obscurity into the momentary notoriety of time, but from a sort of eternity of fame to a sort of eternity of infamy, and sometimes seem to myself to have shown, if indeed it required showing, that between the famous and the infamous there is but one step, if as much as one.

There is in this much of the megalomania which undoubtedly was one of the causes contributory to his disaster. It makes a peculiar contrast with the picture of Wilde, after his release, loafing outside the Café de la Paix, to invite the recognition and the curiosity and the free drinks of chance English tourists, one of whom, questioned as to whether anything had struck him about Wilde, replied: 'Yes, he always wore tartan mittens.' But in what I have quoted there is something more than megalomania. At the time, Wilde's fall reverberated hugely and the echoes of it have not really yet died away. He had, to be sure, enjoyed a very great reputation, as literary reputations go; but it is not often that an English man of letters secures, by whatever means, such a place in the public imagination as this. The thing becomes more peculiar when we repeat that he was not a writer of the first rank or even of marked originality. This is, in short, the problem to be examined.

His first book of importance, the *Poems* of 1881, is in its way a peculiar collection. It is evidently the work of a man of much talent; but it is
exceedingly like a volume of serious parodies. Young poets imitate,
they cannot as a rule help imitating, what they have admired. This is
part of the stage of immaturity and does no harm. But one's first impression on reading these early pieces by Wilde is that a young man who
could imitate so fluently, so copiously and so successfully the manners of
so many different masters ought to be engaged in original work. He
copies even Milton whom, however, he sees through a mist, as it were,
of Wordsworth. This is the opening of his sonnet on the Bulgarian
atrocities:

> Christ, dost thou live indeed? or are thy bones
> Still straitened in their rock-hewn sepulchre?
> And was thy Rising only dreamed by her
> Whose love of thee for all her sin atones?
> For here the air is horrid with men's groans,
> The priests who call upon thy name are slain,
> Dost thou not hear the bitter wail of pain
> From those whose children lie upon the stones?

The very excellence of the thing—for of its kind it is excellent—almost
takes one's breath away. As one goes on one finds more that is surprising.
The combined manners of Keats, Morris and Swinburne come in very
usefully to help a young man, who has absolutely nothing of his own to
say, to three ornate narrative poems. There are ballads reminiscent of
Swinburne and Rossetti. Andrew Lang's attempt to found an English
Pléiade echoes here in a villanelle on Theocritus—of all poets in the
world! Contemporaries in France have their share with *Impression du
Matin* and other pieces. Tennyson too is laid under contribution; and
the best and simplest of the shorter poems is actually an echo of Tom
Hood.

In the ordinary way there would be more malevolence than usefulness in such an analysis as this of the work of a young writer. But in the
ordinary way the young writer, so long as he is thus copying his favourite models, is still plainly learning his job. By the time he has learnt
how to imitate Swinburne or Keats, or whomever it may be, smoothly
and successfully, he has ceased to wish to do anything of the kind. But
for Wilde the styles of other poets were part of his material; and he
sometimes appropriates them with so persuasive an air of having the
right to do it, that one is left at a loss to say whether the results are truly
independent and his own or not.

In the shorter poems, this peculiarity is of little importance, for the poems themselves are of practically none. Wilde's reputation as a poet rests almost entirely on two pieces, both of which are derivative in style and yet both of which have a life of their own. *The Sphinx* gives its author's age as under twenty, which, to speak with frankness, I cannot bring myself to believe. It is much too remarkable an exercise in literary decoration for this to be possible, when one compares it with the other work of the same kind.

It *is* remarkable, and it *is* an exercise. But for Baudelaire and Swinburne it could never have been written. Cato and the fascination of sin, the names of precious stones and other 'stunning' words, as Rossetti called them, a sinister disillusionment with life and hints at strange vices—it is hard to say what in this is the contribution of the poet. Perhaps the form: for the stanza of *In Memoriam* undergoes a definite and interesting change when it is written as a couplet, with the rhymes concealed and not dwelt on. It takes on a different movement, very characteristic and rather impressive. This is, I fancy, Wilde's one invention in literary technique.

But so much will not explain the definite impression made on us that the poem is a valid work of art, and not to be dismissed as derivative or insincere, though both these faults could be shown in it. But what is to be made of such a passage as this?

> Or had you shameful secret guests and did you hurry to your home
> Some Nereid coiled in amber foam with curious rock crystal breasts?
>
> Or did you treading through the froth call to the brown Sidonian
> For tidings of Leviathan, Leviathan or Behemoth?
>
> Or did you when the sun was set climb up the cactus-covered slope
> To meet your swarthy Ethiop whose body was of polished jet?
>
> Or did you while the earthen skiffs dropped down the grey nilotic flats
> At twilight and the flickering bats flew round the temple's triple glyphs
>
> Steal to the border of the bar and swim across the silent lake
> And slink into the vault and make the Pyramid your lupanar
>
> Till from each black sarcophagus rose up the painted swathed dead?
> Or did you lure unto your bed the ivory-horned Tragelaphos?

When the undergraduate (or so, at least, it used to be) reads this for the first time his heart leaps up, for he beholds what an immense amount of entertainment can be got of mere words. And one's instinct still is to say of *The Sphinx*: This is great fun! For it is entirely something, and it is equally certainly nothing on a higher level than that. The extravagance of the decoration is at once self-conscious and naïve. The ideas are mere counters, and the poem expresses no feeling, unless it be a delight in verbal and metrical virtuosity. But as such it exists and has an enduring spark of life in it.

The Ballad of Reading Gaol is a different matter. It was written later in Wilde's life, it describes an actual experience, and it is meant to convey a real feeling. But it too is derivative and its derivations are curious. One can understand that Wilde should again have taken something from Tom Hood for this purpose, but his borrowing from Coleridge is a good deal less easy to explain. Yet it is undoubtedly there:

> They glided past, they glided fast,
>   Like travellers through a mist:
> They mocked the moon in a rigadoon
>   Of delicate turn and twist.
> And with formal pace and loathsome grace
>   The phantoms kept their tryst.
>
> With mop and mow, we saw them go,
>   Slim shadows hand in hand:
> About, about, in ghostly rout
>   They trod a saraband:
> And the damned grotesques made arabesques,
>   Like the wind upon the sand!

This is as self-conscious in its decorative effect as are the passages in which Wilde remembers suddenly and too clearly that he is describing a realistic modern tragedy:

> The Governor was strong upon
>   The Regulations Act:
> The Doctor said that Death was but
>   A scientific fact:
> And twice a day the Chaplain called,
>   And left a little tract.

How are we to reconcile these incongruities and the constant straining of feeling throughout the poem, as in the verses beginning 'Yet each man kills the thing he loves,' with the evident fact that it is a work of power and beauty? Yet it makes a deep impression on almost all who read it, and very much the impression that Wilde intended, of a compassionate revolt against the cruelty of human justice. We can only say that a certain kind of insincerity was natural and essential in Wilde and, for the moment, leave it at that.

The reaching after effect which is the prime force of *The Sphinx* and the disfigurement of *The Ballad of Reading Gaol* is less disconcerting in his prose than in his verse. In prose it can, and very often does, take the form of wit, whereas in verse it takes too often the form of false emotion. And, in so far as Wilde's fame is based on his works at all, it is based on four or five works in prose, on *The Importance of Being Earnest* and *Lady Windermere's Fan*, on *De Profundis* and *Intentions* and *A House of Pomegranates* and *The Picture of Dorian Gray*.

It is here, it seems to me, that his genius, as expressed in his writings, is most often exaggerated. His habit of epigram, which makes a restless glitter over the surface of his plays and stories, can be parallelled from the novels of Disraeli, from whom too he derives his quite conscious and not all fatuous delight in aristocracy and opulence. Some of his sayings are acute and some are shallow; but, as the conversational epigrammatist will, he contrives to make them all look exactly alike.

I adore simple pleasures. They are the last refuge of the complex.
No nice girl should ever waltz with such particularly younger sons! It looks so fast!
Better to take pleasure in a rose than to put its root under a microscope.
Nothing is so dangerous as being too modern. One is apt to grow old-fashioned quite suddenly.

The prose of which such are the high lights is not of the first order, whether in style or in wisdom; and when he aims at beauty it cannot be said that he reaches a much higher level:

But, see, it is dawn already. Draw back the curtains and open the windows wide. How cool the morning air is! Piccadilly lies at our feet like a long riband of silver. A faint purple mist hangs over the Park, and the shadows of the white houses are purple. It is too late to sleep. Let us go down to Covent Garden and look at the roses. Come! I am tired of thought.

Let us then turn to the stories. The fairy-stories are charming; but will it be seriously maintained that they or *Lord Arthur Savile's Crime* are works of a high order? The stories in this second book are excellently ingenious and would be popular at any time and in almost any hands, but they are slight. A trivial thing may be a great work of art, if it displays a passionate delight in triviality; but these do not. And *The Picture of Dorian Gray* is disappointingly little more than ingenious. The idea is magnificent, even if it is a little too bizarre to be the vehicle for very intense feeling. The 'Preface' is almost portentous, the most challenging and sweeping statement of the theory of art for art's sake ever made. But Wilde has sacrificed what might have been a masterpiece to his desire for immediate effect. Tussore silk curtains, opium-scented cigarettes, dressing-tables with large gold-topped bottles on them—these are the unhappy symbols, the first that came to hand, which Wilde employed for the embodiment of what after all was a vision of beauty. There is a book similar in spirit, by one of Wilde's favourite authors, which affords a fair comparison. It is verbose and ill-constructed, but it does to perfection what *Dorian Gray* fails to do. It is *Mademoiselle de Maupin;* and the comparison is fatal to Wilde.

We proceed to the plays, his most successful works. These were written frankly for money; but they are none the worse for that. Of their kind indeed they are very good. All his life he had treated the world as a theatre, and it required no great effort for him to submit himself to theatrical requirements. His stage effects are carried out with a gusto and sweep that make them exhilarating. Look at the curtain for the first act of *Lady Windermere's Fan*:

LADY WINDERMERE

Arthur, if that woman comes here—I warn you—

LORD WINDERMERE

Margaret, you'll ruin us!

LADY WINDERMERE

Us! from this moment my life is separate from yours. But if you wish to avoid a public scandal, write at once to this woman and tell I forbid her to come here!

LORD WINDERMERE

I will not—I cannot—she must come!

LADY WINDERMERE

Then I shall do exactly as I have said. [*Goes R.*] You leave me no choice. [*Exit R.*]

LORD WINDERMERE

[*Calling after her*]. Margaret! Margaret! [*A pause.*] My God! What shall I do? I dare not tell her who this woman really is. The shame would kill her. [*Sinks down into a chair and buries his face in his hands.*]

One asks oneself involuntarily whether Wilde here has his tongue in his cheek or not. The scene is theatrical in the last degree, but effectively, magnificently theatrical. And the same may be said of the dialogue which was the element distinguishing his from the other 'well made' plays of the time. His dialogue of its sort is very fine and, considering that it exists only for its own sake, it is introduced very deftly so as not to give any impression that it retards the action of the play. But it is not dramatic prose of the highest order. It stands to Congreve's prose, for example, just as the scene I have quoted stands to the knocking at the gate in *Macbeth*.

Wilde's plays, if the distinction be permissible, have theatrical rather than dramatic qualities. They exist for effect, not for expression—all, that is to say, except one of them, *The Importance of Being Earnest*. This admirable piece does express something of the author and something which one would hardly have expected to find in him—a simple and light-hearted sense of fun.

It is more genuine than the other plays, and will probably outlive them all.

From this analysis, I have omitted *Salome*, which is, perhaps, taking the whole world together, Wilde's most famous work, a fact not wholly due to Dr. Strauss's use of it as a libretto. It ranks, I think, somewhere with *The Sphinx* and with *Dorian Gray*. The idea is magnificently unexpected; but the execution is only superficial. From the elements of sin and blasphemy which it contains Wilde has made a very striking stage-picture but he had done no more. It is, however, a very characteristic work.

From this brief and rapid examination, I emerge with the verdict that Wilde was a derivative and artificial writer. He aimed constantly at effect rather than at expressing something genuine in himself. He took always the shortest and easiest way to an effect. Not one of his works but has in it the obvious seeds of decay. Yet the figure of Wilde survives; and it seems not unlikely that his legend will preserve some of his writings perhaps beyond their natural span of life.

The explanation is, I think, supplied by himself in *De Profundis*:

I was a man who stood in symbolic relations to the art and culture of my age. I had realised this for myself at the very dawn of my manhood, and had forced my age to realise it afterwards. Few men hold such a position in their own life-time, and have it so acknowledged. It is usually discerned, if discerned at all, by the historian, or the critic, long after both the man and his age have passed away. With me it was different. I felt it myself, and made others feel it. Byron was a symbolic figure, but his relations were to the passion of his age and its weariness of passion. Mine were to something more noble, more permanent, of more vital issue, of larger scope.

The parallel is unfortunate, for what Byron stood for was something decidedly stronger and more vital. But, like him, Wilde was a symbolic figure.

The origin of the movement he represented is not very easy to discover. It sprang perhaps from a revolt of part of the human race against a fate which seemed to be overtaking the whole. In the middle of the nineteenth century the wave of material improvement spread over the world and ugliness and narrowness came in its train. All the countries of Europe, one after another, were given up to industry, railways cut through their fields and the smoke of factory chimneys darkened their skies. Vast mean and degraded populations sprang up which had no songs nor any joy in life. The middle class, trading code of life ruled everywhere; and at once the artist sprang up in passionate reaction.

The reaction took different forms. Ruskin preached that pictures should have a religious effect on those who saw them. Morris, between his day-dreams, laboured for the abandonment of machinery. Poets in France retired to ivory towers and ululated more or less distinctly from the top windows. And soon the rebels began to make themselves deliberately as unlike their enemies as they could. The middle classes applauded virtue, therefore vice was to be exalted. The middle classes preached thrift, therefore waste was to be practised. The middle classes thought art should be instructive, therefore all art was to be perfectly useless. And Baudelaire smoked opium and Verlaine alternated hysterically between religion and wickedness and Gérard de Nerval trailed a lobster after him through the streets of Paris.

The movement became extravagant and was doomed not to persist as it had begun, for it was approaching the evil in an unhelpful manner. But while it lasted it was a very real thing. And into it came Wilde, a young man not at all hysterical, with many talents and in particular a very great talent for histrionics. So he made himself the centre and symbol of all that great and bizarre crusade against bourgeois ideas and morality.

He was not an originator, he was, much as he would have disliked the designation, a populariser. He summarised in his work what was then called *fin de siècle* art, and made it easy for the great public to understand. Almost every aspect of the movement was there. The sensualism of Baudelaire and his hinting at strange vices, Gautier's disinterested immoral adoration of things, hard, bright and sharp-edged, Verlaine's religiosity—all these with dashes of Satanism and cruelty and just so much of the doctrines of Ruskin and Morris as could be made to fit in with the rest without too startling an incongruity.

One might almost say that Wilde was not so much a writer as a museum.

It is not to be said that this view disposes of him either as a legend or as a writer; but it does, I think, explain him. He was artificial and insincere; but there was something genuine in his artificiality and something vital in his insincerity. These were his main qualities, and in both of them he was at heart consistent. He held up his mind as a mirror to a whole side of the life of his time, and in that mirror there may still be seen a wonderfully varied and interesting picture.

So, he having made himself the compendium of this movement, mankind treated him as its leader and turned and crushed him; and his name was removed from playbills and the crowds howled round the Old Bailey on learning that he had been sent to prison. He graciously gave the Decadence one head; and humanity with a brutal but sure instinct promptly cut it off. Life took the opportunity to affirm that art shall not be permitted to declare itself independent of life. For the reverse of his own parallel between himself and Byron is what is true. Byron, by whatever means, proclaimed the revolt of life, passionate, energetic, indignant life, against a world which was unworthy of it. The movement at the head of which Wilde, with incomparable but characteristic arrogance, placed himself, was, though I have called it a revolt, not so much that as an attempt at a secession. The Decadents did not contemplate the conquest of the world for better and nobler ideas. They stated their own superiority and contemptuously stepped aside. It was enough for them to make from time to time wounding remarks on the gross, struggling body of humanity which they had left behind them.

Now the Decadence was doomed to failure, whether it had received this wounding blow in the person of Wilde or not; and it does not rank very high among the movements which in the course of history have at one time and another swept over Europe. But it had in it some of the finest and acutest, if not some of the strongest, spirits of the time. Its achievement was incomplete, fragmentary, unhappy; but it achieved something. And a man who could make himself seem the typical figure of that movement and that achievement is not a man to be neglected.

Wilde, to be sure, deceived himself here as elsewhere. There was probably no really decadent strain in his nature. When, in *Dorian Gray*, he had to suggest abysmal wickedness he failed lamentably to make concrete the vague conception, and his attitude to the conception was all that could be desired from the severest of moralists. What distinguished him was the wax-like character of his mind which received a clear and readable impression of the main elements of his nature. This process of assimilation and simplification made him a leading figure and then a legend; and the legend, as I have said, will very likely make some of his works live longer than would otherwise be natural for them. But the man will always be more important than any of his works; and it will be a long time, I think, before he disappears altogether from memory.

127. Arnold Bennett on Wilde as an outmoded writer

1927

From a signed article, titled 'Books and Persons', *Evening Standard*, 30 June 1927, p. 5; reprinted in *The Savour of Life* (1928).

Bennett (1867–1931), in placing Wilde's comedies, including *The Importance of Being Earnest*, in the same class as such 'cup-and-saucer' comedies as T. W. Robertson's *Caste* (1867), provides his reader with the opportunity of observing—at the very least—the workings of an independent mind.

Oscar Wilde's play, *The Florentine Tragedy*, has been given again in London—at the Arts Theatre Club. It is in blank verse, and very poor blank verse. And according to my recollection it is a very poor play. I will go further and say that it has no value whatever. I think that Wilde's popular vogue is over. In the wide sense of the word he had no popular vogue except a posthumous one. The notion that he received large sums of money for his plays is not based on facts. He made a few thousand pounds out of *The Importance of Being Earnest*, but the other plays, very inferior, did not do much.

Somerset Maugham and Frederick Lonsdale have achieved far more popularity with a single play than Wilde achieved with all his plays

put together. There is as brilliant an originality in the first act of Lonsdale's *Spring Cleaning* as in any act of Wilde's; and more power and
veracity in the first act of Maugham's *Home and Beauty* than in any act
of Wilde's. Moreover, Wilde has to his credit nothing non-theatrical
compararable to Maugham's great (yes, great) novel, *Of Human
Bondage*.

The Importance of Being Earnest is Wilde's best work. I admired it
intensely for many years. I shall not forget my sensations at its first
performance. I said again and again that it was the finest comedy in
English since Sheridan. But when I saw the revival at the Haymarket a
year or two ago—what a mournful disillusion! What a perturbation of
conscience for my critical blindness. I am now inclined to class Wilde
with Robertson as a writer of comedies; certainly I would not put him
higher than the author of *Caste*.

Wilde's real popularity came after his death, and it was, I imagine,
due largely to causes unconnected with artistic merit. (But you never
know.) His books, practically all his books, had an immense sale. At
which I was glad, for Wilde, even if he was not a first-rate writer, had
given keen pleasure to simpletons such as my younger self; and he was
a first-rate figure. If you would realize the European figure he made,
read André Gide's slim volume, *Oscar Wilde. In Memoriam.* (Souvenirs)
(Published by the *Mercure de France*). It displays Wilde at his very best.

Wilde is outmoded: which will annoy his ghost, if ghosts there are,
more than anything else could. His reputation among the lettered
could not possibly survive such a critical examination as, for instance,
Frank Swinnerton addressed to the reputation of R. L. Stevenson—
thereby reducing Stevenson's reputation to about 10 per cent. of its
former size. Certainly 10 per cent. of Wilde's reputation would not
emerge from the cold and fearful inquisition. Wilde's style lacked the
elements of permanence. Even his greater forerunner and exemplar in
preciosity, Walter Pater, has gone under. But whether Pater will rise
again I will not prophesy. I seriously question if he will.

Bibliography

This brief bibliography consists of works which list or describe nineteenth- and twentieth-century criticism, or which give an account of the publishing history of Wilde's works.

ALEXANDER, BEVERLY, 'Oscar Wilde's Plays on the New York Stage: 1883–1950', unpublished Master's essay, Columbia University (1951): a survey of the critical reception of Wilde's plays.

BREUGELMANS, R., 'De Weerklank van Oscar Wilde in Nederland en Vlaanderen (1880–1960)', in *Studia Germanica Gandensia* (1962), iii, 53–144: a survey of translations and performances of Wilde's works in the Netherlands and Flanders and an account of their critical reception.

COWAN, ROBERT ERNEST, and WILLIAM ANDREWS CLARK, JR., editors, *The Library of William Andrews Clark, Jr.: Wilde and Wildeana*, 5 vols (San Francisco, 1922–31): a bibliographical and critical account of the Library which was bequeathed in 1934 to the University of California at Los Angeles. A useful supplement to Mason's bibliography listed below.

HORODISCH, ABRAHAM, *Oscar Wilde's Ballad of Reading Gaol: A Bibliographical Study* (New York, 1954): an account of the English editions and those in translation, with a brief survey of their critical reception.

LEDGER, WALTER, 'Bibliography' in the *Second Collected Edition* of Wilde's works, vol. xii, published by Methuen and Company in 1909, pp. 93–110: describes forty-five different editions of *Salomé*.

MASON, STUART [Christopher Millard], *Bibliography of Oscar Wilde* (1914): contains listings of reviews and articles about Wilde as well as much other material, such as letters, unavailable elsewhere. Indispensable for a study of Wilde's career. Reprinted, with same pagination, in 1967.

Select Index

II TOPICS